CONTEMPORARY
&
CLASSIC ARGUMENTS

A Portable Anthology

Gavin Thomas

CONTEMPORARY
&
CLASSIC ARGUMENTS
A Portable Anthology

SYLVAN BARNET
Professor of English, Tufts University

HUGO BEDAU
Professor of Philosophy, Tufts University

Bedford/St. Martin's   BOSTON   ◆   NEW YORK

For Bedford/St. Martin's

Executive Editor: Stephen A. Scipione
Developmental Editor: John E. Sullivan III
Editorial Assistants: Sarah Whitesel, Amy Hurd
Production Supervisor: Jessie Markland
Project Management: DeMasi Design and Publishing Services
Marketing Manager: Rachel Falk
Cover Design: Donna Lee Dennison
Cover Art: Egg and Sphere© Ryoichi Utsumi/Photonica.
Composition: Pine Tree Composition, Inc.
Printing and Binding: Haddon Craftsmen, an RR Donnelley & Sons
  Company

President: Joan E. Feinberg
Editorial Director: Denise B. Wydra
Director of Marketing: Karen Melton Soeltz
Director of Editing, Design, and Production: Marcia Cohen
Manager, Publishing Services: Emily Berleth

Library of Congress Control Number: 2004107372

Manufactured in the United States of America.

5 4 3 2
k j i h

For information, write: Bedford / St. Martin's, 75 Arlington Street,
Boston, MA 02116   (617-399-4000)

ISBN-10: 0-312-43628-9
ISBN-13: 978-0-312-43628-5

Acknowledgments
Advocates for Cell Phone Safety. "Yes, Prohibit Their Use." Billboard near
  Almeda, California. J. Emilio Flores for *The New York Times.*
G. E. M. Anscombe. "The Criteria of a Just War." Reprinted by permission of
  Dr. MC Gormally. Copyright © MC Gormally.
Judy Brady. "I Want a Wife." From *Ms.,* 1971. Copyright © 1971 by Judy
  Brady. Reprinted by permission of the author.
*Acknowledgments and copyrights are continued at the back of the book
on pages 344–46, which constitute an extension of the copyright page.*

Preface

Contemporary & Classic Arguments: A Portable Anthology is a comparatively brief and inexpensive collection of fifty-four selections, ranging from Plato to the present, with a strong emphasis on contemporary arguments. The contemporary readings are gathered in Part One, which consists of five pro-con debates, and in Part Two, which features six casebooks on the current topics the death penalty, the legal status of drugs, the just war, the limits of privacy, sexual harassment, and whether torture should ever be permitted. The classic arguments—fifteen enduring models for analysis and response—appear in Part Three. All the readings are introduced by headnotes and followed by topics for critical thinking and writing. Additional material on argument can be found at a companion Web site, **bedfordstmartins.com/barnetbedau.**

We want to mention our chief assumptions about the aims of a course that might use this book. Probably most students and instructors would agree that, as critical readers, students should be able to do the following:

- Summarize accurately an argument they have read
- Locate the thesis of an argument
- Locate the assumptions, stated and unstated
- Analyze and evaluate the strength of the evidence and the soundness of the reasoning offered in support of the thesis

- Analyze, evaluate, and account for discrepancies among various readings on a topic (for example, explain why certain facts are used, why others are ignored, or why two sources might interpret the same facts differently)

We trust that the arguments collected in *Contemporary & Classic Arguments* will provide a sufficient, and sufficiently varied, selection of readings for students to practice these critical reading skills and to respond with arguments of their own.

Consider these two quotations, one by Edmund Burke and the other by John Stuart Mill. Burke said, "He that wrestles with us strengthens our nerves, and sharpens our skill. Our antagonist is our helper." Mill said, "He who knows only his own side of the cause knows little." These two quotations continue to reflect the view of argument that underlies this text: In reading an essay, thoughtful readers are engaging in a serious effort to know what the author's ideas are and, having found them, to contribute to a multisided conversation. Thoughtful readers are not setting out to find confirmation for their own views; by listening to others and to their own responses, they hope to enlarge their opinions. They may change their views (perhaps slightly, perhaps radically), but even if they do not drastically change their views, they at least understand why they hold the views they do.

ACKNOWLEDGMENTS

We would like to thank the hundreds of instructors who have taught with *Current Issues and Enduring Questions*, the larger book from which this short book is adapted, through its many editions. Their comments have helped to improve the book you hold. At Bedford/St. Martin's, we thank Joan Feinberg, Denise Wydra, Karen Henry, John Sullivan, and Steve Scipione. They proposed this book and convinced us that it was well worth publishing.

Contents

CONTEMPORARY
&
CLASSIC ARGUMENTS
A Portable Anthology

PART ONE

Debates on Contemporary Issues

1

Affirmative Action: Is It Fair?

TERRY EASTLAND

Terry Eastland, born in Dallas, Texas, and educated at Vanderbilt University, Nashville, Tennessee, and Balliol College, Oxford, is a frequent contributor to conservative journals such as the National Review, American Spectator, Commentary, *and* The Public Interest. *He is the author of several books, including* Religious Liberty in the Supreme Court: The Cases That Define the Debate over Church and State *(1995),* Ending Affirmative Action: The Case for Colorblind Justice *(1996), from which this excerpt is taken, and* Freedom of Expression in the Supreme Court *(2000).*

Ending Affirmative Action

One of the central and hard-won lessons of the fight for colorblindness, lasting more than a century and a quarter, was that distinctions drawn on the basis of race inevitably lead to racial discrimination. That is why the advocates of colorblindness sought the elimination of racial distinctions in the law. They sought to end the source, the raw material, of racial discrimination. The nation was the better for their efforts when, starting in the 1940s, our legal system was strengthened by the addition of a variety of antidiscrimination laws, culminating in the Civil Rights Act of 1964. Soon afterward, the founders of affirmative action, searching for ways to improve the material condition of black Americans and make amends for slavery and segregation, found the constraints of colorblind law inconvenient. They managed to loosen the colorblind strictures of the Civil Rights Act of 1964, and the federal judiciary failed to tighten them in turn. Once preferential treatment was made possible, it spread throughout the public and private sectors, and the targets of numerical affirmative action became more numerous, coming to include Hispanics, Asians, and women.

Defenders of the policy initially promised that it would be temporary—a position that implicitly recognized that it is better not to sort people on the basis of race, that colorblindness is a worthy guide. But with the first step away from colorblindness, further steps came more easily, and in time we heard less often the promise that someday we would renew our previous commitment.

Nonetheless, more than a quarter century of thinking by race and counting by race has served only to confirm and strengthen the case for colorblind law.

We now know that when government has the power to sort people on the basis of race, racial discrimination often results. Preferential treatment is never benign. Whoever would have been admitted to a school, or won the promotion or the contract, but for race, has suffered discrimination—and there is no good discrimination. The nation owes a debt of gratitude to people like Allan Bakke, Brian Weber, Randy Pech, and Cheryl Hopwood, who have brought lawsuits challenging preferential affirmative action. They have courageously kept alive the question of the legality and morality of preferential treatment, providing often lonely witness to the principle at the heart of colorblind law—that no one in America should be discriminated against on account of race.

We know, too, that the effort to regulate on the basis of race can 5 have unanticipated consequences. Where the old advocates of colorblind law were pessimists about the very idea of racial regulation, the founders of affirmative action were optimists, confident of their ability to distinguish between benign and invidious racial classifications. They thought the world could be divided into good and bad people. The bad discriminated against blacks, either intentionally or through seemingly neutral procedures that produced adverse effects. The good—and the founders of affirmative action included themselves in this category— sought to do well by blacks. They were pure in heart, and so they could be trusted not to harm blacks.

But now we know better. It was weak-minded and dangerously naive to think that taking race into account would produce unambiguously good results for those in whose behalf it was done. Many ostensible beneficiaries of affirmative action have testified that preferential treatment often leads to self-doubt, dependency, and entitlement. To be sure, affirmative action doesn't always do that. Sometimes it "works," though the paradox of affirmative action is that its "working" is a function of how soon the recipient quits it entirely and labors under the same rules as everyone else, a sign of genuine equality that is possible only among individuals. But, as the practice of affirmative action has shown, no one knows enough confidently to predict in advance of an act of preferential treatment which effects, for better or worse, it will have upon a given recipient. This negative experience of affirmative action does not constitute an unanswerable argument against it; patients do undergo risky operations. But we do have a choice in the matter; that is, we do not have to take the risk of affirmative action. And once free of it, those now eligible for it would be able to compete and achieve on the same terms as everyone else.

There have been other unanticipated consequences as well, chief among them the stigma produced by affirmative action. Wherever affirmative action operates, the very existence of such a program will lead some people to think that every minority student or every minority employee would not have won opportunity without preferential treatment, a judgment that strips people of the respect due them as individuals. Consider, in the context of higher education, the case of the minority student admitted under affirmative action who would not have won the place without it. This student very well might have been admitted to another school, without the "help" of affirmative action. The problem, however, is that the student admitted under affirmative action is unable to erase its stigma until the individual succeeds in a nonpreferential environment. Even then, however, the number of those who know the nature of the student's achievement is likely to be very small. And the formal, pervasive nature of affirmative action, encouraged and required by so many local, state, and federal government agencies, means that the public will continue to make generalizations about minority advancement simply because it is easy to do so in the absence of particular knowledge. The generalization is that "minority" equals "affirmative action" equals "lower standards." The inference drawn is that affirmative action explains minority success. Tragically, this process of generalization and inference trails the many minorities—perhaps the majority— who make their way without the "help" of any preferential treatment.

Here the negative experience of affirmative action makes a powerful argument for colorblind law. Because affirmative action is stigmatizing, even for those who do not "benefit" from it, it is better to forego affirmative action altogether in favor of procedures for admitting students or hiring workers or awarding contracts that do not brand their targets as inferior and do not provide a basis for generalizing about minority achievement. Such procedures, of course, are those that do not distinguish on the basis of race, that do not "take race into account" in deciding who gets ahead.

Sports, fortunately, is still a world governed by such colorblind rules. No one receives preferential treatment in sports, so no one has self-doubts induced by affirmative action, no one has to "transcend" affirmative action, and no one is stigmatized by affirmative action. No one ever thinks, "Williams is in center field because of affirmative action," or "Lopez is catching because he is Hispanic." Outside of sports—which is to say, in the rest of society—the deeply human desire to be known for individual accomplishment explains why some minorities have made a point of declining participation in programs for which their race or ethnicity makes them eligible. The Hispanic law student at the University of Texas School of Law, whose academic qualifications were good enough to be admitted under the standards governing "white and others," was making an important point when he said that sometimes he wished he was wearing a shirt indicating his academic credentials. Ending affirmative action will create circumstances in which individuals will shine and, just as importantly, be seen to shine, quite on their own merits.

The longer affirmative action remains in place, the more reasons there are to bring it to an end. Of course, past advocates of colorblind law could have told us how hard it would be to quit thinking and counting by race once the racial license had been granted. They knew that the human mind is creative, remarkably capable of coming up with reasons, even quite attractive ones, for why we ought to "take race into account." The founding rationale of affirmative action was to remedy the ill effects of past discrimination against blacks, but this rationale did not easily fit the other groups. So affirmative action was redefined and rejustified in terms of overcoming "underrepresentation" and achieving "diversity." We have also heard the argument that affirmative action is necessary to prevent future discrimination. There have been other reasons offered: Affirmative action is needed to create minority role models, to stimulate the creation of minority businesses, to jump-start economic development in minority communities. With the advent at the local level of minority-dominated governments, minorities have discriminated against nonminorities by fashioning affirmative action programs that, while publicly touted in terms of one or another of the usual rationales, realistically are little more than expressions of racial politics, the ignoble triumph of minority majorities.

The use of race now threatens to produce some truly bizarre results. In large cities where new immigrants congregate, blacks who hold disproportionately more public-sector jobs stand to lose some of those jobs to "underrepresented" Hispanics. Diversity, meanwhile, is a rationale that may allow discrimination against members of traditional minority groups. Even President Clinton has said he would support laying off a black teacher instead of a white teacher if doing so would promote diversity. We cannot escape the fact that by drawing racial and ethnic lines, affirmative action—whatever its rationale—encourages Americans to think of themselves in racial and ethnic terms. That has been a recipe for resentment and chauvinism, neither of which promotes the good health of our democracy.

Fortunately, the Supreme Court has kept the light on, letting us know where home is, even in those cases where it has ruled in support of affirmative action. Those justices of the Supreme Court who consistently voted for affirmative action programs nonetheless refused to endorse group rights or to break in principle with the colorblind tradition. Equality under the Constitution, Justice Brennan wrote, is linked "with the proposition that differences in color or creed, birth or status, are neither significant nor relevant to the way in which such persons are treated." Justice Marshall declared his desire to live in a society "in which the color of a person's skin will not determine the opportunities available to him or her." And Justice Blackmun endorsed a society in which "persons will be regarded as persons," without regard to race or ethnicity.[1]

In recent years the Court has been shining the home light much more brightly. Its decisions in the *Croson* and *Adarand* cases, which speak to every government in the United States, impose strict conditions on the use of racial preferences. These decisions point us in the right direction. Citing Justice Harlan's dissent in *Plessy v. Ferguson* and the opinions in the Japanese Relocation Cases, *Croson* and *Adarand* raise the standard of colorblind law in a context that makes colorblindness even more compelling today than Harlan could have known. He made his argument for colorblind law in the context of a society made up of two races—black and white. Ours today consists of many races and ethnic groups, thanks especially to recent waves of immigration. Law that tries to distinguish among the groups and to favor one over another is bound to fail the country. Instead, we need law that can discourage the natural tendency people have to seek their own kind, law that invites people to minimize and transcend racial and ethnic differences. The best protection for every individual—of whatever race or ethnic background—is to be found in law that does not give effect to any racial views, but, as

---

[1]See Lawrence H. Fuchs, *The American Kaleidoscope: Race, Ethnicity, and the Civic Culture* (Hanover, N.H.: Wesleyan University Press, 1995), p. 456. [All notes are the author's.]

Harlan put it, provides for "equality before the law of all citizens of the United States, without regard to race."

The Supreme Court, however, has left much of the task of ending affirmative action to the American people.[2] That is just as well. Decisions by the elective branches of government to end programs containing preferences would be reached consequent to public debate, not after legal briefs have been submitted. We can take major steps toward recovering colorblind law and principle by enacting measures at the federal and state levels that would deny government the power to favor or slight anyone on account of race. If we do not take such steps, of course, the uncertain political tides may turn back to favor the supporters of affirmative action. Progress toward colorblind law will be much slower, if not impossible, if we rely exclusively on judicial decisions, for the defenders of affirmative action will respond by "mending" programs in ways that better disguise preferences but do not eliminate them. It is possible, too, that judicial progress toward colorblind law could be arrested or even reversed, if there are new Supreme Court appointees with views at odds with those of the majorities in *Croson* and *Adarand*. It falls to us to take action now.

The choice for colorblindness is the choice our own best tradition   15
invites us to make. Our founding charter declares that "all men are created equal" and are "endowed by their Creator with certain unalienable rights," among them "life, liberty, and the pursuit of happiness." We are thereby committed to the proposition that it is individuals who have rights, not groups, and that all individuals enjoy a fundamental equality of rights. The startling character of the United States—and what it has modeled to the rest of the world—is that the individuals who have equal rights may be of any race or ethnic background.

Few Americans have stated the case for equality as cogently as Abraham Lincoln, who did so in an 1858 speech he gave in Chicago in observation of Independence Day. The challenge before Lincoln was to show that the truths of the Declaration of Independence were relevant to the audience before him, which included European immigrants who were not descended from those who wrote the Declaration, fought the Revolution, and framed the Constitution. Having paid honor to the

---

[2]As for whether the Court should declare the Constitution flatly colorblind—a position endorsed by Justices Antonin Scalia and Clarence Thomas—the issue involves complicated and controversial questions, starting with the original meaning of the Fourteenth Amendment. See Jeff Rosen, "The Colorblind Court," *The New Republic*, July 31, 1995, and Andrew Kull, *The Color-Blind Constitution* (Cambridge, Mass.: Harvard University Press, 1992), pp. 221–24.

"men living in that day whom we claim as our fathers and grandfathers," and having linked the principle they contended for to the nation's subsequent prosperity, Lincoln told the audience that "we hold this annual celebration to remind ourselves of all the good done . . . and how it was done and who did it, and how we are historically connected with it." He added that "we go from these meetings in better humor with ourselves — we feel more attached the one to the other, and more firmly bound to the country we inhabit." And, yes, those he was addressing were as much a part of this country as anyone else:

> We have [besides those descended from the founders] . . . among us perhaps half our people who are not descendants at all of these men, they are men who have come from Europe — German, Irish, French, and Scandinavian — men that have come from Europe themselves, or whose ancestors have come hither and settled here, finding themselves our equals in all things. If they look back through this history to trace their connection with those days by blood, they find they have none, they cannot carry themselves back into that glorious epoch and make themselves feel that they are part of us, but when they look through that old Declaration of Independence they find that those old men say that "We hold these truths to be self-evident, that all men are created equal," and then they feel that moral sentiment taught in that day evidences their relation to those men, that it is the father of all moral principle in them, and that they have a right to claim it as though they were blood of the blood, and flesh of the flesh of the men who wrote that Declaration, and so they are.[3]

As Lincoln reminds us, the Declaration included any person from anywhere — the Germans and Swedes and other Europeans whom Lincoln addressed, the slaves Lincoln freed, the Asians who began arriving on our shores just before the nation was about to rend itself in a civil war, the Hispanics from all parts of the globe, Englishmen, American Indians, Jews — in sum, everyone. The Declaration is the great leveler, teaching that the rights of one are the rights of all. It puts us all on the same footing, and it implies the necessity of colorblind law because only that kind of law fully respects the equal rights of all persons, as individuals.

Affirmative action has always been an aberration from our best principles. The time has come to end it.

---

[3]Roy P. Basler, ed., *The Collected Works of Abraham Lincoln* (New Brunswick, N.J.: Rutgers University Press, 1953), vol. 2, pp. 499–500.

Topics for Critical Thinking and Writing

1. Find out, with the help of a reference librarian, what Allan Bakke, Brian Weber, Randy Pech, or Cheryl Hopwood did to warrant commendation from Eastland (para. 4), and write a 250-word essay on what you discover.

2. What, if any, particular programs of affirmative action does Eastland mention and criticize?

3. When Eastland writes (para. 6) that "we do not have to take the risk of affirmative action," what does he mean? How do you think he would reply to someone who disagrees with him?

4. Eastland concentrates on the objections to affirmative action for African Americans; he says little about affirmative action for women. Do you think his objections apply equally well to both groups? Why, or why not?

5. Suppose one argued that affirmative action is a necessary tactic to achieve more racial and cultural diversity on campus among students, faculty, and staff and that such diversity is an end good in itself. How do you think Eastland might reply to such an argument?

6. Head Start programs, established under the Economic Opportunity Act of 1964, help prepare economically disadvantaged students to meet the rigors of academic life in school and college. Do Eastland's criticisms of affirmative action apply to Head Start?

7. Which statement do you think best characterizes Eastland's position? (a) We do not have a problem with racism, so affirmative action was never needed to solve it. (b) We do have a problem with racism, but affirmative action is not the way to solve it. (c) Affirmative action creates a problem of racism where none existed.

8. Read the essay by Burke Marshall and Nicholas deB. Katzenbach (directly following) in defense of affirmative action programs, and write a 1,000-word essay explaining why you think one essay or the other has the better argument overall.

BURKE MARSHALL AND
NICHOLAS DEB. KATZENBACH

Burke Marshall (b. 1922) received his bachelor's and law degrees from Yale University. He was an assistant attorney general from 1961 to 1965 during the Kennedy administration, working on racial issues. He is now an emeritus law professor at Yale. Nicholas deB. Katzenbach (b. 1922) graduated from Princeton

University and received a law degree from Yale. He was attorney general from 1965 to 1966 during the Johnson administration and coauthor of The Political Foundations of International Law *(1961). This essay was first published in the* New York Times Magazine *(February 22, 1998).*

Not Color Blind: Just Blind

Few African American students are likely to enter the great public law schools of California and Texas in the fall. That is the direct, foreseeable consequence of a California referendum and a Texas federal court decision. So concerned were civil rights groups about the popular and legal doctrine that led to this result that they joined together to deny the U.S. Supreme Court the opportunity to decide an apparently definitive affirmative action case involving teachers in Piscataway Township, New Jersey. Do such events—especially Piscataway—foretell the end of affirmative action, or have we simply lost sight of our long-term vision of a color-blind society?

In 1989, the Piscataway school board, faced with the need to lay off a single teacher, chose to lay off a white while retaining an African American of equal seniority and qualifications. The board gave racial diversity, citing its affirmative action policy, as the sole reason for the choice. Its decision was rejected by a federal judge who found the board in violation of the 1964 Civil Rights Act. That ruling was upheld by a federal appellate court. The school board appealed to the Supreme Court. Late last year, with financial assistance from civil rights groups, the board settled the case and withdrew its appeal.

The settlement has since become a kind of raw shorthand in the national debate about affirmative action because its facts serve to make clear the core of that debate. The seeming baldness of the facts plainly told the civil rights groups' leaders that the case should not be permitted to remain in the Supreme Court, and that it would be prudent to use their funds to avoid its doing so. This may be the first time that money has been used directly to take an important public policy issue off the Court's docket.

All this arose because the case was framed to portray person-to-person competition for a job in which race alone was the decisive factor. This aspect fitted neatly with the notion, widespread among opponents of affirmative action, that it creates a zero-sum game in which there is a loser for every winner and that the game is won and lost on the basis of race. Thus it obscures the larger goal of finding and preserving room for blacks in all aspects—economic, political, educational, social—and at all levels of society.

In addition, the case involved a layoff—the loss of a specific, known 5
job—instead of a positive general decision as to what kind and mix of
people are needed in a work force or in a faculty or student body. The
facts fitted in not only with some legal learning—that an affirmative action program should not "unnecessarily trammel" the expectations of
those not included in the program—but also more importantly with the
personalization of the controversy into one in which whites are individually hurt by being deprived of their deserved opportunities, by deliber-
ate and explicit efforts to include blacks.

These aspects of the Piscataway litigation appeared perfect for opponents of affirmative action and a legal land mine for its defenders. The
former believed that the facts of the case would lead a majority of the
Supreme Court to say, about affirmative action in general, that the case
showed its injustices and the malevolent consequences of permitting the
use of race as a factor, certainly as a decisive one, in allocating any
scarce resources, like jobs or admissions to great universities. Strangely
enough, the latter group—the important civil rights organizations and
their lawyers as well as the Clinton administration—saw the case in the
same way. Thus all concerned either hoped or feared that the Court,
when faced with the rejected white teacher, would say: "Enough of this.
It has gone on too long already. This is the end of affirmative action for
any purpose as far as the law is concerned."

Is affirmative action really the unfair black "preference," or "reverse
discrimination," policy that its critics claim and that Piscataway seems
to present so starkly? Have we in fact lost sight of the larger goal of integrating blacks into our society? Or have we been so successful in achieving a "color blind" society about which Martin Luther King dreamed
that the larger goal need no longer concern us?

Those who oppose affirmative action programs do not make such
broad claims. They affirm the goal of an integrated society and do not
contend we have yet achieved it. Critics simply argue that it is morally
and constitutionally wrong to seek its achievement through race-based
programs that give a "preference" to African Americans. Such programs,
they maintain, are essentially wrong for the same reasons that it is
wrong for whites to discriminate against blacks. It denies "equal opportunity" to whites and is antithetical to awarding jobs or promotions or
college admissions on the basis of "merit."

There is no longer any dispute that overt, provable racial bias
against blacks in employment or education should be unlawful. The disputed question is whether overt and provable bias is the only form of
racial bias with which our society should—or can lawfully—be concerned. Certainly that bias—state supported in the Deep South and
rampant throughout the country—was the immediate and most impor-

tant target of the civil rights laws of the 1960s. Equally, the white majority in this country, despite deep-seated feelings of racial superiority, committed itself to achieving an integrated society. That happened, we believe, for the simple reason that it did not seem possible, then or now, for this country to maintain its democratic principles unless we could achieve Dr. King's dream. Is the elimination of overt bias all we need to do to accomplish that end?

The term "affirmative action" was first officially used in 1961 when President Kennedy strengthened an existing executive order prohibiting racial discrimination by government contractors in their employment practices. It was a natural, not a provocative, term to use. In the early '60s, blacks were essentially excluded from every level and every desirable institution of society. In many places they could not enter theaters, restaurants, hotels, or even parts of public libraries, courtrooms, and legislatures. How could that condition possibly have been changed — and the nation as a whole have decided that it should be changed — without taking action affirmatively, positively, deliberately, explicitly to change it?

So it was that there was no real controversy at the national level over the basic idea of acting affirmatively about race, although debate started soon enough, as it should have, over the details of particular steps. But at that time the country saw problems of race as problems to be faced and dealt with as the racial problems they were. The label "affirmative action" became popular perhaps because it suggested that we were at long last dealing with our oldest and most difficult problem. It was applied beyond the Kennedy executive order to a variety of race-based programs, private and public, voluntary as well as legally coerced, that sought to guarantee the employment — or, in the case of educational institutions, the admission — of qualified African Americans. It preceded the Civil Rights Acts of the 1960s and was consciously aimed at racial bias at a time when individuals could not yet sue private employers. But companies' employment of qualified African Americans to insure eligibility for government contracts was measured not individual by individual but by success in achieving reasonable numbers over time.

The technique of setting goals for minority employment is important because of its capacity to deal with all forms of potential bias — overt, concealed, or even inadvertent. Most national corporations have adopted employment goals. They appreciate the economic advantages of expanding and integrating the work force and they understand the need to press hard if the overall goal of inclusion is to be obtained.

The natural inclination of predominantly white male middle managers is to hire and promote one of their own. Most of the time the decision honestly reflects their judgment as to the best candidate without conscious appreciation of how much that judgment may have been conditioned by experience in the largely segregated society we still live in. To hire or promote an African American is often viewed as risky. Will he or she be accepted by fellow workers? A white may be praised for his independence; a like-minded black is seen as not a "team player." If corporations set reasonable hiring and promotion goals and reward management for their achievement, the integration process is speeded up. Public and private policies coincide.

Critics of affirmative action in employment see it not as an effort to create a reasonably integrated work force but as a system for favoring a less-qualified African American over a better-qualified white — a system of "preference" rather than "merit." There are three difficulties with their argument.

First, critics seek to reduce what is administered as a flexible system of hiring and promoting numbers of people into a measurement of one individual against another. Affirmative action programs deal with numbers of people at various times and seek to examine flexibly the results in numbers, not whether individual *A* is better than *B*. Such a program does not examine or re-examine each decision or demand precise achievement of numerical goals; it does not require a "quota," like a sales quota. It thus encourages personnel judgments, tolerating individual mistakes whether a white or a black is the victim.

Second, the critics assume that it is possible precisely to define and measure "merit." The best person for one job may not be the best for another, and vice versa; how does one square individual differences, or the "overqualified" candidate, with merit and the requirements of a particular job? Assuming that we are selecting from a pool of candidates who all meet whatever objective criteria are applicable to job performance, selection of the "best qualified" becomes a matter of subjective judgment by the employer — a judgment that involves weighing such intangibles as personality, leadership ability, motivation, dependability, enthusiasm, attitude toward authority. If critics are claiming that affirmative action has resulted in a less-competent work force because of the hiring and promotion of less-qualified blacks, neither evidence nor experience supports that conclusion.

Third, to argue that affirmative action constitutes a "preference" for African Americans is simply to argue that it distorts what would otherwise be a more efficient and fair system. Since the premise of the argument is that affirmative action constitutes a "preference" for blacks, it is fair to assume that proponents believe a "color blind" system would result in fewer blacks being employed. Why? If the pool of qualified applicants is 10 percent African American, then a color-blind system or an affirmative action program would result in about 10 percent black representation in the work force.

Thus, the word "preference" as critics use it is an effort to convert a broad employment effort into a series of individual choices or comparisons, as in Piscataway, with the additional innuendo that the fact of "preference" means a less-qualified African American will always prevail. That is a serious distortion of affirmative action.

Put differently, opponents of affirmative action in employment believe either that today the playing field is level for all races or that, absent overt racial bias, we should act as if it were. By contrast, most African Americans and many whites believe that bias still exists, though not always overtly, and that affirmative action is simply a guarantee that the playing field is not tilted.

Laws forbidding racial discrimination were relatively easy to administer when the bias was overt and widespread. The more that bias goes underground or, worse yet, is unconscious on the part of the decision maker, who believes his decision is uninfluenced by race, the more difficult and controversial that administration becomes. To label and punish unconscious bias as though it wore a hood may well be offensive. Programs of affirmative action avoid that problem while promoting the integrated society we seek. They minimally interfere with discretion in making particular choices and give management a desirable latitude in exercising particular judgments. 20

The other use of affirmative action most commonly criticized is in college admission. Educational institutions usually create a pool of applicants who meet objective tests designed to determine if the applicant is capable of performing successfully. Tests can reasonably predict first-year performance and do not claim to do more. But selection from the pool is not confined to rank on test scores, and applicants with lower scores are admitted for many reasons. Some applicants are admitted on the basis of judgments about potential and predictions about future performance not unlike those used in employment decisions. A student from a poor school who qualifies may be seen, despite a lower score, as having great motivation and aptitude. In other cases, "merit" is measured by other abilities, like musical or athletic talent. In still others, admissions may be determined by geography, financial ability, relationship to graduates, or relationship to people important in other ways to the institution. And finally, race and national origin may be taken into account and labeled "affirmative action."

If race cannot be taken into account and admission is based on test scores alone, far fewer African Americans will qualify. That was the predictable result in California and Texas, where state institutions were forbidden to take race into account. Again, the word "preference" is unfortunate because critics use it to imply that some kind of racial bias is used to reject better-qualified whites. Most of the students admitted are in fact white, hardly a demonstration of a bias in favor of blacks, and certainly not one that can be equated with past denials of admission to blacks to our best universities.

What proponents of affirmative action in college admissions urge is simply an institutional need for qualified African Americans on the grounds that a diverse student body contributes to educational excellence and to the preparation of students to live in an integrated society. Critics do not question the educational advantage of diversity—though their prescriptions would make its achievement virtually impossible. Further, those African Americans who can qualify for the institutional admissions pool would probably not be as successful as they are without superior motivation and determination—qualities most Americans would associate with merit.

Colleges and professional schools serve as gatekeepers to professional and business careers. If African Americans can successfully do the academic work, they will importantly contribute to the public goal of an integrated society. Studies support the contention that some blacks perform better academically than some whites with better test scores and that African Americans successfully compete for employment at a comparable level with whites upon graduation.

The arguments against this "preference" are similar to those in other affirmative action programs: it is anti-merit and discriminates against whites with higher scores on admissions tests. That argument is not really worth consideration unless one is prepared to argue that all admissions should be measured exclusively by test scores. No one is prepared to go that far. The plea for fairness based on "merit" as measured by test scores appears to be confined to race—a plea that in our society should be regarded with some skepticism.

Affirmative action programs, whether to avoid present bias or to remedy the effects of three centuries of discrimination against African Americans, are race-based. The problems they seek to cure are and always have been race-based. They stem from history—the political, economic, and social domination of blacks by a white majority that regarded blacks as inferior. Undoubtedly there are blacks who are biased against whites and who, given the power to do so, would discriminate against them. Of course, given the power, it would be as morally wrong for them to do so as it has been for whites. But discrimination by blacks against whites is not America's problem. It is not the problem that predominantly white legislatures, businesses, and universities seek to solve through affirmative action programs.

To speak of these white efforts as though they were racially biased against whites and to equate them with the discriminatory practices of the past against African Americans is to steal the rhetoric of civil rights and turn it upside down. For racial bias to be a problem, it must be accompanied by power. Affirmative action programs are race-based not to show preference for one race over another but to resolve that problem. Only if one ignores that purpose and states the matter in Piscataway terms—preferring one individual over another for no reason other than race—does there even appear to be room for argument. If problems of race are to be solved, they must be seen as the race-based problems they are.

It is this aspect of the controversy that recent decisions of the Supreme Court have brought into question. The Equal Protection Clause of the Fourteenth Amendment was designed to insure that former slaves and their descendants were entitled to the same legal protection as white citizens. Like the Thirteenth Amendment abolishing slavery and the Fifteenth guaranteeing the right to vote regardless of race, it was clearly and unequivocally aimed at racial problems—in today's terminology "race based." The Equal Protection Clause has never been viewed as preventing classification of citizens for governmental reasons as long as the legislative classification was "reasonable" in terms of its purpose.

Where that classification involved race, however, the Court determined that it must be given "strict scrutiny." In other words, given our history both before and after the passage of the amendment, the Court understandably thought it wise to regard any racial classifications by overwhelmingly white legislatures with skepticism. When it was satisfied after strict scrutiny that the classification did not have the purpose or effect of discriminating against African Americans or other ethnic minorities, the Court found legislation to be consistent with the amendment. In the context of both our history and that of the amendment, this simply forbade abuse of white political superiority that prejudiced other races or ethnic minorities.

More recently, however, a majority has edged toward pronouncing 30 the Constitution "color blind," coming close to holding legislation that uses any racial classification unconstitutional. Reading the Equal Protection Clause to protect whites as well as blacks from racial classification is to focus upon a situation that does not and never has existed in our society. Unfortunately, it casts doubt upon all forms of racial classification, however benign and however focused upon promoting integration. If such a reading is finally adopted by a majority of the Court, it would put a constitutional pall over all governmental affirmative action programs and even put similar private programs in danger of being labeled "discriminatory" against whites and therefore in violation of existing civil rights legislation—perhaps the ultimate stupidity.

The Court has, in short, never accepted as a national priority—in its terms a "compelling state interest"—the necessary race-based efforts, private and public, to include blacks in the institutional framework that constitutes America's economic, political, educational, and social life. Its recent decisions on the distribution of political power through districting outcomes have precluded race as a major factor while permitting incumbency, party affiliations, random geographic features, and boundaries drawn for obsolete historical reasons. Other lines of cases have similar outcomes for university admissions (as against unfair and educationally irrelevant factors like family ties, athletic prowess, and geography) and employment choices. It is very nearly as if this Court has simply mandated that what is the country's historic struggle against racial oppression and racial prejudice cannot be acted upon in a race-conscious way—that the law must view racial problems observable by all as if oppression and prejudice did not exist and had never existed. The Court's majority, in other words, has come very close to saying—and the hope and fear about the Piscataway case was that it would finally say at last—that courts cannot be permitted to see what is plain to everybody else.

Topics for Critical Thinking and Writing

1. What is a "zero-sum game" (para. 4), and why might it seem that affirmative action involves such a game?

2. The authors suggest that part (most?) of the original purpose behind affirmative action was "the larger goal of integrating blacks into our society" (para. 7). Do the authors explain how this was supposed to work?

3. *Affirmative action* has been defined in law and practice in several different ways. After reading this essay, how would you complete the following definition: "A given program is a program of affirmative action if and only if. . . ." (Hint: Consult your reference librarian about some specific affirmative action program. For example, what made Head Start an example of affirmative action?)

4. The authors offer three replies to critics of affirmative action (paras. 14–18). Which of these replies do you think is most persuasive? Least persuasive? Explain yourself in an essay of 300 words.

5. If it had been within the power of the authors to decide the Piscataway case (paras. 1–6), how do you think they would have decided it?

6. Suppose Jones and Smith are both equally qualified for entrance to a selective college as measured in the usual ways (SAT scores, rank in high school graduating class, teacher recommendations). Only one can be admitted, however. One admission officer argues for admitting Jones because he comes from a remote part of the country and thus would help the college diversify its student body geographically. Another admission officer argues for admitting Smith because she is a member of an ethnic minority and thus would help the college diversify its student body racially. Do you think one of the two kinds of diversity is more important than the other? Why? Which candidate would you prefer to admit, and why?

7. The authors are skeptical about college admissions "based on 'merit'" (para. 25), especially when merit is measured by "test scores." Why are they skeptical? How would you define *merit* as relevant to college admission? (That is, how would you complete the following definition: "An applicant merits admission to a selective college if and only if. . . .") However you define it, would you place great or little emphasis on merit in determining who is admitted to college?

2

Cell Phones: Should Their Use While Driving Be Prohibited?

ADVOCATES FOR CELL PHONE SAFETY

The following essay, untitled, appeared on the Congressional Quarterly's *Web site—www.cq.com—on March 16, 2001.*

Yes, Prohibit Their Use

"There isn't enough evidence to prove that using a cell phone while driving causes accidents."

A lack of statistical data about a problem is not the same thing as a lack of evidence!

The fact is, we have evidence that a problem exists. We don't have statistics—not because they don't exist—but because we don't currently collect them.

The Harvard Center for Risk Analysis published a study (funded by AT&T) in 1999 in which they assigned a crash risk factor to using cell phones. As of summer 2000, it comes out to 450 to 1,000 fatalities each year.

The National Highway Transportation Safety Administration (NHTSA) says that for every fatality, there are 666 property-damage and injury-producing crashes. So we are having somewhere between 300,000 and 650,000 "other" crashes due to cell phones.

We killed 120 kids and small-statured women with airbags and 5 there was a huge government, industry, and societal response. We killed

150 people with Firestone tires, and the response was the same. Both airbags and tires are essential parts of the driving environment. Cell phones are not, so why do we tolerate this problem?

In many states, police are not required to note whether a driver involved in an accident had been on the phone, so statistics linking crashes to phones are hard to come by. Only Oklahoma and Minnesota record that information, but experts say those states' data-collection methods are unreliable.

"The information you need most is not available, because we are not collecting it," said Mark Burris of the University of South Florida's Center for Urban Transportation Research. In November, Japan became one of 14 countries banning handheld phone use while driving. "Accidents caused by the use of mobile phones dropped by 75 percent the next month," Burris noted.

"Cellular telephones are important devices for reporting emergencies."

This is absolutely true, and the law enforcement community supports such use. But emergency calls can and should be made from stopped vehicles. Indeed, most calls relate to witnessing a crash. Under such circumstances, traffic is often stopped, and witnesses attempt to render aid.

The cellular telephone industry often demonstrates its commitment to promoting safety for its customers through the use of information packets included with product purchases or customer billing, and through the occasional television ad. All industries include caveats for product use in the literature that accompanies products. Most of us don't read any of it because we know it is provided to protect companies during litigation.

Topics for Critical Thinking and Writing

1. What do you think of the authors' strategy of using quotations that are then refuted?

2. Do the statistics in paragraphs 3, 4, and 5 impress you, or on the contrary do you feel that (a) they aren't alarmingly large and (b) they may not be accurate? Explain your response.

3. In our view, the final paragraph makes an important point but does not make an effective ending for the essay. Reread the paragraph, thinking about its effectiveness as a concluding paragraph. If you agree with us

that the paragraph is weak, rewrite it—keeping the basic idea—so that
it makes an effective concluding paragraph.

ROBERT W. HAHN AND PAUL TETLOCK

*This essay, from "Driving and Talking Do Mix," was originally
published in* Policy Matters *(November 1999) and reprinted
(without a title) on the* Congressional Quarterly's *Web site—
www.cq.com—on March 16, 2001.*

No, Don't Prohibit Their Use

Check out that guy in the next lane—the one with the cell phone
glued to his ear, who's weaving wildly. Wow, that was close. So close
that Ann Landers just came out in support of a ban on driving and phoning. And Click and Clack, the *Car Talk* guys [on National Public Radio],
are giving away bumper stickers that say "Drive Now, Talk Later."

Legislators are listening. From Victoria, Australia, to Brooklyn,
Ohio, total bans on cell phone calls by drivers have been enacted.
England, Australia, Singapore, and Brazil all restrict car phones to the
hands-free type. And New York City bars calls by taxi drivers.

But does a ban make sense? At first blush, it seems a no-brainer if
cell phones are indeed causing fatal accidents. But lots of activities—
tuning the radio, drinking double lattes, refereeing the sibling wars in
the back seat—can lead to fatal crashes. No one is banning these.

While in-car phoning does increase risk, the benefits far outweigh
the costs. Start with the likely costs of not being able to conduct business
from the car or to call home on the fly. We estimate these costs in lost
time and productivity at about $24 billion—over $200 per household
annually.

The benefits of a ban, of course, would include the decrease in in-   5
juries, property damage, and fatalities. Our best estimate is about 10,000
serious accidents and 100 traffic fatalities—less than 1 percent of the
annual total. Using standard measures of how ordinary people make the
tradeoff between convenience and small risks of large disasters, we
estimate the cost of car phone-induced mayhem at about $1 billion
annually.

Fiddling with our assumptions—reducing the estimated benefits of
car calls, raising the implicit value of lives saved—doesn't change the
bottom line. Nor, for that matter, does assuming that cell phone use is
actually as dangerous as driving after drinking a few beers. Thus, on

balance, the safety purchased with a cell phone ban would simply be too expensive.

Washington and the states should find out what really makes a material difference in the safety of on-board calling. But until we know more, governments should let the 77 million Americans who own cellular phones make their own decisions about when to use them. The market, in the form of consumers, producers, and insurers, is doing pretty well in developing a technology that Americans are finding they can't live without.

Topics for Critical Thinking and Writing

1. What do you think of the opening paragraph? And now that you have read the entire essay, why do you think the authors begin their piece the way they do?

2. The authors use statistics. How impressive are these figures? In paragraph 5, the authors suggest that their "best estimate" of fatalities is "100 traffic fatalities" a year, but the opposing essay (p. 20) suggests that there are "450 to 1,000 fatalities each year." Whose figures do you accept? Why?

3. How would you characterize the tone of the final paragraph? Smug? Earnest? Thoughtful? Or what? And more generally, offer an analysis of this paragraph, pointing out why it is or is not an effective final paragraph.

3

Censorship: Should Public Libraries Filter Internet Sites?

In June 2003 the U.S. Supreme Court upheld (six to three) a federal law that requires public libraries to install filters that block access to pornography on the Internet. The idea was to protect children; adults could presumably ask librarians to unblock the material, and presumably librarians would comply. All nine Justices agreed that restricting the access of children does not in itself violate the First Amendment which guarantees freedom of speech in public forums. The issue was whether the law interferes with the First Amendment rights of adults. Chief Justice Rehnquist, who voted with the majority, said that Internet access does *not* turn a library into a public forum. Libraries, he said, are for "research, learning, and recreational pursuits," and speech in them may be curtailed even without compelling reason, just as a librarian's failure to purchase a particular book—for whatever reasons—does not constitute a violation of the First Amendment. We reprint two arguments, one pro and one con, on the issue. The fact that the Court has decided the issue does not at all imply that one should not continue to debate it.

DAVID BURT

David Burt is a market research manager. This essay was first printed in CQ Researcher, *June 1, 2001, two years before the Supreme Court decided the case.*

Yes, Install Filters

In communities across America, a controversy is raging over how to cope with the problem of library patrons using Internet terminals to access illegal obscenity and child pornography.

Like many libraries, the Broward County, Fla., Public Library relies on "education" and "a policy" to encourage appropriate use of the Internet. But a lawsuit against the library uncovered the problems with such an education/policy approach. The *New Times* of Broward reported that access to Internet pornography in the library had led to 14 incidents of masturbation documented by library and police reports, two incidents of men exposing themselves, and one instance of a man fondling a female patron.

Freedom of Information Act requests have uncovered thousands of other library pornography incidents from all over the country. The Greenville [S.C.] Public Library suffered similar problems. An internal report discovered that "a large number, perhaps 50 percent, of the users on one afternoon were young men going to pornography sites."

Library administrators found that "female staff . . . are intimidated by this activity." One female staffer stated: "I felt dirty coming home at the end of the day."

To stop the illegal activity and restore staff morale, the library board   5 chose to install N2H2 filtering software. Since then, abuse of the Internet has stopped. Further, no patrons have complained about being denied access to legitimate sites.

This experience has been repeated across the county. After watching the failure of the education/policy approach, nearly 4,000 public libraries have chosen to install filtering software. According to a 2000 study by the U.S. National Commission on Libraries and Information Science, 24.6 percent of public libraries now use filters, an increase of 121 percent in two years.

Other research shows the filters are widely popular with the librarians who use them. Library researcher Ken Haycock, who recently studied the use of filters in public libraries, found that 76 percent of public librarians said they were "very/somewhat satisfied" with the decision to install Internet filter software. An eye-popping 90 percent of public librarians using filters responded that the software serves its purpose either "very well" or "somewhat well."

Public libraries don't stock *Hustler* next to *House & Garden* in their magazine section, so why should they offer Hustler.com? They shouldn't. Not when there is a tested, effective solution widely available.

Topics for Critical Thinking and Writing

1. Burt does not address the First Amendment issue of whether filters interfere with an adult's right of access to Internet pornography. Given the facts he sets forth, do you agree that the issue of freedom of access to ideas is irrelevant in this context?

2. In his final paragraph Burt offers an analogy: Just as the library does not stock pornographic magazines, so the library does not need to "offer" online pornography. As we point out in our headnote, Chief Justice Rehnquist made pretty much the same argument. On the other hand, Associate Justice David Souter, voting in the minority, took a different line. Souter said that the proper analogy is not the failure to stock a book; rather, Souter said, the proper analogy "is either to buying a book and then keeping it from adults lacking an acceptable 'purpose' or to buying an encyclopedia and then cutting out pages with anything thought to be unsuitable for all adults." Putting aside the merits of the case as a whole, which (if any) of these comparisons seems valid to you? Explain.

NANCY KRANICH

Nancy Kranich, president of the American Library Association, wrote this essay for CQ Researcher, *which published it along with Burt's essay on June 1, 2001.*

No, Do Not Install Filters

Filters are neither the best nor the only means to protect children using the Internet in libraries. They give parents a false sense of security that their children are protected. No filter protects children from all objectionable content. But all filters block access to critical constitutionally protected speech about many subjects people need to know.

Filters cannot take the place of responsible use, informed by local-based Internet access policies, user-education programs, links to great sites, and safety guidelines. That is why ALA and many other organizations—including the federal Commission on Online Child Protection (COPA) and several filtering companies—oppose federal legislation mandating that libraries and schools utilize Internet-blocking technology. Laws like the Children's Internet Protection Act (CIPA) force libraries in economically disadvantaged areas to use already scarce resources to install expensive and unreliable filtering technologies or lose the vital federal funds they need to end the demoralizing effects of "digital discrimination" in underserved communities.

Thanks to the e-rate and other programs, 95 percent of America's libraries are now online, and libraries are the No. 1 point of access for those without computers at home, work, or school. Librarians have worked hard to ensure that libraries provide a wide spectrum of information to our diverse communities. We do this not only by providing access to both print and online resources but also by instructing people how to use these resources efficiently and safely. We identify great sites for children and adults and schedule computer classes. The vast majority of library patrons use the Internet responsibly, guided by library policies that address appropriate use and invoke disciplinary action for violators. Approximately 95 percent of public libraries already have Internet policies.

Librarians care deeply about children. We have dedicated our careers to ensuring that adults and children enjoy an enriching experience and access to quality materials in libraries. We understand the enormous learning potential of the Internet and appreciate the responsibility we have as a society for ensuring that libraries remain safe and intellectually creative environments for everyone.

This will not be accomplished by imposing Draconian governmental 5 controls over our libraries, but rather by allowing the parents and librarians in our local communities to tailor workable and effective policies to protect children from inappropriate material on the Internet.

Topics for Critical Thinking and Writing

1. In her first paragraph Kranich diminishes the value of filters as a way of protecting children. In your view, does her essay provide adequate support for the view that filters are not the best way to protect children? Explain.

2. In her third paragraph Kranich says: "The vast majority of library patrons use the Internet responsibly, guided by library policies that

address appropriate use and invoke disciplinary action for violators."
Does your public library have such a policy? If so, what is it? Do you
think it is a good one? Explain.

3. In her final paragraph Kranich says that parents and librarians should
   unite "to tailor workable and effective policies to protect children from
   inappropriate material on the Internet." First of all, do you agree that
   children should be protected from some materials? Second, if you do
   agree and if you were serving on a local committee, what proposals
   would you make?

4

Gay Marriages: Should They Be Legalized?

THOMAS B. STODDARD

Thomas B. Stoddard (1948–1997) was executive director of the Lambda Legal Defense and Education Fund, a gay rights organization. In 1995 New York University School of Law established a fellowship in Stoddard's name, honoring him for his work on behalf of gay and lesbian rights. This article is from the op-ed section of the New York Times, *March 4, 1988.*

Gay Marriages: Make Them Legal

"In sickness and in health, 'til death do us part." With those familiar words, millions of people each year are married, a public affirmation of a private bond that both society and the newlyweds hope will endure. Yet for nearly four years, Karen Thompson was denied the company of the one person to whom she had pledged lifelong devotion. Her partner is a woman, Sharon Kowalski, and their home state of Minnesota, like every other jurisdiction in the United States, refuses to permit two individuals of the same sex to marry.

Karen Thompson and Sharon Kowalski are spouses in every respect except the legal. They exchanged vows and rings; they lived together until November 13, 1983 — when Ms. Kowalski was severely injured when her car was struck by a drunk driver. She lost the capacity to walk or to speak more than several words at a time, and needed constant care.

Ms. Thompson sought a court ruling granting her guardianship over her partner, but Ms. Kowalski's parents opposed the petition and obtained sole guardianship. They moved Ms. Kowalski to a nursing home three-hundred miles away from Ms. Thompson and forbade all visits between the two women. Last month, as part of a reevaluation of Ms. Kowalski's mental competency, Ms. Thompson was permitted to visit her partner again. But the prolonged injustice and anguish inflicted on both women hold a moral for everyone.

Marriage, the Supreme Court declared in 1967, is "one of the basic civil rights of man" (and, presumably, of woman as well). The freedom to marry, said the Court, is "essential to the orderly pursuit of happiness."

Marriage is not just a symbolic state. It can be the key to survival, emotional and financial. Marriage triggers a universe of rights, privileges, and presumptions. A married person can share in a spouse's estate even when there is no will. She is typically entitled to the group insurance and pension programs offered by the spouse's employer, and she enjoys tax advantages. She cannot be compelled to testify against her spouse in legal proceedings.

The decision whether or not to marry belongs properly to individuals—not the government. Yet at present, all fifty states deny that choice to millions of gay and lesbian Americans. While marriage has historically required a male partner and a female partner, history alone cannot sanctify injustice. If tradition were the only measure, most states would still limit matrimony to partners of the same race.

As recently as 1967, before the Supreme Court declared miscegenation statutes unconstitutional, sixteen states still prohibited marriages between a white person and a black person. When all the excuses were stripped away, it was clear that the only purpose of those laws was, in the words of the Supreme Court, "to maintain white supremacy."

Those who argue against reforming the marriage statutes because they believe that same-sex marriage would be "antifamily" overlook the obvious: Marriage creates families and promotes social stability. In an increasingly loveless world, those who wish to commit themselves to a relationship founded upon devotion should be encouraged, not scorned. Government has no legitimate interest in how that love is expressed.

And it can no longer be argued—if it ever could—that marriage is fundamentally a procreative unit. Otherwise, states would forbid marriage between those who, by reason of age or infertility, cannot have children, as well as those who elect not to.

As the case of Sharon Kowalski and Karen Thompson demonstrates, sanctimonious illusions lead directly to the suffering of others. Denied the right to marry, these two women are left subject to the whims and prejudices of others, and of the law.

Depriving millions of gay American adults the marriages of their choice, and the rights that flow from marriage, denies equal protection of the law. They, their families and friends, together with fair-minded people everywhere, should demand an end to this monstrous injustice.

Topics for Critical Thinking and Writing

1. Study the essay as an example of ways to argue. What sorts of arguments does Stoddard offer? He does not offer statistics or cite authorities, but what *does* he do in an effort to convince the reader?

2. Stoddard draws an analogy between laws that used to prohibit marriage between persons of different races and laws that still prohibit marriage between persons of the same sex. Evaluate this analogy in an essay of 100 words.

3. Stoddard cites Karen Thompson and Sharon Kowalski (para. 2). Presumably he could have found, if he had wished, a comparable example using two men rather than two women. Do you think the effect of his essay would be better, worse, or the same if his example used men rather than women? Why?

4. Do you find adequate Stoddard's response to the charge that "same sex marriage would be 'antifamily'" (para. 8)? Why, or why not?

5. One widespread assumption is that the family exists to produce children. Stoddard mentions this, but he does not mention that although gay couples cannot produce children, they can (where legally permitted to do so) adopt and rear children and thus fulfill a social need. One partner can even be the natural parent. Do you think he was wise to omit this argument in behalf of same-sex marriages? Why?

6. Think about what principal claims one might make to contradict Stoddard's claims, and then write a 500-word essay defending this proposition: "Lawful marriage should be limited to heterosexual couples." Or if you believe that gay marriages should be legitimized, write an essay offering additional support to Stoddard's essay.

7. Stoddard's whole purpose is to break down the prejudice against same-sex marriages, and he seems to take for granted the appropriateness of monogamy. Yet one might argue against Stoddard that if society opened the door to same-sex marriages, it would be hard to keep the door closed to polygamy or polyandry. Write a 500-word essay exploring this question.

8. Would Stoddard's argument require him to allow marriage between a brother and a sister? A parent and a child? A human being and an animal? Why, or why not?

9. On November 18, 2003, the Massachusetts Supreme Judicial Court (the highest court in the state) ruled 4–3 that the state's constitution gives gay couples the right to marry. The majority opinion held that the state "failed to identify any constitutionally adequate reason for denying civil marriage to same-sex couples." Many legislators and many citizens throughout the country who oppose this decision—including some people who favor "civil unions" for those gays who want recognition of their status—have vowed that they will work for an amendment to the United States Constitution that would limit marriage to the union of a male and a female. In an essay of 500 words indicate why you do or do not favor amending the nation's Constitution so that "marriage" is limited to heterosexual couples.

LISA SCHIFFREN

Lisa Schiffren was a speechwriter for former Vice President Dan Quayle. We reprint an essay that originally was published in the New York Times *on March 23, 1996.*

Gay Marriage, an Oxymoron

As study after study and victim after victim testify to the social devastation of the sexual revolution, easy divorce, and out-of-wedlock motherhood, marriage is fashionable again. And parenthood has transformed many baby boomers into advocates of bourgeois norms.

Indeed, we have come so far that the surprise issue of the political season is whether homosexual "marriage" should be legalized. The Hawaii courts will likely rule that gay marriage is legal, and other states will be required to accept those marriages as valid.

Considering what a momentous change this would be—a radical redefinition of society's most fundamental institution—there has been almost no real debate. This is because the premise is unimaginable to many, and the forces of political correctness have descended on the discussion, raising the cost of opposition. But one may feel the same affection for one's homosexual friends and relatives as for any other and be genuinely pleased for the happiness they derive from relationships while opposing gay marriage for principled reasons.

"Same-sex marriage" is inherently incompatible with our culture's understanding of the institution. Marriage is essentially a lifelong compact between a man and woman committed to sexual exclusivity and the creation and nurture of offspring. For most Americans, the marital union—as distinguished from other sexual relationships and legal and economic partnerships—is imbued with an aspect of holiness. Though many of us are uncomfortable using religious language to discuss social and political issues, Judeo-Christian morality informs our view of family life.

Though it is not polite to mention it, what the Judeo-Christian tradition has to say about homosexual unions could not be clearer. In a diverse, open society such as ours, tolerance of homosexuality is a necessity. But for many, its practice depends on a trick of cognitive dissonance that allows people to believe in the Judeo-Christian moral order while accepting, often with genuine regard, the different lives of homosexual acquaintances. That is why, though homosexuals may believe that they are merely seeking a small expansion of the definition of marriage, the majority of Americans perceive this change as a radical deconstruction of the institution.

Some make the conservative argument that making marriage a civil right will bring stability, an end to promiscuity, and a sense of fairness to gay men and women. But they miss the point. Society cares about stability in heterosexual unions because it is critical for raising healthy children and transmitting the values that are the basis of our culture.

Whether homosexual relationships endure is of little concern to society. That is also true of most childless marriages, harsh as it is to say. Society has wisely chosen not to differentiate between marriages, because it would require meddling into the motives and desires of everyone who applies for a license.

In traditional marriage, the tie that really binds for life is shared responsibility for the children. (A small fraction of gay couples may choose to raise children together, but such children are offspring of one partner and an outside contributor.) What will keep gay marriages together when individuals tire of each other?

Similarly, the argument that legal marriage will check promiscuity by gay males raises the question of how a "piece of paper" will do what the threat of AIDS has not. Lesbians seem to have little problem with monogamy or the rest of what constitutes "domestication," despite the absence of official status.

Finally, there is the so-called fairness argument. The government gives tax benefits, inheritance rights, and employee benefits only to the married. Again, these financial benefits exist to help couples raise children. Tax reform is an effective way to remove distinctions among earners.

If the American people are interested in a radical experiment with same-sex marriages, then subjecting it to the political process is the right route. For a court in Hawaii to assume that it has the power to radically redefine marriage is a stunning abuse of power. To present homosexual

marriage as a fait accompli, without national debate, is a serious political error. A society struggling to recover from thirty years of weakened
norms and broken families is not likely to respond gently to having an
institution central to most people's lives altered.

Topics for Critical Thinking and Writing

1. What is an oxymoron, and why does Schiffren think the phrases *gay
   marriage* and *same-sex marriage* are oxymorons?

2. In paragraph 3 Schiffren refers to "political correctness." How would
   you define that term? So defined, do you think political correctness is
   sometimes objectionable? Always objectionable? Sometimes justifiable?
   Always justifiable?

3. Schiffren defines marriage in paragraph 4 in such a way that a man and
   woman who marry with no intention of having children are deviant.
   She does not imply, however, that such marriages should be prohibited
   by law or otherwise nullified. Does consistency require her to grant that
   while same-sex marriages are no doubt deviant—in the sense of atypi-
   cal or relatively rare—they are nonetheless legitimate?

4. Schiffren refers to "cognitive dissonance" (para. 5). What does she mean
   by this term, and how does she think it plays a role in our society's prevailing attitude toward homosexuality?

5. Schiffren says (para. 7), "Whether homosexual relationships endure is
   of little concern to society" because such relationships do not involve
   nurturing children. By the same token, does society have little concern
   for heterosexual marriages to endure when there are no children involved? Or do you think that there are other considerations that make
   stable intimate relations between consenting adults important to
   society?

6. List the reasons for same-sex marriage unions that Schiffren mentions.
   Which, if any, do you think are significant? Can you think of any reasons that she fails to mention?

7. In her final paragraph, Schiffren deplores the federal court in Hawaii
   that ratified same-sex marriage. Is it the process or the result of this decision to which she mostly objects? Do you agree with her objection? Go
   to your college library, find out the current status of this issue in the
   courts, and write a 500-word paper on the Hawaiian same-sex marriage
   law, how it became law, and what it provides.

8. If gay marriage is recognized as legal, are we necessarily on a slippery
   slope that will bring us to recognition of polygamy or polyandry (per-

haps heterosexual, but perhaps a marriage of a bisexual to a man and also to a woman) and incest. Why, or why not?

9. Schiffren was not replying directly to Thomas B. Stoddard (p. 29), but she probably knew his arguments. Does he make any points that you wish she had faced? If so, what are they? If she were asked to comment on these points by Stoddard, what do you think her responses would be?

10. How would you characterize Schiffren's tone? Haughty? Earnest? Smart-alecky? (You need not come up with a one-word answer; you might say, "She is chiefly X but also sometimes Y.") Do you think her tone will help her to persuade people to accept her views?

5

Gun Control: Would It Really Help?

Sarah Thompson, a retired physician, describes herself thus on her homepage on the Internet: "Dr. Thompson is dedicated to the restoration of full civil liberties and limited constitutional government. She writes [an online] column, "The Righter," which focuses on civil liberties and individual responsibility and action." We reprint here an article that was published in American Gun Review *in October 1997.*

Concealed Carry Prevents Violent Crimes

The right of law-abiding citizens to carry concealed firearms for purposes of self-defense has become a hot and controversial topic. Claims have been made citing everything from "the presence of a firearm in the home increases the risk of homicide by 43 times" to "there are up to 2.5 million defensive uses of private firearms per year, with up to 400,000 lives saved as a result." There are people who feel endangered by the presence of a gun nearby and other people who feel vulnerable when not carrying a gun on their person. Some law enforcement agents welcome the increasing numbers of lawfully armed citizens while others view them as a deadly threat. What and where is the truth in all of this disagreement, and what are the implications for public policy?

Prior to Prohibition, there was virtually no federal gun control, and no concept of guns being "evil." Guns were seen as a threat to society only when they were possessed by blacks, and the history of gun control closely parallels the history of racism in this country. Guns were simply tools, useful for protecting one's livelihood and property, obtaining food for one's family, recreation, and when necessary, self-defense. The gun culture was an accepted and respected part of American life.

However, in a situation similar to the one we face today, Prohibition gave birth to a criminal subculture which depended on violence and guns, terrorizing law-abiding citizens. After Prohibition was repealed, these criminal organizations remained. Rather than attacking crime and criminals, the government passed the National Firearms Act in 1934, which put a $200 "transfer tax" (about $4,000 in 1996 dollars) on certain guns, particularly machine guns and short-barreled shotguns. (For comparison, a short-barreled shotgun cost only about $5!) The Federal Firearms Act followed in 1938, which required firearms dealers to obtain licenses, and started a new federal bureaucracy to "control guns."

The war on guns again escalated after the assassinations of President Kennedy, Senator Robert Kennedy, and the Reverend Martin Luther King in the 1960s. This resulted in the Federal Firearms Act of 1968 which, when compared word for word to the Nazi weapons laws of 1938, is almost identical. In the late 1980s to early 1990s, the attempted assassination of President Reagan and the wounding of his Press Secretary James Brady, and the escalation of violent, firearms-related crimes due to the failed "War on Drugs," have led to an intensification of the "War on Guns." We now have innumerable state and local laws restricting gun ownership, carrying, use, and even appearance, along with federal laws such as the Brady Act and the impending "Brady II."

To enforce these laws, the government needed to get "the people" to   5
support them, to willingly give up their Second Amendment rights and their right to self-defense. To do this, it recruited powerful spokespeople, primarily doctors and the media, to convince people that guns were bad and needed to be banned. Doctors, at least until recently, were highly respected professionals, scientists whose words were above questioning. The same was true of the elite medical journals. Most prestigious of all were the revered doctors and scientists who worked at the huge federal institutes of research. To their enduring shame, some of these doctors were co-opted into helping the government in its "War on Guns."

Doctors, of course, are not superhuman and they have weaknesses like everyone. Many well-meaning doctors just didn't analyze correctly what they were seeing and didn't bother to ask the right questions, since they had been trained to obey medical authorities. For example, doctors who work in emergency rooms see the horrors that misuse of guns can create. They dedicate their lives to saving lives, and watching people, especially young people, die of gunshot wounds is extremely painful. This makes it easy for them to be swayed by emotion and blame the gun instead of the person who misused it. Of course they never see the people who use guns safely and responsibly, and they never see the people whose lives were saved by defensive gun use. It's a very one-sided view.

At the same time, there were other doctors who saw the huge amounts of money being poured into biased gun research and saw the opportunity to get grant money, have their work published, or become famous. All this required was designing research that aided the government's preconceived policy of "proving" that guns were bad in order to disarm the populace. In my opinion there is only one term that applies to people who sell their integrity and their credentials for fame and profit.

Thus since 1987 we have been bombarded with medical "experts" proclaiming that guns were the cause of nearly everything wrong in society. The media gave tremendous coverage to these studies, and reinforced them with emotional and melodramatic stories of lives ruined by guns—by inanimate guns, not by criminals, carelessness, or their own stupidity. People, especially people raised in urban areas who had no experience with guns, believed these stories. No doubt you've heard these claims, and maybe even worried that invoking your Second Amendment rights was a bad idea.

Many of these studies were funded by the National Center for Injury Prevention and Control (NCIPC), a division of the Centers for Disease Control (CDC)—funded, of course, with OUR tax dollars. That's right. Our government officials, sworn to uphold the Constitution, used our money to try to deprive us of one of our most important Constitutional rights. And the NCIPC didn't even pretend to be objective. Dr. Mark Rosenberg, former director of NCIPC, has been quoted avowing his and the CDC's desire to create a public perception of firearms as "dirty, deadly—and banned."

One common excuse for gun control, designed to sound scientific, is [10] that guns are a public health problem, that guns are "pathogens" (germs) which must be eliminated to eliminate the "disease" of gun violence. This simply is not true. To be true, the presence of a gun would cause the disease (violence) in all those exposed to it, and in its absence, violence should not be found. (Every physician is taught the criteria for determining what is or isn't a pathogen early in medical school, so this is inexcusable.) If all those exposed to firearms attempted homicide, our streets truly would be running with blood. Approximately half of all American households own guns, yet few people are involved with homicide or other gun misuse. There are approximately 230 million guns in the United States, more than enough for each adult and teen, yet only a minuscule number of people commit homicide. And if degree of exposure to guns correlated with homicide rates, our police would be the worst offenders.

One often quoted study is the Sloan-Kellerman comparison of Seattle and Vancouver, published in the *New England Journal of Medicine*. Their methodology was simplistic and merely compared the homicide rates in the two cities, then assumed the lower rate in Vancouver was due to gun control. Obviously there are nearly infinite differences in any two cities, yet the study did not control for any differences. The difference in homicide rates could just as easily have been due to economic, cultural, or ethnic variables, differences in laws, age differences, substance abuse, or anything else. Based on their data, one could just as well conclude that the difference was due to the number of movie theaters or eating Twinkies. As a final insult to scientific research, the homicide rates before gun control were not evaluated. Homicide actually increased 25 percent after the institution of the 1977 gun law. . . .

Perhaps the most often quoted myth about the risks of gun ownership is that having a gun in one's home increases one's risk of homicide by a factor of 43. This study, by Kellerman, is full of errors and deceit, and has been widely discredited. Yet the 43 times figure continues to be repeated until it has now achieved the status of "common knowledge." Among the errors, Kellerman did not show that even ONE victim was killed with the gun kept in the home. In fact, at least 49 percent of the victims were killed by someone who did not live in the home and probably had no access to guns kept there. He assumed that the victim of the crime was the one killed, ignoring the possibility that it was the criminal, not the victim, who was killed. Finally, the study showed that substance abuse, family violence, living alone, and living in a rented home were all greater predictors of homicide than was gun ownership. Curiously, the authors have refused to make their data available to other researchers who wish to evaluate the study. Yet, as I mentioned before, this study was funded with our tax dollars.[1]

Fortunately, these fraudulent researchers at the NCIPC were finally exposed in 1996 by a coalition of physicians and criminologists who testified before the House appropriations committee. As a result, the NCIPC's funding for so-called "gun research" was cut from the budget. Of course there were people doing well-designed, accurate research on guns and violence during this period as well. . . . But they weren't doctors, they weren't supported by the government, and the media totally ignored them. They were criminologists, sociologists, lawyers, and their

---

[1] These data have since been released. [*American Gun Review* editor's note.]

studies weren't considered important, especially by the medical establishment.

Gary Kleck's book, *Point Blank: Guns and Violence in America*, was
published in 1991 and received a prestigious criminology award. Although it was generally ignored by both the media and the medical
researchers, it was a turning point. At last there was a comprehensive,
unbiased assessment of the issues surrounding guns and violence that
was available to lay people and researchers alike. In 1995 there was another breakthrough when Kleck and Gertz's study "Armed Resistance to
Crime: The Prevalence and Nature of Self-Defense with a Gun" was published. This study is the first one devoted specifically to the subject of
armed self-defense. Of the nearly 5,000 respondents, 222 reported a defensive gun use within the past 12 months and 313 within the past
5 years. By extrapolating to the total population, he estimated there are
about 2.2 to 2.5 million defensive gun uses by civilians each year, with
1.5 to 1.9 million involving handguns! Four hundred thousand of these
people felt the defensive use of a gun "almost certainly" prevented a
murder. This is ten times the total number of firearms deaths from all
causes in a year! Clearly the risk of allowing civilians to arm themselves
for self-defense pales in comparison to the huge numbers of lives saved.

Now, in the words of David Kopel, "All of the research about
concealed-carry laws has been eclipsed by a comprehensive study by
University of Chicago law professor John Lott, with graduate student
David Mustard." 15

This study goes far beyond any previous study both in its design and
in the comprehensive data collected. Most studies of handgun effects on
crime or violence use either time series or cross-sectional data. Time
series data means that you look at a particular area (for example Salt
Lake County) over time, either continuously or at specified times. Such
studies are open to error due to the time periods chosen. If someone
compared the crime rates in Salt Lake County from 1992 to 1995 (the
year the "shall issue" law became effective), there would likely be little
difference since few people had had the time to obtain the permits to
carry concealed.

Cross-sectional data refers to comparing two or more different
areas at the same time. The accuracy of these studies depends on how
well the areas are matched, and how well the differences between them
are controlled for in the study. As we saw with the Seattle-Vancouver
study, if the cities are not well matched, it is easy to draw, or even create,
the wrong conclusions. In addition, the area one chooses to study is important. Cross-sectional data from states are commonly used, since concealed carry laws are generally passed at the state level. But states are
not uniform at all; they have large cities, small cities, suburban areas,

rural areas, etc. Mixing data from extremely different areas, such as large population centers and rural communities together obscures important information. For example, combining statistics from Salt Lake County (urban) and Kane County (rural) and saying it represents "Utah" actually makes any statistics representing "Utah" quite misleading.

The Lott study solves these problems by using cross-sectional and time series data. They studied every county in the United States continuously from 1977 to 1992, a period of 16 years. Studying counties allowed them to separate urban from rural areas, and a sixteen-year study period is long enough to allow for any temporary, but meaningless, shift in statistics. In addition, the Lott study includes such variables as the type of crime committed, probability of arrest, of conviction, and the length of prison sentences, as well as mandatory sentencing guidelines. It also includes variables such as age, sex, race, income, population and population density. This provides a more detailed, "three-dimensional" picture of the effect of concealed carry permits on crime.

The numbers of arrests and types of crimes were provided by the FBI's Uniform Crime Report, while the information on population was collected from the Census Bureau. Additional information was obtained from state and county officials whenever possible. Other factors which could affect the results such as changes in the laws involving the use of firearms, or sentencing enhancement laws were either eliminated as possibilities or controlled for statistically.

The results of this study show that violent crimes (murder, rape, aggravated assault) decrease dramatically when "shall issue" laws are passed. At the same time, property crimes (auto theft and larceny) increase slightly. This can be explained by habitual criminals changing their preferred method of crime. It makes sense that criminals would switch from crimes where they must confront the victim and thus may get shot, to crimes of stealth where they are much less likely to confront an armed victim. Certainly a small increase in property crimes is a small price to pay for a large savings in human life and health.   20

The statistics are dramatic. Whenever concealed carry laws went into effect in a county during this 16-year period, murders fell by 8.5 percent, rapes by 5 percent, and aggravated assaults by 7 percent. If, in 1992, all states had enacted "shall issue" laws, murders in the United States would have decreased by 1,570. There would have been 4,177 fewer rapes and over 60,000 fewer aggravated assaults. This unequivocally supports the wisdom of our Founding Fathers who guaranteed that our right to keep and bear arms "shall not be infringed."

It means that the bleeding heart gun control advocates, the Sarah Brady types weeping about dead children, and our legislators and presidents who support them, are directly responsible for the deaths of over

1,500 Americans and the rapes of over 4,000 innocent women every single year!

The anti-gunners are unable to find any scientific flaws or errors of analysis in this study. Instead they have attacked the researchers personally, just as they did to the doctors who dared speak the "politically incorrect" truth. There is no place for name-calling in either scientific research or in setting policy that affects millions of lives.

Anti-gunners might ask if allowing concealed carry would cause an increase in accidental deaths. However, the entire number of accidental deaths in the United States in 1992 was 1,409, and only 546 of these occurred in states with concealed carry laws. The total number of accidental handgun deaths per year is less than 200. At most, there would be nine more accidental deaths per year if all states passed concealed carry laws, in contrast to 1,500 lives saved.

Anti-gunners use the argument that if concealed carry were enacted, 25 every minor fender-bender or disagreement would turn into a shoot-out. Over 300,000 permits have been issued in Florida since 1986, but only five violent crimes involving permitted pistols were committed as of December 1995, and none of them resulted in a fatality. There is only one recorded instance of a permitted pistol being used in a shooting following a traffic accident, and in that case a grand jury found that the shooting was justified.

In 1993, private citizens accidentally killed 30 innocent people who they thought were committing a crime, while police killed 330 innocent people. Given the nature of police work, this is not an entirely fair comparison. However, it clearly shows the public can be trusted with concealed pistols.

Another finding is that people who carry concealed handguns protect not only themselves and their families, but the public in general, even that part of the public that protests most loudly against guns. Since by definition a concealed weapon is hidden, a criminal has no way of knowing if a prospective victim is armed, and is therefore less likely to commit a violent crime against any given person.

This is particularly important for women. Women are the victims of a disproportionate number of violent crimes. A woman who carries a gun has a much greater deterrent effect on crime than does a man. Women are usually smaller and weaker than their attackers, and the presence of a firearm equalizes this imbalance. Because the imbalance between a woman and her attacker is much greater, the benefits of carrying are also much greater. A woman carrying a gun decreases the murder rate for women by three to four times the amount a man carrying a gun decreases the murder rate for men.

While numerous studies have attempted to quantify the cost of firearms-related deaths and injuries, this is the first paper to study the economic benefits of allowing concealed carry. For the sake of consistency, the authors based their figures on estimates for the cost of various crimes used by a National Institute of Justice study published in 1996. Costs included loss of life, lost productivity, medical bills, property losses, as well as losses related to fear, pain, suffering, and decreased quality of life.

These figures are based on jury trial awards, which may not be the 30 best way to estimate economic loss. However they are the figures used in anti-gun studies and so the authors chose to use them to more clearly illustrate the economic benefits of gun ownership. The reduction in violent crime caused by concealed weapons permits provides an economic gain of $6.6 billion, compared to a much smaller economic loss of $417 million due to the increase in property crimes. The net gain is still $6.2 billion!

These results may seem like ordinary common sense. Other results seem to go against "common wisdom." For example, it has been traditional to have the most restrictive gun laws in high population, high crime, urban areas such as Los Angeles, New York City, and Washington, D.C. It is common to hear people say that "It's fine for those people who live out in the country to have guns, but people in the city shouldn't have them."

But this study shows that the effect of allowing concealed carry is much greater in high population counties and in high crime counties. For example, the murder rate in very large cities drops by 12 percent when CCW is passed, while it drops by only about 1.6 percent in an average-sized city. Data for rural areas is unreliable since the murder rates in most rural areas are so low that accurate statistical studies cannot be done. An increase from one murder per year to two would show up as a 100 percent increase in the murder rate, which is misleading when compared to cities with daily murders. However, consistent with the earlier comments on criminals switching to "safer" methods of crime, the increase in property crimes in urban areas is also greater than the increase in rural areas.

Contrary to frequently espoused theories about causes of crime, real per capita income showed only a small, though statistically significant, correlation with both violent crimes and property crimes. It would appear that living in a high population density area may contribute more to crime than does poverty, although this requires more study.

Another finding which deserves comment is that the presence of young, black males increases the rate of property crime by 22 percent and violent crime by 5 percent. However, these numbers cannot be accepted completely at face value, nor should they be used to justify racism. The history of gun control in this country reflects the history of racism. The first state and local firearms laws were designed primarily to disarm blacks, and enough damage has already been done. It is necessary to take into account studies showing that young black males are disproportionately arrested and incarcerated for crimes, and that they are disproportionately victims of crimes. In addition, they tend to live in high population areas and have low incomes, both of which are independent factors for increased crime. Finally, in view of recent allegations that the CIA deliberately introduced drugs, guns, and thus crime, into inner city black neighborhoods, more study is necessary before any definite conclusions can be reached. Neither Professor Lott nor I believe that race is a cause of crime. . . .

While it is generally a bad idea to base policy on the results of a 35 single study, the Lott and Mustard study is so well designed and well controlled that it is difficult, if not impossible, to argue with their findings. In addition, their results agree with those of previous researchers, most notably Kleck and Gertz.

Two findings stand out above all. Concealed carrying of firearms by citizens with no prior felony record or history of severe mental illness decreases violent crime, providing a large benefit both to the individuals who carry and the public as a whole. Second, arrests by law enforcement officers have a large deterrent effect on crime, while conviction has a lesser, but still important, effect.

The obvious conclusion is that concealed carry provides a very large benefit to society in terms of lives saved, violent assaults and rapes prevented, and economic savings. At the same time misuse of legally concealed weapons and accidental handgun deaths from concealed weapons are almost non-existent. Thus every effort should be made to facilitate concealed carry by law-abiding citizens. "Shall issue" permit laws should be adopted by all those states that have not yet done so. In particular, large, urban areas should actively encourage arming their good citizens and definitely should not prevent or discourage them from carrying concealed weapons.

Regulations such as gun-free zones which serve only to disarm and/or harass gun owners are counterproductive and should be eliminated at local, state and federal levels. The Supreme Court has already found gun-free school zones unconstitutional and the justices should uphold this finding in light of the current administration's repeated attempts to enact this misguided legislation. Concealed carry permits should be accepted on a reciprocal basis by all states, just as driver's licenses are, under the full faith and credit act of the Constitution.

In view of the negligible incidence of negative events resulting from concealed carry, further studies are indicated to determine whether the extensive background checks and training requirements which most states demand are even necessary. It may be that "Vermont-style" — i.e., universal concealed carry without need for a permit—is more appropriate and would remove both the financial disincentives to lawful carry as well as decrease the demand on the often overworked staff of state permitting agencies and the FBI. Further, the Constitution guarantees the right to keep and bear arms, and many people (including the author) consider the requirement for a permit, which gives them "permission" to exercise what is already an enumerated right to be both unconstitutional and offensive.

Because the beneficial effect of women carrying concealed weapons far outweighs that of men carrying, women should be encouraged to carry, and special classes designed to teach women how to safely use, maintain and carry weapons, along with other self-defense techniques, need to be developed and made widely available. Learning to protect oneself from crime and violence is as important to a woman's health as is learning to detect breast cancer or prevent heart disease. The psychological benefits to women of feeling safe are very significant, but have yet to be studied scientifically. 40

In many areas, including the Salt Lake metropolitan area, there is currently much bad feeling between some law enforcement officers who feel citizens who carry pose a "deadly threat" to them and citizens who feel harassed by police. Lott's study shows that this is not only unnecessary, but counterproductive. Armed citizens can protect themselves, their families and others from violent crimes. Police cannot be everywhere simultaneously, and have no duty to protect individuals. Their role is primarily to investigate crimes after the fact and bring perpetrators to justice. By decreasing the number of violent crimes committed, armed citizens actually decrease the police workload and enable them to be more productive and apprehend a greater percentage of criminals which in turn further decreases crime.

Armed citizens and police who are able to cooperate have a synergistic effect on decreasing crime. Both groups need to acknowledge this, accommodate to the changes in the laws, stop competing, and learn to respect and trust each other. Law enforcement agencies, working with citizens' groups, must develop clear written policies for police and armed citizen interactions and disseminate these policies widely. The self-sufficient, self-protecting gun culture must be restored to its rightful place of respect in society, not demonized as a hotbed of terrorists. The Second Amendment right to keep and bear arms must be unequivocally upheld.

Those who wish to disarm the populace of this country must be exposed for the frauds they are and held responsible morally, if not legally, for the deaths and suffering created by their misguided policies. In the four years since 1992, those who preach gun control have contributed to the deaths of at least six thousand innocent people whose lives they have sworn to protect and whose freedoms they have sworn to uphold.

Topics for Critical Thinking and Writing

1. We think Thompson's opening paragraph is reasonably effective. What is your view of it? Why? After reading her whole article, can you think of ways to improve this introductory paragraph? Do so in a paragraph of not more than 200 words.

2. Suppose someone were to say that Thompson badly distorts the truth when she says that the government wants the public "to willingly give up . . . their right to self-defense" (para. 5). Is it fairer to say that the government wants to *regulate* the ownership, sale, and use of guns, whether for self-defense or any other purpose? How might Thompson reply to this argument?

3. Does Thompson favor unrestricted ownership, sale, and use of guns—handguns as well as long guns?

4. Thompson accuses unnamed doctors of supporting "biased gun research" "to get grant money . . . or become famous" (para. 7). Does she give any examples of such research and such doctors?

5. Ask your reference librarian to help you locate a copy of the gun research by Sloan and Kellerman published in the *New England Journal of Medicine* (para. 11). Has Thompson given a fair account of this research? Write a 300-word essay explaining why or why not.

6. In paragraph 16 and elsewhere, Thompson refers to "'shall issue' laws." What does this phrase mean? How about "CCW" (para. 32)?

7. Thompson claims that the research on comparative gun use in Seattle and Vancouver (para. 11) is of no value because "the cities are not well matched" (para. 17). After consulting with your reference librarian for useful sources of data, write a 500-word essay comparing the two cities, concluding with an account of why you agree or disagree with Thompson about how well matched these two cities are.

8. Thompson reports a decrease in murders in states permitting concealed handguns (para. 20). She does not report on accidental deaths and woundings by persons carrying a concealed weapon (see, however, para. 23). Without information of this sort, how much weight should we attach to the reported decline in murders?

9. Thompson invokes the Second Amendment to the U.S. Constitution (paras. 5, 21, 39, 42). She omits any mention of the opening clause of the amendment, which reads "A well-regulated militia, being necessary to the security of a free State. . . ." No other purpose for owning a gun is explicitly protected by the language of this amendment. How does this translate, if it does, into a right to "keep and bear arms" for other purposes?

10. Thompson claims that enthusiasts for gun control are "directly responsible for the deaths of over 1,500 Americans . . . every single year" (para.

22), and she speaks of those who are "responsible morally, if not legally" for these deaths (para. 43). Since few if any of these enthusiasts ever use, much less own, any guns themselves, how is that they are "directly responsible" for all these deaths?

11. With help from your reference librarian, find out about road rage in an effort to verify Thompson's claim that as of her writing (1997) or more recently, "only one" case has been recorded "of a permitted pistol being used in a shooting following a traffic accident" (para. 25).

12. Thompson is unstinting in her enthusiasm for laws permitting the carrying of concealed weapons; she favors such laws nationwide (paras. 38–40). Is there any reason, however, to believe that if *every* law-abiding citizen carried a concealed weapon, accidental killings and woundings, mistaken judgment about the need to shoot in self-defense, misguided defense of property, and impulsive use of such weapons would remain constant, so that the benefits she touts would be undiminished?

13. What does Thompson mean by the "synergistic effect on decreasing crime" (para. 42)?

NAN DESUKA

Nan Desuka (1957–1985) grew up in Los Angeles. Although she most often wrote about ecology, she occasionally wrote about other controversial topics.

Why Handguns Must Be Outlawed

"Guns don't kill people—criminals do." That's a powerful slogan, much more powerful than its alternate version: "Guns don't kill people—people kill people." But this second version, though less effective, is much nearer to the whole truth. Although accurate statistics are hard to come by, and even harder to interpret, it seems indisputable that large numbers of people, not just criminals, kill, with a handgun, other people. Scarcely a day goes by without a newspaper in any large city reporting that a child has found a gun, kept by the child's parents for self-protection, and has, in playing with this new-found toy, killed himself or a playmate. Or we read of a storekeeper, trying to protect himself during a robbery, who inadvertently shoots an innocent customer. These killers are not, in any reasonable sense of the word, criminals. They are just people who happen to kill people. No wonder the gun lobby prefers the first version of the slogan, "Guns don't kill people—criminals do." This version suggests that the only problem is criminals, not you or me, or our children, and certainly not the members of the National Rifle Association.

Those of us who want strict control of handguns—for me that means the outlawing of handguns, except to the police and related service units—have not been able to come up with a slogan equal in power to "Guns don't kill people—criminals do." The best we have been able to come up with is a mildly amusing bumper sticker showing a teddy bear, with the words "Defend your right to arm bears." Humor can be a powerful weapon (even in writing *on behalf* of gun control, one slips into using the imagery of force), and our playful bumper sticker somehow deflates the self-righteousness of the gun lobby, but doesn't equal the power (again the imagery of force) of "Guns don't kill people—criminals do." For one thing, the effective alliteration of *"criminals"* and *"kill"* binds the two words, making everything so terribly simple. Criminals kill; when there are no criminals, there will be no deaths from guns.

But this notion won't do. Despite the uncertainty of some statistical evidence, everyone knows, or should know, that only about 30 percent of murders are committed by robbers or rapists (Kates, 1978). For the most part the victims of handguns know their assailants well. These victims are women killed by jealous husbands, or they are the women's lovers; or they are drinking buddies who get into a violent argument; or they are innocent people who get shot by disgruntled (and probably demented) employees or fellow workers who have (or imagine) a grudge. Or they are, as I've already said, bystanders at a robbery, killed by a storekeeper. Or they are children playing with their father's gun.

Of course this is not the whole story. Hardened criminals also have guns, and they use them. The murders committed by robbers and rapists are what give credence to Barry Goldwater's quip, "We have a crime problem in this country, not a gun problem" (1975, p. 186). But here again the half-truth of a slogan is used to mislead, used to direct attention away from a national tragedy. Different sources issue different statistics, but a conservative estimate is that handguns annually murder at least fifteen thousand Americans, accidentally kill at least another three thousand and wound at least another hundred thousand. Handguns are easily available, both to criminals and to decent people who believe they need a gun in order to protect themselves from criminals. The decent people, unfortunately, have good cause to believe they need protection. Many parts of many cities are utterly unsafe, and even the tiniest village may harbor a murderer. Senator Goldwater is right in saying there is a crime problem (that's the truth of his half-truth), but he is wrong in saying there is not also a gun problem.

Surely the homicide rate would markedly decrease if handguns were outlawed. The FBI reports (Federal Bureau of Investigation, 1985)   5 that more than 60 percent of all murders are caused by guns, and handguns are involved in more than 70 percent of these. Surely many, even most, of these handgun killings would not occur if the killer had to use a rifle, club, or knife. Of course violent lovers, angry drunks, and deranged employees would still flail out with knives or baseball bats, but some of their victims would be able to run away, with few or no injuries, and most of those who could not run away would nevertheless survive, badly injured but at least alive. But if handguns are outlawed, we are told, responsible citizens will have no way to protect themselves from criminals. First, one should remember that at least 90 percent of America's burglaries are committed when no one is at home. The householder's gun, if he or she has one, is in a drawer of the bedside table, and the gun gets lifted along with the jewelry, adding one more gun to the estimated hundred thousand handguns annually stolen from law-abiding citizens (Shields, 1981). Second, if the householder is at home, and attempts to use the gun, he or she is more likely to get killed or wounded than to kill or deter the intruder. Another way of looking at this last point is to recall that for every burglar who is halted by the sight of a handgun, four innocent people are killed by handgun accidents.

Because handguns are not accurate beyond ten or fifteen feet, they are not the weapons of sportsmen. Their sole purpose is to kill or at least to disable a person at close range. But only a minority of persons killed with these weapons are criminals. Since handguns chiefly destroy the innocent, they must be outlawed—not simply controlled more strictly, but outlawed—to all except to law-enforcement officials. Attempts to control handguns are costly and ineffective, but even if they were cheap and effective stricter controls would not take handguns out of circulation among criminals, because licensed guns are stolen from homeowners and shopkeepers, and thus fall into criminal hands. According to Wright, Rossi, and Daly (1983, p. 181), about 40 percent of the handguns used in crimes are stolen, chiefly from homes that the guns were supposed to protect.

The National Rifle Association is fond of quoting a University of Wisconsin study that says, "gun control laws have no individual or collective effect in reducing the rate of violent crime" (cited in Smith, 1981, p. 17). Agreed—but what if handguns were not available? What if the manufacturer of handguns is severely regulated, and if the guns may be sold only to police officers? True, even if handguns are outlawed, some criminals will manage to get them, but surely fewer petty criminals will have guns. It is simply untrue for the gun lobby to assert that all criminals—since they are by definition lawbreakers—will find ways to get handguns. For the most part, if the sale of handguns is outlawed, guns won't be available, and fewer criminals will have guns. And if fewer criminals have guns, there is every reason to believe that violent crime will decline. A youth armed only with a knife is less likely to try to rob a store than if he is armed with a gun. This commonsense reasoning does not imply that if handguns are outlawed crime will suddenly disappear, or even that an especially repulsive crime such as rape will decrease markedly. A rapist armed with a knife probably has a sufficient weapon. But *some* violent crime will almost surely decrease. And the decrease will probably be significant if in addition to outlawing handguns, severe mandatory punishments are imposed on a person who is found to possess one, and even severer mandatory punishments are imposed on a person who uses one while committing a crime. Again, none of this activity will solve "the crime problem," but neither will anything else, including the "get tough with criminals" attitude of Senator Goldwater. And of course any attempt to reduce crime (one cannot realistically talk of "solving" the crime problem) will have to pay attention to our systems of bail, plea bargaining, and parole, but outlawing handguns will help.

What will the cost be? First, to take "cost" in its most literal sense, there will be the cost of reimbursing gun owners for the weapons they surrender. Every owner of a handgun ought to be paid the fair market value of the weapon. Since the number of handguns is estimated to be between 50 million and 90 million, the cost will be considerable, but it will be far less than the costs—both in money and in sorrow—that result from deaths due to handguns.

Second, one may well ask if there is another sort of cost, a cost to our liberty, to our constitutional rights. The issue is important, and persons who advocate abolition of handguns are blind or thoughtless if they simply brush it off. On the other hand, opponents of gun control do all of us a disservice by insisting over and over that the Constitution guarantees "the right to bear arms." The Second Amendment in the Bill of Rights says this: "A well-regulated militia being necessary to the security of a free State, the right of the people to keep and bear arms shall not be infringed." It is true that the founding fathers, mindful of the British attempt to disarm the colonists, viewed the presence of "a well-regulated militia" as a safeguard of democracy. Their intention is quite clear, even to one who has not read Stephen P. Halbrook's *That Every Man Be Armed*, an exhaustive argument in favor of the right to bear arms. There can be no doubt that the framers of the Constitution and the Bill of Rights believed that armed insurrection was a justifiable means of countering oppression and tyranny. The Second Amendment may be fairly paraphrased thus: "*Because* an organized militia is necessary to the security of the State, the people have the right to possess weapons." But the owners of handguns are not members of a well-regulated militia. Furthermore, nothing in the proposal to ban handguns would deprive citizens of their rifles or other long-arm guns. All handguns, however, even large ones, should be banned. "Let's face it," Guenther W. Bachmann (a vice president of Smith and Wesson) admits, "they are all concealable" (Kennedy, 1981, p. 6). In any case, it is a fact that when gun control laws have been tested in the courts, they have been found to be constitutional. The constitutional argument was worth making, but the question must now be regarded as settled, not only by the courts but by anyone who reads the Second Amendment.

Still, is it not true that "If guns are outlawed, only outlaws will have   10 guns"? This is yet another powerful slogan, but it is simply not true. First, we are talking not about "guns" but about handguns. Second, the police will have guns — handguns and others — and these trained professionals are the ones on whom we must rely for protection against criminals. Of course the police have not eradicated crime; and of course we must hope that in the future they will be more successful in protecting all citizens. But we must also recognize that the efforts of private citizens to protect themselves with handguns have chiefly taken the lives not of criminals but of innocent people.

REFERENCES

Federal Bureau of Investigation (1985). *Uniform crime reports for the United States.* Washington, DC: U.S. Department of Justice.

Goldwater, B. (1975, December). Why gun control laws don't work. *Reader's Digest, 107,* 183–188.

Halbrook, S. P. (1985). *That every man be armed: The evolution of a constitutional right.* Albuquerque: University of New Mexico Press.

Kates, D. B., Jr. (1978, September). Against civil disarming. *Harper's, 257,* 28–33.

Kennedy, E. (1981, October 5). Handguns: Preferred instruments of criminals. *Congressional Record.* Washington, DC: U.S. Government Printing Office.

Shields, P. (1981). *Guns don't die — people do.* New York: Arbor House.

Smith, A. (1981, April). Fifty million handguns. *Esquire, 96,* 16–18.

Wright, J. D., Rossi, P. H., & Daly, K. (1983). *Under the gun.* New York: Aldine.

Topics for Critical Thinking and Writing

1. Reread Desuka's first and last paragraphs, and then in a sentence or two comment on the writer's strategy for opening and closing her essay.

2. On the whole, does the writer strike you as a person who is fair or who at least is trying to be fair? Support your answer by citing specific passages that lead you to your opinion.

3. Many opponents of gun control argue that control of handguns will be a first move down the slippery slope that leads to laws prohibiting private ownership of any sort of gun. Even if you hold this view, state as best you can the arguments that one might offer against it. (Notice that you are asked to offer arguments, not merely an assertion that it won't happen.)

4. Do you agree with Desuka that a reasonable reading of the Second Amendment reveals that individuals do not have a constitutional right to own handguns, even though the founding fathers said that "the right of the people to keep and bear arms shall not be infringed"?

5. Write a 500-word analysis of Desuka's essay, or write a 500-word reply to her essay, responding to her main points.

6. Do you think the prohibition of handguns is feasible? Could it be enforced? Would the effort to enforce it result in worse problems than we already have? Write a 500-word essay defending or attacking the feasibility of Desuka's proposal.

PART TWO

Casebooks on Contemporary Issues

6

The Death Penalty:
Can It Ever Be
Justified?

EDWARD I. KOCH

Edward I. Koch (b. 1924), long active in Democratic politics, was mayor of New York from 1978 to 1989. This essay first appeared in The New Republic *on April 15, 1985.*

Death and Justice: How Capital Punishment Affirms Life

Last December a man named Robert Lee Willie, who had been convicted of raping and murdering an eighteen-year-old woman, was executed in the Louisiana state prison. In a statement issued several minutes before his death, Mr. Willie said: "Killing people is wrong. . . . It makes no difference whether it's citizens, countries, or governments. Killing is wrong." Two weeks later in South Carolina, an admitted killer named Joseph Carl Shaw was put to death for murdering two teenagers. In an appeal to the governor for clemency, Mr. Shaw wrote: "Killing was wrong when I did it. Killing is wrong when you do it. I hope you have the courage and moral strength to stop the killing."

It is a curiosity of modern life that we find ourselves being lectured on morality by cold-blooded killers. Mr. Willie previously had been convicted of aggravated rape, aggravated kidnapping, and the murders of a Louisiana deputy and a man from Missouri. Mr. Shaw committed another murder a week before the two for which he was executed, and admitted mutilating the body of the fourteen-year-old girl he killed. I can't help wondering what prompted these murderers to speak out against killing as they entered the deathhouse door. Did their newfound reverence for life stem from the realization that they were about to lose their own?

Life is indeed precious, and I believe the death penalty helps to affirm this fact. Had the death penalty been a real possibility in the minds of these murderers, they might well have stayed their hand. They might have shown moral awareness before their victims died, and not after. Consider the tragic death of Rosa Velez, who happened to be home when a man named Luis Vera burglarized her apartment in Brooklyn. "Yeah, I shot her," Vera admitted. "She knew me, and I knew I wouldn't go to the chair."

During my twenty-two years in public service, I have heard the pros and cons of capital punishment expressed with special intensity. As a district leader, councilman, congressman, and mayor, I have represented constituencies generally thought of as liberal. Because I support the death penalty for heinous crimes of murder, I have sometimes been the subject of emotional and outraged attacks by voters who find my position reprehensible or worse. I have listened to their ideas. I have weighed their objections carefully. I still support the death penalty. The reasons I maintain my position can be best understood by examining the arguments most frequently heard in opposition.

1. **The death penalty is "barbaric."** Sometimes opponents of capital punishment horrify with tales of lingering death on the gallows, of faulty electric chairs, or of agony in the gas chamber. Partly in response to such protests, several states such as North Carolina and Texas switched to execution by lethal injection. The condemned person is put to death painlessly, without ropes, voltage, bullets, or gas. Did this answer the objections of death penalty opponents? Of course not. On June 22, 1984, the *New York Times* published an editorial that sarcastically attacked the new "hygienic" method of death by injection, and stated that "execution can never be made humane through science." So it's not the method that really troubles opponents. It's the death itself they consider barbaric.

Admittedly, capital punishment is not a pleasant topic. However, one does not have to like the death penalty in order to support it any more than one must like radical surgery, radiation, or chemotherapy in order to find necessary these attempts at curing cancer. Ultimately we may learn how to cure cancer with a simple pill. Unfortunately, that day has not yet arrived. Today we are faced with the choice of letting the cancer spread or trying to cure it with the methods available, methods that one day will almost certainly be considered barbaric. But to give up and do nothing would be far more barbaric and would certainly delay the discovery of an eventual cure. The analogy between cancer and murder is imperfect, because murder is not the "disease" we are trying to cure. The disease is injustice. We may not like the death penalty, but it must be available to punish crimes of cold-blooded murder, cases in which any other form of punishment would be inadequate and, therefore, unjust. If we create a society in which injustice is not tolerated, incidents of murder—the most flagrant form of injustice—will diminish.

2. **No other major democracy uses the death penalty.** No other major democracy—in fact, few other countries of any description—are plagued by a murder rate such as that in the United States. Fewer and fewer Americans can remember the days when unlocked doors were the norm and murder was a rare and terrible offense. In America the murder rate climbed 122 percent between 1963 and 1980. During that same period, the murder rate in New York City increased by almost 400 percent, and the statistics are even worse in many other cities. A study at M.I.T. showed that based on 1970 homicide rates a person who lived in a large American city ran a greater risk of being murdered than an American soldier in World War II ran of being killed in combat. It is not surprising that the laws of each country differ according to differing conditions and traditions. If other countries had our murder problem, the cry for capital punishment would be just as loud as it is here. And I dare say that any other major democracy where 75 percent of the people supported the death penalty would soon enact it into law.

3. **An innocent person might be executed by mistake.** Consider the work of Hugo Adam Bedau, one of the most implacable foes of capital punishment in this country. According to Mr. Bedau, it is "false sentimentality to argue that the death penalty should be abolished because of the abstract possibility that an innocent person might be executed." He cites a study of the seven thousand executions in this country from 1892 to 1971, and concludes that the record fails to show that such cases occur. The main point, however, is this. If government functioned only when the possibility of error didn't exist, government wouldn't function at all. Human life deserves special protection, and one of the best ways to guarantee that protection is to assure that convicted murderers do not kill again. Only the death penalty can accomplish this end. In a recent case in New Jersey, a man named Richard Biegenwald was freed from prison after serving eighteen years for murder; since his release he has been convicted of committing four murders. A prisoner named Lemuel Smith, who, while serving four life sentences for murder (plus two life sentences for kidnapping and robbery) in New York's Green Haven

Prison, lured a woman corrections officer into the chaplain's office and strangled her. He then mutilated and dismembered her body. An additional life sentence for Smith is meaningless. Because New York has no death penalty statute, Smith has effectively been given a license to kill.

But the problem of multiple murder is not confined to the nation's penitentiaries. In 1981, ninety-one police officers were killed in the line of duty in this country. Seven percent of those arrested in the cases that have been solved had a previous arrest for murder. In New York City in 1976 and 1977, eighty-five persons arrested for homicide had a previous arrest for murder. Six of these individuals had two previous arrests for murder, and one had four previous murder arrests. During those two years the New York police were arresting for murder persons with a previous arrest for murder on the average of one every eight and a half days. This is not surprising when we learn that in 1975, for example, the median time served in Massachusetts for homicide was less than two and a half years. In 1976 a study sponsored by the Twentieth Century Fund found that the average time served in the United States for first-degree murder is ten years. The median time served may be considerably lower.

4. **Capital punishment cheapens the value of human life.** On   10
the contrary, it can be easily demonstrated that the death penalty strengthens the value of human life. If the penalty for rape were lowered, clearly it would signal a lessened regard for the victim's suffering, humiliation, and personal integrity. It would cheapen their horrible experience, and expose them to an increased danger of recurrence. When we lower the penalty for murder, it signals a lessened regard for the value of the victim's life. Some critics of capital punishment, such as columnist Jimmy Breslin, have suggested that a life sentence is actually a harsher penalty for murder than death. This is sophistic nonsense. A few killers may decide not to appeal a death sentence, but the overwhelming majority make every effort to stay alive. It is by exacting the highest penalty for the taking of human life that we affirm the highest value of human life.

5. **The death penalty is applied in a discriminatory manner.** This factor no longer seems to be the problem it once was. The appeals process for a condemned prisoner is lengthy and painstaking. Every effort is made to see that the verdict and sentence were fairly arrived at. However, assertions of discrimination are not an argument for ending the death penalty but for extending it. It is not justice to exclude everyone from the penalty of the law if a few are found to be so favored. Justice requires that the law be applied equally to all.

6. **Thou Shalt Not Kill.** The Bible is our greatest source of moral inspiration. Opponents of the death penalty frequently cite the sixth of

the Ten Commandments in an attempt to prove that capital punishment is divinely proscribed. In the original Hebrew, however, the Sixth Commandment reads "Thou Shalt Not Commit Murder," and the Torah specifies capital punishment for a variety of offenses. The biblical viewpoint has been upheld by philosophers throughout history. The greatest thinkers of the nineteenth century—Kant, Locke, Hobbes, Rousseau, Montesquieu, and Mill—agreed that natural law properly authorizes the sovereign to take life in order to vindicate justice. Only Jeremy Bentham was ambivalent. Washington, Jefferson, and Franklin endorsed it. Abraham Lincoln authorized executions for deserters in wartime. Alexis de Tocqueville, who expressed profound respect for American institutions, believed that the death penalty was indispensable to the support of social order. The United States Constitution, widely admired as one of the seminal achievements in the history of humanity, condemns cruel and inhuman punishment, but does not condemn capital punishment.

7. **The death penalty is state-sanctioned murder.** This is the defense with which Messrs. Willie and Shaw hoped to soften the resolve of those who sentenced them to death. By saying in effect, "You're no better than I am," the murderer seeks to bring his accusers down to his own level. It is also a popular argument among opponents of capital punishment, but a transparently false one. Simply put, the state has rights that the private individual does not. In a democracy, those rights are given to the state by the electorate. The execution of a lawfully condemned killer is no more an act of murder than is legal imprisonment an act of kidnapping. If an individual forces a neighbor to pay him money under threat of punishment, it's called extortion. If the state does it, it's called taxation. Rights and responsibilities surrendered by the individual are what give the state its power to govern. This contract is the foundation of civilization itself.

Everyone wants his or her rights, and will defend them jealously. Not everyone, however, wants responsibilities, especially the painful responsibilities that come with law enforcement. Twenty-one years ago a woman named Kitty Genovese was assaulted and murdered on a street in New York. Dozens of neighbors heard her cries for help but did nothing to assist her. They didn't even call the police. In such a climate the criminal understandably grows bolder. In the presence of moral cowardice, he lectures us on our supposed failings and tries to equate his crimes with our quest for justice.

The death of anyone—even a convicted killer—diminishes us all. 15 But we are diminished even more by a justice system that fails to function. It is an illusion to let ourselves believe that doing away with capital punishment removes the murderer's deed from our conscience. The rights of society are paramount. When we protect guilty lives, we give up innocent lives in exchange. When opponents of capital punishment say to the state, "I will not let you kill in my name," they are also saying to murderers: "You can kill in your *own* name as long as I have an excuse for not getting involved."

It is hard to imagine anything worse than being murdered while neighbors do nothing. But something worse exists. When those same neighbors shrink back from justly punishing the murderer, the victim dies twice.

Topics for Critical Thinking and Writing

1. In paragraph 6 Koch draws an analogy between cancer and murder and observes that imperfect as today's cures for cancer are, "to give up and do nothing would be far more barbaric." What is the relevance of this comment in the context of the analogy and the dispute over the death penalty?

2. In paragraph 8 Koch describes a convicted but unexecuted recidivist murderer as someone who "has effectively been given a license to kill." But a license to kill, as in a deer-hunter's license, entitles the holder to engage in lawful killing. (Think of the fictional hero James Bond— Agent 007—who, we are told, had a "license to kill.") What is the difference between having a license and "effectively" having one? How might the opponent of the death penalty reply to Koch's position here?

3. Koch distinguishes between the "median time" served by persons convicted of murder but not sentenced to death and the "average time" they serve, and he adds that the former "may be considerably lower" than the latter (para. 9). Explain the difference between a "median" and an "average". Is knowing one of these statistics more important for certain purposes than the other? Why?

4. Koch identifies seven arguments against the death penalty, and he rejects them all. Which of the seven arguments seems to you to be the strongest objection to the death penalty? Which the weakest? Why? Does Koch effectively refute the strongest argument? Can you think of any argument(s) against the death penalty that he neglects?

5. Koch says he supports the death penalty "for heinous crimes of murder" (para. 4). Does he imply that all murders are heinous crimes or only some? If the latter, what criteria seem to you to be the appropriate ones to distinguish the heinous murders from the rest? Why these criteria?

6. Koch asserts that the death penalty "strengthens the value of human life" (para. 10). Yet opponents of the death penalty often claim the

reverse, arguing that capital punishment undermines the idea that human life is precious. Write an essay of 500 words in which you explain what it means to assert that life is precious and why one of the two positions—support for or opposition to the death penalty—best supports (or is consistent with) this principle.

DAVID BRUCK

David Bruck (b. 1949) graduated from Harvard College and received his law degree from the University of South Carolina. His practice is devoted almost entirely to the defense of persons under death sentence, through the South Carolina Office of Appellate Defense. The essay reprinted here originally appeared on May 20, 1985, in The New Republic *as a response to the essay by Edward I. Koch (p. 55).*

The Death Penalty

Mayor Ed Koch contends that the death penalty "affirms life." By failing to execute murderers, he says, we "signal a lessened regard for the value of the victim's life." Koch suggests that people who oppose the death penalty are like Kitty Genovese's neighbors, who heard her cries for help but did nothing while an attacker stabbed her to death.

This is the standard "moral" defense of death as punishment: Even if executions don't deter violent crime any more effectively than imprisonment, they are still required as the only means we have of doing justice in response to the worst of crimes.

Until recently, this "moral" argument had to be considered in the abstract, since no one was being executed in the United States. But the death penalty is back now, at least in the southern states, where every one of the more than thirty executions carried out over the last two years has taken place. Those of us who live in those states are getting to see the difference between the death penalty in theory, and what happens when you actually try to use it.

South Carolina resumed executing prisoners in January with the electrocution of Joseph Carl Shaw. Shaw was condemned to death for helping to murder two teenagers while he was serving as a military policeman at Fort Jackson, South Carolina. His crime, propelled by mental illness and PCP, was one of terrible brutality. It is Shaw's last words ("Killing was wrong when I did it. It is wrong when you do it. . . .") that so outraged Mayor Koch: He finds it "a curiosity of modern life that we are being lectured on morality by cold-blooded killers." And so it is.

But it was not "modern life" that brought this curiosity into being. It was capital punishment. The electric chair was J. C. Shaw's platform. (The mayor mistakenly writes that Shaw's statement came in the form of a plea to the governor for clemency: Actually Shaw made it only seconds before his death, as he waited, shaved and strapped into the chair, for the switch to be thrown.) It was the chair that provided Shaw with celebrity and an opportunity to lecture us on right and wrong. What made this weird moral reversal even worse is that J. C. Shaw faced his own death with undeniable dignity and courage. And while Shaw died, the TV crews recorded another "curiosity" of the death penalty—the crowd gathered outside the death-house to cheer on the executioner. Whoops of elation greeted the announcement of Shaw's death. Waiting at the penitentiary gates for the appearance of the hearse bearing Shaw's remains, one demonstrator started yelling, "Where's the beef?"

For those who had to see the execution of J. C. Shaw, it wasn't easy to keep in mind that the purpose of the whole spectacle was to affirm life. It will be harder still when Florida executes a cop-killer named Alvin Ford. Ford has lost his mind during his years of death-row confinement, and now spends his days trembling, rocking back and forth, and muttering unintelligible prayers. This has led to litigation over whether Ford meets a centuries-old legal standard for mental competency. Since the Middle Ages, the Anglo-American legal system has generally prohibited the execution of anyone who is too mentally ill to understand what is about to be done to him and why. If Florida wins its case, it will have earned the right to electrocute Ford in his present condition. If it loses, he will not be executed until the state has first nursed him back to some semblance of mental health.[1]

We can at least be thankful that this demoralizing spectacle involves a prisoner who is actually guilty of murder. But this may not always be so. The ordeal of Lenell Jeter—the young black engineer who recently served more than a year of a life sentence for a Texas armed robbery that he didn't commit—should remind us that the system is quite capable of making the very worst sort of mistake. That Jeter was eventually cleared

[1]Florida lost its case to execute Ford. On June 26, 1986, the U.S. Supreme Court ruled that the execution of an insane person violates the Eighth Amendment, which forbids cruel and unusual punishments. Therefore, convicted murderers cannot be executed if they have become so insane that they do not know that they are about to be executed and do not understand the reason for their sentence. If Ford regains his sanity, however, he can be executed. [—Ed.]

is a fluke. If the robbery had occurred at 7 P.M. rather than 3 P.M., he'd have had no alibi, and would still be in prison today. And if someone had been killed in that robbery, Jeter probably would have been sentenced to death. We'd have seen the usual execution-day interviews with state officials and the victim's relatives, all complaining that Jeter's appeals took too long. And Jeter's last words from the gurney would have taken their place among the growing literature of death-house oration that so irritates the mayor.

Koch quotes Hugo Adam Bedau, a prominent abolitionist, to the effect that the record fails to establish that innocent defendants have been executed in the past. But this doesn't mean, as Koch implies, that it hasn't happened. All Bedau was saying was that doubts concerning executed prisoners' guilt are almost never resolved. Bedau is at work now on an effort to determine how many wrongful death sentences may have been imposed: His list of murder convictions since 1900 in which the state eventually *admitted* error is some four hundred cases long. Of course, very few of these cases involved actual executions: The mistakes that Bedau documents were uncovered precisely because the prisoner was alive and able to fight for his vindication. The cases where someone is executed are the very cases in which we're least likely to learn that we got the wrong man.

I don't claim that executions of entirely innocent people will occur very often. But they will occur. And other sorts of mistakes already have. Roosevelt Green was executed in Georgia two days before J. C. Shaw. Green and an accomplice kidnapped a young woman. Green swore that his companion shot her to death after Green had left, and that he knew nothing about the murder. Green's claim was supported by a statement that his accomplice made to a witness after the crime. The jury never resolved whether Green was telling the truth, and when he tried to take a polygraph examination a few days before his scheduled execution, the state of Georgia refused to allow the examiner into the prison. As the pressure for symbolic retribution mounts, the courts, like the public, are losing patience with such details. Green was electrocuted on January 9, while members of the Ku Klux Klan rallied outside the prison.

Then there is another sort of arbitrariness that happens all the time. 10 Last October, Louisiana executed a man named Ernest Knighton. Knighton had killed a gas station owner during a robbery. Like any murder, this was a terrible crime. But it was not premeditated, and is the sort of crime that very rarely results in a death sentence. Why was Knighton electrocuted when almost everyone else who committed the same offense was not? Was it because he was black? Was it because his victim and all twelve members of the jury that sentenced him were white? Was it because Knighton's court-appointed lawyer presented no evidence on his behalf at his sentencing hearing? Or maybe there's no reason except bad luck. One thing is clear: Ernest Knighton was picked out to die the way a fisherman takes a cricket out of a bait jar. No one cares which cricket gets impaled on the hook.

Not every prisoner executed recently was chosen that randomly. But many were. And having selected these men so casually, so blindly, the death penalty system asks us to accept that the purpose of killing each of them is to affirm the sanctity of human life.

The death penalty states are also learning that the death penalty is easier to advocate than it is to administer. In Florida, where executions have become almost routine, the governor reports that nearly a third of his time is spent reviewing the clemency requests of condemned prisoners. The Florida Supreme Court is hopelessly backlogged with death cases. Some have taken five years to decide, and the rest of the Court's work waits in line behind the death appeals. Florida's death row currently holds more than 230 prisoners. State officials are reportedly considering building a special "death prison" devoted entirely to the isolation and electrocution of the condemned. The state is also considering the creation of a special public defender unit that will do nothing else but handle death penalty appeals. The death penalty, in short, is spawning death agencies.

And what is Florida getting for all of this? The state went through almost all of 1983 without executing anyone: Its rate of intentional homicide declined by 17 percent. Last year Florida executed eight people—the most of any state, and the sixth highest total for any year since Florida started electrocuting people back in 1924. Elsewhere in the United States last year, the homicide rate continued to decline. But in Florida, it actually rose by 5.1 percent.

But these are just the tiresome facts. The electric chair has been a centerpiece of each of Koch's recent political campaigns, and he knows better than anyone how little the facts have to do with the public's support for capital punishment. What really fuels the death penalty is the justifiable frustration and rage of people who see that the government is not coping with violent crime. So what if the death penalty doesn't work? At least it gives us the satisfaction of knowing that we got one or two of the sons of bitches.

Perhaps we want retribution on the flesh and bone of a handful of 15 convicted murderers so badly that we're willing to close our eyes to all of the demoralization and danger that come with it. A lot of politicians think so, and they may be right. But if they are, then let's at least look honestly at what we're doing. This lottery of death both comes from and encourages an attitude toward human life that is not reverent, but reckless.

And that is why the mayor is dead wrong when he confuses such fury with justice. He suggests that we trivialize murder unless we kill murderers. By that logic, we also trivialize rape unless we sodomize rapists. The sin of Kitty Genovese's neighbors wasn't that they failed to stab her attacker to death. Justice does demand that murderers be punished. And common sense demands that society be protected from them. But neither justice nor self-preservation demands that we kill men whom we have already imprisoned.

The electric chair in which J. C. Shaw died earlier this year was built in 1912 at the suggestion of South Carolina's governor at the time, Cole Blease. Governor Blease's other criminal justice initiative was an impassioned crusade in favor of lynch law. Any lesser response, the governor insisted, trivialized the loathsome crimes of interracial rape and murder. In 1912, a lot of people agreed with Governor Blease that a proper regard for justice required both lynching and the electric chair. Eventually we are going to learn that justice requires neither.

Topics for Critical Thinking and Writing

1. After three introductory paragraphs, Bruck devotes two paragraphs to Shaw's execution. In a sentence or two, state the point he is making in his discussion of this execution. Then in another sentence or two (or three), indicate the degree to which this point refutes Edward I. Koch's argument.

2. In paragraph 7, Bruck refers to the case of Lenell Jeter, an innocent man who was condemned to a life sentence. Evaluate this point as a piece of evidence used to support an argument against the death penalty.

3. In paragraph 8, Bruck says that "the state eventually *admitted* error" in some four hundred cases. He goes on: "Of course, very few of these cases involved actual executions." How few is "very few"? Why do you suppose Bruck doesn't specify the number? If it is only, say, two, in your opinion does that affect Bruck's point?

4. Discussing the case of Roosevelt Green (para. 9), Bruck points out that Green offered to take a polygraph test but "the state of Georgia refused to allow the examiner into the prison." In a paragraph evaluate the state's position on this matter.

5. In paragraph 13 Bruck points out that although "last year" (1984) the state executed eight people, the homicide rate in Florida rose 5.1 percent, whereas elsewhere in the United States the homicide rate declined.

What do you make of these figures? What do you think Edward I. Koch (p. 55) would make of them?

6. In his next-to-last paragraph Bruck says that Koch "suggests that we trivialize murder unless we kill murderers. By that logic, we also trivialize rape unless we sodomize rapists." Do you agree that this statement brings out the absurdity of Koch's thinking?

7. Evaluate Bruck's final paragraph (a) as a concluding paragraph and (b) as a piece of argumentation.

8. Bruck, writing early in 1985, stresses that all the "more than thirty" executions in the nation "in the last two years" have taken place in the South (para. 3). Why does he think this figure points to a vulnerability in Koch's argument? Would Bruck's argument here be spoiled if some executions were to occur outside of the South? (By the way, where exactly have most of the recent executions in the nation occurred?)

9. Bruck argues that the present death-penalty system—in practice even if not in theory—utterly fails to "affirm the sanctity of human life" (para. 11). Do you think Bruck would, or should, concede that at least in theory it is possible for a death-penalty system to be no more offensive to the value of human life than, say, a system of imprisonment is offensive to the value of human liberty or a system of fines is offensive to the value of human property?

10. Can Bruck be criticized for implying that cases like those he cites— Shaw, Ford, Green, and Knightson, in particular—are the rule rather than the exception? Does either Bruck or Koch cite any evidence to help settle this question?

11. Write a paragraph explaining which of these events seems to you to be the more unseemly: a condemned prisoner, on the threshold of execution, lecturing the rest of us on the immorality of killing; or the crowd that bursts into cheers outside a prison when it learns that a scheduled execution has been carried out.

POTTER STEWART

After the U.S. Supreme Court decided Furman v. Georgia *in 1972, requiring states either to abolish the death penalty or revise their statutes to avoid the "arbitrariness" to which the Court objected in* Furman, *state legislatures reacted in one of two ways. A few states enacted mandatory death penalties, giving the trial court no alternative to a death sentence once the defendant was convicted. Most states, including Georgia, tightened up their procedures by imposing new requirements on the trial and appellate courts in death penalty cases. In 1976 these new statutes were challenged, and in a series of decisions the Court (by a seven to two majority) settled two crucial questions: (1) The death penalty was not "a per se [as such] violation" of the Eighth Amendment (prohibiting "cruel and unusual punishments") and the Fourteenth Amendment (guaranteeing "equal protection of the laws"), and (2) several kinds of new death penalty statutes were constitutionally unobjectionable. The most important of these cases was* Gregg v. Georgia; *we reprint excerpts from the majority opinion by Associate Justice Potter Stewart (1915–1985). (Justice Stewart had voted against the death penalty in* Furman, *but four years later he switched sides, evidently believing that his objections of 1972 were no longer relevant.) In the following opinion, the citations referring to legal documents have been omitted.*

Gregg v. Georgia

The Georgia statute, as amended after our decision in *Furman v. Georgia*, retains the death penalty for six categories of crime: murder, kidnapping for ransom or where the victim is harmed, armed robbery, rape, treason, and aircraft hijacking. The capital defendant's guilt or innocence is determined in the traditional manner, either by a trial judge or a jury, in the first stage of a bifurcated trial. . . .

After a verdict, finding, or plea of guilty to a capital crime, a presentence hearing is conducted before whoever made the determination of guilt. The sentencing procedures are essentially the same in both bench and jury trials. At the hearing:

> [T]he judge [or jury] shall hear additional evidence in extenuation, mitigation, and aggravation of punishment, including the record of any prior criminal convictions and pleas of guilty or pleas of nolo contendere of the defendant, or the absence of any prior conviction and pleas: Provided, however, that only such evidence in aggravations as the State has made known to the defendant prior to his trial shall be admissible. The judge [or jury] shall also hear argument by the defendant or his counsel and the prosecuting attorney . . . regarding the punishment to be imposed.

The defendant is accorded substantial latitude as to the types of evidence that he may introduce. Evidence considered during the guilt stage may be considered during the sentencing stage without being resubmitted.

In the assessment of the appropriate sentence to be imposed the judge is also required to consider or to include in his instructions to the jury "any mitigating circumstances or aggravating circumstances otherwise authorized by law and any of [ten] statutory aggravating circumstances which may be supported by the evidence. . . ." The scope of the nonstatutory aggravating or mitigating circumstances is not delineated in the statute. Before a convicted defendant may be sentenced to death, however, except in cases of treason or aircraft hijacking, the jury, or the trial judge in cases tried without a jury, must find beyond a reasonable doubt one of the ten aggravating circumstances specified in the statute.[1] The sentence of death may be imposed only if the jury (or judge) finds one of the statutory aggravating circumstances and then elects to impose that sentence. If the verdict is death the jury or judge must specify the aggravating circumstance(s) found. In jury cases, the trial judge is bound by the jury's recommended sentence.

In addition to the conventional appellate process available in all criminal cases, provision is made for special expedited direct review by the Supreme Court of Georgia of the appropriateness of imposing the sentence of death in the particular case. The court is directed to consider "the punishment as well as any errors enumerated by way of appeal," and to determine

1. whether the sentence of death was imposed under the influence of passion, prejudice, or any other arbitrary factor, and
2. whether, in cases other than treason or aircraft hijacking, the evidence supports the jury's or judge's finding of a statutory aggravating circumstance as enumerated in §27.2534.1 (b), and
3. whether the sentence of death is excessive or disproportionate to the penalty imposed in similar cases, considering both the crime and the defendant.

If the court affirms a death sentence, it is required to include in its decision reference to similar cases that it has taken into consideration. . . . We now consider specifically whether the sentence of death for the crime of murder is a per se violation of the Eighth and Fourteenth Amendments to the Constitution. We note first that history and precedent strongly support a negative answer to this question.

The imposition of the death penalty for the crime of murder has a long history of acceptance both in the United States and in England. The common-law rule imposed a mandatory death sentence on all convicted murderers. And the penalty continued to be used into the twentieth century by most American states, although the breadth of the common-law rule was diminished, initially by narrowing the class of murders to be punished by death and subsequently by widespread adoption of laws expressly granting juries the discretion to recommend mercy.

It is apparent from the text of the Constitution itself that the existence of capital punishment was accepted by the Framers. At the time the Eighth Amendment was ratified, capital punishment was a common sanction in every state. Indeed, the First Congress of the United States enacted legislation providing death as the penalty for specified crimes. The Fifth Amendment, adopted at the same time as the Eighth, contemplated the continued existence of the capital sanction by imposing certain limits on the prosecution of capital cases:

> No person shall be held to answer for a capital, or otherwise infamous crime, unless on a presentment or indictment of a Grand Jury . . . ; nor shall any person be subject for the same offense to be twice put in jeopardy of life or limb; . . . nor be deprived of life, liberty, or property, without due process of law. . . .

And the Fourteenth Amendment, adopted over three-quarters of a century later, similarly contemplates the existence of the capital sanction in providing that no state shall deprive any person of "life, liberty, or property" without due process of law.

Four years ago, the petitioners in *Furman* and its companion cases predicated their argument primarily upon the asserted proposition that standards of decency had evolved to the point where capital punishment no longer could be tolerated. The petitioners in those cases said, in effect, that the evolutionary process had come to an end, and that standards of decency required that the Eighth Amendment be construed finally as prohibiting capital punishment for any crime regardless of its depravity and impact on society. This view was accepted by two Justices. Three other Justices were unwilling to go so far; focusing on the procedures by which convicted defendants were selected for the death penalty rather than on the actual punishment inflicted, they joined in the conclusion that the statutes before the Court were constitutionally invalid.

The petitioners in the capital cases before the Court today renew the "standards of decency" argument, but developments during the four years since *Furman* have undercut substantially the assumptions upon which their argument rested. Despite the continuing debate, dating back to the nineteenth century, over the morality and utility of capital punishment, it is now evident that a large proportion of American society continues to regard it as an appropriate and necessary criminal sanction.

The most marked indication of society's endorsement of the death 10 penalty for murder is the legislative response to *Furman*. The legislatures of at least thirty-five states have enacted new statutes that provide for the death penalty for at least some crimes that result in the death of another person. And the Congress of the United States, in 1974, enacted a statute providing the death penalty for aircraft piracy that results in death. . . .

In the only statewide referendum occurring since *Furman* and brought to our attention, the people of California adopted a constitutional amendment that authorized capital punishment, in effect negating a prior ruling by the Supreme Court of California in *People v. Anderson*, that the death penalty violated the California Constitution.

The jury also is a significant and reliable objective index of contemporary values because it is so directly involved. . . .

It may be true that evolving standards have influenced juries in recent decades to be more discriminating in imposing the sentence of death. But the relative infrequency of jury verdicts imposing the death sentence does not indicate rejection of capital punishment per se. Rather, the reluctance of juries in many cases to impose the sentence may well reflect the humane feeling that this most irrevocable of sanctions should be reserved for a small number of extreme cases. Indeed, the actions of juries in many states since *Furman* are fully compatible with the legislative judgments, reflected in the new statutes, as to the continued utility and necessity of capital punishment in appropriate cases. At the close of 1974 at least 254 persons had been sentenced to death since *Furman*, and by the end of March 1976, more than 460 persons were subject to death sentences. . . .

The death penalty is said to serve two principal social purposes: retribution and deterrence of capital crimes by prospective offenders.

In part, capital punishment is an expression of society's moral outrage at particularly offensive conduct. This function may be unappealing to many, but it is essential in an ordered society that asks its citizens to rely on legal processes rather than self-help to vindicate their wrongs.

15

> The instinct for retribution is part of the nature of man, and channeling that instinct in the administration of criminal justice serves an important purpose in promoting the stability of a society governed by law. When people begin to believe that organized society is unwilling or unable to impose upon criminal offenders the punishment they "deserve," then there are sown the seeds of anarchy—of self-help, vigilante justice, and lynch law. *Furman v. Georgia* (Stewart, J., concurring).

"Retribution is no longer the dominant objective of the criminal law," *Williams v. New York*, but neither is it a forbidden objective nor one inconsistent with our respect for the dignity of men. . . . Indeed, the decision that capital punishment may be the appropriate sanction in extreme cases is an expression of the community's belief that certain crimes are themselves so grievous an affront to humanity that the only adequate response may be the penalty of death.[2]

Statistical attempts to evaluate the worth of the death penalty as a deterrent to crimes by potential offenders have occasioned a great deal of debate. The results simply have been inconclusive. As one opponent of capital punishment has said:

> [A]fter all possible inquiry, including the probing of all possible methods of inquiry, we do not know, and for systematic and easily visible reasons cannot know, what the truth about this "deterrent" effect may be. . . .
>
> The inescapable flaw is . . . that social conditions in any state are not constant through time, and that social conditions are not the same in any two states. If an effect were observed (and the observed effects, one way or another, are not large) then one could not at all tell whether any of this effect is attributable to the presence or absence of capital punishment. A "scientific"—that is to say, a soundly based— conclusion is simply impossible, and no methodological path out of this tangle suggests itself. C. Black, *Capital Punishment: The Inevitability of Caprice and Mistake* 25–26 (1974).

Although some of the studies suggest that the death penalty may not function as a significantly greater deterrent than lesser penalties, there is no convincing empirical evidence either supporting or refuting this view. We may nevertheless assume safely that there are murderers, such as those who act in passion, for whom the threat of death has little or no deterrent effect. But for many others, the death penalty undoubtedly is a significant deterrent. There are carefully contemplated murders, such as murder for hire, where the possible penalty of death may well enter into the cold calculus that precedes the decision to act.[3] And there are some categories of murder, such as murder by a life prisoner, where other sanctions may not be adequate. . . .

In sum, we cannot say that the judgment of the Georgia legislature that capital punishment may be necessary in some cases is clearly wrong. Considerations of federalism, as well as respect for the ability of a legislature to evaluate, in terms of its particular state, the moral consensus concerning the death penalty and its social utility as a sanction, require us to conclude, in the absence of more convincing evidence, that the infliction of death as a punishment for murder is not without justification and thus is not unconstitutionally severe.

Finally, we must consider whether the punishment of death is disproportionate in relation to the crime for which it is imposed. There is no question that death as a punishment is unique in its severity and irrevocability. But we are concerned here only with the imposition of capital punishment for the crime of murder, and when a life has been taken deliberately by the offender,[4] we cannot say that the punishment is invariably disproportionate to the crime. It is an extreme sanction, suitable to the most extreme of crimes.

We hold that the death penalty is not a form of punishment that   20 may never be imposed, regardless of the circumstances of the offense, regardless of the character of the offender, and regardless of the procedure followed in reaching the decision to impose it. . . .

While some have suggested that standards to guide a capital jury's sentencing deliberations are impossible to formulate, the fact is that such standards have been developed. When the drafters of the Model Penal Code faced this problem, they concluded "that it is within the realm of possibility to point to the main circumstances of aggravation and of mitigation that should be weighed *and weighed against each other* when they are presented in a concrete case" (emphasis in original). While such standards are by necessity somewhat general, they do provide guidance to the sentencing authority and thereby reduce the likelihood that it will impose a sentence that fairly can be called capricious or arbitrary. Where the sentencing authority is required to specify the factors it relied upon in reaching its decision, the further safeguard of meaningful appellate review is available to ensure that death sentences are not imposed capriciously or in a freakish manner.

In summary, the concerns expressed in *Furman* that the penalty of death not be imposed in an arbitrary or capricious manner can be met by a carefully drafted statute that ensures that the sentencing authority is given adequate information and guidance. As a general proposition these concerns are best met by a system that provides for a bifurcated proceeding at which the sentencing authority is apprised of the information relevant to the imposition of sentence and provided with standards to guide its use of the information.

For the reasons expressed in this opinion, we hold that the statutory system under which Gregg was sentenced to death does not violate the Constitution. Accordingly, the judgment of the Georgia Supreme Court is affirmed.

NOTES

1. The statute provides in part:
    (a) The death penalty may be imposed for the offenses of aircraft hijacking or treason, in any case.

(b) In all cases of other offenses for which the death penalty may be authorized, the judge shall consider, or he shall include in his instructions to the jury for it to consider, any mitigating circumstances or aggravating circumstances otherwise authorized by law and any of the following statutory aggravating circumstances which may be supported by the evidence:

   (1) The offense of murder, rape, armed robbery, or kidnapping was committed by a person with a prior record of conviction for a capital felony, or the offense of murder was committed by a person who has a substantial history of serious assaultive criminal convictions.

   (2) The offense of murder, rape, armed robbery, or kidnapping was committed while the offender was engaged in the commission of another capital felony, or aggravated battery, or the offense of murder was committed while the offender was engaged in the commission of burglary or arson in the first degree.

   (3) The offender by his act of murder, armed robbery, or kidnapping knowingly created a great risk of death to more than one person in a public place by means of a weapon or device which would normally be hazardous to the lives of more than one person.

   (4) The offender committed the offense of murder for himself or another, for the purpose of receiving money or any other thing of monetary value.

   (5) The murder of a judicial officer, former judicial officer, district attorney or solicitor or former district attorney or solicitor during or because of the exercise of his official duty.

   (6) The offender caused or directed another to commit murder or committed murder as an agent or employee of another person.

   (7) The offense of murder, rape, armed robbery, or kidnapping was outrageously or wantonly vile, horrible or inhuman in that it involved torture, depravity of mind, or an aggravated battery to the victim.

   (8) The offense of murder was committed against any peace officer, corrections employee or fireman while engaged in the performance of his official duties.

   (9) The offense of murder was committed by a person in, or who has escaped from, the lawful custody of a peace officer or place of lawful confinement.

  (10) The murder was committed for the purpose of avoiding, interfering with, or preventing a lawful arrest or custody in a place of lawful confinement, of himself or another.

(c) The statutory instructions as determined by the trial judge to be warranted by the evidence shall be given in charge and in writing to the jury for its deliberation. The jury, if its verdict be a recommendation of death, shall designate in writing, signed by the foreman of the jury, the aggravating circumstance or circumstances which it found beyond a reasonable doubt. In non-jury cases the judge shall make such designation. Except in cases of treason or aircraft hijacking, unless at least one of the statutory aggravating circumstances enumerated is so found, the death penalty shall not be imposed.

The Supreme Court of Georgia recently held unconstitutional the portion of the first circumstance encompassing persons who have a "substantial history of serious assaultive criminal convictions" because it did not set "sufficiently 'clear and objective standards.'"

2. Lord Justice Denning, Master of the Rolls of the Court of Appeal in England, spoke to this effect before the British Royal Commission on Capital Punishment:

> Punishment is the way in which society expresses its denunciation of wrongdoing: and, in order to maintain respect for law, it is essential that the punishment inflicted for grave crimes should adequately reflect the revulsion felt by the great majority of citizens for them. It is a mistake to consider the objects of punishment as being deterrent or reformative or preventive and nothing else. . . . The truth is that some crimes are so outrageous that society insists on adequate punishment, because the wrong-doer deserves it, irrespective of whether it is a deterrent or not.

A contemporary writer has noted more recently that opposition to capital punishment "has much more appeal when the discussion is merely academic than when the community is confronted with a crime, or a series of crimes, so gross, so heinous, so cold-blooded that anything short of death seems an inadequate response." Raspberry, Death Sentence, *Washington Post*, Mar. 12, 1976, p. A27, cols. 5–6.

3. Other types of calculated murders, apparently occurring with increasing frequency, include the use of bombs or other means of indiscriminate killings, the extortion murder of hostages or kidnap victims, and the execution-style killing of witnesses to a crime.

4. We do not address here the question whether the taking of the criminal's life is a proportionate sanction where no victim has been deprived of life — for example, when capital punishment is imposed for rape, kidnapping, or armed robbery that does not result in the death of any human being.

Topics for Critical Thinking and Writing

1. What features of Georgia's new death penalty statute does Justice Stewart point to in arguing that the new statute will prevent the problems found in the old statute?

2. Since the new Georgia statute upheld by the Supreme Court in its *Gregg* decision does nothing to affect the discretion the prosecutor has in deciding whether to seek the death penalty in a murder case, and nothing to affect the complete discretion the governor has in deciding whether to extend clemency, can it be argued that despite the new death-penalty statutes like Georgia's, the problems that gave rise to the decision in *Furman* will probably reappear?

3. How important do you think public opinion is in determining what the Bill of Rights means? Does it matter to the meaning of "cruel and unusual punishment" that most Americans profess to favor the death penalty? (Think of parallel cases: Does it matter to the meanings of "due process of law," "the right to bear arms," "an impartial jury"—all protected by the Bill of Rights—what a majority of the public thinks?)

4. In 1976, when the Supreme Court decided *Gregg*, it also decided *Woodson v. North Carolina*. In *Woodson*, the Court held unconstitutional under the Eighth and Fourteenth Amendments a *mandatory* death penalty for anyone convicted of first-degree murder. Do you think North Carolina's statute was a reasonable response to objections to the death penalty at the time of *Furman* based on the alleged arbitrary and discriminatory administration of that penalty? Why, or why not?

5. Stewart mentions the kinds of murder where he thinks the death penalty might be a better deterrent than life imprisonment. What are they? What reasons might be given for or against agreeing with him?

6. A year after *Gregg* was decided, the Supreme Court ruled in *Coker v. Georgia* that the death penalty for rape was unconstitutional under the Eighth and Fourteenth Amendments. Do you think that Stewart's opinion in *Gregg* silently implies that *only* murder is punishable by death? (What about a death penalty for treason? Espionage? Kidnapping for ransom? Large-scale illegal drug trafficking?) In an essay of 500 words, argue either for or against that conclusion.

HARRY BLACKMUN

Harry Blackmun (1908–1999) was born in Nashville, Illinois, and educated at Harvard, where he received his undergraduate and law degrees. He was appointed to the United States Supreme Court in 1970 as a conservative, but when he retired in 1994, he was regarded as a liberal. Blackmun became a national figure in 1973 when he wrote the majority opinion in Roe v. Wade, *a case that (although it placed limits on abortion) asserted that the right to privacy includes "a woman's decision whether or not to terminate her pregnancy." We reprint his dissent from the Supreme Court's order denying review in a Texas death-penalty case,*

Callins v. Collins, 510 U.S. 1141 (1994). In his first sentence, Blackmun says that Callins "will be executed by the State of Texas," and though in 1994 Callins received a stay of execution, he, in fact, was executed in 1997.

Dissenting Opinion in *Callins v. Collins*

Bruce Edwin Callins will be executed by the State of Texas. . . . Intravenous tubes attached to his arms will carry the instrument of death, a toxic fluid designed specifically for the purpose of killing human beings. The witnesses, standing a few feet away, will behold Callins, no longer a defendant, an appellant, or a petitioner, but a man, strapped to a gurney, and seconds away from extinction.

Within days, or perhaps hours, the memory of Callins will begin to fade. The wheels of justice will churn again, and somewhere, another jury or another judge will have the unenviable task of determining whether some human being is to live or die.

We hope, of course, that the defendant whose life is at risk will be represented by competent counsel, someone who is inspired by the awareness that a less-than-vigorous defense truly could have fatal consequences for the defendant. We hope that the attorney will investigate all aspects of the case, follow all evidentiary and procedural rules, and appear before a judge who is still committed to the protection of defendants' rights even now, as the prospect of meaningful judicial oversight has diminished. In the same vein, we hope that the prosecution, in urging the penalty of death, will have exercised its discretion wisely, free from bias, prejudice, or political motive and will be humbled, rather than emboldened, by the awesome authority conferred by the State.

But even if we can feel confident that these actors will fulfill their roles to the best of their human ability, our collective conscience will remain uneasy. Twenty years have passed since this Court declared that the death penalty must be imposed fairly, and with reasonable consistency or not at all (see *Furman v. Georgia*, 1972), and, despite the effort of the states and courts to devise legal formulas and procedural rules to meet this daunting challenge, the death penalty remains fraught with arbitrariness, discrimination, caprice, and mistake.

This is not to say that the problems with the death penalty today are   5
identical to those that were present twenty years ago. Rather, the problems that were pursued down one hole with procedural rules and verbal formulas have come to the surface somewhere else, just as virulent and

pernicious as they were in their original form. Experience has taught us that the constitutional goal of eliminating arbitrariness and discrimination from the administration of death . . . can never be achieved without compromising an equally essential component of fundamental fairness: individualized sentencing. (See *Lockett v. Ohio,* 1978.)

It is tempting, when faced with conflicting constitutional commands, to sacrifice one for the other or to assume that an acceptable balance between them already has been struck. In the context of the death penalty, however, such jurisprudential maneuvers are wholly inappropriate. The death penalty must be imposed "fairly, and with reasonable consistency, or not at all." (*Eddings v. Oklahoma,* 1982).

To be fair, a capital sentencing scheme must treat each person convicted of a capital offense with that "degree of respect due the uniqueness of the individual. . . ." That means affording the sentencer the power and discretion to grant mercy in a particular case, and providing avenues for the consideration of any and all relevant mitigating evidence that would justify a sentence less than death.

Reasonable consistency, on the other hand, requires that the death penalty be inflicted evenhandedly, in accordance with reason and objective standards, rather than by whim, caprice, or prejudice.

Finally, because human error is inevitable and because our criminal justice system is less than perfect, searching appellate review of death sentences and their underlying convictions is a prerequisite to a constitutional death penalty scheme.

On their face, these goals of individual fairness, reasonable consistency, and absence of error appear to be attainable: Courts are in the very business of erecting procedural devices from which fair, equitable, and reliable outcomes are presumed to flow. Yet, in the death penalty area, this Court, in my view, has engaged in a futile effort to balance these constitutional demands and now is retreating not only from the *Furman* promise of consistency and rationality but from the requirement of individualized sentencing as well.

Having virtually conceded that both fairness and rationality cannot be achieved in the administration of the death penalty (*McClesky v. Kemp,* 1987), the Court has chosen to deregulate the entire enterprise, replacing, it would seem, substantive constitutional requirements with mere aesthetics and abdicating its statutorily and constitutionally imposed duty to provide meaningful judicial oversight to the administration of death by the states.

From this day forward, I no longer shall tinker with the machinery of death. For more than twenty years I have endeavored—indeed, I have struggled, along with a majority of this Court—to develop procedural and substantive rules that would lend more than the mere appearance of fairness to the death penalty endeavor. . . . Rather than continue to coddle the Court's delusion that the desired level of fairness has been achieved and the need for regulation eviscerated, I feel morally and intellectually obligated simply to concede that the death penalty experiment has failed. It is virtually self-evident to me now that no combination of procedural rules or substantive regulations ever can save the death penalty from its inherent constitutional deficiencies. The basic question—does the system accurately and consistently determine which defendants "deserve" to die?—cannot be answered in the affirmative. . . . The problem is that the inevitability of factual, legal, and moral error gives us a system that we know must wrongly kill some defendants, a system that fails to deliver the fair, consistent and reliable sentences of death required by the Constitution. . . .

There is little doubt now that *Furman*'s essential holding was correct. Although most of the public seems to desire, and the Constitution appears to permit, the penalty of death, it surely is beyond dispute that if the death penalty cannot be administered consistently and rationally, it may not be administered at all. . . .

Delivering on the *Furman* promise, however, has proved to be another matter. *Furman* aspired to eliminate the vestiges of racism and the effects of poverty in capital sentencing; it deplored the "wanton" and "random" infliction of death by a government with constitutionally limited power. *Furman* demanded that the sentencer's discretion be directed and limited by procedural rules and objective standards in order to minimize the risk of arbitrary and capricious sentences of death.

In the years following *Furman*, serious efforts were made to comply   15 with its mandate. State legislatures and appellate courts struggled to provide judges and juries with sensible and objective guidelines for determining who should live and who should die. Some states attempted to define who is "deserving" of the death penalty through the use of carefully chosen adjectives, reserving the death penalty for those who commit crimes that are "especially heinous, atrocious, or cruel," or "wantonly vile, horrible, or inhuman." Other states enacted mandatory death penalty statutes, reading *Furman* as an invitation to eliminate sentencer discretion altogether. . . .

Unfortunately, all this experimentation and ingenuity yielded little of what *Furman* demanded. It soon became apparent that discretion could not be eliminated from capital sentencing without threatening the fundamental fairness due a defendant when life is at stake. Just as contemporary society was no longer tolerant of the random or discriminatory infliction of the penalty of death . . . evolving standards of decency required due consideration of the uniqueness of each individual defendant when imposing society's ultimate penalty.

This development in the American conscience would have presented no constitutional dilemma if fairness to the individual could be achieved without sacrificing the consistency and rationality promised in *Furman*. But over the past two decades, efforts to balance these competing constitutional commands have been to no avail. Experience has shown that the consistency and rationality promised in *Furman* are inversely related to the fairness owed the individual when considering a sentence of death. A step toward consistency is a step away from fairness. . . .

While one might hope that providing the sentencer with as much relevant mitigating evidence as possible will lead to more rational and consistent sentences, experience has taught otherwise. It seems that the decision whether a human being should live or die is so inherently subjective, rife with all of life's understandings, experiences, prejudices, and passions, that it inevitably defies the rationality and consistency required by the Constitution. . . .

The consistency promised in *Furman* and the fairness to the individual demanded in *Lockett* are not only inversely related but irreconcilable in the context of capital punishment. Any statute or procedure that could effectively eliminate arbitrariness from the administration of death would also restrict the sentencer's discretion to such an extent that the sentencer would be unable to give full consideration to the unique characteristics of each defendant and the circumstances of the offense.

By the same token, any statute of procedure that would provide the 20 sentencer with sufficient discretion to consider fully and act upon the unique circumstances of each defendant would "thro(w) open the back door to arbitrary and irrational sentencing." . . .

In my view, the proper course when faced with irreconcilable constitutional commands is not to ignore one or the other, nor to pretend that the dilemma does not exist, but to admit the futility of the effort to harmonize them. This means accepting the fact that the death penalty cannot be administered in accord with our Constitution. . . .

Perhaps one day this Court will develop procedural rules or verbal formulas that actually will provide consistency, fairness, and reliability in a capital-sentencing scheme. I am not optimistic that such a day will come. I am more optimistic, though, that this Court eventually will conclude that the effort to eliminate arbitrariness while preserving fairness "in the infliction of (death) is so plainly doomed to failure that it and the death penalty must be abandoned altogether." (*Godfrey v. Georgia*, 1980. . . .) I may not live to see that day, but I have faith that eventually it will arrive. The path the Court has chosen lessens us all.

Topics for Critical Thinking and Writing

1. Who is the "we" to whom Blackmun refers when he says "We hope . . ." (para. 3)? We on the U.S. Supreme Court? We who are inclined to support the death penalty? We the people of Texas? We Americans? Or is this merely the so-called editorial "we" and of no substantive significance at all?

2. What does Blackmun mean by contrasting "procedural and substantive rules" of law (para. 12)?

3. Assuming for the sake of argument that Blackmun's criticisms of what he elsewhere called "the machinery of death" are correct, what do you think accounts for the failure of the criminal justice system in death-penalty states over the past generation (since *Furman v. Georgia* was decided in 1972) to operate "fairly, and with reasonable consistency" (para. 6) in accordance with "reason and objective standards" (para. 8)?

4. What does Blackmun mean when he says that "consistency and rationality" in death-penalty cases are "inversely related to the fairness owed the individual" offender (para. 17)?

5. Blackmun claims that the appellate courts (of Texas? of all death-penalty states? of the federal government?) have failed to give "meaningful judicial oversight to the administration of death by the states" (para. 11). After reading Blackmun's opinion, explain in an essay of 500 words what you think such "meaningful oversight" ought to involve.

HELEN PREJEAN

Sister Helen Prejean, born in Baton Rouge, has been a member of the Order of the Sisters of St. Joseph of Medaille since 1957. In 1993, she achieved international fame with her book Dead Man Walking: An Eyewitness Account of the Death Penalty in the United States, *based on her experiences counseling prisoners on death row in Louisiana prisons. An excerpt is printed here. A film with the same title, starring Susan Sarandon (as Sister Helen) and Sean Penn, was released in 1995. When confronted with the argument that the death penalty is appropriate revenge for society to take on a murderer, Sister Helen said, "I would not want my death avenged — especially by government, which can't be trusted to control its own bureaucrats or collect taxes equitably or fill a pothole, much less decide which of its citizens to kill." The title is the editors'.*

Executions Are Too Costly — Morally

I think of the running debate I engage in with "church" people about the death penalty. "Proof texts" from the Bible usually punctuate these discussions without regard for the cultural context or literary genre of the passages invoked. (Will D. Campbell, a Southern Baptist minister and writer, calls this use of scriptural quotations "biblical quarter-backing.")

It is abundantly clear that the Bible depicts murder as a crime for which death is considered the appropriate punishment, and one is hard-pressed to find a biblical "proof text" in either the Hebrew Testament or the New Testament which unequivocally refutes this. Even Jesus' admonition "Let him without sin cast the first stone," when he was asked the appropriate punishment for an adulteress (John 8:7)—the Mosaic law prescribed death—should be read in its proper context. This passage is an "entrapment" story, which sought to show Jesus' wisdom in besting his adversaries. It is not an ethical pronouncement about capital punishment.

Similarly, the "eye for eye" passage from Exodus, which pro-death penalty advocates are fond of quoting, is rarely cited in its original context, in which it is clearly meant to limit revenge.

The passage, including verse 22, which sets the context reads:

> If, when men come to blows, they hurt a woman who is pregnant and she suffers a miscarriage, though she does not die of it, the man responsible must pay the compensation demanded of him by the woman's master; he shall hand it over after arbitration. But should she die, you shall give life for life, eye for eye, tooth for tooth, hand for hand, foot for foot, burn for burn, wound for wound, stroke for stroke. (Exodus 21:22–25)

In the example given (patently patriarchal: the woman is considered 5 the negotiable property of her male master), it is clear that punishment is to be measured out according to the seriousness of the offense. If the child is lost but not the mother, the punishment is less grave than if both mother and child are lost. *Only* an eye for an eye, *only* a life for a life is the intent of the passage. Restraint was badly needed. It was not uncommon for an offended family or clan to slaughter entire communities in retaliation for an offense against one of their members.

Even granting the call for restraint in this passage, it is nonetheless clear—here and in numerous other instances throughout the Hebrew Bible—that the punishment for murder was death.

But we must remember that such prescriptions of the Mosaic Law were promulgated in a seminomadic culture in which the preservation of a fragile society—without benefit of prisons and other institutions—demanded quick, effective, harsh punishment of offenders. And we should note the numerous other crimes for which the Bible prescribes death as punishment:

contempt of parents (Exodus 21:15, 17; Leviticus 24:17);

trespass upon sacred ground (Exodus 19:12–13; Numbers 1:51; 18:7);

sorcery (Exodus 22:18; Leviticus 20:27);

bestiality (Exodus 22:19; Leviticus 20:15–16);

sacrifice to foreign gods (Exodus 22:20; Deuteronomy 13:1–9);

profaning the sabbath (Exodus 31:14);

adultery (Leviticus 20:10; Deuteronomy 22:22–24);

incest (Leviticus 20:11–13);

homosexuality (Leviticus 20:13);

and prostitution (Leviticus 21:19; Deuteronomy 22:13–21).

And this is by no means a complete list.

But no person with common sense would dream of appropriating such a moral code today, and it is curious that those who so readily invoke the "eye for an eye, life for life" passage are quick to shun other biblical prescriptions which also call for death, arguing that modern societies have evolved over the three thousand or so years since biblical times and no longer consider such exaggerated and archaic punishments appropriate.

Such nuances are lost, of course, in "biblical quarterbacking," and more and more I find myself steering away from such futile discussions. Instead, I try to articulate what I personally believe about Jesus and the ethical thrust he gave to humankind: an impetus toward compassion, a preference for disarming enemies without humiliating and destroying them, and a solidarity with poor and suffering people.

So, what happened to the impetus of love and compassion Jesus set blazing into history?

The first Christians adhered closely to the way of life Jesus had taught. They died in amphitheaters rather than offer homage to worldly emperors. They refused to fight in emperors' wars. But then a tragic diversion happened, which Elaine Pagels has deftly explored in her book *Adam, Eve, and the Serpent:* in 313 C.E. (Common Era) the Emperor Constantine entered the Christian church.

Pagels says, "Christian bishops, once targets for arrest, torture, and execution, now received tax exemptions, gifts from the imperial treasury, prestige, and even influence at court; the churches gained new wealth, power and prominence." Unfortunately, the exercise of power practiced by Christians in alliance with the Roman Empire—with its unabashed allegiance to the sword—soon bore no resemblance to the purely moral persuasion that Jesus had taught.

In the fifth century, Pagels points out, Augustine provided the theo- 15 logical rationale the church needed to justify the use of violence by church and state governments. Augustine persuaded church authorities that "original sin" so damaged every person's ability to make moral choices that external control by church and state authorities over people's lives was necessary and justified. The "wicked" might be "coerced by the sword" to "protect the innocent," Augustine taught. And thus was legitimated for Christians the authority of secular government to "control" its subjects by coercive and violent means—even punishment by death.

In the latter part of the twentieth century, however, two flares of hope—Mohandas K. Gandhi and Martin Luther King—have demonstrated that Jesus' counsel to practice compassion and tolerance even toward one's enemies can effect social change. Susan Jacoby, analyzing the moral power that Gandhi and King unleashed in their campaigns for social justice, finds a unique form of aggression:

"'If everyone took an eye for an eye,' Gandhi said, 'the whole world would be blind.' But Gandhi did not want to take anyone's eye; he wanted to force the British out of India. . . .'"

Nonviolence and nonaggression are generally regarded as interchangeable concepts—King and Gandhi frequently used them that way—but nonviolence, as employed by Gandhi in India and by King in the American South, might reasonably be viewed as a highly disciplined form of aggression. If one defines aggression in the primary dictionary sense of "attack," nonviolent resistance proved to be the most powerful attack imaginable on the powers King and Gandhi were trying to overturn. The writings of both men are filled with references to love as a powerful force against oppression, and while the two leaders were not using the term "force" in the military sense, they certainly regarded nonviolence as a tactical weapon as well as an expression of high moral principle. The root meaning of Gandhi's concept of *satyagraha* . . . is "holding on to truth" . . . Gandhi also called *satyagraha* the "love force" or "soul force" and explained that he had discovered "in the earliest stages that pursuit of truth did not permit violence being inflicted on one's opponent, but that he must be weaned from error by patience and sympathy. . . . And patience means self-suffering." So the doctrine came to mean vindication of truth, not by the infliction of suffering on the opponent, but on one's self.

King was even more explicit on this point: the purpose of civil disobedience, he explained many times, was to force the defenders of segregation to commit brutal acts in public and thus arouse the conscience of the world on behalf of those wronged by racism. King and Gandhi did not succeed because they changed the hearts and minds of southern sheriffs and British colonial administrators (although they did, in fact, change some minds) but because they *made the price of maintaining control too high for their opponents* [emphasis mine].

That, I believe, is what it's going to take to abolish the death penalty in this country: we must persuade the American people that government killings are too costly for us, not only financially, but—more important—morally.

The death penalty *costs* too much. Allowing our government to kill citizens compromises the deepest moral values upon which this country was conceived: the inviolable dignity of human persons.

I have no doubt that we will one day abolish the death penalty in   20 America. It will come sooner if people like me who know the truth about executions do our work well and educate the public. It will come slowly if we do not. Because, finally, I know that it is not a question of malice or ill will or meanness of spirit that prompts our citizens to support executions. It is, quite simply, that people don't know the truth of what is going on. That is not by accident. The secrecy surrounding executions makes it possible for executions to continue. I am convinced that if executions were made public, the torture and violence would be unmasked, and we would be shamed into abolishing executions. We would be embarrassed at the brutalization of the crowds that would gather to watch a man or woman be killed. And we would be humiliated to know that visitors from other countries—Japan, Russia, Latin America, Europe—were watching us kill our own citizens—we, who take pride in being the flagship of democracy in the world.

Topics for Critical Thinking and Writing

1. Suppose you interpret the "eye for eye" passage from Exodus (paras. 3–6) not as a "call for restraint" but as support for the death penalty. Does that mean no exceptions whatsoever—that everyone who kills another must be sentenced to death and executed? Would that require

abandoning the distinction between murder and manslaughter or between first- and second-degree murder?

2. Prejean lists ten different crimes for which the Bible prescribes death as the punishment (para. 7) and says "no person with common sense would dream of appropriating [them] today" (para. 9). Do you agree? In an essay of 500 words, defend or criticize the proposition that the death penalty ought to be confined to the crime of first-degree murder.

3. Do you think that someone who endorses the biblical doctrine of "life for life, eye for eye" (para. 4) is also required by consistency to endorse the death penalty for some or all of the ten nonhomicidal crimes Prejean mentions (para. 7)? Explain.

4. In deciding whether to impose the death penalty for serious crimes, what guidance do you think a secular society, such as ours, ought to accept from the Bible? In an essay of 500 words, defend or criticize this thesis: "Biblical teachings ought to play a central role in deciding how we use the death penalty."

5. Prejean does not propose any alternative to the death penalty. Presumably she would favor some form of imprisonment for crimes involving death. She claims that the death penalty is inconsistent with "the inviolable dignity of human persons" (para. 19). Does consistency require her also to reject flogging? Solitary confinement in prison? Life imprisonment without the possibility of parole? Write a 500-word essay on this theme: "Severe Punishment and the Inviolable Dignity of Human Persons."

6. Prejean thinks that if executions were made public, Americans would soon decide to oppose the death penalty (para. 20). Do you agree? Write a 500-word essay for or against the following proposition: "Executions held in public would soon lead to public rejection of the death penalty."

CASEY JOHNSON

When the U.S. Supreme Court in 2001 refused to hear a case challenging the death penalty for minors, the New York Times Magazine *invited two young students to offer their views, pro and con, and we reprint the two essays. The issue remains unresolved.*

Yes, The Death Penalty Should Apply to Juveniles

I've always believed in "an eye for an eye and a tooth for a tooth." All people need to be accountable for their actions, including juveniles.

The death penalty is a fair punishment for those who murder—even if they were under 18 when they killed. I don't believe that killers can be rehabilitated, even if they are young.

Since August, my classmates and I have corresponded with death-row inmates in Texas as part of a class we're taking on the criminal-justice system. I have been repeatedly shocked and disappointed to see how the inmates lie about their cases. Their inability to be truthful even when they are already in jail has reinforced my opinion.

I don't feel any sympathy for someone who kills; I don't care how old they are. It would be one thing if they were 4 or 5 years old and didn't know right from wrong, but a 16-year-old should know better. If a killer has the intellectual ability to understand that what he or she did was wrong, then that killer must pay with his or her life.

In the biblical story of the Garden of Eden, God tells Adam and Eve not to eat the fruit, but they eat it anyway. So Adam and Eve are banned from the Garden of Eden—one strike and they are out. This principle should hold true for murderers of any age—one strike and you are out.

Furthermore, why should taxpayers pay to feed, house, and clothe a murderer for life? Killers with life sentences live better than our home-less people or those who work and are poor and deprived.

If you take a life, it cannot be given back. The ultimate punishment for murder should be death, even for teenagers.

—Casey Johnson, 18

EMMA WELCH

No, The Death Penalty Should Not Apply to Juveniles

Minors cannot vote or run for office, and in most cases they cannot live without guardians. Minors cannot even hold bank accounts or sign legal contracts without the consent of their adult custodians.

These restrictions recognize the fact that juveniles cannot—and should not—be held legally responsible for their actions. Why then do so many states choose to execute criminals whose crimes were commit-ted before the age of 18? Is death not the ultimate in responsibility? If 16-year-olds cannot open bank accounts in their own names, why can they pay for crimes with their lives? This is a double standard.

It is with good reason that there are restrictions placed on teenagers. Scientific studies show that teenagers lack the ability to sense the great weight that their decisions can have. Sixteen-year-olds can certainly differentiate between right and wrong, but they often lack a fully developed awareness of the consequences of their actions. This is the very quality that distinguishes a responsible adult from a child. The American Bar Association, a professional association for lawyers, agrees. It believes that children are inherently different from adults in their level of responsibility for their actions.

The international community also finds the juvenile death penalty immoral. Executing a minor violates respected international treaties. These treaties recognize that society cannot force someone with an underdeveloped sense of the consequences of their actions to pay with their lives for those actions. A judicial system that takes the life of a child does not truly uphold justice.

—Emma Welch, 17

Topics for Critical Thinking and Writing

1. Johnson seems to concede (para. 3) that if a killer is "4 or 5 years old" and doesn't "know right from wrong," then the death penalty for such a youngster would be inappropriate. How old do you think a murderer might be, according to Johnson, before he or she crosses the threshold of responsibility?

2. Johnson bolsters his case for the death penalty by drawing a parallel to the way God punishes Adam and Eve by expelling them from the Garden of Eden (para. 4). How do you think Johnson would react to the way God decrees punishment for the murderer Cain (Genesis 4:8–16)?

3. Johnson claims that life behind bars is often better than the conditions the homeless endure. What should we infer from this? That we should make life in prison more like life on the streets? Or that we should improve the lot of the homeless? Or both? Or neither?

4. Welch says (para. 2) that "juveniles cannot . . . be held legally responsible for their actions." Doesn't this imply that she ought to favor no punishment at all for offenders under eighteen—and isn't that position implausible on its face?

5. Welch mentions several activities that are available to adults but not to minors—anyone under eighteen (para. 1). Can you see any differences between these things and the eligibility for the death penalty of a sixteen-year-old?

6. Is it misleading to protest the execution of a "minor" when what is really being protested is the execution of someone now in his twenties or thirties (or even older) but who committed murder when he was under eighteen?

ALEX KOZINSKI AND SEAN GALLAGHER

Alex Kozinski is a judge on the Ninth U.S. Circuit Court of Appeals. Sean Gallagher was his law clerk when the two of them wrote this essay, published in the New York Times *on March 8, 1995.*

For an Honest Death Penalty

It is a staple of American politics that there is very strong support for the death penalty; in opinion polls, roughly 70 percent consistently favor it. Yet the popular will on this issue has been thwarted.

To be sure, we have many capital trials, convictions, and death sentences; we have endless and massively costly appeals; and a few people do get put to death every year. But compared to the number of death sentences, the number of executions is minuscule, and the gap is widening fast.

In 1972, the Supreme Court struck down all existing death penalty statutes and emptied the nation's death rows. Almost immediately states began passing death penalty laws to comply with the Court's reinterpretation of the Eighth Amendment. Since then more than 5,000 men and a handful of women have been given the death sentence; about 2,000 of those sentences have been set aside; fewer than 300 have been carried out.

THE WILL OF THE MAJORITY THWARTED

The reasons are complex, but they boil down to this: The Supreme Court's death penalty case law reflects an uneasy accommodation between the will of the popular majority, who favor capital punishment, and the objections of a much smaller—but ferociously committed—minority, who view it as a barbaric anachronism.

Assuaging death penalty opponents, the Court has devised a number of extraordinary safeguards applicable to capital cases; but responding to complaints that these procedures were used for obstruction and delay, it has also imposed various limitations and exceptions to these safeguards. This pull and tug has resulted in a procedural structure—   5 what Justice Harry A. Blackmun called a "machinery of death"—that is remarkably time-consuming, painfully cumbersome, and extremely expensive.

No one knows precisely how large a slice of our productive resources we force-feed to this behemoth, but we can make some educated guesses. To begin with, while 80 to 90 percent of all criminal cases end in plea bargains, capital cases almost always go to trial, and the trials are vastly more complex than their noncapital counterparts. If the defendant is sentenced to death, the case shuttles between the state and Federal courts for years, sometimes decades.

The Robert Alton Harris case, for example, found its way to the California Supreme Court six times; it was reviewed in Federal district court on five occasions, and each time it was appealed to the Ninth Circuit. The U.S. Supreme Court reviewed the case once on the merits, though on five other occasions it considered and declined Mr. Harris's request for review. Before Mr. Harris was executed in 1992, his case was reviewed by at least thirty judges and justices on more than twenty occasions over thirteen years.

State and local governments pay for the prosecution as well as for the defense team—which consists of at least two lawyers and a battery of investigators and experts; much of this money is spent even if the defendant eventually gets a lesser sentence. California reportedly spends $90 million a year on the death penalty. Once the case gets into Federal court, the United States starts picking up the defense tab and the sums can be daunting. In one recent case, a Federal district court paid defense lawyers more than $400,000, which didn't include the appeal or petition to the Supreme Court. Our own estimate is that death cases, on the average, cost taxpayers about a million dollars more than their noncapital counterparts. With 3,000 or so inmates on death row, to paraphrase Senator Everett Dirksen, pretty soon you get into real money.

Another significant cost is the burden on the courts. More than a quarter of the opinions published by the California Supreme Court from 1987 to 1993 involved death penalty cases. Since capital appeals are mandatory while appeals in other cases are discretionary, much of this burden is borne by other litigants who must vie for a diminished share of that court's attention. Estimating the judicial resources devoted to a capital case in the Federal courts is difficult, but a fair guess would be ten times those in other cases.

Perhaps the most significant cost of the death penalty is the lack of   10 finality. Death cases raise many more issues, and far more complex issues, than other criminal cases; convictions are attacked with more gusto and reviewed with more vigor in the courts. As a result, fully 40 percent of the death sentences imposed since 1972 have been vacated, sometimes five, ten or fifteen years after trial. One worries about the effect on the families of the victims, who have to endure the possibility—often the reality—of retrials, evidentiary hearings and last-minute stays of execution for years after the crime.

What are we getting in return? Even though we devote vast resources to the task, we come nowhere near executing the number of people we put on death row, and probably never will. We sentence about 250 inmates to death every year but have never executed more than forty. Just to keep up with the number of new death row inmates, states would have to sextuple the pace of executions; to eliminate the backlog, there would have to be one execution a day for the next twenty-six years.

This reality moots much of the traditional debate about the death penalty. Death penalty opponents have certainly not won the popular battle: despite relentless assaults, the public remains firmly committed to capital punishment. Nor have opponents won the moral battle: most of us continue to believe that those who show utter contempt for human life by committing remorseless, premeditated murder justly forfeit the right to their own life.

Other arguments against the death penalty also fall flat. For example, the fear that an innocent person may be convicted also applies to noncapital cases; no one, after all, can give back the twenty years someone wrongfully spends behind bars. Our system is therefore heavily geared to give the criminal defendant the benefit of the doubt. Wrongfully convicted defendants are rare; wrongfully convicted capital defendants are even rarer. The case where the innocent defendant is saved from the electric chair because the one-armed man shows up and confesses happens only in the movies.

Death penalty opponents are winning the war nevertheless. Unable to stop the majority altogether, they have managed to vastly increase the cost of imposing the death penalty while reducing the rate of executions to a trickle. This trend is not likely to be reversed. Even if we were willing to double or triple the resources we devote to the death penalty, even if we could put all other civil and criminal cases handled by the state and Federal courts on the back burner, it would be to no avail.

The great stumbling block is the lawyers: the jurisprudence of death 15 is so complex, so esoteric, so harrowing, this is the one area where there aren't nearly enough lawyers willing and able to handle all the current cases. In California, for example, almost half the pending death penalty appeals—more than 100—are on hold because the state can't find lawyers to handle them.

We are thus left in a peculiar limbo: we have constructed a machine that is extremely expensive, chokes our legal institutions, visits repeated trauma on victims' families, and ultimately produces nothing like the benefits we would expect from an effective system of capital punishment. This is surely the worst of all worlds.

Only two solutions suggest themselves, one judicial and the other political. The judicial solution would require a wholesale repudiation of the Supreme Court's death penalty jurisprudence. This is unlikely to happen. Over the last quarter-century, the Court has developed a substantial body of case law, consisting of some four score opinions, premised on the proposition that death *is* different and we must exercise extraordinary caution before taking human life. As we learned a few years back in the area of abortion, conservative justices are reluctant to reverse such major constitutional judgments.

A political solution may be no easier to achieve, but it's all we have left. The key to any such solution lies with the majority, precisely those among us who consistently strive for imposition of the death penalty for an ever-widening circle of crimes.

The majority must come to understand that this is a self-defeating tactic. Increasing the number of crimes punishable by death, widening the circumstances under which death may be imposed, obtaining more guilty verdicts and expanding death row populations will do nothing to insure that the very worst members of our society are put to death. The majority must accept that we may be willing and able to carry out thirty, forty, maybe fifty executions a year but that we cannot—will not— carry out one a day, every day, for the foreseeable future.

Once that reality is accepted, a difficult but essential next step is to 20 identify where we want to spend our death penalty resources. Instead of adopting a very expansive list of crimes for which the death penalty is an option, state legislatures should draft narrow statutes that reserve the death penalty for only the most heinous criminals. Everyone on death row is very bad, but even within that depraved group, it's possible to make moral judgments about how deeply someone has stepped down the rungs of Hell. Hitler was worse than Eichmann, though both were unspeakably evil by any standard; John Wayne Gacy, with two dozen or so brutal deaths on his conscience, must be considered worse than John Spenkelink, who killed only once.

Differentiating among depraved killers would force us to do some painful soul-searching about the nature of human evil, but it would have three significant advantages. First, it would mean that in a world of limited resources and in the face of a determined opposition, we will sentence to death only those we intend to execute. Second, it would insure that those who suffer the death penalty are the worst of the very bad— mass murderers, hired killers, airplane bombers, for example. This must be better than loading our death rows with many more than we can possibly execute, and then picking those who will die essentially at random.

Third, a political solution would put the process of accommodating divergent viewpoints back into the political arena, where it belongs. This would mean that the people, through their elected representatives, would reassert meaningful control over the process, rather than letting the courts and chance perform the accommodation on an ad hoc, irrational basis.

It will take a heroic act of will for the majority to initiate a political compromise on this emotionally charged issue. But as with democracy itself, the alternatives are much worse.

Topics for Critical Thinking and Writing

1. The authors, writing in 1995, reported that "roughly 70 percent" of the American public "consistently favor" the death penalty (para. 1). Consult the reference librarian in your college library, and verify whether this is true according to the most recent public-opinion polls (Gallup, Harris, or other polling agencies).

2. The authors say that "compared to the number of death sentences, the number of executions is minuscule" (para. 2). Verify this claim by consulting the most recent issue of *Capital Punishment* (issued by the U.S. Department of Justice, Bureau of Justice Statistics). Exactly how many death sentences and executions occurred last year?

3. The authors cite the case of Robert Alton Harris and the multiple reviews his conviction and sentence received in the state and federal courts (para. 7). Is the reader supposed to infer from this case that (a) the courts are being manipulated by a convicted murderer who doesn't want to die, (b) the courts give extraordinary attention to capital cases to avoid making an irreversible mistake, or (c) neither of the above?

4. The authors say, "One worries about the effect [of these delays] on the families of the victims" (para. 10). This concern for the victims' families assumes that the defendants are guilty and were proved guilty by fair trials. Is it equally appropriate to worry about the effect on the families of defendants who were not guilty or were not proved guilty by a fair trial?

5. The authors identify three costs associated with the death penalty in this country (paras. 8–10). How would you rank their relative importance? Explain your view in an essay of 250 words.

6. The authors refer to "the benefits we would expect from an effective system of capital punishment" (para. 16), but they never tell us what those benefits are. Write a 500-word essay on this topic: "The (Alleged) Benefits of an Ideal Death-Penalty System."

7. Why do the authors insist that increasing the number of crimes punishable by death or increasing the number of persons sentenced to death "will do nothing to insure that the very worst members of our society are put to death" (para. 19)?

8. What is the "political solution" (para. 22) to the death penalty in our society that the authors favor? Do you agree or disagree with them? Why? Explain your position in an essay of 350 words.

7

Drugs: Should Their Sale and Use Be Legalized?

WILLIAM J. BENNETT

William J. Bennett, born in Brooklyn in 1943, was educated at Williams College, the University of Texas, and Harvard Law School. Today he is most widely known as the author of The Book of Virtues: A Treasury of Great Moral Stories *(1993), but he has also been a public servant, Secretary of Education, and a director of the National Drug Control Policy. In 1989, during his tenure as "drug czar," he delivered at Harvard the address that we reprint. Among his recent publications are* The Broken Hearth: Reversing the Moral Collapse of the American Family *(2001) and* Why We Fight: Moral Duty and the War on Terrorism *(2002).*

Drug Policy and the Intellectuals

. . . The issue I want to address is our national drug policy and the intellectuals. Unfortunately, the issue is a little one-sided. There is a very great deal to say about our national drug policy, but much less to say about the intellectuals—except that by and large, they're against it. Why they should be against it is an interesting question, perhaps more a social-psychological question than a properly intellectual one. But whatever the reasons, I'm sorry to say that on properly intellectual grounds the arguments mustered against our current drug policy by America's intellectuals make for very thin gruel indeed.

94

I should point out, however, that in the fields of medical and scientific research, there is indeed serious and valuable drug-related work going on. But in the great public policy debate over drugs, the academic and intellectual communities have by and large had little to contribute, and little of that has been genuinely useful or for that matter mentally distinguished.

The field of national drug policy is wide open for serious research and serious thinking on both the theoretical and the practical levels; treatment and prevention; education; law enforcement and the criminal-justice system; the proper role of the federal government versus state and local jurisdictions; international diplomacy and foreign intelligence — these are only a few of the areas in which complex questions of policy and politics need to be addressed and resolved if our national drug strategy is to be successful. But apart from a handful of exceptions — including Mark Moore and Mark Kleiman here at the Kennedy School, and Harvard's own, or ex-own, James Q. Wilson — on most of these issues the country's major ideas factories have not just shut down, they've hardly even tooled up.

It's not that most intellectuals are indifferent to the drug issue, though there may be some of that, too. Rather, they seem complacent and incurious. They've made up their minds, and they don't want to be bothered with further information or analysis, further discussion or debate, especially when it comes from Washington. What I read in the opinion columns of my newspaper or in my monthly magazine or what I hear from the resident intellectual on my favorite television talk show is something like a developing intellectual consensus on the drug question. That consensus holds one or both of these propositions to be self-evident: (a) *that the drug problem in America is absurdly simple, and easily solved;* and (b) *that the drug problem in America is a lost cause.*

As it happens, each of these apparently contradictory propositions   5
is false. As it also happens, both are disputed by the *real* experts on drugs in the United States — and there are many such experts, though not the kind the media like to focus on. And both are disbelieved by the American people, whose experience tells them, emphatically, otherwise.

The consensus has a political dimension, which helps account for its seemingly divergent aspect. In some quarters of the far Right there is a tendency to assert that the drug problem is essentially a problem of the inner city, and therefore that what it calls for, essentially, is quarantine. "If those people want to kill themselves off with drugs, let them kill themselves off with drugs," would be a crude but not too inaccurate way of summarizing this position. But this position has relatively few adherents. On the Left, it is something else, something much more prevalent. There we see whole cadres of social scientists, abetted by whole armies of social workers, who seem to take it as catechism that the problem facing us isn't drugs at all, it's poverty, or racism, or some other equally large and intractable social phenomenon. If we want to eliminate the drug problem, these people say, we must first eliminate the "root causes" of drugs, a hopelessly daunting task at which, however, they also happen to make their living. Twenty-five years ago, no one would have suggested that we must first address the root causes of racism before fighting segregation. We fought it, quite correctly, by passing laws against unacceptable conduct. The causes of racism was an interesting question, but the moral imperative was to end it as soon as possible and by all reasonable means: education, prevention, the media and not least of all, the law. So too with drugs.

What unites these two views of the drug problem from opposite sides of the political spectrum is that they issue, inevitably, in a policy of neglect. To me that is a scandalous position, intellectually as well as morally scandalous. For I believe, along with those I have named as the real experts on drugs, and along with most Americans, that the drug problem is not easy but difficult—very difficult in some respects. But at the same time, and again along with those same experts and with the American people, I believe it is not a lost cause but a solvable one. I will return to this theme, but let me pause here to note one specific issue on which the Left/Right consensus has lately come to rest; a position around which it has been attempting to build national sentiment. That position is legalization.

It is indeed bizarre to see the likes of Anthony Lewis and William F. Buckley lining up on the same side of an issue; but such is the perversity that the so-called legalization debate engenders. To call it a "debate," though, suggests that the arguments in *favor* of drug legalization are rigorous, substantial, and serious. They are not. They are, at bottom, a series of superficial and even disingenuous ideas that more sober minds recognize as a recipe for a public policy disaster. Let me explain.

Most conversations about legalization begin with the notion of "taking the profit out of the drug business." But has anyone bothered to examine carefully how the drug business works? As a recent *New York Times* article vividly described, instances of drug dealers actually earning huge sums of money are relatively rare. There are some who do, of course, but most people in the crack business are the low-level "runners" who do not make much money at all. Many of them work as prostitutes or small-time criminals to supplement their drug earnings. True, a lot of naive kids are lured into the drug world by visions of a life filled with big money and fast cars. That's what they think the good life holds for them. But the reality is far different. Many dealers, in the long run, wind up smoking more crack than they sell. Their business becomes a form of slavery: long hours, dangerous work, small pay, and, as the *Times* pointed out, no health benefits either. In many cases, steady work at McDonald's over time would in fact be a step *up* the income scale for these kids. What does straighten them out, it seems, is not a higher minimum wage, or less stringent laws, but the dawning realization that dealing drugs invariably leads to murder or to prison. And that's exactly why we have drug laws—to make drug use a wholly unattractive choice.

Legalization, on the other hand, removes that incentive to stay away 10 from a life of drugs. Let's be honest—there are some people who are going to smoke crack whether it is legal or illegal. But by keeping it illegal, we maintain the criminal sanctions that persuade most people that the good life cannot be reached by dealing drugs.

The big lie behind every call for legalization is that making drugs legally available would "solve" the drug problem. But has anyone actually thought about what that kind of legalized regime would look like? Would crack be legal? How about PCP? Or smokable heroin? Or ice? Would they all be stocked at the local convenience store, perhaps just a few blocks from an elementary school? And how much would they cost? If we taxed drugs and made them expensive, we would still have the black market and crime problems that we have today; if we sold them cheap to eliminate the black market cocaine at, say, $10 a gram—then we would succeed in making a daily dose of cocaine well within the allowance budget of most sixth-graders. When pressed, the advocates of legalization like to sound courageous by proposing that we begin by legalizing marijuana. But they have absolutely nothing to say on the tough questions of controlling other, more powerful drugs, and how they would be regulated.

As far as marijuana is concerned, let me say this: I didn't have to become drug czar to be opposed to legalized marijuana. As Secretary of Education I realized that, given the state of American education, the last thing we needed was a policy that made widely available a substance that impairs memory, concentration, and attention span; why in God's name foster the use of a drug that makes you stupid?

Now what would happen if drugs were suddenly made legal? Legalization advocates deny that the amount of drug use would be affected. I would argue that if drugs are easier to obtain, drug use will soar. In fact, we have just undergone a kind of cruel national experiment in which drugs became cheap and widely available: That experiment is called the crack epidemic. When powder cocaine was expensive and hard to get, it was found almost exclusively in the circles of the rich, the famous, or the privileged. Only when cocaine was dumped into the country, and a $3 vial of crack could be bought on street corners did we see cocaine use skyrocket, this time largely among the poor and disadvantaged. The lesson is clear: If you're in favor of drugs being sold in stores like aspirin, you're in favor of boom times for drug users and drug addicts. With legalization, drug use will go up, way up.

When drug use rises, who benefits and who pays? Legalization advocates think that the cost of enforcing drug laws is too great. But the real question—the question they never ask—is what does it cost not to enforce those laws. The price that American society would have to pay for legalized drugs, I submit, would be intolerably high. We would have more drug-related accidents at work, on the highways, and in the airways. We would have even bigger losses in worker productivity. Our hospitals would be filled with drug emergencies. We would have more school kids on dope, and that means more dropouts. More pregnant women would buy legal cocaine, and then deliver tiny, premature infants. I've seen them in hospitals across the country. It's a horrid form of child abuse, and under a legalization scheme, we will have a lot more of it. For those women and those babies, crack has the same effect whether it's legal or not. Now, if you add to that the costs of treatment, social welfare, and insurance, you've got the price of legalization. So I ask you again, who benefits, who pays?

What about crime? To listen to legalization advocates, one might think that street crime would disappear with the repeal of our drug laws. They haven't done their homework. Our best research indicates that most drug criminals were into crime well before they got into drugs. Making drugs legal would just be a way of subsidizing their habit. They would continue to rob and steal to pay for food, for clothes, for entertainment. And they would carry on with their drug trafficking by undercutting the legalized price of drugs and catering to teenagers, who, I assume, would be nominally restricted from buying drugs at the corner store.

All this should be old news to people who understand one clear lesson of prohibition. When we had laws against alcohol, there was less consumption of alcohol, less alcohol-related disease, fewer drunken brawls, and a lot less public drunkenness. And contrary to myth, there is no evidence that Prohibition caused big increases in crime. No one is suggesting that we go back to Prohibition. But at least we should admit that legalized alcohol, which is responsible for some 100,000 deaths a year, is hardly a model for drug policy. As Charles Krauthammer has pointed out, the question is not which is worse, alcohol or drugs. The question is can we accept both legalized alcohol *and* legalized drugs? The answer is no.

So it seems to me that on the merits of their arguments, the legalizers have no case at all. But there is another, crucial point I want to make on this subject, unrelated to costs or benefits. Drug use—especially heavy drug use—destroys human character. It destroys dignity and autonomy, it burns away the sense of responsibility, it subverts productivity, it makes a mockery of virtue. As our Founders would surely recognize, a citizenry that is perpetually in a drug-induced haze doesn't bode well for the future of self-government. Libertarians don't like to hear this, but it is a truth that everyone knows who has seen drug addiction up close. And don't listen to people who say drug users are only hurting themselves: They hurt parents, they destroy families, they ruin friendships. And let me remind this audience, here at a great university, that drugs are a threat to the life of the mind; anyone who values that life should have nothing but contempt for drugs. Learned institutions should regard drugs as the plague.

That's why I find the surrender of many of America's intellectuals to arguments for drug legalization so odd and so scandalous. For the past three months, I have been traveling the country, visiting drug-ridden neighborhoods, seeing treatment and prevention programs in action, talking to teachers, cops, parents, kids. These, it seems, are the real drug experts—they've witnessed the problem firsthand. But unlike some prominent residents of Princeton, Madison, Cambridge, or Palo Alto, they refuse to surrender. They are in the community, reclaiming their neighborhoods, working with police, setting up community activities, getting addicts into treatment, saving their children.

Too many American intellectuals don't know about this and seem not to want to know. Their hostility to the national war on drugs is, I think, partly rooted in a general hostility to law enforcement and criminal justice. That's why they take refuge in pseudosolutions like legalization, which stress only the treatment side of the problem. Whenever discussion turns to the need for more police and stronger penalties, they cry that our constitutional liberties are in jeopardy. Well, yes, they are in jeopardy, but not from drug *policy:* On this score, the guardians of our Constitution can sleep easy. Constitutional liberties are in jeopardy, instead, from drugs themselves, which every day scorch the earth of our common freedom. Yes, sometimes cops go too far, and when they do they should be held accountable. But these excursions from the law are the exception. Meanwhile drug dealers violate our rights everyday as a rule, as a norm, as their modus operandi. Why can't our civil libertarians see that?

When we are not being told by critics that law enforcement threat- 20 ens our liberties, we are being told that it won't work. Let me tell you that law enforcement does work and why it must work. Several weeks ago I was in Wichita, Kansas, talking to a teenage boy who was now in his fourth treatment program. Every time he had finished a previous round of treatment, he found himself back on the streets, surrounded by the same cheap dope and tough hustlers who had gotten him started in the first place. He was tempted, he was pressured, and he gave in. Virtually any expert on drug treatment will tell you that, for most people, no therapy in the world can fight temptation on that scale. As long as drugs are found on any street corner, no amount of treatment, no amount of education can finally stand against them. Yes, we need drug treatment and drug education. But drug treatment and drug education need law enforcement. And that's why our strategy calls for a bigger criminal justice system: as a form of drug *prevention*.

To the Americans who are waging the drug war in their own front yards every day, this is nothing new, nothing startling. In the San Jose section of Albuquerque, New Mexico, just two weeks ago, I spoke to Rudy Chavez and Jack Candelarla, and police chief Sam Baca. They had wanted to start a youth center that would keep their kids safe from the depredations of the street. Somehow it never worked—until together they set up a police station right in the heart of drug-dealing territory. Then it worked. Together with the cops, the law-abiding residents cleared the area, and made it safe for them and their children to walk outside their homes. The youth center began to thrive.

Scenes like this are being played out all across the country. I've seen them in Tulsa, Dallas, Tampa, Omaha, Des Moines, Seattle, New York. Americans—many of them poor, black, or Hispanic—have figured out what the armchair critics haven't. Drugs may threaten to destroy their neighborhoods, but *they* refuse to stand by and let it happen. *They* have discovered that it is possible not only to fight back, but to win. In some elite circles, the talk may be only of the sad state of the helpless and the hopeless, but while these circles talk on, the helpless and the hopeless themselves are carrying out a national drug policy. They are fighting back.

When I think of these scenes I'm reminded of what John Jacob, president of the Urban League, said recently: Drugs are destroying more black families than poverty ever did. And I'm thankful that many of these poor families have the courage to fight drugs now, rather than declaring themselves passive victims of root causes.

America's intellectuals—and here I think particularly of liberal intellectuals—have spent much of the last nine years decrying the social programs of two Republican administrations in the name of the defenseless poor. But today, on the one outstanding issue that disproportionately hurts the poor—that is wiping out many of the poor—where are the liberal intellectuals to be found? They are on the editorial and op-ed pages, and in magazines like this month's *Harper's*, telling us with an ignorant sneer that our drug policy won't work. Many universities, too, which have been quick to take on the challenges of sexism, racism, and ethnocentrism, seem content on the drug issue to wag a finger at us, or to point it mindlessly at American society in general. In public policy schools, there is no shortage of arms control scholars. Isn't it time we had more drug control scholars?

The current situation won't do. The failure to get serious about the   25
drug issue is, I think, a failure of civic courage—the kind of courage shown by many who have been among the main victims of the drug scourge. But it betokens as well a betrayal of the self-declared mission of intellectuals as the bearers of society's conscience. There may be reasons for this reluctance, this hostility, this failure. But I would remind you that not all crusades led by the U.S. government, enjoying broad popular support, are brutish, corrupt, and sinister. What is brutish, corrupt, and sinister is the murder and mayhem being committed in our cities' streets. One would think that a little more concern and serious thought would come from those who claim to care so deeply about America's problems.

So I stand here this afternoon with a simple message for America's pundits and academic cynics: Get serious about drug policy. We are grappling with complicated, stubborn policy issues, and I encourage you to join us. Tough work lies ahead, and we need serious minds to focus on how we should use the tools that we have in the most effective way.

I came to this job with realistic expectations. I am not promising a drug-free America by next week, or even by next year. But that doesn't mean that success is out of reach. Success will come—I've seen a lot of it already—in slow, careful steps. Its enemies are timidity, petulance, false expectations. But its three greatest foes remain surrender, despair, and neglect. So, for the sake of their fellow citizens, I invite America's deep thinkers to get with the program, or at the very least, to get in the game.

Topics for Critical Thinking and Writing

1. In paragraph 6, Bennett draws a parallel between racism and drug abuse and suggests that society ought to fight the one (drug abuse) as it successfully fought the other (racism). What do you think of this parallel? Explain.

2. Bennett identifies two propositions on the issue of drug abuse that he believes are accepted by "consensus" thinking in America (para. 4). What are these propositions, and what is Bennett's view of them? How does he try to convince the reader to agree with him?

3. What are Bennett's main objections to solving the problem of drug abuse by legalizing drugs?

4. At the time he gave this lecture, Bennett was a cigarette smoker trying to break the habit. Do you see any inconsistency in his opposing legalized marijuana and tolerating (and even using) legalized tobacco?

5. What measures besides stricter law enforcement does Bennett propose for wide-scale adoption to reduce drug abuse? Why does he object to relying only on such measures?

6. Bennett is known to be (or to have been) a heavy gambler, a high roller. On one occasion he said to the press, "It is true that I have gambled large sums of money. . . . I have done too much gambling, and this is not an example I wish to set." Does his admitted heavy gambling weaken his arguments about drugs?

JAMES Q. WILSON

James Q. Wilson is Collins Professor of Management and Public Policy at the University of California at Los Angeles. He is the author of Thinking about Crime *(1975),* Bureaucracy *(1989), and* Crime: Public Policies for Crime Control *(2002), the coauthor of* Crime and Human Nature *(1985), and the coeditor of* Drugs and Crime *(1990). The essay that we reprint appeared originally in February 1990 in* Commentary, *a conservative magazine.*

Against the Legalization of Drugs

In 1972, the president appointed me chairman of the National Advisory Council for Drug Abuse Prevention. Created by Congress, the Council was charged with providing guidance on how best to coordinate the national war on drugs. (Yes, we called it a war then, too.) In those days, the drug we were chiefly concerned with was heroin. When I took office, heroin use had been increasing dramatically. Everybody was worried that this increase would continue. Such phrases as "heroin epidemic" were commonplace.

That same year, the eminent economist Milton Friedman published an essay in *Newsweek* in which he called for legalizing heroin. His argument was on two grounds: As a matter of ethics, the government has no right to tell people not to use heroin (or to drink or to commit suicide); as a matter of economics, the prohibition of drug use imposes costs on society that far exceed the benefits. Others, such as the psychoanalyst Thomas Szasz, made the same argument.

We did not take Friedman's advice. (Government commissions rarely do.) I do not recall that we even discussed legalizing heroin, though we did discuss (but did not take action on) legalizing a drug, cocaine, that many people then argued was benign. Our marching orders were to figure out how to win the war on heroin, not to run up the white flag of surrender.

That was 1972. Today, we have the same number of heroin addicts that we had then—half a million, give or take a few thousand. Having that many heroin addicts is no trivial matter; these people deserve our attention. But not having had an increase in that number for over fifteen years is also something that deserves our attention. What happened to the "heroin epidemic" that many people once thought would overwhelm us?

The facts are clear: A more or less stable pool of heroin addicts has been getting older, with relatively few new recruits. In 1976 the average age of heroin users who appeared in hospital emergency rooms was about twenty-seven; ten years later it was thirty-two. More than two-thirds of all heroin users appearing in emergency rooms are now over the age of thirty. Back in the early 1970s, when heroin got onto the national political agenda, the typical heroin addict was much younger, often a teenager. Household surveys show the same thing—the rate of opiate use (which includes heroin) has been flat for the better part of two decades. More fine-grained studies of inner-city neighborhoods confirm this. John Boyle and Ann Brunswick found that the percentage of young blacks in Harlem who use heroin fell from 8 percent in 1970–71 to about 3 percent in 1975–76.

Why did heroin lose its appeal for young people? When the young blacks in Harlem were asked why they stopped, more than half mentioned "trouble with the law" or "high cost" (and high cost is, of course, directly the result of law enforcement). Two-thirds said that heroin hurt their health; nearly all said they had had a bad experience with it. We need not rely, however, simply on what they said. In New York City in 1973–75, the street price of heroin rose dramatically and its purity sharply declined, probably as a result of the heroin shortage caused by the success of the Turkish government in reducing the supply of opium base and of the French government in closing down heroin-processing laboratories located in and around Marseilles. These were short-lived gains for, just as Friedman predicted, alternative sources of supply—mostly in Mexico—quickly emerged. But the three-year heroin shortage interrupted the easy recruitment of new users.

Health and related problems were no doubt part of the reason for the reduced flow of recruits. Over the preceding years, Harlem youth had watched as more and more heroin users died of overdoses, were poisoned by adulterated doses, or acquired hepatitis from dirty needles. The word got around: Heroin can kill you. By 1974 new hepatitis cases and drug-overdose deaths had dropped to a fraction of what they had been in 1970.

Alas, treatment did not seem to explain much of the cessation in drug use. Treatment programs can and do help heroin addicts, but treatment did not explain the drop in the number of *new* users (who by definition had never been in treatment) nor even much of the reduction in the number of experienced users.

No one knows how much of the decline to attribute to personal observation as opposed to high prices or reduced supply. But other evidence suggests strongly that price and supply played a large role. In 1972 the National Advisory Council was especially worried by the prospect that U.S. servicemen returning to this country from Vietnam would bring their heroin habits with them. Fortunately, a brilliant study by Lee Robins of Washington University in St. Louis put that fear to rest. She measured drug use of Vietnam veterans shortly after they had returned home. Though many had used heroin regularly while in Southeast Asia, most gave up the habit when back in the United States. The reason: Here, heroin was less available and sanctions on its use were more pronounced. Of course, if a veteran had been willing to pay enough—which might have meant traveling to another city and would certainly have meant making an illegal contact with a disreputable dealer in a threatening neighborhood in order to acquire a (possibly) dangerous dose— he could have sustained his drug habit. Most veterans were unwilling to pay this price, and so their drug use declined or disappeared.

RELIVING THE PAST

Suppose we had taken Friedman's advice in 1972. What would have 10 happened? We cannot be entirely certain, but at a minimum we would have placed the young heroin addicts (and, above all, the prospective addicts) in a very different position from the one in which they actually found themselves. Heroin would have been legal. Its price would have been reduced by 95 percent (minus whatever we chose to recover in taxes). Now that it could be sold by the same people who make aspirin, its quality would have been assured—no poisons, no adulterants. Sterile hypodermic needles would have been readily available at the neighborhood drugstore, probably at the same counter where the heroin was sold. No need to travel to big cities or unfamiliar neighborhoods— heroin could have been purchased anywhere, perhaps by mail order.

There would no longer have been any financial or medical reason to avoid heroin use. Anybody could have afforded it. We might have tried to prevent children from buying it, but as we have learned from our efforts to prevent minors from buying alcohol and tobacco, young people have a way of penetrating markets theoretically reserved for adults. Returning Vietnam veterans would have discovered that Omaha and Raleigh had been converted into the pharmaceutical equivalent of Saigon.

Under these circumstances, can we doubt for a moment that heroin use would have grown exponentially? Or that a vastly larger supply of new users would have been recruited? Professor Friedman is a Nobel Prize–winning economist whose understanding of market forces is profound. What did he think would happen to consumption under his legalized regime? Here are his words: "Legalizing drugs might increase the number of addicts, but it is not clear that it would. Forbidden fruit is attractive, particularly to the young."

Really? I suppose that we should expect no increase in Porsche sales if we cut the price by 95 percent, no increase in whiskey sales if we cut the price by a comparable amount—because young people only want fast cars and strong liquor when they are "forbidden." Perhaps Friedman's uncharacteristic lapse from the obvious implications of price theory can be explained by a misunderstanding of how drug users are recruited. In his 1972 essay he said that "drug addicts are deliberately made by pushers, who give likely prospects their first few doses free." If drugs were legal it would not pay anybody to produce addicts, because everybody would buy from the cheapest source. But as every drug expert knows, pushers do not produce addicts. Friends or acquaintances do. In fact, pushers are usually reluctant to deal with nonusers because a nonuser could be an undercover cop. Drug use spreads in the same way any fad or fashion spreads: Somebody who is already a user urges his friends to try, or simply shows already-eager friends how to do it.

But we need not rely on speculation, however plausible, that lowered prices and more abundant supplies would have increased heroin usage. Great Britain once followed such a policy and with almost exactly those results. Until the mid-1960s, British physicians were allowed to prescribe heroin to certain classes of addicts. (Possessing these drugs without a doctor's prescription remained a criminal offense.) For many years this policy worked well enough because the addict patients were typically middle-class people who had become dependent on opiate painkillers while undergoing hospital treatment. There was no drug culture. The British system worked for many years, not because it prevented drug abuse but because there was no problem of drug abuse that would test the system.

All that changed in the 1960s. A few unscrupulous doctors began 15 passing out heroin in wholesale amounts. One doctor prescribed almost six hundred thousand heroin tablets—that is, over thirteen pounds — in just one year. A youthful drug culture emerged with a demand for drugs far different from that of the older addicts. As a result, the British government required doctors to refer users to government-run clinics to receive their heroin.

But the shift to clinics did not curtail the growth in heroin use. Throughout the 1960s the number of addicts increased—the late John Kaplan of Stanford estimated by fivefold—in part as a result of the diversion of heroin from clinic patients to new users on the streets. An addict would bargain with the clinic doctor over how big a dose he would receive. The patient wanted as much as he could get, the doctor wanted to give as little as was needed. The patient had an advantage in this conflict because the doctor could not be certain how much was really needed. Many patients would use some of their "maintenance" dose and sell the remaining part to friends, thereby recruiting new addicts. As the clinics learned of this, they began to shift their treatment away from heroin and toward methadone, an addictive drug that, when taken orally, does not produce a "high" but will block the withdrawal pains associated with heroin abstinence.

Whether what happened in England in the 1960s was a miniepidemic or an epidemic depends on whether one looks at numbers or at rates of change. Compared to the United States, the numbers were small. In 1960 there were sixty-eight heroin addicts known to the British government; by 1968 there were two thousand in treatment and many more who refused treatment. (They would refuse in part because they did not want to get methadone at a clinic if they could get heroin on the street.) Richard Hartnoll estimates that the actual number of addicts in England is five times the number officially registered. At a minimum, the number of British addicts increased by thirtyfold in ten years; the actual increase may have been much larger.

In the early 1980s the numbers began to rise again, and this time nobody doubted that a real epidemic was at hand. The increase was estimated to be 40 percent a year. By 1982 there were thought to be twenty thousand heroin users in London alone. Geoffrey Pearson reports that many cities—Glasgow, Liverpool, Manchester, and Sheffield among them—were now experiencing a drug problem that once had been largely confined to London. The problem, again, was supply. The country was being flooded with cheap, high-quality heroin, first from Iran and then from Southeast Asia.

The United States began the 1960s with a much larger number of heroin addicts and probably a bigger at-risk population than was the case in Great Britain. Even though it would be foolhardy to suppose that the British system, if installed here, would have worked the same way or with the same results, it would be equally foolhardy to suppose that a combination of heroin available from leaky clinics and from street dealers who faced only minimal law-enforcement risks would not have produced a much greater increase in heroin use than we actually experienced. My guess is that if we had allowed either doctors or clinics to prescribe heroin, we would have had far worse results than were produced in Britain, if for no other reason than the vastly larger number of addicts with which we began. We would have had to find some way to police thousands (not scores) of physicians and hundreds (not dozens) of clinics. If the British civil service found it difficult to keep heroin in the hands of addicts and out of the hands of recruits when it was dealing with a few hundred people, how well would the American civil service have accomplished the same tasks when dealing with tens of thousands of people?

BACK TO THE FUTURE

Now cocaine, especially in its potent form, crack, is the focus of attention. Now as in 1972 the government is trying to reduce its use. Now as then some people are advocating legalization. Is there any more reason to yield to those arguments today than there was almost two decades ago?[1]   20

I think not. If we had yielded in 1972 we almost certainly would have had today a permanent population of several million, not several hundred thousand, heroin addicts. If we yield now we will have a far more serious problem with cocaine.

Crack is worse than heroin by almost any measure. Heroin produces a pleasant drowsiness and, if hygienically administered, has only the physical side effects of constipation and sexual impotence. Regular heroin use incapacitates many users, especially poor ones, for any productive work or social responsibility. They will sit nodding on a street corner, helpless but at least harmless. By contrast, regular cocaine use leaves the user neither helpless nor harmless. When smoked (as with crack) or injected, cocaine produces instant, intense, and short-lived euphoria. The experience generates a powerful desire to repeat it. If the drug is readily available, repeat use will occur. Those people who progress to "bingeing" on cocaine become devoted to the drug and its

---

[1]I do not here take up the question of marijuana. For a variety of reasons—its widespread use and its lesser tendency to addict—it presents a different problem from cocaine or heroin. For a penetrating analysis, see Mark Kleiman, *Marijuana: Costs of Abuse, Costs of Control* (Greenwood Press, 217 pp.). [Author's note.]

effects to the exclusion of almost all other considerations—job, family, children, sleep, food, even sex. Dr. Frank Gawin at Yale and Dr. Everett Ellinwood at Duke report that a substantial percentage of all high-dose, binge users become uninhibited, impulsive, hypersexual, compulsive, irritable, and hyperactive. Their moods vacillate dramatically, leading at times to violence and homicide.

Women are much more likely to use crack than heroin, and if they are pregnant, the effects on their babies are tragic. Douglas Besharov, who has been following the effects of drugs on infants for twenty years, writes that nothing he learned about heroin prepared him for the devastation of cocaine. Cocaine harms the fetus and can lead to physical deformities or neurological damage. Some crack babies have for all practical purposes suffered a disabling stroke while still in the womb. The long-term consequences of this brain damage are lowered cognitive ability and the onset of mood disorders. Besharov estimates that about thirty thousand to fifty thousand such babies are born every year, about seven thousand in New York City alone. There may be ways to treat such infants, but from everything we now know the treatment will be long, difficult, and expensive. Worse, the mothers who are most likely to produce crack babies are precisely the ones who, because of poverty or temperament, are least able and willing to obtain such treatment. In fact, anecdotal evidence suggests the crack mothers are likely to abuse their infants.

The notion that abusing drugs such as cocaine is a "victimless crime" is not only absurd but dangerous. Even ignoring the fetal drug syndrome, crack-dependent people are, like heroin addicts, individuals who regularly victimize their children by neglect, their spouses by improvidence, their employers by lethargy, and their co-workers by carelessness. Society is not and could never be a collection of autonomous individuals. We all have a stake in ensuring that each of us displays a minimal level of dignity, responsibility, and empathy. We cannot, of course, coerce people into goodness, but we can and should insist that some standards must be met if society itself—on which the very existence of the human personality depends—is to persist. Drawing the line that defines those standards is difficult and contentious, but if crack and heroin use do not fall below it, what does?

The advocates of legalization will respond by suggesting that my picture is overdrawn. Ethan Nadelmann of Princeton argues that the risk of legalization is less than most people suppose. Over twenty million Americans between the ages of eighteen and twenty-five have tried cocaine (according to a government survey), but only a quarter million use it daily. From this Nadelmann concludes that at most 3 percent of all young people who try cocaine develop a problem with it. The implication is clear: Make the drug legal and we only have to worry about 3 percent of our youth.

The implication rests on a logical fallacy and a factual error. The fallacy is this: The percentage of occasional cocaine users who become binge users *when the drug is illegal* (and thus expensive and hard to find) tells us nothing about the percentage who will become dependent when the drug is legal (and thus cheap and abundant). Drs. Gawin and Ellinwood report, in common with several other researchers, that controlled or occasional use of cocaine changes to compulsive and frequent use "when access to the drug increases" or when the user switches from snorting to smoking. More cocaine more potently administered alters, perhaps sharply, the proportion of "controlled" users who become heavy users.

The factual error is this: The federal survey Nadelmann quotes was done in 1985, *before* crack had become common. Thus the probability of becoming dependent on cocaine was derived from the responses of users who snorted the drug. The speed and potency of cocaine's action increases dramatically when it is smoked. We do not yet know how greatly the advent of crack increases the risk of dependency, but all the clinical evidence suggests that the increase is likely to be large.

It is possible that some people will not become heavy users even when the drug is readily available in its most potent form. So far there are no scientific grounds for predicting who will and who will not become dependent. Neither socioeconomic background nor personality traits differentiate between casual and intensive users. Thus, the only way to settle the question of who is correct about the effect of easy availability on drug use, Nadelmann or Gawin and Ellinwood, is to try it and see. But the social experiment is so risky as to be no experiment at all, for if cocaine is legalized and if the rate of its abusive use increases dramatically, there is no way to put the genie back in the bottle, and it is not a kindly genie.

HAVE WE LOST?

Many people who agree that there are risks in legalizing cocaine or heroin still favor it because, they think, we have lost the war on drugs. "Nothing we have done has worked" and the current federal policy is just "more of the same." Whatever the costs of greater drug use, surely they would be less than the costs of our present, failed efforts.

That is exactly what I was told in 1972 — and heroin is not quite as bad a drug as cocaine. We did not surrender and we did not lose. We did not win, either. What the nation accomplished then was what most efforts to save people from themselves accomplish: The problem was contained and the number of victims minimized, all at a considerable cost in law enforcement and increased crime. Was the cost worth it? I think so, but others may disagree. What are the lives of would-be addicts worth? I recall some people saying to me then, "Let them kill themselves." I was appalled. Happily, such views did not prevail.

Have we lost today? Not at all. High-rate cocaine use is not commonplace. The National Institute of Drug Abuse (NIDA) reports that less than 5 percent of high-school seniors used cocaine within the last thirty days. Of course this survey misses young people who have dropped out of school and miscounts those who lie on the questionnaire, but even if we inflate the NIDA estimate by some plausible percentage, it is still not much above 5 percent. Medical examiners reported in 1987 that about 1,500 died from cocaine use; hospital emergency rooms reported about 30,000 admissions related to cocaine abuse.

These are not small numbers, but neither are they evidence of a nationwide plague that threatens to engulf us all. Moreover, cities vary greatly in the proportion of people who are involved with cocaine. To get city-level data we need to turn to drug tests carried out on arrested persons, who obviously are more likely to be drug users than the average citizen. The National Institute of Justice, through its Drug Use Forecasting (DUF) project, collects urinalysis data on arrestees in twenty-two cities. As we have already seen, opiate (chiefly heroin) use has been flat or declining in most of these cities over the last decade. Cocaine use has gone up sharply, but with great variation among cities. New York, Philadelphia, and Washington, D.C., all report that two-thirds or more of their arrestees tested positive for cocaine, but in Portland, San Antonio, and Indianapolis the percentage was one-third or less.

In some neighborhoods, of course, matters have reached crisis proportions. Gangs control the streets, shootings terrorize residents, and drug dealing occurs in plain view. The police seem barely able to contain matters. But in these neighborhoods—unlike at Palo Alto cocktail parties—the people are not calling for legalization, they are calling for help. And often not much help has come. Many cities are willing to do almost anything about the drug problem except spend more money on it. The federal government cannot change that; only local voters and politicians can. It is not clear that they will.

It took about ten years to contain heroin. We have had experience with crack for only about three or four years. Each year we spend perhaps $11 billion on law enforcement (and some of that goes to deal with marijuana) and perhaps $2 billion on treatment. Large sums, but not sums that should lead anyone to say, "We just can't afford this any more."

The illegality of drugs increases crime, partly because some users 35
turn to crime to pay for their habits, partly because some users are stim-

ulated by certain drugs (such as crack or PCP) to act more violently or ruthlessly than they otherwise would, and partly because criminal organizations seeking to control drug supplies use force to manage their markets. These also are serious costs, but no one knows how much they would be reduced if drugs were legalized. Addicts would no longer steal to pay black-market prices for drugs, a real gain. But some, perhaps a great deal, of that gain would be offset by the great increase in the number of addicts. These people, nodding on heroin or living in the delusion-ridden high of cocaine, would hardly be ideal employees. Many would steal simply to support themselves, since snatch-and-grab, opportunistic crime can be managed even by people unable to hold a regular job or plan an elaborate crime. Those British addicts who get their supplies from government clinics are not models of law-abiding decency. Most are in crime, and though their per-capita rate of criminality may be lower thanks to the cheapness of their drugs, the total volume of crime they produce may be quite large. Of course, society could decide to support all unemployable addicts on welfare, but that would mean that gains from lowered rates of crime would have to be offset by large increases in welfare budgets.

Proponents of legalization claim that the costs of having more addicts around would be largely if not entirely offset by having more money available with which to treat and care for them. The money would come from taxes levied on the sale of heroin and cocaine.

To obtain this fiscal dividend, however, legalization's supporters must first solve an economic dilemma. If they want to raise a lot of money to pay for welfare and treatment, the tax rate on the drugs will have to be quite high. Even if they themselves do not want a high rate, the politicians' love of "sin taxes" would probably guarantee that it would be high anyway. But the higher the tax, the higher the price of the drug, and the higher the price the greater the likelihood that addicts will turn to crime to find the money for it and that criminal organizations will be formed to sell tax-free drugs at below-market rates. If we managed to keep taxes (and thus prices) low, we would get that much less money to pay for welfare and treatment and more people could afford to become addicts. There may be an optimal tax rate for drugs that maximizes revenue while minimizing crime, bootlegging, and the recruitment of new addicts, but our experience with alcohol does not suggest that we know how to find it.

THE BENEFITS OF ILLEGALITY

The advocates of legalization find nothing to be said in favor of the current system except, possibly, that it keeps the number of addicts

smaller than it would otherwise be. In fact, the benefits are more substantial than that.

First, treatment. All the talk about providing "treatment on demand" implies that there is a demand for treatment. That is not quite
right. There are some drug-dependent people who genuinely want treatment and will remain in it if offered; they should receive it. But there are
far more who want only short-term help after a bad crash; once stabi-
lized and bathed, they are back on the street again, hustling. And even
many of the addicts who enroll in a program honestly wanting help drop
out after a short while when they discover that help takes time and commitment. Drug-dependent people have very short time horizons and a
weak capacity for commitment. These two groups—those looking for a
quick fix and those unable to stick with a long-term fix—are not easily
helped. Even if we increase the number of treatment slots—as we
should—we would have to do something to make treatment more effective.

One thing that can often make it more effective is compulsion.   40
Douglas Anglin of UCLA, in common with many other researchers, has
found that the longer one stays in a treatment program, the better the
chances of a reduction in drug dependency. But he, again like most
other researchers, has found that dropout rates are high. He has also
found, however, that patients who enter treatment under legal compulsion stay in the program longer than those not subject to such pressure.
His research on the California civil commitment program, for example,
found that heroin users involved with its required drug-testing program
had over the long term a lower rate of heroin use than similar addicts
who were free of such constraints. If for many addicts compulsion is a
useful component of treatment, it is not clear how compulsion could be
achieved in a society in which purchasing, possessing, and using the
drug were legal. It could be managed, I suppose, but I would not want to
have to answer the challenge from the American Civil Liberties Union
that it is wrong to compel a person to undergo treatment for consuming
a legal commodity.

Next, education. We are now investing substantially in drug-
education programs in the schools. Though we do not yet know for certain what will work, there are some promising leads. But I wonder how
credible such programs would be if they were aimed at dissuading children from doing something perfectly legal. We could, of course, treat
drug education like smoking education: Inhaling crack and inhaling tobacco are both legal, but you should not do it because it is bad for you.
That tobacco is bad for you is easily shown; the Surgeon General has
seen to that. But what do we say about crack? It is pleasurable, but de-
voting yourself to so much pleasure is not a good idea (though perfectly

legal)? Unlike tobacco, cocaine will not give you cancer or emphysema, but it will lead you to neglect your duties to family, job, and neighborhood? Everybody is doing cocaine, but you should not?

Again, it might be possible under a legalized regime to have effective drug-prevention programs, but their effectiveness would depend heavily, I think, on first having decided that cocaine use, like tobacco use, is purely a matter of practical consequences; no fundamental moral significance attaches to either. But if we believe—as I do—that dependency on certain mind-altering drugs *is* a moral issue and that their illegality rests in part on their immorality, then legalizing them undercuts, if it does not eliminate altogether, the moral message.

That message is at the root of the distinction we now make between nicotine and cocaine. Both are highly addictive; both have harmful physical effects. But we treat the two drugs differently, not simply because nicotine is so widely used as to be beyond the reach of effective prohibition, but because its use does not destroy the user's essential humanity. Tobacco shortens one's life, cocaine debases it. Nicotine alters one's habits, cocaine alters one's soul. The heavy use of crack, unlike the heavy use of tobacco, corrodes those natural sentiments of sympathy and duty that constitute our human nature and make possible our social life. To say, as does Nadelmann, that distinguishing morally between tobacco and cocaine is "little more than a transient prejudice" is close to saying that morality itself is but a prejudice.

THE ALCOHOL PROBLEM

Now we have arrived where many arguments about legalizing drugs begin: Is there any reason to treat heroin and cocaine differently from the way we treat alcohol?

There is no easy answer to that question because, as with so many human problems, one cannot decide simply on the basis either of moral principles or of individual consequences; one has to temper any policy by a commonsense judgment of what is possible. Alcohol, like heroin, cocaine, PCP, and marijuana, is a drug—that is, a mood-altering substance—and consumed to excess it certainly has harmful consequences: auto accidents, barroom fights, bedroom shootings. It is also, for some people, addictive. We cannot confidently compare the addictive powers of these drugs, but the best evidence suggests that crack and heroin are much more addictive than alcohol.

Many people, Nadelmann included, argue that since the health and financial costs of alcohol abuse are so much higher than those of cocaine or heroin abuse, it is hypocritical folly to devote our efforts to preventing cocaine or drug use. But as Mark Kleiman of Harvard has pointed out, this comparison is quite misleading. What Nadelmann is doing is showing that a *legalized* drug (alcohol) produces greater social harm than *illegal* ones (cocaine and heroin). But of course. Suppose that in the 1920s we had made heroin and cocaine legal and alcohol illegal. Can anyone doubt that Nadelmann would now be writing that it is folly to continue our ban on alcohol because cocaine and heroin are so much more harmful?

And let there be no doubt about it—widespread heroin and cocaine use are associated with all manner of ills. Thomas Bewley found that the mortality rate of British heroin addicts in 1968 was twenty-eight times as high as the death rate of the same age group of nonaddicts, even though in England at the time an addict could obtain free or low-cost heroin and clean needles from British clinics. Perform the following mental experiment: Suppose we legalized heroin and cocaine in this country. In what proportion of auto fatalities would the state police report that the driver was nodding off on heroin or recklessly driving on a coke high? In what proportion of spouse-assault and child-abuse cases would the local police report that crack was involved? In what proportion of industrial accidents would safety investigators report that the forklift or drill-press operator was in a drug-induced stupor or frenzy? We do not know exactly what the proportion would be, but anyone who asserts that it would not be much higher than it is now would have to believe that these drugs have little appeal except when they are illegal. And that is nonsense.

An advocate of legalization might concede that social harm—perhaps harm equivalent to that already produced by alcohol—would follow from making cocaine and heroin generally available. But at least, he might add, we would have the problem "out in the open" where it could be treated as a matter of "public health." That is well and good, *if* we knew how to treat—that is, cure—heroin and cocaine abuse. But we do not know how to do it for all the people who would need such help. We are having only limited success in coping with chronic alcoholics. Addictive behavior is immensely difficult to change, and the best methods for changing it—living in drug-free therapeutic communities, becoming faithful members of Alcoholics Anonymous or Narcotics Anonymous—require great personal commitment, a quality that is, alas, in short supply among the very persons—young people, disadvantaged people—who are often most at risk for addiction.

Suppose that today we had, not fifteen million alcohol abusers, but half a million. Suppose that we already knew what we have learned from our long experience with the widespread use of alcohol. Would we make whiskey legal? I do not know, but I suspect there would be a lively debate. The Surgeon General would remind us of the risks alcohol poses to pregnant women. The National Highway Traffic Safety Administration would point to the likelihood of more highway fatalities caused by drunk drivers. The Food and Drug Administration might find that there is a nontrivial increase in cancer associated with alcohol consumption. At the same time the police would report great difficulty in keeping illegal whiskey out of our cities, officers being corrupted by bootleggers, and alcohol addicts often resorting to crime to feed their habit. Libertarians, for their part, would argue that every citizen has a right to drink anything he wishes and that drinking is, in any event, a "victimless crime."

However the debate might turn out, the central fact would be that 50 the problem was still, at that point, a small one. The government cannot legislate away the addictive tendencies in all of us, nor can it remove completely even the most dangerous addictive substances. But it can cope with harms when the harms are still manageable.

SCIENCE AND ADDICTION

One advantage of containing a problem while it is still containable is that it buys time for science to learn more about it and perhaps to discover a cure. Almost unnoticed in the current debate over legalizing drugs is that basic science has made rapid strides in identifying the underlying neurological processes involved in some forms of addiction. Stimulants such as cocaine and amphetamines alter the way certain brain cells communicate with one another. That alteration is complex and not entirely understood, but in simplified form it involves modifying the way in which a neurotransmitter called dopamine sends signals from one cell to another.

When dopamine crosses the synapse between two cells, it is in effect carrying a message from the first cell to activate the second one. In certain parts of the brain that message is experienced as pleasure. After the message is delivered, the dopamine returns to the first cell. Cocaine apparently blocks this return, or "reuptake," so that the excited cell and others nearby continue to send pleasure messages. When the exaggerated high produced by cocaine-influenced dopamine finally ends, the brain cells may (in ways that are still a matter of dispute) suffer from an extreme lack of dopamine, thereby making the individual unable to experience any pleasure at all. This would explain why cocaine users often feel so depressed after enjoying the drug. Stimulants may also affect the way in which other neurotransmitters, such as serotonin and noradrenaline, operate.

Whatever the exact mechanism may be, once it is identified it becomes possible to use drugs to block either the effect of cocaine or its tendency to produce dependency. There have already been experiments using desipramine, imipramine, bromocriptine, carbamazepine, and other chemicals. There are some promising results.

Tragically, we spend very little on such research, and the agencies funding it have not in the past occupied very influential or visible posts in the federal bureaucracy. If there is one aspect of the "war on drugs" metaphor that I dislike, it is its tendency to focus attention almost exclusively on the troops in the trenches, whether engaged in enforcement or treatment, and away from the research-and-development efforts back on the home front where the war may ultimately be decided.

I believe that the prospects of scientists in controlling addiction will 55 be strongly influenced by the size and character of the problem they face. If the problem is a few hundred thousand chronic, high-dose users of an illegal product, the chances of making a difference at a reasonable cost will be much greater than if the problem is a few million chronic users of legal substances. Once a drug is legal, not only will its use increase but many of those who then use it will prefer the drug to the treatment: They will want the pleasure, whatever the cost to themselves or their families, and they will resist—probably successfully—any effort to wean them away from experiencing the high that comes from inhaling a legal substance.

IF I AM WRONG . . .

No one can know what our society would be like if we changed the law to make access to cocaine, heroin, and PCP easier. I believe, for reasons given, that the result would be a sharp increase in use, a more widespread degradation of the human personality, and a greater rate of accidents and violence.

I may be wrong. If I am, then we will needlessly have incurred heavy costs in law enforcement and some forms of criminality. But if I am right, and the legalizers prevail anyway, then we will have consigned millions of people, hundreds of thousands of infants, and hundreds of neighborhoods to a life of oblivion and disease. To the lives and families destroyed by alcohol we will have added countless more destroyed by cocaine, heroin, PCP, and whatever else a basement scientist can invent.

Human character is formed by society; indeed, human character is inconceivable without society, and good character is less likely in a bad society. Will we, in the name of an abstract doctrine of radical individualism, and with the false comfort of suspect predictions, decide to take the chance that somehow individual decency can survive amid a more general level of degradation?

I think not. The American people are too wise for that, whatever the academic essayists and cocktail-party pundits may say. But if Americans today are less wise than I suppose, then Americans at some future time will look back on us now and wonder, what kind of people were they that they could have done such a thing?

Topics for Critical Thinking and Writing

1. Wilson objects to the idea that using cocaine is a "victimless crime" (para. 24; see also para. 49). A crime is said to be "victimless" when the offender consents to the act and those who do not consent are not harmed. Why does it matter to Wilson, do you think, whether using illegal drugs is a victimless crime?

2. Wilson accuses Ethan Nadelmann, an advocate of legalization, of committing "a logical fallacy and a factual error" (para. 26). What is the fallacy, and what is the error?

3. Wilson raises the question of whether we "won" or "lost" the war on heroin in the 1970s and whether we will do any better with the current war on cocaine (paras. 30–31). What would you regard as convincing evidence that we are winning the war on drugs? Losing it?

4. In his criticism of those who would legalize drugs, Wilson points to what he regards as an inescapable "economic dilemma" (para. 37). What is this dilemma? Do you see any way around it?

5. Economists tell us that we can control the use of a good or service by controlling the cost (thus probably reducing the demand), by ignoring the cost and controlling the supply, or by doing both. In the war on drugs, which of these three economic strategies does Wilson apparently favor, and why?

MILTON FRIEDMAN

Milton Friedman, winner of a Nobel Prize in economics, was born in Brooklyn in 1912. Educated at Rutgers University, the University of Chicago, and Columbia University, Friedman, a leading conservative economist, has had considerable influence on economic thought in America through his academic and popular writings. We reprint a piece that appeared in the New York Times *in 1998.*

There's No Justice in the War on Drugs

Twenty-five years ago, President Richard M. Nixon announced a "War on Drugs." I criticized the action on both moral and expediential grounds in my *Newsweek* column of May 1, 1972, "Prohibition and Drugs":

> On ethical grounds, do we have the right to use the machinery of government to prevent an individual from becoming an alcoholic or a drug addict? For children, almost everyone would answer at least a qualified yes. But for responsible adults, I, for one, would answer no. Reason with the potential addict, yes. Tell him the consequences, yes. Pray for and with him, yes. But I believe that we have no right to use force, directly or indirectly, to prevent a fellow man from committing suicide, let alone from drinking alcohol or taking drugs.

That basic ethical flaw has inevitably generated specific evils during the past quarter century, just as it did during our earlier attempt at alcohol prohibition.

1. **The use of informers.** Informers are not needed in crimes like robbery and murder because the victims of those crimes have a strong incentive to report the crime. In the drug trade, the crime consists of a transaction between a willing buyer and willing seller. Neither has any incentive to report a violation of law. On the contrary, it is in the self-interest of both that the crime not be reported. That is why informers are needed. The use of informers and the immense sums of money at stake inevitably generate corruption—as they did during Prohibition. They also lead to violations of the civil rights of innocent people, to the shameful practices of forcible entry and forfeiture of property without due process.

    As I wrote in 1972: "Addicts and pushers are not the only ones corrupted. Immense sums are at stake. It is inevitable that some relatively low-paid police and other government officials—and some high-paid ones as well—will succumb to the temptation to pick up easy money."

2. **Filling the prisons.** In 1970, 200,000 people were in prison.   5
Today, 1.6 million people are. Eight times as many in absolute number, six times as many relative to the increased population. In addition, 2.3 million are on probation and parole. The attempt to prohibit drugs is by far the major source of the horrendous growth in the prison population.

There is no light at the end of that tunnel. How many of our citizens do we want to turn into criminals before we yell "enough"?

3. **Disproportionate imprisonment of blacks.** Sher Hosonko, at the time Connecticut's director of addiction services, stressed this effect of drug prohibition in a talk given in June 1995:

> Today in this country, we incarcerate 3,109 black men for every 100,000 of them in the population. Just to give you an idea of the drama in this number, our closest competitor for incarcerating black men is South Africa. South Africa—and this is pre–Nelson Mandela and under an overt public policy of apartheid—incarcerated 729 black men for every 100,000. Figure this out: In the land of the Bill of Rights, we jail over four times as many black men as the only country in the world that advertised a political policy of apartheid.

4. **Destruction of inner cities.** Drug prohibition is one of the most important factors that have combined to reduce our inner cities to their present state. The crowded inner cities have a comparative advantage for selling drugs. Though most customers do not live in the inner cities, most sellers do. Young boys and girls view the swaggering, affluent drug dealers as role models. Compared with the returns from a traditional career of study and hard work, returns from dealing drugs are tempting to young and old alike. And many, especially the young, are not dissuaded by the bullets that fly so freely in disputes between competing drug dealers—bullets that fly only because dealing drugs is illegal. Al Capone epitomizes our earlier attempt at Prohibition; the Crips and Bloods epitomize this one.

5. **Compounding the harm to users.** Prohibition makes drugs exorbitantly expensive and highly uncertain in quality. A user must associate with criminals to get the drugs, and many are driven to become criminals themselves to finance the habit. Needles, which are hard to get, are often shared, with the predictable effect of spreading disease. Finally, an addict who seeks treatment must confess to being a criminal in order to qualify for a treatment program. Alternatively, professionals who treat addicts must become informers or criminals themselves.

6. **Undertreatment of chronic pain.** The Federal Department of 10 Health and Human Services has issued reports showing that two-thirds of all terminal cancer patients do not receive adequate pain medication, and the numbers are surely higher in nonterminally ill patients. Such serious undertreatment of chronic pain is a direct result of the Drug Enforcement Agency's pressures on physicians who prescribe narcotics.

7. **Harming foreign countries.** Our drug policy has led to thousands of deaths and enormous loss of wealth in countries like Colombia,

Peru, and Mexico, and has undermined the stability of their governments. All because we cannot enforce our laws at home. If we did, there would be no market for imported drugs. There would be no Cali cartel. The foreign countries would not have to suffer the loss of sovereignty involved in letting our "advisers" and troops operate on their soil, search their vessels, and encourage local militaries to shoot down their planes. They could run their own affairs, and we, in turn, could avoid the diversion of military forces from their proper function.

Can any policy, however high-minded, be moral if it leads to widespread corruption, imprisons so many, has so racist an effect, destroys our inner cities, wreaks havoc on misguided and vulnerable individuals, and brings death and destruction to foreign countries?

Topics for Critical Thinking and Writing

1. State in one sentence the thesis of Friedman's essay.

2. Which of the seven reasons Friedman cites in favor of revising our "war on drugs" do you find most convincing? Explain why, in a short essay of 100 words.

3. Friedman distinguishes between "moral and expediential" objections to current drug policy (para. 1). What does he mean by this distinction? Which kind of objection do you think is the most persuasive? Why?

4. If a policy, a practice, or an individual act is unethical or immoral, then it violates some ethical standard or moral norm. What norms or standards does Friedman think that our current drug policy violates?

5. Does Friedman favor a policy on addictive (and currently illegal) drugs that is like our policy on alcohol? Explain in an essay of 250 words how the two policies might differ.

ELLIOTT CURRIE

Elliott Currie, a graduate of Roosevelt University in Chicago, was a lecturer in the Legal Studies Program at the University of California, Berkeley, and vice chair of the Eisenhower Foundation in Washington, D.C., an organization that supports drug-abuse-prevention programs. We reprint an essay that appeared in the journal Dissent *in 1993; the essay is a slightly revised version of a chapter that first appeared in one of Currie's books,* Reckoning: Drugs, the Cities, and the American Future *(1993).*

Toward a Policy on Drugs

One of the strongest implications of what we now know about the causes of endemic drug abuse is that the criminal-justice system's effect on the drug crisis will inevitably be limited. That shouldn't surprise us in the 1990s; it has, after all, been a central argument of drug research since the 1950s. Today, as the drug problem has worsened, the limits of the law are if anything even clearer. But that does not mean that the justice system has no role to play in a more effective strategy against drugs. Drugs will always be a "law-enforcement problem" in part, and the real job is to define what we want the police and the courts to accomplish.

We will never, for reasons that will shortly become clear, punish our way out of the drug crisis. We can, however, use the criminal-justice system, in small but significant ways, to improve the prospects of drug users who are now caught in an endless loop of court, jail, and street. And we can use law enforcement, in small but significant ways, to help strengthen the ability of drug-ridden communities to defend themselves against violence, fear, and demoralization. Today the criminal-justice system does very little of the first and not enough of the second. But doing these things well will require far-reaching changes in our priorities. Above all, we will have to shift from an approach in which discouraging drug use through punishment and fear takes central place to one that emphasizes three very different principles: the reintegration of drug abusers into productive life, the reduction of harm, and the promotion of community safety.

This is a tall order, but, as we shall see, something similar is being practiced in many countries that suffer far less convulsing drug problems than we do. Their experience suggests that a different and more humane criminal-justice response to drugs is both possible and practical. Today, there is much debate about the role of the justice system in a rational drug policy—but for the most part, the debate is between those who would intensify the effort to control drugs through the courts and prisons and those who want to take drugs out of the orbit of the justice system altogether. I do not think that either approach takes sufficient account of the social realities of drug abuse; and both, consequently, exaggerate the role of regulatory policies in determining the shape and seriousness of the problem. But those are not the only alternatives. In between, there is a range of more promising strategies—what some Europeans call a "third way"—that is more attuned to those realities and more compatible with our democratic values.

One response to the failure of the drug war has been to call for more of what we've already done—even harsher sentences, still more money for jails and prisons—on the grounds that we have simply not provided enough resources to fight the war effectively. That position is shared by the Bush administration and many Democrats in Congress as well. But the strategy of upping the ante cannot work; and even to attempt it on a large scale would dramatically increase the social costs that an overreliance on punishment has already brought. We've seen that the effort to contain the drug problem through force and fear has already distorted our justice system in fundamental ways and caused a rippling of secondary costs throughout the society as a whole. Much more of this would alter the character of American society beyond recognition. And it would not solve the drug problem.

Why wouldn't more of the same do the job?   5

To understand why escalating the war on drugs would be unlikely to make much difference—short of efforts on a scale that would cause unprecedented social damage—we need to consider how the criminal-justice system is, in theory, *supposed* to work to reduce drug abuse and drug-related crime. Criminologists distinguish between two mechanisms by which punishment may decrease illegal behavior. One is "incapacitation," an unlovely term that simply means that locking people up will keep them—as long as they are behind bars—from engaging in the behavior we wish to suppress. The other is "deterrence," by which we mean either that people tempted to engage in the behavior will be persuaded otherwise by the threat of punishment ("general deterrence"), or that individuals, once punished, will be less likely to engage in the behavior again ("specific deterrence"). What makes the drug problem so resistant to even very heavy doses of criminalization is that neither mechanism works effectively for most drug offenders—particularly those most heavily involved in the drug subcultures of the street.

The main reason why incapacitation is unworkable as a strategy against drug offenders is that there are so many of them that a serious attempt to put them all—or even just the "hard core"—behind bars is unrealistic, even in the barest fiscal terms. This is obvious if we pause to recall the sheer number of people who use hard drugs in the United States. Consider the estimates of the number of people who have used drugs during the previous year provided annually by the NIDA (National Institute on Drug Abuse) Household Survey—which substantially *understates* the extent of hard-drug use. Even if we exclude the more than 20 million people who used marijuana in the past year, the number of hard-drug users is enormous: the survey estimates over six million cocaine users in 1991 (including over a million who used crack), about 700,000 heroin users, and 5.7 million users of hallucinogens and inhalants. Even if we abandon the aim of imprisoning less serious hard-drug users, thus allowing the most conservative accounting of the costs of incapacitation, the problem remains staggering: by the lowest estimates, there are no fewer than two million hard-core abusers of cocaine and heroin alone.

If we take as a rough approximation that about 25 percent of America's prisoners are behind bars for drug offenses, that gives us roughly 300,000 drug offenders in prison at any given point—and this after several years of a hugely implemented war mainly directed at lower-level dealers and street drug users. We have seen what this flood of offenders has done to the nation's courts and prisons, but what is utterly sobering is that even this massive effort at repression has barely scratched the surface: according to the most optimistic estimate, we may at any point be incarcerating on drug-related charges about one-eighth of the country's hard-core cocaine and heroin abusers. And where drug addiction is truly endemic, the disparity is greater. By 1989 there were roughly 20,000 drug offenders on any given day in New York State's prisons, but there were an estimated 200,000 to 250,000 *heroin* addicts in New York City alone. To be sure, these figures obscure the fact that many prisoners behind bars for *non*drug offenses are also hard-core drug users; but the figures are skewed in the other direction by the large (if unknown) number of active drug dealers who are not themselves addicted.

Thus, though we cannot quantify these proportions with any precision, the basic point should be clear: the pool of *serious* addicts and active dealers is far, far larger than the numbers we now hold in prison—even in the midst of an unprecedented incarceration binge that has made us far and away the world's leader in imprisonment rates.

What would it mean to expand our prison capacity enough to put the *majority* of hard-core users and dealers behind bars for long terms? To triple the number of users and low-level dealers behind bars, even putting two drug offenders to a cell, would require about 300,000 new cells. At a conservative estimate of about $100,000 per cell, that means a $30 billion investment in construction alone. If we then assume an equally conservative estimate of about $25,000 in yearly operating costs per inmate, we add roughly $15 billion a year to our current costs. Yet this would leave the majority of drug dealers and hard-core addicts still on the streets and, of course, would do nothing to prevent new ones from emerging in otherwise unchanged communities to take the place of those behind bars.

It is not entirely clear, moreover, what that huge expenditure would, in fact, accomplish. For if the goal is to prevent the drug dealing and other crimes that addicts commit, the remedy may literally cost more than the disease. Although drug addicts do commit a great deal of crime, most of them are very minor ones, mainly petty theft and small-time drug dealing. This pattern has been best illuminated in the study of Harlem heroin addicts by Bruce Johnson and his co-workers. Most of the street addicts in this study were "primarily thieves and small-scale drug distributors who avoided serious crimes, like robbery, burglary, assault." The average income per nondrug crime among these addicts was $35. Even among the most criminally active group—what these researchers called "robber-dealers"—the annual income from crime amounted on average to only about $21,000, and for the great majority—about 70 percent—of less active addict-criminals, it ranged from $5,000 to $13,000. At the same time, the researchers estimated that the average cost per day of confining one addict in a New York City jail cell was roughly $100, or $37,000 a year. Putting these numbers together, Johnson and his co-workers came to the startling conclusion that it would cost considerably more to lock up all of Harlem's street addicts than to simply let them continue to "take care of business" on the street.

If we cannot expect much from intensified criminalization, would the legalization of hard drugs solve the drug crisis?

No: it would not. To understand why, we need to consider the claims for legalization's effects in the light of what we know about the roots and meanings of endemic drug abuse. First, however, we need to step back in order to sort out exactly what we *mean* by "legalization"—a frustratingly vague and often confused term that means very different things to different interpreters. Many, indeed, who argue most vehemently one way or the other about the merits of legalization are not really clear just what it is they are arguing *about*.

At one end of the spectrum are those who mean by legalization the total deregulation of the production, sale, and use of all drugs—hard and soft. Advocates of this position run the gamut from right-wing economists to some staunch liberals, united behind the principle that government has no business interfering in individuals' choice to ingest whatever substances they desire. Most who subscribe to that general view would add several qualifiers: for example, that drugs (like alcohol) should not be sold to minors, or that drug advertising should be regulated or prohibited, or (less often) that drugs should be sold only in government/run stores, as alcohol is in some states. But these are seen as necessary, if sometimes grudging, exceptions to the general rule that private drug transactions should not be the province of government intervention. For present purposes, I will call this the "free-market" approach to drug control, and describe its central aim as the "deregulation" of the drug market.

Another approach would not go so far as to deregulate the drug 15 trade, but would opt for the controlled dispensation of drugs to addicts who have been certified by a physician, under strict guidelines as to amounts and conditions of use. Something like this "medical model," in varying forms, guided British policy toward heroin after the 1920s. Under the so-called British system, addicts could receive heroin from physicians or clinics—but the private production and distribution of heroin was always subject to strong penalties, as was the use of the drug except in its medical or "pharmaceutical" form. (A small-scale experiment in cocaine prescription is presently being tried in the city of Liverpool.) Since the seventies, the British have largely abandoned prescribing heroin in favor of methadone—a synthetic opiate that blocks the body's craving for heroin but, among other things, produces less of a pleasurable "high" and lasts considerably longer. The practice of dispensing methadone to heroin addicts came into wide use in the United States in the 1960s and remains a major form of treatment. Methadone prescription, of course, does not "legalize" heroin, and the possession or sale of methadone itself is highly illegal outside of the strictly controlled medical relationship.

Still another meaning sometimes given to legalization is what is more accurately called the "decriminalization" of drug *use*. We may continue to define the production and sale of certain drugs as crimes and subject them to heavy penalties, but not punish those who only *use* the drugs (or have small amounts in their possession), or punish them very lightly—with small fines, for example, rather than jail. Something close to this is the practice in Holland, which is often wrongly perceived as a country that has legalized drugs. Though drug use remains technically illegal, Dutch policy is to focus most law-enforcement resources on sales, especially on larger traffickers, while dealing with users mainly through treatment programs and other social services, rather than the police and courts.

Another aspect of Dutch policy illustrates a further possible meaning of legalization: we may selectively decriminalize *some* drugs, in some amounts, and not others. The Dutch, in practice—though not in law—have tolerated both sale and use of small amounts of marijuana and hashish, but not heroin or cocaine. A German court has recently ruled that possession of small amounts of hashish and marijuana is not a crime, and, indeed, marijuana possession has largely been decriminalized in some American states, though usually as a matter of practical policy rather than legislation.

Let me make my own view clear. I think much would be gained if we followed the example of some European countries and moved toward decriminalization of the drug user. I also think there is a strong argument for treating marijuana differently from the harder drugs, and that there is room for careful experiment with strictly controlled medical prescription for some addicts. For reasons that will become clear, decriminalization is not a panacea; it will not end the drug crisis, but it could substantially decrease the irrationality and inhumanity of our present punitive war on drugs.

The free-market approach, on the other hand, is another matter entirely. Some variant of that approach is more prominent in drug-policy debates in the United States than in other developed societies, probably because it meshes with a strongly individualistic and antigovernment political culture. Indeed, the degree to which the debate over drug policy has been dominated by the clash between fervent drug "warriors" and equally ardent free-market advocates is a peculiarly American phenomenon. Much of that clash is about philosophical principles, and addressing those issues in detail would take more space than we have. My aim here is simply to examine the empirical claims of the free-market perspective in the light of what we know about the social context of drug abuse. Here the free-market view fails to convince. It greatly exaggerates the benefits of deregulation while simultaneously underestimating the potential costs.

There is no question that the criminalization of drugs produces negative secondary consequences—especially in the unusually punitive form that criminalization has taken in the United States. Nor is there much question that this argues for a root-and-branch rethinking of our current punitive strategy—to which we'll return later in this essay—especially our approach to drug *users*.

But proponents of full-scale deregulation of hard drugs also tend to gloss over the very real primary costs of drug abuse—particularly on the American level—and to exaggerate the degree to which the multiple pathologies surrounding drug use in America are simply an unintended result of a "prohibitionist" regulatory policy. No country now legalizes the sale of hard drugs. Yet no other country has anything resembling the American drug problem. That alone should tell us that more than prohibition is involved in shaping the magnitude and severity of our drug crisis. But there is more technical evidence as well. It confirms that much (though, of course, not all) of the harm caused by endemic drug abuse is intrinsic to the impact of hard drugs themselves (and the street cultures in which drug abuse is embedded) within the context of a glaringly unequal, depriving, and deteriorating society. And it affirms that we will not substantially reduce that harm without attacking the social roots of the extraordinary demand for hard drugs in the United States. Just as we cannot punish our way out of the drug crisis, neither will we escape its grim toll by deregulating the drug market.

The most important argument for a free-market approach has traditionally been that it would reduce or eliminate the crime and violence now inextricably entwined with addiction to drugs and with the drug trade. In this view it is precisely the illegality of drug use that is responsible for drug-related crime—which, in turn, is seen as by far the largest part of the overall problem of urban violence. Criminal sanctions against drugs, as one observer insists, "cause the bulk of murders and property crime in major urban areas." Because criminalization makes drugs far more costly than they would otherwise be, addicts are forced to commit crimes in order to gain enough income to afford their habits. Moreover, they are forced to seek out actively criminal people in order to obtain their drugs, which exposes them to even more destructive criminal influences. At the same time, the fact that the drug trade is illegal means both that it is hugely profitable and that the inevitable conflicts and disputes over "turf" or between dealers and users cannot be resolved or moderated by legal mechanisms, and hence are usually resolved by violence.

For all of these reasons, it is argued, outlawing drugs has the unintended, but inevitable, effect of causing a flood of crime and urban violence that would not exist otherwise and sucking young people, especially, into a bloody drug trade. If we legalize the sale and use of hard drugs, the roots of drug-related violence would be severed, and much of the larger crisis of criminal violence in the cities would disappear.

But the evidence suggests that although this view contains an element of truth, it is far too simplistic—and that it relies on stereotypical assumptions about the relationship between drugs and crime that have been called into serious question since the classic drug research of the 1950s. In particular, the widely held notion that most of the crime committed by addicts can be explained by their need for money to buy illegal drugs does not fit well with the evidence.

In its popular form, the drugs-cause-crime argument is implicitly 25 based on the assumption that addict crime is caused by pharmacological compulsion—as a recent British study puts it, on a kind of "enslavement" model in which the uncontrollable craving for drugs forces an otherwise law-abiding citizen to engage in crime for gain. As we've seen, however, a key finding of most of the research into the meaning of drug use and the growth of drug subcultures since the 1950s has been that the purely pharmacological craving for drugs is by no means the most important motive for drug use. Nor is it clear that those cravings are typically so uncontrollable that addicts are in any meaningful sense "driven" to crime to satisfy them.

On the surface, there is much to suggest a strong link between crime and the imperatives of addiction. The studies of addict crime by John Ball and Douglas Anglin and their colleagues show not only that the most heavily addicted commit huge numbers of crimes, but also that their crime rates seem to increase when their heroin use increases and to fall when it declines. Thus, for example, heroin addicts in Ball's study in Baltimore had an average of 255 "crime days" per year when they were actively addicted, versus about 65 when they were not. In general, the level of property crime appears in these studies to go up simultaneously with increasing intensity of drug use. One explanation, and perhaps the most common one, is that the increased need for money to buy drugs drives addicts into more crime.

But a closer look shows that things are considerably more complicated. To begin with, it is a recurrent finding that most people who both abuse drugs and commit crimes began committing the crimes *before* they began using drugs—meaning that their need for drugs cannot have caused their initial criminal involvement (though it may have accelerated it later). George Vaillant's follow-up study of addicts and alcoholics found, for example, that, unlike alcoholics, heroin addicts had typically been involved in delinquency and crime well before they began their career of substance abuse. While alcoholics seemed to become involved in crime as a *result* of their abuse of alcohol, more than half of the heroin addicts (versus just 5 percent of the alcoholics) "were known to have been delinquent *before* drug abuse." A federal survey of drug use among prison inmates in 1986, similarly, found that three-fifths of those who had ever used a "major drug" regularly—that is, heroin, cocaine, methadone, PCP, or LSD—had not done so until after their first arrest.

Other studies have found that for many addicts, drug use and crime seem to have begun more or less *independently* without one clearly causing the other. This was the finding, for example, in Charles Faupel and Carl Klockars's study of hard-core heroin addicts in Wilmington, Delaware. "All of our respondents," they note, "reported some criminal activity prior to their first use of heroin." Moreover, "perhaps most importantly, virtually all of our respondents reported that they believed that their criminal and drug careers began independently of one another, although both careers became intimately interconnected as each evolved."

More recent research shows that the drugs-crime relationship may be even more complex than this suggests. It is not only that crime may precede drug use, especially heavy or addictive use, or that both may emerge more or less independently; it is also likely that there are several *different* kinds of drugs-crime connections among different types of drug users. David Nurco of the University of Maryland and his colleagues, for example, studying heroin addicts in Baltimore and New York City, found that nine different kinds of addicts could be distinguished by the type and severity of their crimes. Like earlier researchers, they found that most addicts committed large numbers of crimes — mainly drug dealing and small-scale property crime, notably shoplifting, burglary, and fencing. Others were involved in illegal gambling and what the researchers called "deception crimes" — including forgery and con games — and a relatively small percentage had engaged in violent crime. On the whole, addicts heavily involved in one type of crime were not likely to be involved in others; as the researchers put it, they tended to be either "dealers or stealers," but rarely both. About 6 percent of the addicts, moreover, were "uninvolved" — they did not commit crimes either while addicted or before, or during periods of nonaddiction interspersed in the course of their longer addiction careers.

The most troubling group of addicts — what the researchers called 30 "violent generalists" — were only about 7 percent of the total sample, but they were extremely active — and very dangerous; they accounted for over half of all the violent crimes committed by the entire sample. Moreover, revealingly, the violent generalists were very active in serious crime *before* they became addicted to narcotics as well as during periods of nonaddiction thereafter — again demonstrating that the violence was not dependent on their addiction itself. Nurco and his colleagues measured the addicts' criminal activity by what they called "crime days" per year. Addicts were asked how many days they had committed each of several types of crime; since on any given day they might have committed more than one type of crime, the resulting figure could add up to more than the number of days in the year. The violent generalists averaged an astonishing 900 crime days a year over the course of their careers. The rates were highest during periods when they were heavily addicted to drugs. But even *before* they were addicted, they averaged 573 crime days, and 491 after their addiction had ended. Indeed, the most active group of violent generalists engaged in more crime *prior* to addiction than any other group did *while* addicted. And they continued to commit crimes — often violent ones — long after they had ceased to be addicted to narcotics.

None of this is to deny that serious addiction to heroin or other illegal drugs can accelerate the level of crime among participants in the drug culture, or stimulate crime even in some users who are otherwise not criminal. Higher levels of drug use *do* go hand in hand with increased crime, especially property crime. Certainly, many addicts mug, steal, or sell their bodies for drugs. The point is that—as the early drug researchers discovered in the 1950s—both crime and drug abuse tend to be spawned by the same set of unfavorable social circumstances, and they interact with one another in much more complex ways than the simple addiction-leads-to-crime view proposes. Simply providing drugs more easily to people enmeshed in the drug cultures of the cities is not likely to cut the deep social roots of addict crime.

If we take the harms of drug abuse seriously, and I think we must, we cannot avoid being deeply concerned about anything that would significantly increase the availability of hard drugs within the American social context; and no one seriously doubts that legalization would indeed increase availability, and probably lower prices for many drugs. In turn, increased availability—as we know from the experience with alcohol—typically leads to increased consumption, and with it increased social and public-health costs. A growing body of research, for example, shows that most alcohol-related health problems, including deaths from cirrhosis and other diseases, were far lower during Prohibition than afterward, when per capita alcohol consumption rose dramatically (by about 75 percent, for example, between 1950 and 1980). It is difficult to imagine why a similar rise in consumption—and in the associated public-health problems—would not follow the full-scale legalization of cocaine, heroin, methamphetamine, and PCP (not to mention the array of as yet undiscovered "designer" drugs that a legalized corporate drug industry would be certain to develop).

If consumption increased, it would almost certainly increase most among the strata already most vulnerable to hard-drug use—thus exacerbating the social stratification of the drug crisis. It is among the poor and near-poor that offsetting measures like education and drug treatment are least effective and where the countervailing social supports and opportunities are least strong. We would expect, therefore, that a free-market policy applied to hard drugs would produce the same results it has created with the *legal* killer drugs, tobacco and alcohol—namely, a widening disparity in use between the better-off and the disadvantaged. And that disparity is already stunning. According to a recent study by Colin McCord and Howard Freeman of Harlem Hospital, between 1979 and 1981—that is, *before* the crack epidemic of the eighties—Harlem blacks were 283 times as likely to die of drug dependency as whites in the general population. Drug deaths, combined with deaths from cirrhosis, alcoholism, cardiovascular disease, and homicide, helped to give black men in Harlem a shorter life expectancy than men in Bangladesh. This is the social reality that the rather abstract calls for the legalization of hard-drug sales tend to ignore.

Topics for Critical Thinking and Writing

1. Currie claims that "Drugs will always be a 'law-enforcement problem'" (para. 1). Why do you think he believes this? Is the evidence he offers adequate to support this troubling judgment?

2. Currie mentions what he regards as "small but significant ways" (para. 2) to reduce the place of drugs in our lives. What are they? Why do you think he doesn't mention (a) curbing the manufacture of illegal addictive drugs, (b) vigorously reducing imports of illegal addictive drugs into the United States, and (c) aggressively educating the public on the harm that illegal addictive drugs cause their users?

3. Why does Currie think that "escalating the war on drugs," with its reliance on "incapacitation" and "deterrence," is doomed to ineffectiveness (para. 6)? Are you persuaded? Explain.

4. Currie eventually states his own views (para. 18). Do you think the essay would have been more effective if he had stated his views in his opening paragraph? Why, or why not?

5. Currie stresses the uniqueness of the drug problem in the United States. What do you think explains "the magnitude and severity of our drug crisis" (para. 21)? Farmers in other countries produce more illegal addictive drugs than ours do. Other countries have graver problems of poverty than we do. Gross manifest disparities between rich and poor are not unique to the United States. So what's the explanation? Does Currie tell us?

6. Why does Currie reject the drugs-cause-crime argument (para. 24)?

8

The Just War: What Are the Criteria?

G. E. M. ANSCOMBE

Gertrude Elizabeth Margaret Anscombe (1919–2001) taught philosophy at Cambridge University, where she had been a post graduate student of Ludwig Wittgenstein and later an editor of his collected works. She was widely admired for her trenchant style and original and unfashionable (but superbly argued) views. We reprint a short extract from her essay "The Justice of the Present War Examined," written in 1939 at the outset of World War II. The essay appears in her book Ethics, Religion, and Politics, *published by the University of Minnesota Press in 1981.*

The Criteria of a Just War

In these days the authorities claim the right to control not only the policy of the nation but also the actions of every individual within it; and their claim has the support of a large section of the people of the country, and of a peculiar force of emotion. This support is gained, and this emotion caused by the fact that they are "evil things" that we are fighting against. That they are evil we need have no doubt; yet many of us still feel distrust of these claims and these emotions lest they blind men to their duty of considering carefully, before they act, the justice of the things they propose to do. Men can be moved to fight by being made to hate the deeds of their enemies; but a war is not made just by the fact that one's enemies' deeds are hateful. Therefore it is our duty to resist passion and to consider carefully whether all the conditions of a just war are satisfied in this present war, lest we sin against the natural law by participating in it. . . .

There are seven conditions which must be all fulfilled for a war to be just:

1. There must be a just occasion: that is, there must be violation of, or attack upon, strict rights.
2. The war must be made by a lawful authority: that is, when there is no higher authority, a sovereign state.
3. The warring state must have an upright intention in making war: it must not declare war in order to obtain, or inflict anything un-just.
4. Only right means must be used in the conduct of the war.
5. War must be the only possible means of righting the wrong done.
6. There must be a reasonable hope of victory.
7. The probable good must outweigh the probable evil effects of the war.

Topics for Critical Thinking and Writing

1. Do you think the American Revolution was a just war, given the criteria of a just war as Anscombe defines them?
2. How about the Spanish-American War? The Korean War? Our Civil War?
3. Do you think that Anscombe's seven criteria are equally important? Explain.

PETER STEINFELS

Peter Steinfels writes a regular column called Beliefs on religious issues for the New York Times. *The column we reprint was origi-nally published there on March 1, 2003.*

The Just War Tradition
and the Invasion of Iraq

War is justified only as a last resort; all peaceful alternatives must be exhausted.

That is one of the pillars of the venerable tradition of moral reasoning known as just-war theory, now being cited on every side of the debate about invading Iraq; and however straightforward and sensible the notion of going to war only as a last resort may sound in principle, the world is demonstrating how difficult it is to apply in practice.

To begin with, the problem is both rhetorical—in the sense of persuasive use of language—and logical. The criterion of "last resort" has been invoked by opponents of virtually every American military action in recent times, from the Persian Gulf to Bosnia, Kosovo and, most recently, Afghanistan; and one has to grant that the opponents can appeal to a kind of logic that makes their opposition unassailable.

In the latest issue of *The New York Review of Books*, that logic is explained and challenged by Michael Walzer, the political scientist whose book *Just and Unjust Wars* has become a classic in the field.

"Lastness," he writes, "is never actually reached in real life: it is always possible to do something else, or to do it again, before doing whatever it is that comes last." One more diplomatic initiative, one more peace conference, one more appeal to world opinion, one more nonmilitary form of pressure—the last resort is always just over the horizon. 5

This kind of argument is reminiscent of the ancient philosophical conundrum in which Achilles can never overtake a tortoise that has a head start because every time Achilles reaches a point where the tortoise has been, the tortoise will have moved on; or, in a different, modern version, first Achilles must reach half the distance between himself and the tortoise, then half of that, and half of that, and half of that, and on to infinity, without ever reaching the tortoise.

In the real world, of course, Achilles overtakes the tortoise even if the diminishing distance can be divided infinitely. In the real world, endless diplomatic initiatives can reach a point of diminishing returns, indeed of negative returns. Why would anyone strain the moral criterion of last resort, as a significant number of religious people do, in a way that makes it clear that virtually no military action, short of repelling perhaps a full-scale enemy attack already launched on the nation's territory, would ever meet it?

The reason is not mysterious. A good number of those invoking the just-war criterion of last resort are in reality absolute pacifists opposed to all use of armed force. Or they are what their critics call functional pacifists, not exactly avowing principled pacifism but just never encountering an American use of force they could not denounce. Or they are what might be called isolationist pacifists, for whom nothing except being subjected to that full-scale attack would be irrefutable evidence that the moment of last resort had arrived.

Of course, when pacifists of these various kinds demand the continuation of weapons inspections and surveillance in Iraq as peaceful alternatives to war that are not yet exhausted, they put themselves in a funny position. They know that those inspections are occurring only because of the mobilization of American (and British) military forces. Yet not long ago the same people were opposing that very military mobilization on the basis that all peaceful alternatives had not yet been exhausted.

So for all the talk of going to war only as a last resort, is this criterion really meaningless? Is the principle that war can be morally justified only if all peaceful alternatives have been exhausted a moral standard that can logically never be met? 10

There is an old Latin maxim in legal and moral reasoning that seems pertinent here: *abusus non tollitusum,* abuse does not nullify use. For those like Professor Walzer who value the just-war tradition as a disciplined way to think about the morality of war, the fact that some people have stretched the criterion of last resort to the breaking point in order to support their foregone conclusions does not invalidate it.

The criterion, these just-war theorists say, is essentially a prudential one. Establishing what is or is not a last resort is a matter not of abstract mathematical demonstration but of practical, concrete wisdom, acquired through experience and reflection.

War must be the last resort, Professor Walzer writes, "because of the unpredictable, unexpected, unintended and unavoidable horrors that it regularly brings." As for the notion of lastness, it is essentially "cautionary," he states: "look hard for alternatives before you 'let loose the dogs of war.'"

As a matter of fact, when it comes to Iraq, Professor Walzer believes that "even at this last minute, there still are alternatives, and that is the best argument against going to war." The alternatives he outlines in *The New York Review* focus on containment and control—maintaining the economic sanctions, the no-flight zones and the United Nations inspections almost indefinitely—and on fashioning a strong international system that would take responsibility, including military responsibility, for those tasks.

Others, of course, disagree, including both those who would rely more on deterring Iraq's use of arms rather than on preventing their development, and those who have come to see war as the only solution. That argument is being conducted elsewhere, indeed everywhere. What 15 is significant for the just-war tradition is that Professor Walzer himself, despite his admonitions against strained renderings of the last-resort criterion, still considers it central to the current debate.

Topics for Critical Thinking and Writing

1. Does G. E. M. Anscombe (p. 132) include among her seven criteria for a just war the criterion of "last resort" on which Steinfels concentrates (para. 1)?

2. Does inclusion of the "last-resort" criterion in any list of criteria for a just war make the requirements so vague as to be useless? Discuss in an essay of 250 words.

3. Steinfels discusses various kinds of pacifism (paras. 8–9). What does the tone of his discussion suggest about whether he accepts or rejects one of these positions? Explain.

4. What does Steinfels mean when he describes the last-resort criterion as "prudential" (para. 12)? Do you agree or disagree?

GEORGE A. LOPEZ

George A. Lopez is director of policy studies and a senior fellow at the Joan B. Kroc Institute of International Peace Studies at the University of Notre Dame. His essay reprinted here originally appeared in Commonweal *for September 27, 2002, several months before the American invasion of Iraq. In his third paragraph Lopez uses two Latin terms:* ad bellum *("to war") and* in bello *("in war").* Ad bellum *concerns relate to whether it is appropriate to go to war;* in bello *concerns are the moral rules governing conduct in a war—for instance, treatment of civilians.*

Iraq and Just-War Thinking

The Washington view about war with Iraq has moved precipitously from "a rumor of war" to "foregone conclusion." Although prominent policy makers, including Republicans, have questioned the wisdom of the Bush administration's call for regime change, many end their remarks with, "the president has yet to make the case"—anticipating, of course, that he will.

No one can pretend that just-war principles have ever governed U.S. foreign policy. But in recent years, debates about the use of force—in the Persian Gulf, in Bosnia and Kosovo, and in response to September 11—have been informed, at least partially, by the ethical criteria of the just-war tradition. But a focus on these criteria was visibly lacking at the Senate Foreign Relations committee hearings on Iraq in July and August. And National Security Adviser Condoleezza Rice observed recently that removing Saddam Hussein from power might be the *moral obligation* of the United States, without specifying the moral grounds. Does the just-war tradition have any relevance to the decision to go to war with Iraq?

American culture generally—and decision makers in particular—rarely accept what some just-war thinkers consider a foundation stone: there is a "presumption against the use of force," and who regard the just-war criteria as impediments to which exceptions might be made in a specific case. Yet others understand the just-war tradition as permitting the use of force once certain conditions are met. In practice then, just-war thinking becomes a *pro forma* checklist to be met by decision makers who want U.S. citizens to consider the use of force moral and legal. Often enough, at the top of their checklist sits the selection of a norm-laden *nom de guerre,* Operation Just Cause (Panama), or Operation Enduring Freedom (Afghanistan), signifying an adherence to *ad bellum* concerns. The preponderance of the checklist focuses on the *in bello* problems of proportionate response, avoidance of civilian casualties, and insuring that war is a last resort. This checklist approach was clearly manifest in the congressional debates that preceded the war against Iraq in 1990–91.

Catholic intellectuals and church leaders have contributed to the checklist mentality by failing to respond to the changing conduct of war. In contrast, "The Challenge of Peace," the Catholic bishops' 1983 pastoral letter, made a substantive and politically effective contribution to U.S. thinking about the morality of nuclear weapons and war-fighting doctrines by directly linking these security challenges to dictates about the just-war responsibility of U.S. decision makers. The two letters that followed (the bishops' 1994 anniversary reflection on "The Challenge of Peace," and "Living with Faith and Hope after September 11") had their strengths, but neither provided a compelling and comprehensive framework tied to the genuine security concerns of Americans. Now we face, according a Defense Department "Nuclear Posture Review," leaked last February, the possibility of a pre-emptive strike on Iraq and the possible use of low-yield nuclear weapons to destroy hardened Iraqi bunkers. In these circumstances, we desperately need the contemporary equivalent of the bishops' 1984 letter, which noted that the moral acceptance of policies (in this case, deterrence policy) be strictly conditioned. We need a bold restatement of their central message: "peacemaking is no longer an optional commitment of faith."

In a world with only one superpower, U.S. Catholics must thoroughly debate the meaning, scope, and relevance of just-war thinking. Whatever the uncertainties and real threat of terrorism today, virtually no existing war scenario places this country at risk—militarily, politically, or socially. While there can be rightful concern about the number of American lives lost in battle, the major moral dilemmas facing the country right now lie in the damage levels that could be inflicted on Iraq and the conditions under which we proclaim victory. Such an unbalanced military situation is unprecedented. Yet it has not led to any reassessment by Catholic leaders of what might constitute a "just war" for the United States in these circumstances. Our failure to think ahead is coming back to haunt us in an atmosphere of the "foregone conclusion" of war with Iraq.

To understand the specific challenges that have gone unmet and have helped to create the untenable situation faced by just-war thinking, consider the last dozen years, and the wars in the Persian Gulf, Kosovo, and Afghanistan. Three unresolved dilemmas—one regarding *ad bellum* concerns, the other two *in bello* controversies—make up the legacy of the three U.S. wars. These dilemmas challenge the ability of the just-war tradition to prohibit or to limit the character of a new war against Iraq. The first area of concern lies in the *ad bellum* criteria of right authority. The Gulf War, Kosovo, and Afghanistan were all fought under *ad bellum* criteria to defend and re-establish important international norms. Yet only in the case of the Gulf War did the United States seek and receive authorization of the international community via a UN Security Council Resolution authorizing the use of force.

The unwillingness of the U.S. to seek Security Council endorsement in the Kosovo case generated criticism, while similar U.S. inaction was a surprise in the war against Afghanistan. Amid mounting criticism of projected unilateral U.S. military action, the Bush administration now indicates it seeks such authority from the Council. But the Council may only provide authorization for military action aimed at potential weapons facilities, and only after an inspection phase has fizzled. If the UN does not grant the United States authority to wage a war aimed at regime change, will President Bush accept this as right authority limiting U.S. policy? Or will the United States argue that, its attempt at Security Council consensus having failed, it has exhausted the last possible peaceful means to resolve the dispute with Iraq, and thus "has the right" to wage war?

The two *in bello* concerns at stake are dynamically interrelated. Our failure to clarify just-war thinking on these matters during the past decade will prove costly if a war with Iraq ensues. The first controversy—one with a cruel irony—lies in use of precision-guided munitions (PGMs), or "smart weapons." In response to legal and ethical concerns about the civilian casualties in war, the United States developed PGMs, which now assure that the accidental bombing of unintended targets rarely occurs. When it does, it has usually resulted from faulty intelligence in the identification of targets, not as a result of cross winds or poor pilot judgment. Thus, there has been a real and significant reduction in the loss of civilian life during warfare. This use of PGMs, however, has driven the United States into an ethical trap. Given the near certainty that bombers can hit any target without concern for inadvertent civilian death, U.S. war planners have been able to expand, over the last decade, the list of targets considered "military" and acceptable for bombing. In the Persian Gulf War, the decision to destroy urban-based infrastructure was justified by the logic that such aerial bombardment destroys the energy, economic, and communication capacity of the civilian structure for war, thus isolating the enemy's leadership from its troops and from civilian society. The more infrastructure destroyed, the more quickly the enemy is willing to surrender, or so the theory goes.

The ethical fallacy here is that the war is more humane because it is shortened by the expanded and intense destruction of electric grid systems, water treatment facilities, waste disposal systems, and bridges that carry fiber-optic cables. In a world of "smart weapons," all of these areas are now defined as targets of military necessity (because they can be bombed without large numbers of civilian casualties). Such facilities, which would have been targeted in an earlier era only if a nation was engaged in carpet bombing or "total war," have now been made accessible targets by the "humane" nature of the weapons. This thinking is fundamental to the air-land battle strategy adopted in the Gulf War and, undoubtedly, it will be a key component of another war with Iraq. If the United States were committed to fully rebuilding the infrastructure it destroys in such assaults, the ethical quandary might be lessened. But our track record in the first war against Iraq does not inspire confidence. Moreover, this trend toward target expansion is directly related to a second crisis of *in bello* criteria.

With the Gulf War, massive aerial superiority and the success of PGMs led to a relatively quick end to the fighting. Thus when the U.S./UN-Iraq armistice was signed at the end of February 1991, the number of Iraqi civilian deaths due to the war was rather limited. But by the end of 1991, almost as many Iraqis (some would estimate more) had died from the results of bombing as died during the six weeks of actual fighting. By the end of 1992, more than a hundred thousand Iraqi civilians died from the lack of clean water and sewage disposal, and the breakdown of electrical service to hospitals.

Ironically then, civilian deaths as collateral damage and noncombatant casualties occur in the wake of war, as a result of bombing during the war. Vulnerable populations, especially children, not killed by wartime bombing, now may die months later due to wartime decisions about what facilities to destroy. Just-war thinking, and ethical analysis in general, have not focused on this cumbersome reality. Thus, we have few guidelines to contribute to the debates about the ethical parameters that ought to guide the search for targeting, or the moral culpability related to "civilian fatalities"—or the more antiseptic term, "collateral damage."

As we move to a point where war appears to be a "foregone conclusion," reflective American Catholics must ask why the just-war tradition fails to capture the minds and thus guide the discussion of pundits and politicians? John Courtney Murray may have provided part of the answer in 1958 when he wrote that the failure of leaders to employ "the Catholic doctrine of war initially rises from the fact that it has for so long not been used, even by Catholics. That is, it has not been made the basis for a sound critique of public policies, and as a means for the formation of a right public opinion."

I have argued two points: that the guiding frame of any debate—to presume against the use of force—has been lost in the public square; and that the use of PGMs has created a dynamic which generates new and unexpected civilian casualties. As a result, we now face a situation that strikes at the heart of what Augustine and Aquinas sought to prevent centuries ago. How Catholics attempt to form "right public opinion" about war with Iraq in the coming months will determine the future relevance of the just-war tradition in American politics.

Topics for Critical Thinking and Writing

1. Does Lopez accept, ignore, or dispute G. E. M. Anscombe's seven criteria of a just war (p. 133)?

2. Lopez remarks that "just-war principles have [never] governed U.S. foreign policy" (para. 2). Do you agree? If so, how is this to be best explained?

3. What does Lopez mean by the contrast between *ad bellum* concerns and *in bello* concerns (paras. 3 and 6)?

4. Do the criteria for a just war have special relevance for Catholic moral thinking, or are they equally relevant to the moral thinking of Protestants, Jews, agnostics, and atheists? Explain.

5. Does Lopez seem optimistic or pessimistic about the relevance of just-war thinking to current American foreign policy?

WILLIAM A. GALSTON

William A. Galston is on the faculty of the Institute for Philosophy and Public Policy at the University of Maryland. His most recent book is Liberal Pluralism *(2002). The essay we reprint first appeared in* Philosophy and Public Policy Quarterly, *vol. 22, no. 4 (fall 2002), several months before the United States invaded Iraq. A slightly different version appeared in* The American Prospect *(September 23, 2002).*

The Perils of Preemptive War

INTRODUCTION

On June 1, 2002, at West Point, President George W. Bush set forth a new doctrine for U.S. security policy. The successful strategies of the Cold War era, he declared, are ill suited to national defense in the twenty-first century. Deterrence means nothing against terrorist networks; containment will not thwart unbalanced dictators possessing weapons of mass destruction. We cannot afford to wait until we are attacked. In today's circumstances, Americans must be ready to take "preemptive action" to defend our lives and liberties.

On August 26, 2002, Vice President Dick Cheney forcefully applied this new doctrine to Iraq. Saddam Hussein, he stated, is bolstering the country's chemical and biological capabilities and is aggressively pursuing nuclear weapons. "What we must not do in the face of a mortal threat," he declared, "is to give in to wishful thinking or willful blindness. . . . Deliverable weapons of mass destruction in the hands of a terror network or murderous dictator or the two working together constitutes as grave a threat as can be imagined. The risks of inaction are far greater than the risks of action."

After an ominous silence lasting much of the summer, a debate about U.S. policy toward Iraq has finally begun. Remarkably, Democratic elected officials are not party to it. Some agree with Bush administration hawks; others have been intimidated into acquiescence or silence. The Senate Foreign Relations Committee hearings yielded questions rather than answers and failed to prod Democratic leaders into declaring their position. Meanwhile, Democratic political consultants are advising their clients to avoid foreign policy and to wage their campaigns on the more hospitable turf of corporate fraud and prescription drugs. The memory of the Gulf War a decade ago, when the vast majority of Democrats ended up on the wrong side of the debate, deters many from reentering the fray today.

The Democratic Party's abdication has left the field to Republican combatants—unilateralists versus multilateralists, ideologues versus "realists." The resulting debate has been intense but narrow, focused primarily on issues of prudence rather than principle.

ARGUMENTS FROM PRUDENCE

This is not to suggest that the prudential issues are unimportant, or   5
that the intra-Republican discord has been less than illuminating. Glib analogies between Iraq and Afghanistan and cocky talk about a military cakewalk have given way to more sober assessments. President Bush's oft-repeated goal of "regime change" would likely require 150,000 to 200,000 U.S. troops, allies in the region willing to allow us to preposition and supply those forces and bloody street battles in downtown Baghdad. With little left to lose, Saddam Hussein might carry out a "Samson scenario" by equipping his Scud missiles with chemical or biological agents and firing them at Tel Aviv. Senior Israeli military and intelligence officials doubt that Israeli Prime Minister Ariel Sharon would defer to U.S. calls for restraint, as Yitzhak Shamir's government did during the Gulf War. Israeli retaliation could spark a wider regional conflagration.

Assume that we can surmount these difficulties. The Bush administration's goal of regime change is the equivalent of our World War II aim of unconditional surrender, and it would have similar postwar consequences. We would assume total responsibility for Iraq's territorial integrity, for the security and basic needs of its population, and for the reconstruction of its system of governance and political culture. This would require an occupation measured in years or even decades. Whatever our intentions, nations in the region (and elsewhere) would view our continuing presence through the historical prism of colonialism. *The Economist,* which favors a U.S. invasion of Iraq, nonetheless speaks of the "imperial flavour" of such a potential occupation.

But the risks would not end there. The Bush administration and its supporters argue that the overthrow of Saddam Hussein would shift the political balance in our favor throughout the Middle East (including among the Palestinians). Henry Kissinger is not alone in arguing that the road to solving the Israeli-Palestinian conflict leads through Baghdad, not the other way around. More broadly, say the optimists, governments in the region would see that opposing the United States carries serious risk, and that there is more to be gained from cooperating with us. Rather than rising up in injured pride, the Arab "street" would respect our resolve and move toward moderation, as would Arab leaders.

Perhaps so. But it does not take much imagination to conjure a darker picture, and the performance of our intelligence services in the region does not inspire confidence in the factual basis of the optimists' views. If a wave of public anger helped Islamic radicals unseat Pakistan's General Pervez Musharraf, for example, we would have exchanged a dangerous regime seeking nuclear weapons for an even more dangerous regime that possesses them.

All this, and I have not yet mentioned potential economic and diplomatic consequences. Even a relatively short war would likely produce an oil-price spike that could tip the fragile global economy into recession. Moreover, unlike the Gulf War, which the Japanese and Saudis largely financed, the United States would have to go it alone this time, with an estimated price tag of U.S. $60 billion for the war and $15 billion to $20 billion per year for the occupation.

Our closest allies have spoken out against an invasion of Iraq. 10 Gerhard Schröder, leading a usually complaisant Germany but locked in a tough re-election fight, had gone so far as to label this possibility an "adventure," sparking a protest from our ambassador. Some Bush administration officials seem not to believe that our allies' views matter all that much. Others argue, more temperately, that the Europeans and other protesters will swallow their reservations after the fact, when they can see the military success of our action and its positive consequences. They may be right. But it is at least as likely that this disagreement will widen the already sizeable gap between European and American worldviews. Generations of young people could grow up resenting and resisting America, as they did after the Vietnam War. Whether or not these trends in the long run undermine our alliances, they could have a range of negative short-term consequences, including diminished intelligence sharing and cooperation.

BROADER IMPLICATIONS

Republicans have at least raised these prudential issues. For the most part, however, they have ignored broader questions of principle. But these questions cannot be evaded. An invasion of Iraq would be one of the most fateful deployments of American power since World War II. A global strategy based on the new Bush doctrine of preemption means the end of the system of international institutions, laws and norms that we have worked to build for more than half a century. To his credit, Kissinger recognizes this; he labels Bush's new approach "revolutionary" and declares, "Regime change as a goal for military intervention challenges the international system." The question is whether this revolution in international doctrine is justified and wise.

I think not. What is at stake is nothing less than a fundamental shift in America's place in the world. Rather than continuing to serve as first among equals in the postwar international system, the United States would act as a law unto itself, creating new rules of international engagement without the consent of other nations. In my judgment, this new stance would ill serve the long-term interests of the United States.

There is a reason why President Bush could build on the world's sympathy in framing the U.S. response to al Qaeda after September 11, and why his father was able to sustain such a broad coalition to reverse Saddam Hussein's invasion of Kuwait. In those cases our policy fit squarely within established doctrines of self-defense. By contrast, if we seek to overthrow Saddam Hussein, we will act outside the framework of global security that we have helped create.

In the first place, we are a signatory to (indeed, the principal drafter of) the United Nations Charter, which explicitly reserves to sovereign nations "the inherent right of individual or collective self-defense," but only in the event of armed attack. Unless the administration establishes Iraqi complicity in the terrorism of 9/11, it cannot invoke self-defense, as defined by the charter, as the justification for attacking Iraq. And if evidence of Iraqi involvement exists, the administration has a responsibility to present it to Congress, the American people and the world, much as John F. Kennedy and Adlai Stevenson did to justify the U.S. naval blockade of Cuba during the 1962 missile crisis.

The broader structure of international law creates additional obstacles to an invasion of Iraq. To be sure, such law contains a doctrine of "anticipatory self-defense," and there is an ongoing argument concerning its scope. Daniel Webster, then secretary of state, offered the single most influential statement of the doctrine in 1837: There must be shown "a necessity of self-defense . . . instant, overwhelming, leaving no choice of means, and no moment for deliberation." Some contemporary scholars adopt a more permissive view. But even if that debate were resolved in the manner most favorable to the Bush administration, the concept of anticipatory self-defense would still be too narrow to support an attack on Iraq: The threat to the United States from Iraq is not sufficiently specific, clearly enough established or shown to be imminent.

The Bush doctrine of preemption goes well beyond the established bounds of anticipatory self-defense, as many supporters of the administration's Iraq policy privately concede. (They argue that the United States needs to make new law, using Iraq as a precedent.) If the administration wishes to argue that terrorism renders the imminence criterion obsolete, it must do what it has thus far failed to do—namely, to show that Iraq has both the capability of harming us and a serious intent to do so. The abstract logical possibility that Saddam Hussein could transfer weapons of mass destruction to stateless terrorists is not enough. If we cannot make our case, the world will see anticipatory self-defense as an international hunting license.

JUST WAR THEORY

We must also examine the proposed invasion of Iraq through the prism of just war theories developed by philosophers and theologians over a period of centuries. Just war theory begins with the proposition that universal moral reasoning can and should be applied to the activity of war, thereby helping us determine together whether a particular use of force is just or unjust. One of its most distinguished contemporary exponents, Michael Walzer, puts it this way: First strikes can occasionally be justified before the moment of imminent attack, if we have reached the point of "sufficient threat." This concept has three dimensions: "a manifest intent to injure, a degree of active preparation that makes that intent a positive danger, and a general situation in which waiting, or doing anything other than fighting, greatly magnifies the risk." The potential injury, moreover, must be of the gravest possible nature: the loss of territorial integrity or political independence.

Saddam Hussein may well endanger the survival of his neighbors, but he poses no such risk to the United States. And he knows full well that complicity in a 9/11-style terrorist attack on the United States would justify, and swiftly evoke, a regime-ending response. During the Gulf War, we invoked this threat to deter him from using weapons of mass destruction against our troops, and there is no reason to believe that this strategy would be less effective today. Dictators have much more to lose than do stateless terrorists; that is why deterrence directed against them has a good chance of working.

In short, the U.S. cannot claim it undertakes a war of national defense. Iraq has not attacked the U.S. and, in spite of determined efforts by some in the administration, it is not yet clearly implicated in attacks on us by others. The just war tradition suggests that four criteria exist that can justify preemption, and each of them is a continuum of possibilities rather than an on/off switch. These criteria are (1) the severity of the threat; (2) the degree of probability of the threat; (3) the imminence of the threat; and (4) the cost of delay. But if one tests the proposed intervention in Iraq against these criteria, I suggest one finds the following: (1) the threat is high in the worst case—that is, the acquisition of transferable nuclear weapons; (2) the probability of the threat is contested—many experts have argued that a transfer of nuclear weapons by Saddam Hussein to terrorists is contrary not only to his past behavior but also to his clear and present interests; (3) no one has argued that the threat of attack is imminent; and (4) the cost of delay is low if it is measured in months as the U.S. tries to exhaust other options.

According to this four-part analysis, then, the case has not been 20 made that Iraq poses a sufficient threat to justify a preemptive strike. Further, in its segue from al Qaeda to Saddam Hussein, and from defense to preemption, the Bush administration has shifted its focus from stateless foes to state-based adversaries, and from terrorism in the precise sense to the possession of weapons of mass destruction. Each constitutes a threat. But they are not the same threat and do not warrant the same response. It serves no useful purpose to pretend that they are seamlessly connected, let alone one and the same.

The United Nations, international law, just war theory—it is not hard to imagine the impatience with which policy makers will greet arguments made on these bases. The first duty of every government, they will say, is to defend the lives and security of its citizens. The elimination of Saddam Hussein and, by extension, every regime that threatens to share weapons of mass destruction with anti-American terrorists, comports with this duty. To invoke international norms designed for a different world is to blind ourselves to the harsh necessities of international action in this new era of terrorism. Now that we have faced the facts about the axis of evil, it would be a dereliction of duty to shrink from their consequences for policy. Even if no other nation agrees, we have a duty to the American people to go it alone. The end justifies—indeed requires—the means.

These are powerful claims, not easily dismissed. But even if an invasion of Iraq succeeds in removing a threat here and now, it is not clear whether a policy of preemption would make us safer in the long run. Specifically, we must ask how the new norms of international action we employ would play out as nations around the world adopt them and shape them to their own purposes. (And they *will*; witness the instant appropriation of the United States' antiterrorism rhetoric by Russia and India, among others.) It is an illusion to believe that the United States can employ new norms of action while denying the rights of others to do so as well.

Also at stake are competing understandings of the international system and of our role within it. Some administration officials appear to believe that alliances and treaties are in the main counterproductive, constraining us from most effectively pursuing our national interest. Because the United States enjoys unprecedented military, economic and technological preeminence, we can do best by going it alone. The response to these unilateralists is that that there are many goals that we cannot hope to achieve without the cooperation of others. To pretend otherwise is to exchange short-term gains for long-term risks.

Even after we acknowledge the important distinctions between domestic and international politics, the fact remains: No push for international cooperation can succeed without international law and, therefore, without treaties that build the institutions for administering that law. This is one more reason, if one were needed, why the United States must resist the temptation to set itself apart from the system of international law. It will serve us poorly in the long run if we offer public justifications for an invasion of Iraq that we cannot square with established international legal norms.

BUT *IF* THERE BE WAR . . .

I have argued that war with Iraq *is* avoidable and *should be* avoided. 25 But if the U.S. does go to war, I contend that there are better and worse ways of prosecuting such a war. The U.S. must make a visible and credible effort to explore and exhaust all other *reasonable* options — not logically possible options — but all reasonable ones. The U.S. also must state a public rationale that focuses on enforcement within some viable international system. And most important of all, if regime change means the unconditional surrender of Iraq and abdication by Saddam Hussein of all reins of power, then the U.S. must commit itself to doing for Iraq what it did for Germany after World War II. The U.S. must commit itself to political, economic, and social reconstruction of Iraq such that a decent regime capable of standing on its own will be the likely outcome of U.S. efforts. If that means an occupation measured in decades rather than months, and it means the expenditures of tens of billions of dollars a year in order to sustain that — then we must commit ourselves to that here and now, because if what we really have in mind is the destruction and abandonment of a nation, that, in my judgment, is absolutely the worst outcome imaginable.

We are the most powerful nation on earth, but we must remember we are not invulnerable. I conclude by stressing that to safeguard our own security, we need the assistance of the allies whose doubts we scorn, and the protection of the international restraints against which we chafe. We must therefore resist the easy seduction of unilateral action. In the long run, our interests will best be served by an international system that is as law-like and collaborative as possible, given the reality that we live in a world of sovereign states.

Topics for Critical Thinking and Writing

1. What is the difference, if any, between preventive war and preemptive war?

2. What does Galston mean by a "Samson scenario" (para. 5), and to what is he alluding?

3. Galston equates "regime change" with "unconditional surrender" (para. 6). Yet *regime change* implies that even though the ruling regime changes, some things in the society will remain unchanged. What might such things be?

4. Prior to the invasion of Iraq by U.S. troops in the spring of 2003, some worried that such an invasion would look like colonial imperialism (para. 6). Have subsequent events proved this to be a reasonable worry or not?

5. Explain in an essay of 100 words the contrast Galston draws between "prudential" worries about invading Iraq and "questions of principle" (para. 11).

6. Why does Galston think that justifying a U.S.-led invasion of Iraq on the ground of "anticipatory self-defense" (paras. 15–16) is unreasonable?

7. Why does Galston think that using the concept of just war (para. 17) to defend a U.S. invasion of Iraq will fail?

8. Examine the concept of a just war under the criteria Galston proposes (para. 19) and under the criteria that G. E. M. Anscombe proposes (p. 133). Are there any important differences between the two sets of criteria? Explain in an essay of 250 words.

9. What is the difference, if any, between responding to a "sufficient threat" (para. 17) and acting out of "anticipatory self-defense" (para. 15)?

10. What do the "unilateralists" want as the main features of our foreign policy, according to Galston (paras. 23 and 26), and why does Galston oppose unilateralism?

ANDREW SULLIVAN

Andrew Sullivan, the conservative senior editor at The New Republic, *has written from a Roman Catholic perspective on a wide variety of issues—though on gay marriage he takes a liberal position. This essay originally appeared in the March 3, 2003, issue of* Time.

Yes, a War Would Be Moral

The strongest emotional appeal of the movement opposing a war against Saddam Hussein is the idea that peace should always be given the moral benefit of the doubt over war. War is always "failure," as French President Jacques Chirac has put it. Most religious leaders— from the Pope on down—have argued that peace is almost always morally preferable to war, and that this war—whatever its strategic or political justification—would be simply unjust. Indeed, many of these authorities have gone right up to the edge of saying that peace under any circumstance deserves not only a chance but an almost infinite number of chances before we resort to force of arms. But this ignores the fact that some wars are obviously moral. The war against Hitler killed millions—but it was just.

No sane person, after all, is opposed to peace as such. The question is, Peace at what risk? Peace on whose terms? Peace for how long? Looked at this way, war is not only sometimes a moral option—as theologians have long argued. Sometimes it's the only moral option we have. In some ways, this war is a textbook example of that. First off, we are not initiating a war. We are not the aggressor. We are still in a long process of defense. It's hard to remember now, but this war is not a new one. It's merely the continuation of one begun in 1990 by Saddam when he invaded Kuwait. Recall that when that war was won 12 years ago, no peace treaty was signed. Instead, a truce was arranged on a clear and unequivocal condition: that Saddam completely disarm himself of weapons of mass destruction. Since no one—not even the U.N. inspectors—believes that such disarmament has happened, the truce no longer holds.

The issue is therefore not whether to start a war. It is whether to end one by rewarding the aggressor and simply ignoring his infractions of the truce. Such a policy, inasmuch as it clearly rewards unprovoked violence, is immoral and imprudent. Have we exhausted every single alternative to war? Well, we have spent the past 12 years trying to find peaceful ways to get Saddam to live up to his promises. Waves of inspections, countless resolutions, occasional use of targeted force under the Clinton Administration, crippling economic sanctions and finally an attempt under U.N. Resolution 1441 to give Saddam a last, last chance to disarm. He was told nearly four months ago by a unanimous U.N. Security Council that he had to disarm immediately and completely. He still hasn't. I can't think of any recent war that tried so hard for so long to give peace a chance. This isn't so much a "rush to war," as some have bizarrely called it. It's an endless, painstaking, nail-biting crawl.

But can the war be legitimate without the sanction of the U.N.? Of course it can. Traditional just-war theory leaves the responsibility for grave decisions like these to the relevant authorities—the parties to the dispute and the countries planning to take action. We do not live under a world government. We live under a system in which nation states wield authorities in cooperation with one another. A coalition of the willing—a majority of the states in Europe, the U.S., Britain and other countries—easily qualifies as a legitimate source of authority for launching war.

Is there a credible alternative? Well, there is one obvious alternative   5 to war: continuation of economic sanctions on Iraq. But these sanctions have long been abused by Saddam to allow him to finance his weapons programs while leaving thousands of innocent Iraqis, including children, to starve or die for lack of good medical care. Is it moral to allow this intense suffering to continue indefinitely while we congratulate ourselves for giving "peace" a chance? Is it more moral to maintain that horror indefinitely rather than to try to win a quick war to depose Saddam, free the Iraqi people from tyranny and end the sanctions?

War is an awful thing. But it isn't the most awful thing. No one disputes the evil of Saddam's brutal police state. No one doubts that he would get and use weapons of mass destruction if he could. No one can guarantee that he would not help Islamist terrorists get exactly those weapons to use against the West or his own regional enemies. No one disputes that the Iraqi people would be better off under almost any other regime than the current one—or that vast numbers of them, including almost every Iraqi exile, endorse a war to remove the tyrant. If we can do so with a minimum of civilian casualties, if we do all we can to encourage democracy in the aftermath, then this war is not only vital for our national security. It is a moral imperative. And those who oppose it without offering any credible moral alternative are not merely wrong and misguided. They are helping to perpetuate a deep and intolerable injustice.

Topics for Critical Thinking and Writing

1. Consider Sullivan's argument in light of G. E. M. Anscombe's seven criteria for a just war (p. 133). Does he accept, dispute, or ignore these criteria? Discuss this issue in an essay of 250 words.

2. Do you think that Sullivan regards the war against Iraq as "a last resort" in the sense in which Peter Steinfels (p. 134) uses that term?

3. Sullivan says, "War is an awful thing. But it isn't the most awful thing" (para. 6). What things do you think he might believe are more awful? Do you agree?

9

Privacy:
What Are Its Limits?

AMITAI ETZIONI

Amitai Etzioni, university professor at George Washington University, previously taught sociology at Columbia University for twenty years. He is the editor of The Responsive Community *(1991) and the author of more than a dozen books, including* The Limits of Privacy *(1999). Etzioni served as senior advisor to the White House from 1979 to 1980 and as the president of the American Sociological Association from 1994 to 1995.*

Less Privacy Is Good for Us (and You)

Despite the fact that privacy is not so much as mentioned in the Constitution and that it was only shoehorned in some thirty-four years ago, it is viewed by most Americans as a profound, inalienable right.

The media is loaded with horror stories about the ways privacy is not so much nibbled away as it is stripped away by bosses who read your e-mail, neighbors who listen in on your cell phones, and E-Z passes that allow tollbooth operators to keep track of your movements. A typical headline decries the "End of Privacy" (Richard A. Spinello, in an issue of *America*, a Catholic weekly) or "The Death of Privacy" (Joshua Quittner, in *Time*).

It is time to pay attention to the other half of the equation that defines a good society: concerns for public health and safety that entail some rather justifiable diminution of privacy.

Take the HIV testing of infants. New medical data—for instance, evidence recently published by the prestigious *New England Journal of Medicine*—show that a significant proportion of children born to mothers who have HIV can ward off this horrible disease but only on two conditions: that their mothers not breast-feed them and that they immediately be given AZT. For this to happen, mothers must be informed that they have HIV. An estimated two-thirds of infected mothers are unaware. However, various civil libertarians and some gay activists vehemently oppose such disclosure on the grounds that when infants are tested for HIV, in effect one finds out if the mother is a carrier, and thus her privacy is violated. While New York State in 1996, after a very acrimonious debate, enacted a law that requires infant testing and disclosure of the findings to the mother, most other states have so far avoided dealing with this issue.

Congress passed the buck by asking the Institute of Medicine (IOM) to conduct a study of the matter. The IOM committee, dominated by politically correct people, just reported its recommendations. It suggested that all pregnant women be asked to consent to HIV testing as part of routine prenatal care. There is little wrong with such a recommendation other than it does not deal with many of the mothers who are drug addicts or otherwise live at society's margins. Many of these women do not show up for prenatal care, and they are particularly prone to HIV, according to a study published in the American Health Association's *Journal of School Health*. To save the lives of their children, they must be tested at delivery and treated even if this entails a violation of mothers' privacy.

Recently a suggestion to use driver's licenses to curb illegal immigration has sent the Coalition for Constitutional Liberties, a large group of libertarians, civil libertarians, and privacy advocates, into higher orbit than John Glenn ever traversed. The coalition wrote:

> This plan pushes us to the brink of tyranny, where citizens will not be allowed to travel, open bank accounts, obtain health care, get a job, or purchase firearms without first presenting the proper government papers.
>
> The authorizing section of the law . . . is reminiscent of the totalitarian dictates by Politburo members in the former Soviet Union, not the Congress of the United States of America.

Meanwhile, Wells Fargo is introducing a new device that allows a person to cash checks at its ATM machines because the machines recognize faces. Rapidly coming is a whole new industry of so-called biometrics that uses natural features such as voice, hand design, and eye pattern to recognize a person with the same extremely high reliability provided by the new DNA tests.

It's true that as biometrics catches on, it will practically strip Americans of anonymity, an important part of privacy. In the near future, a person who acquired a poor reputation in one part of the country will find it much more difficult to move to another part, change his name, and gain a whole fresh start. Biometrics see right through such assumed identities. One may hope that future communities will become more tolerant of such people, especially if they openly acknowledge the mistakes of their past and truly seek to lead a more prosocial life. But they will no longer be able to hide their pasts.

Above all, while biometrics clearly undermines privacy, the social benefits it promises are very substantial. Specifically, each year at least half a million criminals become fugitives, avoiding trial, incarceration, or serving their full sentences, often committing additional crimes while on the lam. People who fraudulently file for multiple income tax refunds using fake identities and multiple Social Security numbers cost the nation between $1 billion and $5 billion per year. Numerous divorced parents escape their financial obligations to their children by avoiding detection when they move or change jobs. (The sums owed to children are variously estimated as running between $18 billion to $23 billion a year.) Professional and amateur criminals, employing fraudulent identification documentation to make phony credit card purchases, cost credit card companies and retail businesses an indeterminate number of billions of dollars each year. The United States loses an estimated $18 billion a year to benefit fraud committed by illegal aliens using false IDs. A 1998 General Accounting Office report estimates identity fraud to cost $10 billion annually in entitlement programs alone.

People hired to work in child care centers, kindergartens, and 10 schools cannot be effectively screened to keep out child abusers and sex offenders, largely because when background checks are conducted, convicted criminals escape detection by using false identification and aliases. Biometrics would sharply curtail all these crimes, although far from wipe them out singlehandedly.

The courts have recognized that privacy must be weighed against considerations of public interest but have tended to privilege privacy and make claims for public health or safety clear several high hurdles. In recent years these barriers have been somewhat lowered as courts have become more concerned with public safety and health. Given that these often are matters of state law and that neither legislatures nor courts act in unison, the details are complex and far from all pointing in one direction. But, by and large, courts have allowed mandatory drug testing of those who directly have the lives of others in their hands, including pilots, train engineers, drivers of school buses, and air traffic controllers, even though such testing violates their privacy. In case after case, the courts have disregarded objections to such tests by civil libertarians who argue that such tests constitute "suspicionless" searches, grossly violate privacy, and—as the ACLU puts it—"condition Americans to a police state."

All this points to a need to recast privacy in our civic culture, public policies, and legal doctrines. We should cease to treat it as unmitigated good, a sacred right (the way Warren and Brandeis referred to in their famous article and many since) or one that courts automatically privilege.

Instead, privacy should rely squarely on the Fourth Amendment, the only one that has a balance built right into its text. It recognizes both searches that wantonly violate privacy ("unreasonable" ones) and those that enhance the common good to such an extent that they are justified, even if they intrude into one's privacy. Moreover, it provides a mechanism to sort out which searches are in the public interest and which violate privacy without sufficient cause, by introducing the concept of warrants issued by a "neutral magistrate" presented with "probable cause." Warrants also limit the invasion of privacy "by specification of the person to be seized, the place to be searched, and the evidence to be sought." The Fourth may have become the Constitutional Foundation of privacy a long time ago if it was not for the fact that *Roe v. Wade* is construed as a privacy right, and touching it provokes fierce opposition. The good news, though, is that even the advocates of choice in this area are now looking to base their position on some other legal grounds, especially the Fourteenth Amendment.

We might be ready to treat privacy for what it is: one very important right but not one that trumps most other considerations, especially of public safety and health.

Topics for Critical Thinking and Writing

1. Etzioni says that the right of privacy "was only shoehorned" into the Constitution "some thirty-four years ago" (para. 1)—that is, in 1965. Look up the U.S. Supreme Court case of *Griswold v. Connecticut,* and write a 250-word essay explaining how this right figured in that decision.

2. Who are the "politically correct people" to whom the author refers (para. 5)? What determines whether a policy or a practice is politically correct?

3. Etzioni obviously favors some invasions of privacy—but on what grounds? Where and why does he draw the line between justifiable and unjustifiable invasions of privacy? Write a 250-word essay answering that question.

4. The author takes for granted the value of privacy—that is, the value each of us attaches to keeping truths about ourselves from becoming public knowledge. Is the value of privacy only or mainly in its role as a means to other ends? Or is there something about privacy of intrinsic value in itself? Explain your own views in an essay of 500 words.

5. Who should bear the burden of persuasion: those who want to violate someone's privacy or those who do not want their privacy invaded, even for a good cause?

6. Ask your reference librarian to help you locate the "famous article" by Samuel Warren and Louis Brandeis (para. 12) that initially and influentially defended the right to privacy. What were the circumstances in which they defended this right, and what arguments did they offer to that purpose?

NADINE STROSSEN

Nadine Strossen, president of the American Civil Liberties Union since 1991 and professor of law at New York Law School, published the following essay on IntellectualCapital.com in 1998. It evoked an abundant response, from which we reprint (following her essay) a selection of e-mails, including a response by Strossen.

Everyone Is Watching You

In 1949, a young English author named Eric Blair opened his latest novel with a scene in an apartment building where on each landing, a poster with an "enormous face gazed from the wall. It was so contrived that the eyes follow you about when you move."

You probably know Blair better by his pen name—George Orwell. The book, of course, was *1984,* and the poster bore the now-clichéd caption, "Big Brother is watching you." But even Blair's vivid imagination did not accurately predict the future. Today, the more appropriate caption would be, "Everyone Is Watching You."

"Everyone" includes banks, automated teller machines, parking lots, shopping centers, stadiums, and convenience stores. Also government offices, schools, businesses, and workplaces. Whether cruising through a toll booth, or buying a gallon of milk, or strolling in the park, private citizens increasingly are forfeiting their privacy whenever they venture out of their homes—or even, for that matter, while we are at home.

Consider the chilling story of Barbara Katende, who recently told the *New York Times* that she had spotted a camera on a rooftop about 200 yards from her apartment. A rooftop she had seen, but not thought about, every time she stood before her sixth-floor window with the blinds open, lounging around in her underwear or in nothing at all. The camera monitors traffic. But it has a powerful zoom lens and can turn in any direction. A technician who controls traffic cameras from a Manhattan studio told the *Times*, "If you can see the Empire State Building, we can see you."

Cities all over the country, including our nation's capital, are in-   5 stalling cameras to record citizens' every coming-and-going on the streets, sidewalks, and parks. In Tempe, Arizona, officials struck a rotating camera—nicknamed "Sneaky Peak"—atop the municipal building. Why? Why not? "It's the biggest hit on our Web page," a Tempe official told the *Washington Post*.

Even more chillingly, new "face recognition" technology makes it possible to instantly identify individuals who are captured on video through complicated searches of facial images stored in government databases. As CNN commented, this is "a wonderful way for government to spy on its citizens who went to the antigovernment rally."

Why the mania for surveillance? Many claim that we need to trade privacy for safety. But even many law-enforcement officials believe, based on their actual experience, that video surveillance does not effectively detect or deter crime.

A number of cities that previously used video cameras—for example, Miami Beach, Florida, Newark, New Jersey, White Plains, New York, and Fredricksburg, Virginia—have abandoned them, concluding that they were not worth the expense. Surveillance cameras that had been mounted for 22 months in New York City's Times Square led to only 10 arrests before they were dismantled, prompting the *New York Times* to dub them, "one of the greatest flops along the Great White Way."

Even in Blair's United Kingdom, where video-surveillance cameras   10 are the most pervasive and powerful, the government itself has concluded that they have not demonstrably improved public safety. As noted by a report in the *Telegraph*, "A series of studies, including one by the Home Office itself, suggest that" video surveillance "has merely pushed crime into others areas or that its initial impact fades rapidly."

Just last September, the police department in Oakland, California, urged the city council to reject a video-surveillance project that the police department itself initially had recommended, but about which it had second thoughts—in terms of both privacy and efficiency. As Oakland's police chief told the city council, "There is no conclusive way to establish that the presence of video surveillance cameras resulted in the prevention or reduction of crime."

Moreover, responding to a detailed letter of concern from the American Civil Liberties Union, the Oakland city attorney concluded that a "method of surveillance may be no greater than that which can be achieved by the naked eye. [T]he California Supreme Court has held that 'precious liberties' . . . do not simply shrink as the government acquires new means of infringing upon them.'"

I applaud the California supreme court's ruling, which echoes the pro-privacy principles first declared by U.S. Supreme Court Justice Louis Brandeis in a famous 1928 dissent. Unfortunately, the Brandeisian view of privacy—which he defined as "the right to be let alone, the most comprehensive of rights"—remains a minority position among current judges. The Supreme Court, for example, has held that the Constitution only protects expectations of privacy that society considers "reasonable." This creates a downward spiral: The more government and others invade our privacy, the fewer "reasonable expectations" of privacy we have, which means that government and others may intrude even further into our privacy, etc., etc.

Given the foreshortened view of constitutional privacy that is currently enforced by our courts, we have to develop other avenues of legal protection—most importantly, federal and state statutes. Here, too, we now have only a patchwork of protection.

We must, therefore, take political and other direct action to remedy 15 the current lack of legal protection against the ubiquitous electronic "peeping Toms." Urge your community to oppose cameras in public places. If you notice a camera in an odd place, find out why it is there and what it is supposed to be recording. Tell businesses that record every transaction on camera that you will not be shopping there anymore. Before taking a job, let the employer know that you object to secret taping. And, most importantly, urge your elected officials to introduce laws limiting surveillance.

E-mail Responses to Nadine Strossen

Here we give a selection of e-mail responses that Strossen's article (p. 155) evoked. Typographical errors have not been corrected.

5/28/98

Dave

We have had the cop on the corner for over a hundred years, watching. He had a circle of vision of about 200 yards diameter. If the young lady in the story had lived in that 200 yard circle, she would have been observed by the government. What has changed is that the circle of vision is now about 2000 yards diameter. That and the cop on the corner of 50–100 years ago would have walked over to the womans house and ask her to act responsibly. All a camera can do is replace 100 cops on the corner with one. The garantee of the government is to be secure in our person and our homes, and it was done to provide for the pursuit of happiness. A camera can help to provide that security and that avenue of pursuit. The real question I have is this: is the decision of police departments to abandon video surveilance an outcome of Rodney King?

5/29/98

Merwyn R. Markel

There still are some situations where individuals may have no reasonable expectation of privacy. These include public areas and unshaded 6th floor windows in urban areas, where they may easily be seen, and may want to be seen, by others. Government has as much right to post cameras as to patrol police officers in the former former areas, and for some strange reason I can't get too concerned about people parading semi-nude and nude and then complaining when they are observed in the latter areas.

5/29/98

Merwyn R. Markel

By insisting government curtail its observation in public areas does ACLU really want to protect the right of persons to conduct criminal activities out of sight of law enforcement personnel?

5/29/98

Wilson Lee, San Diego, CA

Merwyn, I don't think the ACLU is arguing that criminals should be allowed to commit crimes, but rather that there are better ways—which don't infringe upon our privacy rights—to enforce laws against criminal behavior than using blanket video surveillance. Those cameras are pretty much equivalent to warrantless searches of innocent people.

5/30/98

Merwyn R. Markel

Wilson Lee: I don't think you adequately dealt with my first post. Cameras in public places don't "search" innocent people; they mearly record what is there for anyone present to see. I can't escape the conclusion that the ACLU just wants goverment to give criminals what the ACLU considers a sporting chance. Of course without using video cameras, government has and continues to unjustifiably if not illegally intrude on the privacy of its citizens. Some of the ways it does so include: (a) gathering information about them that they do not vluntarily disclose, whether or not it then discloses that information to unauthorized parties for political or other unauthorized purposes, and (b) obtaining information from citizens under the promise that it will not be used to their detrament, and then breaking that promise. Category (a) includes EEOC's requirement that all employers of 15 or more persons gather and report the percentages of "minorities" and females they employ, and the 500 FBI files on political opponents that just happened to be turned over to White House personnel. Example (b) includes a government agency asking an employment applicant to disclose his race and sex on a document it promises to use only for "statistical puropses" and then managing to associate it with the applicant anyway to deny him a job he was better qualified for than the successful applicant. Now why, do you suppose, Nadine and the ACLU don't mention such intrusions of our privacy?

5/30/98

Wilson Lee, San Diego, CA

Merwyn: Perhaps calling surveillance cameras warrantless searches may have been hyperbolic on my part. But I still think we have some reasonable expectations of privacy, even in public places. And I'm not sure a surveillance camera is equivalent in power to posting police officers. For one, a police officer wouldn't be able to search databases to instantly identify the faces of those being surveilled. The point is not that criminals will get away with more without surveillance. That may be true, to a certain extent. But having some crimes go unpunished costs our society less than giving the government more power. Even if you ignore the issue of constitutional rights, on purely pragmatic terms, surveillance fails the test because its efficacy in preventing crime is unproven, simlar to how capital punishment fails as a deterrent (but that's a debate for another article). I agree that we should be able to keep control over our private information. I can't speak for the ACLU, but I imagine that the lack of mention of such other privacy violations in the article does not imply that they don't take issue with them.

5/31/98

Merwyn R. Markel

Wilson Lee: You say "surveilence fails the test [of fairness or constitutionality, I assume] because its efficacy in preventing crime is unproven." I humbly suggest that we don't need "proof" to justify doing what seems reasonable, even when its constutionality is challenged. I'd like to see a judicial decision that says otherwise. It is reasonable to believe that many if not all criminals would not commit their crimes if they thought they were being observed doing so by law enforcement officers or recorded doing so by law enforcement cameras. It is also resonable to believe that such surveilence will assist government law enforcement personnel to detect and apprehend criminals, which is still a prime responsibility of government. The "proof" Nadine mentions is, assumining her claims about it are correct, merely "proof" that in specific past situations electronic surveilence was found—correctly or incorrectly—to deter crime less than certain government officials thought justified by the cost. That says nothing about the efficacy of other past or future surveilence programs or situations. The efficacy of science to prove something today and the opposite tomorrow hardly needs proof. For similar reasons, I welcome future discussions about capital punishment.

6/1/98
Nadine Strossen

A couple of you . . . make a point that is often raised in opposition to pro-privacy arguments, namely: If you've got nothing to hide, why should you care about privacy? This is a variation on the theme that only criminals would benefit from increasing privacy protection. Nothing could be further from the truth. I pride myself on being a law-abiding person, and on holding myself to high moral standards even in arenas where no one can observe my behavior. In other words, it is extremely important to me that I conduct myself consistent with my own moral standards especially when I am being judged only by my own conscience, rather than for the benefit of some outside observer/evaluator. . . . So, when I want to stop someone from observing my behavior, it's not because I believe my behavior is illegal or immoral. Rather, it's because my behavior is my private business—and that of the others with whom I affirmatively choose to share it. Think of this analogy: I'm not ashamed of my nude body, but that doesn't mean I want government or private Peeping Toms to look at it! In short, I—and every other law-abiding citizen—has something very important to hide: our privacy.

Topics for Critical Thinking and Writing

1. Do you consider surveillance cameras in "banks, automated teller machines, parking lots, shopping centers, stadiums, and convenience stores" (para. 3) an unreasonable invasion of your privacy? Explain.

2. Strossen refers to "a famous 1928 dissent" by Justice Brandeis (para. 13). The case is *Olmstead v. United States*. With the help of your reference librarian, locate a copy of this case, and read Brandeis's dissent. Then summarize it in an essay of 250 words.

3. The U.S. Supreme Court has held, Strossen tells us, "that the Constitution only protects expectations of privacy that society considers 'reasonable'" (para. 13). Look back at paragraph 4, in which Strossen tells us that Barbara Katende sometimes stood nude before her sixth-floor window. Would you say that Katende had a "reasonable" expectation of privacy? Why, or why not?

4. "Dave" offers a comparison with "50–100 years ago." How convincing do you find this argument? Why?

5. "Dave" also mentions Rodney King. Who is he, and why is it apt to mention him in the context?

6. Two of the letter writers, "Dave" and "Merwyn R. Markel" draw an analogy between police observation and camera observation. Do you think the analogy is a good one, or not? Explain your view in an essay of 250 words.

7. Do you agree with "Wilson Lee" (5/29/98) that surveillance "cameras are pretty much equivalent to warrantless searches of innocent people"? In your response, consider also the later postings that we print.

8. "Merwyn R. Markel" ends his posting of 5/30/98 with a question. What do you think his own answer to the question would be?

9. "Wilson Lee" (5/30/98) says that "having some crimes go unpunished costs our society less than giving the government more power." How would you support or refute this assertion?

10. Write a response to Nadine Strossen's posting of 6/1/98 (but don't send it). Consider especially the analogy that she offers.

11. Strossen recommends that you "tell businesses that record every transaction on camera that you will not be shopping there anymore" (para. 15). Is this reasonable advice? Are you prepared to follow it? Why, or why not?

JUDITH WAGNER DECEW

Judith Wagner DeCew is a professor of philosophy and associate dean at Clark University, Worcester, Massachusetts. She has served on the faculty at the Massachusetts Institute of Technology and has been a research fellow at the Bunting Institute and also at Harvard Law School. Her book In Pursuit of Privacy: Law, Ethics, and the Rise of Technology *(1997), from which this selection is drawn, was nominated for the Herbert Jacob Book Prize of the Law and Society Association.*

The Feminist Critique of Privacy

... There has been extensive debate among philosophers and legal theorists about what privacy means, whether and how it can be defined, and the scope of protection it can and should afford. Reactions to recent Supreme Court confirmation hearings have made it clear that many in the public and in Congress are unwilling to give up the privacy protection they currently enjoy. They view privacy, as I do, as a valuable shield for protecting a sphere within which we can act free of scrutiny and intrusion by others.

In contrast, many feminists have called attention to the "darker side of privacy," citing its potential to shield domination, repression, degradation, and physical harm to women and others without power. It might be thought that this feminist critique of privacy is powerful enough to defeat my thesis that we can and must view privacy as a meaningful concept with significant value for a wide range of claims associated with tort, Fourth Amendment, and other constitutional law. I argue ... , to the contrary, that we may support many concerns raised by the feminist critique of privacy without abandoning the concept of privacy and the significant benefits a strong right of privacy affords.

Perhaps the most prominent version of this critique of privacy is articulated by Catharine MacKinnon. She begins by observing that

> the idea of privacy embodies a tension between precluding public exposure or governmental intrusion on the one hand, and autonomy in the sense of protecting personal self-action on the other. This is a tension, not just two facets of one right. The liberal state resolves this tension by identifying the threshold of the state at its permissible extent of penetration into a domain that is considered free by definition: the private sphere. By this move the state secures "an inviolable personality" by ensuring "autonomy of control over the intimacies of personal identity."[1] The state does this by centering its self-restraint on body and home, especially bedroom. By staying out of marriage and the family—essentially meaning sexuality, that is, heterosexuality—from contraception through pornography to the abortion decision, the law of privacy proposes to guarantee individual bodily integrity, personal exercise of moral intelligence, and freedom of intimacy. But have women's rights to access to those values been guaranteed? The law of privacy instead translates traditional liberal values into the

The full text has been edited, and the endnotes have accordingly been renumbered. [—Ed.]

rhetoric of individual rights as a means of subordinating those rights to specific social imperatives.[2]

MacKinnon is of course correct that privacy has developed in law to protect both (i) an "individual interest in avoiding disclosure of personal matters," as well as limiting governmental intrusion on and regulation of these matters, and (ii) an "interest in independence in making certain kinds of important decisions" regarding body, home, and lifestyle.[3] Many legal theorists have taken these to be clearly separable interests, whereas I have argued [elsewhere] that there are deeper similarities and connections between the two than is usually acknowledged.[4] Following most legal theorists, MacKinnon treats protection from public exposure and governmental intrusion as separate from and in tension with protection of autonomous decision making. Perhaps her reason is that she finds these goals incompatible: safeguarding (i) precludes guaranteeing (ii).

A serious difficulty, MacKinnon believes, is that the state merges these two interests by drawing the line where state intrusion is no longer justified at those matters concerning body, home, and the heterosexual family, asserting that in this way it is protecting personal autonomy. But, MacKinnon continues, the move to ensure autonomy in intimate relations with respect to the body, home, and family relations does nothing to help women, since the values of individual bodily integrity, exercise of moral intelligence, and freedom of intimacy are not guaranteed to women. The fundamental flaw, according to MacKinnon, is that underlying privacy protection in the law is a liberal ideal of the private: as long as the public does not interfere, autonomous individuals interact freely and equally. But this presumes that women are, like men, free and equal, an assumption MacKinnon finds patently false. When the private is defined as personal, intimate, autonomous, and individual, it is on her view defined by reference to characteristics most feminists believe women do not possess. The law of privacy thus presumes a liberal conception of rights with false assumptions about women. Moreover, privacy is just one instance where our legal system fails to recognize and take into account the preexisting oppression and inequality of women. For MacKinnon, privacy represents yet another domain where women are deprived of power and are deprived of recourse under the law, all on the suspect theory that "the government best promotes freedom when it stays out of existing social relationships."[5]

MacKinnon continues her argument in even stronger language: 5

For women the measure of the intimacy has been the measure of the oppression. This is why feminism has had to explode the private. This is why feminism has seen the personal as the political. The private is public for those for whom the personal is political. In this sense, for women there is no private, either normatively or empirically. Feminism confronts the fact that women have no privacy to lose or to guarantee. Women are not inviolable. Women's sexuality is not only violable, it is—hence, women are—seen in and as their violation. To confront the fact that women have no privacy is to confront the intimate degradation of women as the public order. The doctrinal choice of privacy in the abortion context thus reaffirms and reinforces what the feminist critique of sexuality criticizes: the public/private split.[6]

MacKinnon appears to be making two distinct but related claims here. The first is that women have no privacy, and hence protecting privacy provides no benefit at all for women. Privacy protection may even be a positive detriment to women, giving men the legal right to treat their wives and partners (and children) unequally or even brutally.[7] The second claim is that feminism has demonstrated the importance of criticizing the split between public and private domains, and thus "has had to explode the private." Let us consider each in turn.

Why is it that women have no privacy to lose or guarantee? MacKinnon's answer appears to be that because women are violable and violated, they have no zone of autonomy within which to control their destinies. In particular, in the realm of sexuality, often viewed as a paradigmatic example of the private, women do not have control. Men can and often do maintain their power over women in such intimate circumstances. Although sexual intimacy, and activities within the home and family, may be private in the sense of being withheld from public view and shielded from governmental intrusion, they are not private in the sense of being areas where women have control over their decision making.

This argument is easily refuted. Note first that I have already shown, contrary to MacKinnon, that although privacy law does in part protect one's ability to make intimate and personal choices, it does not follow that privacy is merely equivalent to autonomy or control over decision making. Privacy and autonomy are distinct concepts and can and should be differentiated.[8] Second, even if women do in fact often lose control in the domain of intimate sexual relations, it does not follow that they have no interest in the value of protecting a zone for autonomous decision making. MacKinnon often repeats her claim that women have no privacy that can be taken away. That women are in fact violated in private contexts, however, implies nothing about the worth of protecting a zone within which they can have the power to limit intrusions and violations. In short, descriptive facts about actual limitations on privacy fail to imply anything about the normative value of seeking privacy protection for women.

MacKinnon's second point in this passage underscores the importance of rejecting the public/private split. The public/private distinction has captured the imagination of many feminist scholars. In fact a substantial portion of feminist theory and political struggle over the past two hundred years has been concerned with deconstructing the traditional notion, going back as far as Aristotle, of a public (male) political realm and a private (female) domestic realm.[9] Some of the most influential work in feminist political theory, philosophy, and legal theory takes this paradigm as its starting point in analyzing women's oppression. Carole Pateman goes so far as to claim that the public/private dichotomy "is, ultimately, what the feminist movement is about."[10] Yet despite this emphasis on the public/private distinction, it is difficult to clarify what the feminist critique of it entails. Feminist scholars such as Ruth Gavison and Pateman have made clear that there is no single or privileged version.[11] There are, to the contrary, a multiplicity of interwoven ways of understanding attacks on the public/private dichotomy. As regards MacKinnon in particular, it is not clear what she means by the need to "explode" the private. She appears to believe there is no distinction between public and private because there is no private realm for women at all. Does she also mean to say that there *should* be no public/private distinction? . . .

I believe we can agree with MacKinnon that whenever distinguishing public and private realms renders the domestic arena unsuitable for scrutiny, then the distinction works to the detriment of women. But what is the alternative? If the line between public and private is sometimes indeterminate, does it follow that nothing is or should be private? If there is no distinction between public and private, is everything public? Should every part of our lives be open to public appraisal? Indeed, on one interpretation of MacKinnon's view that we must "explode" the public/private distinction and that "the private is public," we must totally reject any realm of the private and apparently must conclude that everything is public. Thus rejection of the dichotomy is accomplished by collapsing the private into the public. Others have viewed this as a plausible reading of the feminist critique of privacy. For example, in a recent discussion of the public and private, Jean Bethke Elshtain describes one form of the feminist critique:

> In its give-no-quarter form in radical feminist argument, any distinction between the personal and the political was disdained. Note that the claim was not that the personal and political are interrelated in ways previously hidden by male-dominated political ideology and

practice, or that the personal and political might be analogous to each other along certain axes of power and privilege. Rather, there was a collapse of one into the other: The personal *is* political. Nothing personal was exempt from political definition, direction, and manipulation—not sexual intimacy, not love, not parenting. The total collapse of public and private as central distinctions in an enduring democratic drama followed, at least in theory. The private sphere fell under a thoroughgoing politicized definition. Everything was grist for a voracious publicity mill; nothing was exempt, there was nowhere to hide.[12]

A similar understanding of the feminist critique of privacy is echoed by Ruth Gavison, who observes, "Usually, when the dichotomy between public and private is challenged, the argument is that all is (or should be) public." Yet Gavison quickly notes that feminists often equivocate when confronted with the implications of this rejection of the public/private split:

> But once we look at particular questions, it is rare to find feminists who argue consistently either that everything should be regulated by the state, or that the family and all other forms of intimate relationships should disappear in favor of public communities that . . . police the different ways in which members interact. When pushed, feminists explicitly deny this is their ideal. . . . [I]t is hard to specify even one context or dimension of the distinction in which the claim is that the whole category of the private is useless.[13]

Thus, even if women are often vulnerable and exploited in the private, domestic sphere, we may ask whether it follows that women have *no* interest in values of accessibility privacy as freedom from intrusion and expressive privacy as control over certain intimate and personal decisions and relationships. Are there *no* contexts in which women wish to keep the state out of their lives? MacKinnon often writes as if she would respond affirmatively, especially in her argument against privacy protection and in favor of equality analysis in feminist jurisprudence.[14] Nevertheless, I suspect the answer must be no, even for MacKinnon. Anita Allen has suggested that an analogy between privacy and liberty is helpful here. Just as the harm that results from the exercise of individual liberty does not lead to the rejection of liberty, similarly there is inadequate reason to reject privacy completely based on harm done in private.[15]

MacKinnon believes that the public/private distinction perpetuates the subjection of women in the domestic sphere, encouraging a policy of nonintervention by the state. She seems then to be making a further point as well: that male power over women is affirmatively embodied in privacy law. In the words of Susan Moller Okin, "The protection of the privacy of a domestic sphere in which inequality exists is the protection of the right of the strong to exploit and abuse the weak."[16] Batterers and child molesters rely on the shroud of secrecy that surrounds abuse to maintain their power. Thus many have worked to make the state more responsive to the abuse of women by rejecting legal privacy protection for the family. MacKinnon concludes,

> The right of privacy is a right of men "to be let alone" to oppress women one at a time. It embodies and reflects the private sphere's existing definition of womanhood. This instance of liberalism—applied to women as if they were persons, gender neutral—reinforces the division between public and private which is not gender neutral. It is an ideological division that lies about women's shared experience. . . . It polices the division between public and private, a very material division that keeps the private beyond public redress and depoliticizes women's subjection within it.[17]

The insights of this critique of privacy underscore how important it is to take care when viewing public and private categories differently. Feminists have correctly identified the ways in which the distinction can be dangerous if it is used to devalue the work of women in domestic roles, to silence them politically by categorizing them as having no public voice or value, and to allow the continuation of abuse and degradation under the cover of a private sphere unavailable for public censure. Thus MacKinnon and other feminists are right to urge that the distinction not be used to justify differential social and legal treatment of women. The "privacy" of the family, for example, should not be invoked to mask exploitation and battering of family members.

On one hand, it seems clear that defenders of privacy have too often ignored the role of *individual* male power, and sexual and physical abuse, in domestic contexts. On the other hand, focus on domestic violence ignores *state-sponsored* expressions of control over women. Consider, for example, intrusions such as government sterilization programs and the interventions involved in state control over welfare programs, including the withdrawal of benefits from women upon the birth of additional children.[18]

Consequently, this first interpretation of MacKinnon's sweeping critique may ultimately lead to a view stronger than she means to endorse. Rejecting the public/private distinction in this way obscures the difference between individual and institutional expressions of (male) power.

On this reading, MacKinnon highlights the very real existence of domination by individual men over women, then argues for the rejection of privacy, and thereby implies everything should remain public. In doing so, she fails to address the need to differentiate between justified and unjustified uses of state power over individuals.[19] Governmental regulation might refer to reasonable laws regarding family matters, such as giving women the right to charge husbands with rape. Or it might mean that the state will reveal and regulate all the embarrassing details. There is, moreover, an important difference between a government that protects a woman's decision to charge her husband with rape and one that forces her to do so. Evaluating the justifiability of state intervention requires specifying what kind of regulation is at issue.[20] We may decry violations of women by individual men, and may well defend the role of the state to intervene—reasonably, firmly, and effectively—given evidence of domestic violence. Exploitation and abuse *should* be matters of public concern. But that need not imply that there is never value in making a distinction between public and private. We need not be committed to the view that there should be *no* limitations on state interference in individual, personal, and intimate affairs. We need not be pushed to agree that there should be *no* private realm within which women can live their lives free from state policing and intrusion.

In short, on this first interpretation of her critique of privacy, MacKinnon correctly emphasizes the need to limit individual violations and intrusions on women by men, but at the same time she underemphasizes the need to limit intrusions by the state.

Some may believe, however, that this first interpretation of MacKinnon's argument is unsympathetic and actually misses a central point of the feminist critique of privacy. Other readers of MacKinnon's critique dispute the view that rejecting the public/private split merely collapses one side of the dichotomy onto the other.[21] On this alternative interpretation, that is neither the feminist point nor an implication of the feminist position. To the contrary, feminists want to do away with the whole public/private dichotomy *as it has been understood in the past.* Thus feminists stress that they do not intend to have the state insinuating itself into the most intimate parts of people's lives. They are instead emphasizing that the state must stop ignoring the unbelievable abuses that have been protected in the name of privacy; this is, they believe, a position that is not captured by the public/private distinction as it has been known and used. According to this account, whether or not it is successfully captured by MacKinnon, feminists are talking about a position that bypasses the public/private distinction in a different way. . . .

Carole Pateman reiterates the feminist challenge to the separation and opposition between public and private spheres as central categories of political liberalism, where domestic family life is paradigmatically private. Pateman believes that "the dichotomy between the private and the public obscures the subjection of women to men within an apparently universal, egalitarian and individualist order.... The essential feminist argument is that the doctrine of 'separate but equal,' and the ostensible individualism and egalitarianism of liberal theory, obscure the patriarchal reality of a social structure of inequality and the domination of women by men."[22] But she emphasizes that feminists reject the claim that a public/private dichotomy is inevitable:

> They [feminists] argue that a proper understanding of liberal social life is possible only when it is accepted that the two spheres, the domestic (private) and civil society (public) held to be separate and opposed, are inextricably interrelated; they are the two sides of the single coin of liberal-patriarchalism.... [Furthermore,] feminist critiques insist that an alternative to the liberal conception must also encompass the relationship between public and domestic life.[23]

What is needed, on Pateman's view, is a feminist theoretical perspective that takes account of social relationships between men and women within the context of interpretations of both the public and the private. Work by political theorists such as John Stuart Mill,[24] as well as practical experience from the feminist movement, has shown that women's place in the private sphere cannot simply be augmented by extending to women a role in the public sphere. The spheres are not additive but integrally related. As Pateman notes, "These feminist critiques of the dichotomy between private and public stress that the categories refer to two *interrelated* dimensions of the structure of liberal-patriarchalism; they do not necessarily suggest that no distinction can or should be drawn between the personal and political aspects of social life" (emphasis mine).[25] In sum, Pateman views the feminist critique of privacy as stressing rejection of the dichotomy *as it has been understood,* but she concludes that the "separate" worlds of private and public life are closely interrelated and that both are necessary dimensions of a future, democratic feminist social order. An adequate account, after acknowledging that public and private are not necessarily in harmony, will develop a social theory in which these categories are distinct but interrelated, rather than totally separate or opposed.

Pateman's approach also highlights another dimension of feminist perspectives on the public/private split. The well-known slogan "the personal is political" is often taken to be one of feminism's most significant lessons. Whom one sleeps with, whether one has an abortion, whether one seeks reproduction-assisting technologies, whether one is a religious fundamentalist, and so on—all these choices have political implications. Moreover, personal circumstances and family life are regulated and structured by public factors, including legislation concerning rape and sexuality, marriage and divorce, and policies on child care and welfare. What feminists are trying to articulate in this strand of argument is that the public/private dichotomy is misleading in critical ways because it fails to reflect the interconnections between public and private. . . .

Clearly the feminist critique of privacy is multifaceted, and there is no question that . . . Pateman acknowledge[s] the difficulties of the public/private dichotomy and the damaging effects of accepting it as it has been defended in the past. Both, however, appear to agree that absent domination and abuse, there may be great value for women as well as men in preserving a sanctuary where we can live free from scrutiny and the pressure to conform, free to express our identities through relationships and choices about our bodies and lifestyles, without government intrusion. Nevertheless, this clearly leads to a challenge for . . . Pateman, as well as other feminists like Gavison, Allen, Elshtain, and myself, who are unwilling to jettison privacy completely. Given the lingering influence, in our culture and law, of the separate spheres analysis—that women belong in the home and men in public positions—it may take much time and effort to address the difficulties of preserving the two spheres in some form while extricating them from their gendered past and gendered connotations.[26] Perhaps MacKinnon believes that these difficulties are insurmountable.

It is now clear, however, that the feminist critique of privacy, on [20] either of the interpretations I have examined, does not undermine my defense of a broad conception of privacy. Exploding the public/private distinction by collapsing it to leave all public is an unacceptable and even dangerous alternative, granting excessive power to the state. While we may often find it difficult to determine when official intervention is warranted, defending privacy as a shield to ward off unjustified individual and institutional intrusions in our personal lives remains an essential component of both our moral and legal systems if we are to preserve both peace of mind and bodily integrity. Alternatively, recognizing the insidious effects of the dichotomy, including the continued subordination of women, and rejecting the distinction as it has been understood in the past are compatible with retaining a meaningful concept of privacy in a theory of a new social order as envisioned by such feminists as . . . Pateman.

NOTES

1. Tom Gerety, "Redefining Privacy," 12 *Harvard Civil Rights–Civil Liberties Law Review* 233, 236 (1977).

2. Catharine MacKinnon, *Toward a Feminist Theory of the State* (Cambridge: Harvard University Press, 1989), 187. In this passage, she cites Kenneth I. Karst, "The Freedom of Intimate Association," 89 *Yale Law Journal* 624 (1980); Tom Grey, "Eros, Civilization, and the Burger Court," 43 *Law and Contemporary Problems* 83 (1980); and others.
3. Whalen v. Roe, 429 U.S. 589, 599, 600 (1977).
4. For example, see Louis Henkin, "Privacy and Autonomy," 74 *Columbia Law Review* 1410 (1974), and Hyman Gross, "The Concept of Privacy," 42 *New York Law Review* 34 (1967), on the separation of the interests. See also Judith Wagner DeCew, "The Scope of Privacy in Law and Ethics," *Law and Philosophy* 5 (1986), 145–173, on connections between them. Others who take this latter view include Ferdinand Schoeman, *Privacy and Social Freedom* (Cambridge: Cambridge University Press, 1992), and Julie Inness, *Privacy, Intimacy, and Isolation* (Oxford: Oxford University Press, 1992).
5. MacKinnon, *Toward a Feminist Theory of the State*, 164–165.
6. Ibid., 191.
7. The old rape shield laws, for example, made it impossible for women to claim their husbands had raped them.
8. See . . . William Parent, "Privacy, Morality, and the Law," *Philosophy and Public Affairs* 12 (1983), 269–288, for examples and discussion of this point.
9. See Carole Pateman, "Feminist Critiques of the Public/Private Dichotomy," in *The Disorder of Women: Democracy, Feminism, and Political Theory* (Stanford: Stanford University Press, 1989), 127, for example, on enfranchising women.
10. Ibid., 118. Also quoted in Susan Moller Okin, *Justice, Gender, and the Family* (New York: Basic Books, 1989), 111.
11. See Ruth Gavison, "Feminism and the Public/Private Distinction," 45 *Stanford Law Review* 1 (1992). She reviews and carefully assesses many different interpretations of the feminist critique of the public/private distinction.
12. Jean Bethke Elshtain, *Democracy on Trial* (New York: Basic Books, 1995), 43.
13. Gavison, "Feminism and the Public/Private Distinction," 28, 28–29.
14. Another who seems to endorse this view is Supreme Court Justice Ruth Bader Ginsberg, "Some Thoughts on Autonomy and Equality in Relation to *Roe v. Wade*," 63 *North Carolina Law Review* 375 (1985). See also Kenneth L. Karst, "Foreword: Equal Citizenship under the Fourteenth Amendment," 91 *Harvard Law Review* 1 (1977). For replies to this approach, see Gavison, "Feminism and the Public/Private Distinction," 31–35.
15. Anita Allen, *Uneasy Access: Privacy for Women in a Free Society* (Totowa, N.J.: Rowman and Littlefield, 1988), 40. But see my review of her book in *Philosophical Review* 101 (1992), 709–711, describing why this reply is incomplete.

16. Okin, *Justice, Gender, and the Family*, 174. See also MacKinnon, *Toward a Feminist Theory of the State*, 244.

17. MacKinnon, *Toward a Feminist Theory of the State*, 194.

18. See, for example, Frances Olsen, "The Myth of State Intervention in the Family," 18 *University of Michigan Journal of Law Reform* 835 (1985), for an explanation of the government's pervasive involvement in black women's lives. I am grateful to Barbara Schulman for stressing this distinction.

19. Jean Bethke Elshtain's critique of this feminist view is related to my own yet differs in that it is based on political considerations. Calling attention to a serious problem that puts democracy on trial, she writes, "if there are no distinctions between public and private, personal and political, it follows that there can be no differentiated activity or set of institutions that are genuinely political, the purview of citizens and the bases of order, legitimacy, and purpose in a democratic community" (*Democracy on Trial*, 44).

20. See the proceedings of Changing Perspectives of the Family, a symposium held April 16, 1994, at the Constitutional Law Resource Center at Drake University, Des Moines, Iowa, for a contemporary discussion of the implications of changing perspectives of the family in both constitutional law and family law and for a discussion of the degree to which the state may organize and control intimate relationships.

21. I am indebted to Joan Callahan for emphasizing the importance of this interpretation.

22. Pateman, "Feminist Critiques," 120.

23. Ibid., 121–122, 123.

24. John Stuart Mill, *The Subjection of Women* (1869; reprint, Indianapolis: Hackett, 1988).

25. Pateman, "Feminist Critiques," 133.

26. I owe this point to Diana Meyers. She has suggested that the debate over privacy may have an important pragmatic dimension as well. Those who believe the battery of women is so pervasive, and the need to expose it to stop the abuse so urgent, that it almost always compromises women's autonomy (whether women acknowledge that or not) will be drawn to MacKinnon's full-blown critique of privacy. Those who believe domestic violence, despite its severity, can be addressed without giving up the value of privacy will be attracted to a more moderate approach.

Topics for Critical Thinking and Writing

1. In the second paragraph, DeCew refers to "claims [of privacy] associated with tort [and] Fourth Amendment" issues. What do you think these claims might be?

2. The author tells us that "Privacy and autonomy are distinct concepts" (para. 7). How does she distinguish them? Write a 500-word essay on the theme "Privacy versus Autonomy."

3. What do you think MacKinnon means when she says that feminism "has had to explode the private" (para. 5)? On what basis does she claim that "women have no privacy to lose or guarantee" (para. 6)? Do you agree? Explain.

4. Explain what DeCew means by the "public/private split" (para. 8). Does she accept or reject this "split"?

5. The author mentions the slogan "the personal is political" (para. 18). Explain in a sentence or two what you think this slogan means.

10

Sexual Harassment: Is There Any Doubt about What It Is?

TUFTS UNIVERSITY

Many colleges and universities have drawn up statements of policy concerning sexual harassment. The following statement is fairly typical in that it seeks to define sexual harassment, to suggest ways of stopping it (these range from informal discussion to a formal grievance procedure), and to indicate resources that can provide help.

What Is Sexual Harassment?

Sexual harassment is a form of sex discrimination and violates federal and state law and university policy. Tufts University, its agents, supervisory employees, employees, and students shall be held liable for their acts of sexual harassment and are subject to appropriate university disciplinary action and personal liability. Sexual harassment is prohibited at Tufts University.

Sexual harassment, whether between people of different sexes or the same sex, is defined to include but is not limited to, unwanted sexual advances, unwelcome requests for sexual favors, and other behavior of a sexual nature when:

1. submission to such conduct is made either explicitly or implicitly a term and condition of an individual's employment or academic status; or

2. submission to, or rejection of, such conduct by an individual is used as a basis for employment or academic decisions affecting him or her; or

3. such conduct, whether verbal or physical, has the purpose or effect of unreasonably interfering with the individual's work or academic performance or of creating an intimidating, hostile, or offensive environment in which to work or to learn.

Any member of the Tufts community who feels that he or she has been sexually harassed should feel free to use the procedure described in this pamphlet without threat of intimidation, retaliation, or harassment.

WHO ARE THE PARTICIPANTS?

Sexual harassment can involve

- instructor and instructor
- professor and student
- teaching assistant and student
- supervisor and employee
- student and student
- staff member and student
- other relationships among colleagues, peers, and co-workers

The following behavior may constitute sexual harassment: 5

- lewd remarks, whistles, or personal reference to one's anatomy
- unwanted physical contact such as patting, pinching, or constant brushing against a person's body
- subtle or overt pressure for sexual favors
- persistent and offensive sexual jokes and comments
- display of pictures of a sexual nature
- persistent and unwanted requests for dates
- e-mail messages of an offensive sexual nature

The consequences to a person responsible for sexual harassment can include

- termination
- demotion

- denial of a promotion
- suspension
- letter of reprimand

It is unlawful to retaliate against an employee or student for filing a complaint of sexual harassment or for cooperating in an investigation of a complaint of sexual harassment.

HOW TO STOP SEXUAL HARASSMENT

If you are experiencing some form of sexual harassment, you need to know that Tufts provides several options to assist you. Since each situation is as distinct as the persons involved, the preferences of the complainant—including the need for confidentiality—will determine which option is most appropriate. Both informal and formal resolution options are available at Tufts. The only alternative we do not recommend is that you do nothing.

If you believe you are being or have been sexually harassed, you should consider taking the following steps immediately:

1. You may want to keep track of dates, places, times, witnesses, and the nature of the harassment. Save any letters, cards, or notes in a safe place.
2. Seek the advice of or report the incident to any of the individuals listed as sexual harassment resource persons. You may also seek the assistance of the Counseling Center, campus chaplains, Health Services psychiatrist, or Health Services counselor.

You may also consider using the following strategies:

1. Say "no" to your harasser. Say it firmly without smiling and apologizing.
2. Tell your harasser, in writing, that you object to this behavior. Describe the specific behaviors which are offensive or threatening, and keep a copy.
3. Utilize the Tufts University sexual harassment grievance procedure.

WHERE TO FIND HELP

On each campus there are university sexual harassment resource persons who are available to provide informal and formal resolution options.

Efforts will be made to protect your confidentiality. Each, however, has a duty to assure resolution and report the incident to the Office of Equal Opportunity, which may limit the ability to maintain confidentiality. The Tufts University sexual harassment resource persons are: [At this point the brochure gives a list of names of Tufts deans and organizations (for instance, Asian American Center; Health Education Program; Lesbian, Gay, Bisexual Resource Center) as well as outside organizations (for instance, Equal Employment Opportunity Commission), with telephone numbers.]

RESOLUTION BY INFORMAL DISCUSSION

Any student or employee who believes that he/she has been sexually harassed should first attempt to resolve the problem through discussion with the other party. In cases in which discussing the problem with that person presents particular stress or difficulties, the complainant has the right to consult on an informal basis with a supervisor, an administrator, the Office of Equal Opportunity, Human Resources, or a sexual harassment resource person. Efforts will be made to protect your confidentiality. The complainant may bring an associate to that meeting if desired. If there has been no resolution within a reasonable period of time, the sexual harassment grievance procedure shall then be instituted if desired.

SEXUAL HARASSMENT GRIEVANCE PROCEDURE

If the problem has not been resolved to the satisfaction of the complainant through informal discussion, she/he has the right to file a grievance in accordance with the following procedure.

A. Where to File the Grievance?

If the person alleged to be responsible for the harassment is:

1. a staff member or an administrator — file with the vice president for Human Resources or campus Human Resources manager;
2. a faculty member — file with the appropriate dean of college/school or provost;
3. a student — file with the appropriate dean of students or dean of the college/school.

B. What Should Be Filed?

The grievance should be in writing and should summarize the 15 harassment complained of, the person alleged to be responsible, and the resolution sought.

C. When Should the Grievance Be Filed?

The grievance should normally be filed within ninety (90) days of the incident(s) giving rise to the complaint. The university may extend this period if it finds that there are extenuating circumstances.

D. How Will the Grievance Be Processed?

1. If the person alleged to be responsible for the harassment is a student, the grievance will be processed through the discipline procedure applicable to that student.

2. If the person alleged to be responsible for the harassment is a staff member, administrator, or faculty member, the person with whom the grievance is filed will notify the special assistant to the president for affirmative action, who will attempt to resolve it by discussion, investigation, or other steps that he/she deems appropriate. The special assistant to the president for affirmative action may appoint a hearing panel to review the matter. The complainant will be informed by the special assistant to the president for affirmative action or his/her designee of the action taken.

3. If a hearing panel is appointed, it will conduct an investigation which may, if the panel deems appropriate, include a hearing. The findings and recommendations of the panel will be sent to the president.

4. The president or his/her designee will review the findings and recommendations of the panel and may review other facts relating to the grievance. The decision of the president or his/her designee is binding and shall not be subject to review under any other grievance procedure in effect at Tufts University.

Topics for Critical Thinking and Writing

1. Where, if at all, would you draw the line between harmless, inoffensive flirtation and sexual harassment?

2. For an act to qualify as sexual harassment, is it, or should it be, necessary that the aggressor persist in behavior the victim doesn't want after the victim has said "Stop!"? What position does the Tufts policy take on this issue?

3. Evaluate the four-part grievance procedure described in the Tufts statement. Can you think of ways it might be improved to be fairer? More efficient? Should the accused have the right to face his or her accusers?

Should the victim's testimony require corroboration? Explain your answers to these questions in an essay of 500 words.

4. The list headed "Who Are the Participants?" does not include "student and instructor" or "student and staff member," though it includes "instructor and student" and "staff member and student." Can you conceive of situations in which a student harasses an instructor or a staff member?

5. If your school has a comparable statement of policy, study it closely, partly by comparing it with the Tufts policy. Then (assuming that your school's statement does not in every respect satisfy you), set forth (with supporting reasons) the revisions you would make in it.

ELLEN GOODMAN

Ellen Goodman, educated at Radcliffe College, worked as a reporter for Newsweek *and the* Detroit Free Press. *Since 1967 she has written for the* Boston Globe, *and since 1972 her column has been nationally syndicated. The essay that we reprint appeared in the* Boston Globe *in October 1991.*

The Reasonable Woman Standard

Since the volatile mix of sex and harassment exploded under the Capitol dome, it hasn't just been senators scurrying for cover. The case of the professor and judge has left a gender gap that looks more like a crater.[1]

We have discovered that men and women see this issue differently. Stop the presses. Sweetheart, get me rewrite.

On the *Today* show, Bryant Gumbel asks something about a man's right to have a pinup on the wall and Katie Couric says what she thinks of that. On the normally sober *MacNeil/Lehrer* hour the usual panel of legal experts doesn't break down between left and right but between male and female.

---

[1] Professor Anita Hill, of the University of Oklahoma Law School, accused Clarence Thomas of sexually harassing her while he was her supervisor. The accusations were made before the Senate Judiciary Committee in hearings to confirm Thomas's appointment to a seat on the U.S. Supreme Court. During the televised hearings, several senators were widely regarded as having treated Hill badly. [—Ed.]

On a hundred radio talk shows, women are sharing experiences and men are asking for proof. In ten thousand offices, the order of the day is the nervous joke. One boss asks his secretary if he can still say "good morning," or is that sexual harassment. Heh, heh. The women aren't laughing.

Okay boys and girls, back to your corners. Can we talk? Can we   5
hear?

The good news is that women have stopped rolling their eyes at each other and started speaking out. The bad news is that we may each assume the other gender not only doesn't understand but can't understand. "They don't get it" becomes "they can't get it."

Let's start with the fact that sexual harassment is a concept as new as date rape. Date rape, that should-be oxymoron, assumes a different perspective on the part of the man and the woman. His date, her rape. Sexual harassment comes with some of the same assumptions. What he labels sexual, she labels harassment.

This produces what many men tend to darkly call a "murky" area of the law. Murky however is a step in the right direction. When everything was clear, it was clearly biased. The old single standard was [a] male standard. The only options a working woman had were to grin, bear it, or quit.

Sexual harassment rules are based on the point of view of the victim, nearly always a woman. The rules ask, not just whether she has been physically assaulted, but whether the environment in which she works is intimidating or coercive. Whether she feels harassed. It says that her feelings matter.

This, of course, raises all sorts of hackles about women's *feelings*,   10
women's *sensitivity*. How can you judge the sensitivity level of every single woman you work with? What's a poor man to do?

But the law isn't psychiatry. It doesn't adapt to individual sensitivity levels. There is a standard emerging by which the courts can judge these cases and by which people can judge them as well. It's called "the reasonable woman standard." How would a reasonable woman interpret this? How would a reasonable woman behave?

This is not an entirely new idea, although perhaps the law's belief in the reasonableness of women is. There has long been a "reasonable man" in the law not to mention a "reasonable pilot," a "reasonable innkeeper," a "reasonable train operator."

Now the law is admitting that a reasonable woman may see these situations differently than a man. That truth—available in your senator's mailbag—is also apparent in research. We tend to see sexualized situations from our own gender's perspective. Kim Lane Scheppele, a political science and law professor at the University of Michigan, summarizes the miscues this way: "Men see the sex first and miss the coercion. Women see the coercion and miss the sex."

Does that mean that we are genetically doomed to our double vision? Scheppele is quick to say no. Our justice system rests on the belief that one person can get in another's head, walk in her shoes, see things from another perspective. And so does our hope for change.

If a jury of car drivers can understand how a "reasonable pilot" would see one situation, a jury of men can see how a reasonable woman would see another event. The crucial ingredient is empathy.   15

Check it out in the office tomorrow. He's coming on, she's backing off, he keeps coming. Read the body language. There's a *Playboy* calendar on the wall and a PMS joke in the boardroom and the boss is just being friendly. How would a reasonable woman feel?

At this moment, when the air is crackling with hostility and consciousness-raising has the hair sticking up on the back of many necks, guess what? Men can "get it." Reasonable men.

Topics for Critical Thinking and Writing

1. Goodman is a journalist, which means in part that her writing is lively. Point to two or three sentences that you would not normally find in a textbook, and evaluate them. (Example: "Okay boys and girls, back to your corners," para. 5.) Are the sentences you have selected effective? Why, or why not?

2. Why does Goodman describe date rape as a "should-be oxymoron" (para. 7)?

3. In paragraphs 11 and 12 Goodman speaks of "the reasonable woman standard." In recent years several cases have come to the courts in which women have said that they are harassed by posters of nude women in the workplace. Such posters have been said to create an "intimidating, hostile, or offensive environment." (a) What do you think Goodman's opinion of these cases would be? (b) Imagine that you are a member of the jury deciding such a case. What is your verdict? Why?

4. According to Goodman's account of the law (paras. 8–13), the criterion for sexual harassment is whether the "reasonable woman" would regard the "environment" in which she works (or studies) as "intimidating" or "coercive," thus causing her to "feel harassed." In a 500-word essay describe three hypothetical cases, one of which you believe clearly involves sexual harassment, a second that clearly does not, and a third that is a borderline case.

5. Given what Goodman says about sexual harassment, can men be victims of sexual harassment? Why, or why not?

ELLEN FRANKEL PAUL

Ellen Frankel Paul teaches political science at Bowling Green State University. Among the many books that she has written, edited, or coedited are Equity and Gender *(1989),* Self-Interest *(1997),* Democracy *(1999), and* The Right to Privacy *(2000). The essay that we reprint here was originally published in* Society *in 1991.*

Bared Buttocks and Federal Cases

Women in American society are victims of sexual harassment in alarming proportions. Sexual harassment is an inevitable corollary to class exploitation; as capitalists exploit workers, so do males in positions of authority exploit their female subordinates. Male professors, supervisors, and apartment managers in ever increasing numbers take advantage of the financial dependence and vulnerability of women to extract sexual concessions.

These are the assertions that commonly begin discussions of sexual harassment. For reasons that will be adumbrated below, dissent from the prevailing view is long overdue. Three recent episodes will serve to frame this disagreement.

Valerie Craig, an employee of Y & Y Snacks, Inc., joined several coworkers and her supervisor for drinks after work one day in July of 1978. Her supervisor drove her home and proposed that they become more intimately acquainted. She refused his invitation for sexual relations, whereupon he said that he would "get even" with her. Ten days after the incident she was fired from her job. She soon filed a complaint of sexual harassment with the Equal Employment Opportunity Commission (EEOC), and the case wound its way through the courts. Craig prevailed, the company was held liable for damages, and she received back pay, reinstatement, and an order prohibiting Y & Y from taking reprisals against her in the future.

Carol Zabowicz, one of only two female forklift operators in a West Bend Company warehouse, charged that her coworkers over a four-year period 1978–1982 sexually harassed her by such acts as: asking her whether she was wearing a bra; two of the men exposing their buttocks between ten and twenty times; a male coworker grabbing his crotch and making obscene suggestions or growling; subjecting her to offensive and abusive language; and exhibiting obscene drawings with her initials on them. Zabowicz began to show symptoms of physical and psychological stress, necessitating several medical leaves, and she filed a sexual harassment complaint with the EEOC. The district court judge remarked that "the sustained, malicious, and brutal harassment meted out . . . was more than merely unreasonable; it was malevolent and outrageous." The company knew of the harassment and took corrective action only after the employee filed a complaint with the EEOC. The company, was, therefore, held liable, and Zabowicz was awarded back pay for the period of her medical absence, and a judgment that her rights were violated under the Civil Rights Act of 1964.

On September 17, 1990, Lisa Olson, a sports reporter for the *Boston Herald,* charged five football players of the just-defeated New England Patriots with sexual harassment for making sexually suggestive and offensive remarks to her when she entered their locker room to conduct a post-game interview. The incident amounted to nothing short of "mind rape," according to Olson. After vociferous lamentations in the media, the National Football League fined the team and its players $25,000 each. The National Organization for Women called for a boycott of Remington electric shavers because the owner of the company, Victor Kiam, also own[ed] the Patriots and allegedly displayed insufficient sensitivity at the time when the episode occurred.

All these incidents are indisputably disturbing. In an ideal world—one needless to say far different from the one that we inhabit or are ever likely to inhabit—women would not be subjected to such treatment in the course of their work. Women, and men as well, would be accorded respect by coworkers and supervisors, their feelings would be taken into account, and their dignity would be left intact. For women to expect reverential treatment in the workplace is utopian, yet they should not have to tolerate outrageous, offensive sexual overtures and threats as they go about earning a living.

One question that needs to be pondered is: What kinds of undesired sexual behavior should women be protected against by law? That is, what kind of actions are deemed so outrageous and violate a woman's rights to such extent that the law should intervene, and what actions should be considered inconveniences of life, to be morally condemned but not adjudicated? A subsidiary question concerns the type of legal remedy appropriate for the wrongs that do require redress. Before directly addressing these questions, it might be useful to diffuse some of the hyperbole adhering to the sexual harassment issue.

Surveys are one source of this hyperbole. If their results are accepted at face value, they lead to the conclusion that women are disproportionately victims of legions of sexual harassers. A poll by the Albuquerque *Tribune* found that nearly 80 percent of the respondents reported that they or someone they knew had been victims of sexual harassment. The Merit Systems Protection Board determined that 42 percent of the women (and 14 percent of men) working for the federal government had experienced some form of unwanted sexual attention between 1985 and 1987, with unwanted "sexual teasing" identified as the most prevalent form. A Defense Department survey found that 64 percent of women in the military (and 17 percent of the men) suffered "uninvited and unwanted sexual attention" within the previous year. The United Methodist Church established that 77 percent of its clergywomen experienced incidents of sexual harassment, with 41 percent of these naming a pastor or colleague as the perpetrator, and 31 percent mentioning church social functions as the setting.

A few caveats concerning polls in general, and these sorts of polls in particular, are worth considering. Pollsters looking for a particular social ill tend to find it, usually in gargantuan proportions. (What fate would lie in store for a pollster who concluded that child abuse, or wife beating, or mistreatment of the elderly had dwindled to the point of negligibility!) Sexual harassment is a notoriously ill-defined and almost infinitely expandable concept, including everything from rape to unwelcome neck massaging, discomfiture upon witnessing sexual overtures directed at others, yelling at and blowing smoke in the ears of female subordinates, and displays of pornographic pictures in the workplace. Defining sexual harassment, as the United Methodists did, as "any sexually related behavior that is unwelcome, offensive or which fails to respect the rights of others," the concept is broad enough to include everything from "unsolicited suggestive looks or leers [or] pressures for dates" to "actual sexual assaults or rapes." Categorizing everything from rape to "looks" as sexual harassment makes us all victims, a state of affairs satisfying to radical feminists, but not very useful for distinguishing serious injuries from the merely trivial.

Yet, even if the surveys exaggerate the extent of sexual harassment, however defined, what they do reflect is a great deal of tension between the sexes. As women in ever increasing numbers entered the workplace in the last two decades, as the women's movement challenged alleged male hegemony and exploitation with ever greater intemperance, and as women entered previously all-male preserves from the board rooms to the coal pits, it is lamentable, but should not be surprising, that this tension sometimes takes sexual form. Not that sexual harassment on the job, in the university, and in other settings is a trivial or insignificant matter, but a sense of proportion needs to be restored and, even more importantly, distinctions need to be made. In other words, sexual harassment must be deideologized. Statements that paint nearly all women as victims and all men and their patriarchal, capitalist system as perpetrators, are ideological fantasy. Ideology blurs the distinction between being injured — being a genuine victim — and merely being offended. An example is this statement by Catharine A. MacKinnon, a law professor and feminist activist:

> Sexual harassment perpetuates the interlocked structure by which women have been kept sexually in thrall to men and at the bottom of the labor market. Two forces of American society converge: men's control over women's sexuality and capital's control over employees' work lives. Women historically have been required to exchange sexual services for material survival, in one form or another. Prostitution and marriage as well as sexual harassment in different ways institutionalize this arrangement.

Such hyperbole needs to be diffused and distinctions need to be drawn. Rape, a nonconsensual invasion of a person's body, is a crime clear and simple. It is a violation of the right to the physical integrity of the body (the right to life, as John Locke or Thomas Jefferson would have put it). Criminal law should and does prohibit rape. Whether it is useful to call rape "sexual harassment" is doubtful, for it makes the latter concept overly broad while trivializing the former.

Intimidation in the workplace of the kind that befell Valerie Craig — that is, extortion of sexual favors by a supervisor from a subordinate by threatening to penalize, fire, or fail to reward — is what the courts term *quid pro quo*[1] sexual harassment. Since the mid-1970s, the federal courts have treated this type of sexual harassment as a form of sex discrimination in employment proscribed under Title VII of the Civil Rights Act of 1964. A plaintiff who prevails against an employer may receive such equitable remedies as reinstatement and back pay, and the court can order the company to prepare and disseminate a policy against sexual harassment. Current law places principal liability on the company, not the harassing supervisor, even when higher management is unaware of the harassment and, thus, cannot take any steps to prevent it.

Quid pro quo sexual harassment is morally objectionable and analogous to extortion: The harasser extorts property (i.e., use of the woman's body) through the leverage of fear for her job. The victim of such behavior should have legal recourse, but serious reservations can be held

---

[1] ***quid pro quo*** This for that, or one thing in return for another (Latin). [—Ed.]

about rectifying these injustices through the blunt instrument of Title VII: In egregious cases the victim is left less than whole (for back pay will not compensate her for ancillary losses), and no prospects for punitive damages are offered to deter would-be harassers. Even more distressing about Title VII is the fact that the primary target of litigation is not the actual harasser, but rather the employer. This places a double burden on a company. The employer is swindled by the supervisor because he spent his time pursuing sexual gratification and thereby impairing the efficiency of the workplace by mismanaging his subordinates, and the employer must endure lengthy and expensive litigation, pay damages, and suffer loss to its reputation. It would be fairer to both the company and the victim to treat sexual harassment as a tort—that is, as a private wrong or injury for which the court can assess damages. Employers should be held vicariously liable only when they know of an employee's behavior and do not try to redress it.

As for the workplace harassment endured by Carol Zabowicz—the bared buttocks, obscene portraits, etc.—that too should be legally redressable. Presently, such incidents also fall under the umbrella of Title VII, and are termed hostile environment sexual harassment, a category accepted later than *quid pro quo* and with some judicial reluctance. The main problem with this category is that it has proven too elastic: cases have reached the courts based on everything from off-color jokes to unwanted, persistent sexual advances by coworkers. A new tort of sexual harassment would handle these cases better. Only instances above a certain threshold of egregiousness or outrageousness would be actionable. In other words, the behavior that the plaintiff found offensive would also have to be offensive to the proverbial "reasonable man" of the tort law. That is, the behavior would have to be objectively injurious rather than merely subjectively offensive. The defendant would be the actual harasser not the company, unless it knew about the problem and failed to act. Victims of scatological jokes, leers, unwanted offers of dates, and other sexual annoyances would no longer have their day in court.

A distinction must be restored between morally offensive behavior 15 and behavior that causes serious harm. Only the latter should fall under the jurisdiction of criminal or tort law. Do we really want legislators and judges delving into our most intimate private lives, deciding when a look is a leer, and when a leer is a Civil Rights Act offense? Do we really want courts deciding, as one recently did, whether a school principal's disparaging remarks about a female school district administrator was sexual harassment and, hence, a breach of Title VII, or merely the act of a spurned and vengeful lover? Do we want judges settling disputes such as the one that arose at a car dealership after a female employee turned down a male coworker's offer of a date and his colleagues retaliated by calling her offensive names and embarrassing her in front of customers? Or another case in which a female shipyard worker complained of an "offensive working environment" because of the prevalence of pornographic material on the docks? Do we want the state to prevent or compensate us for any behavior that someone might find offensive? Should people have a legally enforceable right not to be offended by others? At some point, the price for such protection is the loss of both liberty and privacy rights.

Workplaces are breeding grounds of envy, personal grudges, infatuation, and jilted loves, and beneath a fairly high threshold of outrageousness, these travails should be either suffered in silence, complained of to higher management, or left behind as one seeks other employment. No one, female or male, can expect to enjoy a working environment that is perfectly stress-free, or to be treated always and by everyone with kindness and respect. To the extent that sympathetic judges have encouraged women to seek monetary compensation for slights and annoyances, they have not done them a great service. Women need to develop a thick skin in order to survive and prosper in the workforce. It is patronizing to think that they need to be recompensed by male judges for seeing a few pornographic pictures on a wall. By their efforts to extend sexual harassment charges to even the most trivial behavior, the radical feminists send a message that women are not resilient enough to ignore the run-of-the-mill, churlish provocation from male coworkers. It is difficult to imagine a suit by a longshoreman complaining of mental stress due to the display of nude male centerfolds by female coworkers. Women cannot expect to have it both ways: equality where convenient, but special dispensations when the going gets rough. Equality has its price and that price may include unwelcome sexual advances, irritating and even intimidating sexual jests, and lewd and obnoxious colleagues.

Egregious acts—sexual harassment per se—must be legally redressable. Lesser but not trivial offenses, whether at the workplace or in other more social settings, should be considered moral lapses for which the offending party receives opprobrium, disciplinary warnings, or penalties, depending on the setting and the severity. Trivial offenses, dirty jokes, sexual overtures, and sexual innuendoes do make many women feel intensely discomfited, but, unless they become outrageous through persistence or content, these too should be taken as part of life's annoyances. The perpetrators should be either endured, ignored, rebuked, or avoided, as circumstances and personal inclination dictate.

Whether Lisa Olson's experience in the locker room of the New England Patriots falls into the second or third category is debatable. The media circus triggered by the incident was certainly out of proportion to the event.

As the presence of women on road gangs, construction crews, and oil rigs becomes a fact of life, the animosities and tensions of this transition period are likely to abate gradually. Meanwhile, women should "lighten up," and even dispense a few risqué barbs of their own, a sure way of taking the fun out of it for offensive male bores.

Topics for Critical Thinking and Writing

1. Reread the first paragraph, trying *not* to bring to it your knowledge of what Paul says in the rest of the essay. What was your response? Then, in light of what you know about the entire essay, explain Paul's strategy in beginning this way.

2. Paul occasionally uses a word that probably is not part of everyone's vocabulary, such as "adumbrated" (paragraph 2), "adjudicated" (7), "hegemony" (10), "deideologized" (10), and "ancillary" (13). What is your response? Is the essay needlessly obscure? Are some words not part of everyday speech but appropriate here? Explain.

3. How, if at all, does Paul define *sexual harassment* (see especially paras. 9–10)? How would you define it? Consider what is common to the three cases of sexual harassment with which Paul opens her essay (paras. 3–5).

4. Paul asserts that women ought to be prepared to encounter a certain amount of inappropriate behavior in the workplace. Are you satisfied with the reasons she gives? Explain.

5. Paul thinks Title VII places an unfair burden on employers whose employees are guilty of sexual harassment because the employer may not know about the employee's misbehavior (paras. 12–13). Suppose one argues that employers ought to know about such harassment and ought to take steps to prevent it. How might Paul reply?

6. Paul distinguishes between "offensive behavior" and harm (para. 15) and the behavior that causes each. Can you think of cases of sexual harassment (actual or hypothetical) in which the distinction is blurred? If so, explain.

7. If you have read Ellen Goodman's "The Reasonable Woman Standard" (p. 179), compare Goodman's views with Paul's. On what significant points do they disagree?

SARAH J. McCARTHY

As Sarah J. McCarthy indicates in this essay, she is the owner of a small restaurant. The essay originally appeared in the December 9, 1991, issue of Forbes, *a magazine that reports on business and financial issues.*

Cultural Fascism

On the same day that Ted Kennedy asked forgiveness for his personal "shortcomings," he advocated slapping lottery-size punitive damages on small-business owners who may be guilty of excessive flirting or whose employees may be guilty of talking dirty. Senator Kennedy expressed regrets that the new civil rights bill caps punitive damages for sexual harassment as high as $300,000 (depending on company size), and he promises to push for increases next year. Note that the senators have voted to exempt themselves from punitive damages.

I am the owner of a small restaurant/bar that employs approximately twenty young males whose role models range from Axl Rose to John Belushi. They work hard in a high-stress, fast-paced job in a hot kitchen and at times they are guilty of colorful language. They have also been overheard telling Pee-Wee Herman jokes and listening to obnoxious rock lyrics. They have discussed pornography and they have flirted with waitresses. One chef/manager has asked out a pretty blonde waitress probably a hundred times in three years. She seems to enjoy the game, but always says no. Everyone calls everyone else "Honey"—it's a ritual, a way of softening what sound like barked orders: "I need the medium-rare shish kebab *now!*"

"Honey" doesn't mean the same thing here as it does in women's studies departments or at the EEOC.[1] The auto body shop down the street has pinups. Perhaps under the vigilant eyes of the feminist political correctness gestapo we can reshape our employees' behavior so they act more like nerds from the Yale women's studies department. The gestapo will not lack for potential informers seeking punitive damages and instant riches.

With the Civil Rights Bill of 1991 we are witnessing the most organized and systematic assault on free speech and privacy since the McCarthy era. The vagueness of the sexual harassment law, combined with our current litigation explosion, is a frightening prospect for small businesses. We are now financially responsible for sexually offensive

[1] **EEOC** Equal Employment Opportunity Commission. [—Ed.]

verbal behavior, even if we don't know it is occurring, under a law that provides no guidelines to define "offensive" and "harassment." This is a cultural fascism unmatched since the Chinese communists outlawed hand-holding, decorative clothing, and premarital sex.

This law is detrimental even to the women it professes to help. I am   5
a feminist, but the law has made me fearful of hiring women. If one of our cooks or managers—or my husband or sons—offends someone, it could cost us $100,000 in punitive damages and legal expenses. There will be no insurance fund or stockholders or taxpayers to pick up the tab.

When I was a feminist activist in the 1970s, we knew the dangers of a pedestal—it was said to be as confining as any other small place. As we were revolted and outraged by the woman-hatred in violent pornography, we reminded each other that education, not laws, was the solution to our problems. In Women against Sexist Violence in Pornography and Media, in Pittsburgh, we were well aware of the dangers of encroaching on the First Amendment. Free speech was, perhaps more than anything else, what made our country grow into a land of enlightenment and diversity. The lesbians among us were aware that the same laws used to censor pornography could be used against them if their sexual expressions were deemed offensive.

We admired powerful women writers such as Marge Piercy and poets like Robin Morgan who swooped in from nowhere, writing break-your-chains poems about women swinging from crystal chandeliers like monkeys on vines and defecating in punch bowls. Are we allowed to talk about these poems in the current American workplace?

The lawyers—the prim women and men who went to the politically correct law schools—believe with sophomoric arrogance that the solution to all the world's problems is tort litigation. We now have eternally complicated questions of sexual politics judged by the shirting standards of the reasonable prude.

To the leadership of the women's movement: You do women a disservice. You ladies—and I use that term intentionally—have trivialized the women's movement. You have made us ladies again. You have not considered the unintended effects of your sexual harassment law. You are saying that too many things men say and do with each other are too rough-and-tumble for us. Wielding the power of your $300,000 lawsuits, you are frightening managers into hiring men over women. I know that I am so frightened. You have installed a double pane of glass on the glass ceiling with the help of your white knight and protector, Senator Kennedy.

You and your allies tried to lynch Clarence Thomas. You alienate   10
your natural allies. Men and women who wanted to work shoulder to

shoulder with you are now looking over their shoulders. You have made women into china dolls that if broken come with a $300,000 price tag. The games, intrigue, nuances, and fun of flirting have been made into criminal activity.

We women are not as delicate and powerless as you think. We do not want victim status in the workplace. Don't try to foist it on us.

Topics for Critical Thinking and Writing

1. Reread McCarthy's opening paragraph. What is her point? How effective do you think this paragraph is as the opening of an argumentative essay?

2. In her third paragraph McCarthy speaks of "the feminist political correctness gestapo." What does she mean by this phrase, and why does she use it?

3. In paragraph 8 McCarthy refers to "tort litigation." Explain the phrase.

4. In her second paragraph McCarthy suggests that in "a high-stress, fast-paced" environment with young (and presumably not highly educated) males, "colorful language," dirty jokes, and "obnoxious rock lyrics" are to be expected. Would you agree that a woman who takes a job in such an environment cannot reasonably complain that this sort of behavior constitutes sexual harassment? Explain.

5. How do you think McCarthy would define sexual harassment? That is, how according to her views should we complete the following sentence: "Person A sexually harasses person B if and only if . . ."?

6. Read the essay by Ellen Goodman (p. 179), and explain in a brief essay of 100 words where she and McCarthy differ. With whom do you agree? Why?

11

Torture: Is It Ever Justifiable?

CLINTON R. VAN ZANDT

Clinton R. Van Zandt is a security consultant. This essay was paired with the next essay when it was originally published in CQ Researcher *on April 18, 2003.*

It Should Be Permissible to Torture Suspected Terrorists to Gather Information

In man's search for truth down through the ages, "trial by ordeal" often has been resorted to when a suspect refused to talk. In recent times, however, numerous nations and international bodies have legislated against the intentional infliction of pain or suffering in an attempt to gain information or a confession.

Most civilized people would say they oppose the inhuman or degrading treatment of another human being. But what happens when there is a so-called "ticking time bomb"—a situation when a suspect is thought to have time-sensitive information affecting the lives of thousands—or even millions—of people? When the ticking bomb is factored into the equation, the physical and psychological rules of engagement suddenly become a sticky sea of gray for many otherwise absolutists.

The U.S. once taught friendly governments how to extract information from prisoners by the use of coercive techniques known as "stress and duress." Interview strategies were designed to exhaust the individual's ability to resist while providing him with the rationalization he needed to cooperate.

In the war against terrorism, we seek to gain intelligence about our adversary of immediate as well as long-term strategic value. In both cloak-and-dagger missions and law-enforcement operations, there may come a time when our nation must quickly try to obtain information critical to the lives of millions of people from a person who refuses to talk.

To remain a nation based upon the rule of law, the United States   5
needs to establish a court at the national level before which the government could argue that torture was essential to extract critical information. The court would be required to rule on the matter immediately, and if in agreement, it would be able to issue a "duress-interview warrant" allowing the authorities to do whatever was necessary to obtain the needed information from the prisoner. There would be no appeal process and no public or media scrutiny. The authority of the court would be absolute.

In short, the overriding public-safety issue would take precedence over a prisoner's human rights. Without such a mechanism, we are left with conventional methods of interrogation while watching the seconds on the time bomb tick away, as the only person who might know how to stop the clock remains mute and simply awaits our fate. And lastly, should time allow, we still need to verify and corroborate the information before we act on it.

Topics for Critical Thinking and Writing

1. Does Van Zandt offer the reader any reason in favor of torture except as the best way to deal with a "ticking time bomb" scenario (para. 1)?

2. Van Zandt favors a national court to judge the government's claims that torture in a given case is necessary (para. 5). Do you believe that such a court would adequately respect the civil liberties of suspects? Explain.

3. Compare the provisions of the special court that Van Zandt favors creating with the quasi-military courts proposed by Attorney General John Ashcroft after September 11, 2001, to deal with suspected terrorists. Were the Ashcroft special courts intended to pass judgment on government proposals to use torture? What is the status today of the Ashcroft proposal?

VINCENT IACOPINO

Vincent Iacopino, M.D., Ph.D., is director of research for Physicans for Human Rights. This essay was originally paired with the preceding essay when it was first published in CQ Researcher *on April 18, 2003.*

It Should Not Be Permissible to Torture Suspected Terrorists to Gather Information

Torture cannot be justified by any government, for any reason, despite recent reports of U.S. officials and others attempting to justify such practices. Torture is unequivocally prohibited in international law. This legal and moral imperative was established in the aftermath of Nazi war crimes as a rhetorical statement of moral and human identity. Under the U.N. Convention Against Torture, the United States is obligated to prohibit torture, ensure prompt and impartial investigations and prosecute perpetrators. Additionally, on countless occasions the State Department's Country Report on Human Rights Practices has criticized governments that torture, in some cases the same practices the U.S. is now accused of committing in its "war on terrorism."

Those now advocating the use of torture risk undermining principles of justice and the rule of law in what appears to be an unfortunate public display of arrogance and ignorance:

- Torture does not make any one person or society safer or more secure. States that torture undermine their authority and legitimacy. Also, U.S. sanctioning of any form of torture will escalate its already widespread use.

- Those currently arguing in the abstract for torture only under "special circumstances" or with "humane limitations" know very little of the horror they are prescribing. Even seemingly innocuous methods of torture such as hooding can be terrorizing—for example, when combined with a mock execution or other psychological methods. Moreover, hypothetical "limits" on torture cannot be ensured in the absence of independent monitoring of all interactions with detainees and investigation and prosecution of all allegations of torture—conditions that torturers do not permit.

- Labeling torture as a "stress and duress" interrogation technique does not alter the brutality that it represents.

- "Ticking bomb" scenarios are naive, abstract fantasies that serve to assuage the moral conscience of perpetrators and collaborators.

Acts of terror must be prevented and punished. To consider using acts of torture that the world has deemed unacceptable under any circumstance is profoundly disturbing. Torture will never serve the interests of justice because it undermines the dignity of us all. We all lose when the "war on terrorism" ends up threatening the protection of human rights.

The United States must be neither silent nor, in any way, complicit with such practices, or, indeed, we risk losing that which we seek to preserve—our humanity.

Topics for Critical Thinking and Writing

1. What is a "'ticking bomb' scenario" (para. 2)? In 250 words or less, write such a scenario. Why does Iacopino describe such hypotheticals as "naive, abstract fantasies"? Do you agree with his evaluation of those hypotheticals? Explain in 500 words.

2. What methods of interrogation of suspected terrorists do you think Iacopino would tolerate? Suppose they fail—then what?

3. It is often said that terrorists have forfeited any right to be treated humanely by virtue of their readiness to murder the innocent. Iacopino evidently rejects this reasoning (even though he never mentions it). Write a short essay explaining how you think Iacopino might respond to this argument.

PHILIP B. HEYMANN

Philip B. Heymann, former United States deputy attorney general, is a professor at Harvard Law School. This essay was first published in the Boston Globe *on February 16, 2002, paired with the essay by Alan M. Dershowitz that we reprint after Heymann's essay.*

Torture Should Not Be Authorized

Authorizing torture is a bad and dangerous idea that can easily be made to sound plausible. There is a subtle fallacy embedded in the traditional "ticking bomb" argument for torture to save lives.

That argument goes like this. First, I can imagine dangers so dire that I might torture or kill guilty or innocent persons if I was quite sure that was necessary and sufficient to prevent those dangers. Second, very many feel this way, although differing in the circumstances and the certainty level they would want. Therefore, the "ticking bomb" argument concludes, everyone wants a system for authorizing torture or murder; we need only debate the circumstances and the level of certainty.

This conclusion, leading to abandonment of one of the few worldwide legal prohibitions, leaves out the fact that I do not have faith in the authorizing system for finding the required circumstances with any certainty because the costs of errors are born by the suspect tortured, not by those who decide to torture him. The conclusion also ignores the high probability that the practice of torture will spread unwisely if acceptance of torture with the approval of judges is substituted for a flat, worldwide prohibition.

The use of torture would increase sharply if there were "torture warrants." Any law enforcement or intelligence official who tortures a prisoner in the United States now is very likely to be prosecuted and imprisoned.

Punches may be thrown, but anything we think of as "torture" is   5 considered an inexcusable practice. That revulsion will disappear if we make torture acceptable and legal whenever a judge accepts the judgment of intelligence officials that: (1) there is a bomb; (2) the suspect knows where it is; (3) torture will get the truth, not a false story, out of him before the bomb explodes; (4) the bomb won't be moved in the meantime. Every individual who believes in his heart, however recklessly, that those conditions (or others he thinks are just as compelling) are met will think there is nothing seriously wrong with torture.

Professor Alan Dershowitz wants to bet that judges will say "no" in a high enough percentage of cases of "ticking bombs" that whatever moral force their refusal has will offset the legitimating and demoralizing effects of authorizing occasional torture. It's a bad bet.

Judges have deferred to the last several thousand requests for national security wiretaps and they would defer here. The basis of their decisions, information revealing secret "sources and methods" of intelligence gathering, would not be public. And if the judge refused, overrode the judgment of agents who thought lives would be lost without torture, and denied a warrant, why would that decision be more likely to be accepted and followed by agents desperate to save lives than the flat ban on torture we now have?

How many false positives do you want to accept? You would get six false positives out of 10 occasions of torture even in the extraordinarily unlikely event that the intelligence officers convince the judge that they were really 80 percent sure of each of the above four predictions.

And even if you would tolerate this number of false positives if torture were in fact the only way to get the needed information to defuse the bomb, there are frequently other promising ways (such as emergency searches or stimulating conversations over tapped phones) that will be abandoned or discounted if torture is available.

Finally, if we approve torture in one set of circumstances, isn't every 10 country then free to define its own exceptions, applicable to Americans as well as its own citizens? Fear of that led us to accept the Geneva Convention prohibiting torture of a prisoner of war, although obtaining his information might save dozens of American lives.

As to preventing terrorism, torture is an equally bad idea. Torture is a prescription for losing a war for support of our beliefs in the hope of reducing the casualties from relatively small battles.

Dershowitz misunderstands my argument. I do not accept torture either "off the books" with a wink at the secret discretion of the torturers or on the open authority of the judges from whom they might seek authorization. I predict so many types of harms to so many people and to the nation from any system that authorizes torture, either secretly or openly, that I would prohibit it. The overall, longer-term cost of any system authorizing torture, openly or tacitly, would far outweigh its occasional, short-term benefits.

Topics for Critical Thinking and Writing

1. Heymann alludes to a slippery slope argument against torture (para. 4). Formulate that argument in an essay of 100 words.

2. Heymann worries that "torture warrants" (para. 4) would erode the strong feelings against torture that the public and its officials now have. What evidence, if any, does he have to confirm his claim about such warrants? Do you have any evidence that might confirm his claim?

3. What is a "false positive" (para. 8), and why are they so important in the debate over the morality of torture? Explain in an essay of 250 words.

4. Both Vincent Iacopino (p. 194) and Heymann absolutely oppose torture no matter what the circumstances. Yet they argue their cases with different reasons, different emphases, and different tones. Discuss these features of their essays in an essay of your own.

ALAN M. DERSHOWITZ

Alan M. Dershowitz, educated at Brooklyn College and Yale Law School, is a professor at Harvard Law School. Among his books are Why Terrorism Works *(2000) and* Shouting Fire: Civil Liberties in a Turbulent Era *(2002). The essay that we reprint here originally appeared in the* Boston Globe *on February 16, 2002, paired with the preceding essay by Philip B. Heymann.*

Yes, It Should Be "On the Books"

Professor Philip Heymann and I share a common goal: to eliminate torture from the world, or at the very least to reduce it to an absolute minimum.

The real disagreement between us seems to be over whether the use of torture, under these extreme circumstances, would be worse if done in secret without being incorporated into our legal system—or worse if it required a torture warrant to be issued by a judge.

This is truly a choice of evils, with no perfect resolution. However, I insist that any extraordinary steps contemplated by a democracy must be done "on the books."

Of course there is the risk of false positives and ever expanding criteria. But these evils would exist whether torture was conducted off or on the books.

A carefully designed judicial procedure is more likely to reduce the   5
amount of torture actually conducted, by creating accountability and leaving a public record of every warrant sought and granted.

The legal historian John Langbein has shown that there was far more torture in Medieval France than England because in France the practice was left to the discretion of local officials, whereas in England it required an extraordinary warrant, which was rarely granted.

Heymann suggests that "any law enforcement and intelligence official who tortures a prisoner in the United States now is very likely to be prosecuted and imprisoned."

I believe that a police officer who tortured and successfully prevented a terrorist attack would not be prosecuted, and if he were, he would be acquitted.

Indeed, in a case decided in 1984, the Court of Appeals for the 11th circuit commended police officers who tortured a kidnapper into disclosing the location of his victim.

Although there was no evidence that the victim's life was in immi- 10
nent danger, the court described the offending police officers as "a
group of concerned officers acting in a reasonable manner to obtain information in order to protect another individual from bodily harm or
death."

Elsewhere in the opinion, they described the "reasonable manner"
as including "choking him until he revealed where [the victim] was
being held." These police officers were not prosecuted. Under my proposal, no torture warrant could have been granted in such as case.

Our nation has had extensive experience with "off the book" actions.
President Nixon authorized an off the book "plumbers" operation to
break into homes and offices.

President Reagan authorized an off the book foreign policy that cul-
minated in the Iran-Contra debacle.

President Eisenhower and Kennedy apparently authorized off the
book attempts to assassinate Fidel Castro.

The road to tyranny is paved by executive officials authorizing ac- 15
tions which they deem necessary to national security, without subjecting
these actions to the check and balance of legislative approval, judicial
imprimatur, and public accountability.

We are a nation of laws, and if the rule of law means anything, it
means that no action regardless of how unpalatable, must ever be taken
outside of the rule of law. If the action is to be taken, it must be deemed
lawful. If it cannot be deemed lawful it should not be taken.

Unless we are prepared to authorize the issuance of a torture warrant in the case of the ticking bomb, we should not torture, even if that
means that innocent people may die. If we want to prevent the death of
hundreds of innocent people by subjecting one guilty person to non-
lethal pain, then we must find a way to justify this exception to the otherwise blanket prohibition against torture.

All the evils of torture would be multiplied if we were to accept the
way of the hypocrite, by proclaiming loudly that we are against it but
subtly winking an eye of approval when it is done. Hypocrisy too, is con-
tagious.

Several years ago, an Israeli prime minister reprimanded security
officials for bringing him "unwanted information of misdeeds by Shin
Bet" (the Israeli FBI).

A wise professor commented on this action in the following 20
words: "That strategy is extremely dangerous to democratic values, because it is designed to prevent oversight and to deny accountability to
the public."

That wise professor was Philip Heymann.

Topics for Critical Thinking and Writing

1. Dershowitz occasionally appears on television, and he strikes many viewers as overly aggressive and self-satisfied. What image of himself (a matter of ethos) does he project in this essay? Support your view by pointing to specific passages that help to establish his persona.

2. The White House regularly tells us that Saddam Hussein used torture, and that our government is morally superior. Would Dershowitz's proposal put us at the level of those tyrannies that we oppose? Explain.

3. In paragraph 16 Dershowitz says that "we are a nation of laws," and he proposes that a law be passed that would allow torture to be used in certain extreme cases. Is he in effect saying that in some circumstances the police should act in a criminal fashion, and that we should say it is OK by passing a law approving of such behavior? If we had such a law, we could of course still say "We are a nation of law," but whom would we be kidding? Your view?

MICHAEL LEVIN

Michael Levin, educated at Michigan State University and Columbia University, has taught philosophy at Columbia and now at City College of the City University of New York. Levin has written numerous papers for professional journals and a book entitled Metaphysics and the Mind-Body Problem *(1979). His most recent book (with Laurence Thomas) is* Sexual Orientation and Human Rights *(1999). The following essay is intended for a general audience.*

The Case for Torture

It is generally assumed that torture is impermissible, a throwback to a more brutal age. Enlightened societies reject it outright, and regimes suspected of using it risk the wrath of the United States.

I believe this attitude is unwise. There are situations in which torture is not merely permissible but morally mandatory. Moreover, these situations are moving from the realm of imagination to fact.

Death: Suppose a terrorist has hidden an atomic bomb on Manhattan Island which will detonate at noon on July 4 unless. . . . (here follow the usual demands for money and release of his friends from jail).

Suppose, further, that he is caught at 10 A.M. of the fateful day, but—preferring death to failure—won't disclose where the bomb is. What do we do? If we follow due process—wait for his lawyer, arraign him—millions of people will die. If the only way to save those lives is to subject the terrorist to the most excruciating possible pain, what grounds can there be for not doing so? I suggest there are none. In any case, I ask you to face the question with an open mind.

Torturing the terrorist is unconstitutional? Probably. But millions of lives surely outweigh constitutionality. Torture is barbaric? Mass murder is far more barbaric. Indeed, letting millions of innocents die in deference to one who flaunts his guilt is moral cowardice, an unwillingness to dirty one's hands. If *you* caught the terrorist, could you sleep nights knowing that millions died because you couldn't bring yourself to apply the electrodes?

Once you concede that torture is justified in extreme cases, you have   5
admitted that the decision to use torture is a matter of balancing innocent lives against the means needed to save them. You must now face more realistic cases involving more modest numbers. Someone plants a bomb on a jumbo jet. He alone can disarm it, and his demands cannot be met (or if they can, we refuse to set a precedent by yielding to his threats). Surely we can, we must, do anything to the extortionist to save the passengers. How can we tell 300, or 100, or 10 people who never asked to be put in danger, "I'm sorry, you'll have to die in agony, we just couldn't bring ourselves to . . ."

Here are the results of an informal poll about a third, hypothetical, case. Suppose a terrorist group kidnapped a newborn baby from a hospital. I asked four mothers if they would approve of torturing kidnappers if that were necessary to get their own newborns back. All said yes, the most "liberal" adding that she would like to administer it herself.

I am not advocating torture as punishment. Punishment is addressed to deeds irrevocably past. Rather, I am advocating torture as an acceptable measure for preventing future evils. So understood, it is far less objectionable than many extant punishments. Opponents of the death penalty, for example, are forever insisting that executing a murderer will not bring back his victim (as if the purpose of capital punishment were supposed to be resurrection, not deterrence or retribution). But torture, in the cases described, is intended not to bring anyone back but to keep innocents from being dispatched. The most powerful argument against using torture as a punishment or to secure confessions is that such practices disregard the rights of the individual. Well, if the individual is all that important—and he is—it is correspondingly important to protect the rights of individuals threatened by terrorists. If life is so valuable that it must never be taken, the lives of the innocents must be saved even at the price of hurting the one who endangers them.

Better precedents for torture are assassination and pre-emptive attack. No Allied leader would have flinched at assassinating Hitler, had that been possible. (The Allies did assassinate Heydrich.) Americans would be angered to learn that Roosevelt could have had Hitler killed in 1943—thereby shortening the war and saving millions of lives—but refused on moral grounds. Similarly, if nation A learns that nation B is about to launch an unprovoked attack, A has a right to save itself by destroying B's military capability first. In the same way, if the police can by torture save those who would otherwise die at the hands of kidnappers or terrorists, they must.

Idealism: There is an important difference between terrorists and their victims that should mute talk of the terrorists' "rights." The terrorist's victims are at risk unintentionally, not having asked to be endangered. But the terrorist knowingly initiated his actions. Unlike his victims, he volunteered for the risks of his deed. By threatening to kill for profit or idealism, he renounces civilized standards, and he can have no complaint if civilization tries to thwart him by whatever means necessary.

Just as torture is justified only to save lives (not extort confessions or recantations) it is justifiably administered only to those *known* to hold innocent lives in their hands. Ah, but how can the authorities ever be sure they have the right malefactor? Isn't there a danger of error and abuse? Won't We turn into Them?

Questions like these are disingenuous in a world in which terrorists proclaim themselves and perform for television. The name of their game is public recognition. After all, you can't very well intimidate a government into releasing your freedom fighters unless you announce that it is your group that has seized its embassy. "Clear guilt" is difficult to define, but when 40 million people see a group of masked gunmen seize an airplane on the evening news, there is not much question about who the perpetrators are. There will be hard cases where the situation is murkier. Nonetheless, a line demarcating the legitimate use of torture can be drawn. Torture only the obviously guilty, and only for the sake of saving innocents, and the line between Us and Them will remain clear.

There is little danger that the Western democracies will lose their way if they choose to inflict pain as one way of preserving order. Paralysis in the face of evil is the greater danger. Some day soon a terrorist will threaten tens of thousands of lives, and torture will be the only way to save them. We had better start thinking about this.

Topics for Critical Thinking and Writing

1. In his first four paragraphs, Levin uses hypothetical cases (these are also commonly called *invented instances*), and he pretty much assumes you agree in these cases that torture is acceptable. (For this presumed agreement, see the first sentence in para. 5.) Do you agree? If not, why?

2. In paragraph 11 Levin asserts that although "There will be hard cases" where the situation is murky, "Nonetheless, a line demarcating the legitimate use of torture can be drawn." He then draws the line: "Torture only the obviously guilty, and only for the sake of saving innocents, and the line between Us and Them will remain clear." His essay is built on hypothetical cases. Can you invent a hypothetical case where the line between Us and Them is *not* clear?

3. Levin ends his essay by saying, "Some day soon a terrorist will threaten tens of thousands of lives, and torture will be the only way to save them." Given the fact that he wrote this essay in 1982, can we say that time has refuted this argument?

4. Is it reasonable to reply to Levin that we never know that the accused both is really guilty and will break under torture and therefore that torture is never justified? Why, or why not?

5. Let's look now at some matters of style. Evaluate Levin's title and his first two paragraphs. Notice that the first paragraph ends with a relatively long sentence and the second paragraph begins with a relatively short sentence. What is the effect of this sequence?

6. In paragraph 7, Levin says that "Opponents of the death penalty, for example, are forever insisting that executing a murderer will not bring back his victim." Suppose instead of "are forever insisting" he had said "sometimes argue." What would be the difference in tone—the difference in the speaker's voice and therefore in your sense of what sort of person the speaker is? What does Levin gain or lose by writing the sentence as he does?

PART THREE

Classic Arguments

PLATO

Plato (427–347 B.C.), an Athenian aristocrat by birth, was the student of one great philosopher (Socrates) and the teacher of another (Aristotle). His legacy of more than two dozen dialogues — imaginary discussions between Socrates and one or more other speakers, usually young Athenians — has been of such influence that the whole of Western philosophy can be characterized, A. N. Whitehead wrote, as "a series of footnotes to Plato." Plato's interests encompassed the full range of topics in philosophy: ethics, politics, logic, metaphysics, epistemology, aesthetics, psychology, and education.

The selection reprinted here, Crito, *is the third of four dialogues telling the story of the final days of Socrates (469–399 B.C.). The first in the sequence,* Euthyphro, *portrays Socrates in his typical role, questioning someone about his beliefs (in this case, the young aristocrat, Euthyphro). The discussion is focused on the nature of piety, but the conversation breaks off before a final answer is reached — perhaps none is possible — because Socrates is on his way to stand trial before the Athenian assembly. He has been charged with "preaching false gods" (heresy) and "corrupting the youth" by causing them to doubt or disregard the wisdom of their elders. (How faithful to any actual event or discussion* Euthyphro *and Plato's other Socratic dialogues really are, scholars cannot say with assurance.)*

In Apology, *the second dialogue in the sequence, Plato (who remains entirely in the background, as he does in all the dialogues) recounts Socrates' public reply to the charges against him. During the speech, Socrates explains his life, reminding his fellow citizens that if he is (as the oracle had pronounced) "the wisest of men," then it is only because he knows that he doesn't know what others believe or pretend they do know. The dialogue ends with Socrates being found guilty and duly sentenced to death.*

The third in the series is Crito, *but we will postpone comment on it for a moment and glance at the fourth dialogue,* Phaedo, *in which Plato portrays Socrates' final philosophical discussion. The topic, appropriately, is whether the soul is immortal. It ends with Socrates, in the company of his closest friends, bidding them a last farewell and drinking the fatal cup of hemlock.*

Crito, *the whole text of which is reprinted here, is the debate provoked by Crito, an old friend and admirer of Socrates. He visits Socrates in prison and urges him to escape while he still has the chance. After all, Crito argues, the guilty verdict was wrong and unfair, few Athenians really want to have Socrates put to death, his family and friends will be distraught, and so forth.*

Socrates will not have it. He patiently but firmly examines each of Crito's arguments and explains why it would be wrong to follow his advice.

Plato's Crito thus ranks with Sophocles' tragedy Antigone as one of the first explorations in Western literature of the perennial theme of our responsibility for obeying laws that challenge our conscientious moral convictions. Antigone concludes that she must disobey the law of Creon, tyrant of Thebes; Socrates concludes that he must obey the law of democratic Athens. In Crito, we have not only a superb illustration of Socratic dialogue and argument but also a portrait of a virtuous thinker at the end of a long life, reflecting on its course and on the moral principles that have guided him. We see Socrates living an "examined life," the only life he thought was worth living.

This translation is by Hugh Tredennick.

Crito

(**SCENE:** *A room in the State prison at Athens in the year 399 B.C. The time is half an hour before dawn, and the room would be almost dark but for the light of a little oil lamp. There is a pallet bed against the back wall. At the head of it a small table supports the lamp; near the foot of it Crito is sitting patiently on a stool. He is an old man, kindly, practical, simple-minded; at present he is suffering from acute emotional strain. On the bed lies Socrates asleep. He stirs, yawns, opens his eyes, and sees Crito.)*

SOCRATES: Here already, Crito? Surely it is still early?

CRITO: Indeed it is.

SOCRATES: About what time?

CRITO: Just before dawn.

SOCRATES: I wonder that the warder paid any attention to you.   5

CRITO: He is used to me now, Socrates, because I come here so often; besides, he is under some small obligation to me.

SOCRATES: Have you only just come, or have you been here for long?

CRITO: Fairly long.

SOCRATES: Then why didn't you wake me at once, instead of sitting by my bed so quietly?

CRITO: I wouldn't dream of such a thing, Socrates. I only wish I were not   10 so sleepless and depressed myself. I have been wondering at you, because I saw how comfortably you were sleeping; and I deliberately didn't wake you because I wanted you to go on being as comfortable as you could. I have often felt before in the course of my life how fortunate you are in your disposition, but I feel it more than ever now in your present misfortune when I see how easily and placidly you put up with it.

SOCRATES: Well, really, Crito, it would be hardly suitable for a man of my age to resent having to die.

CRITO: Other people just as old as you are get involved in these misfortunes, Socrates, but their age doesn't keep them from resenting it when they find themselves in your position.

SOCRATES: Quite true. But tell me, why have you come so early?

CRITO: Because I bring bad news, Socrates; not so bad from your point of view, I suppose, but it will be very hard to bear for me and your other friends, and I think that I shall find it hardest of all.

SOCRATES: Why, what is this news? Has the boat come in from Delos—   15
the boat which ends my reprieve when it arrives?[1]

CRITO: It hasn't actually come in yet, but I expect that it will be here today, judging from the report of some people who have just arrived from Sunium and left it there. It's quite clear from their account that it will be here today; and so by tomorrow, Socrates, you will have to—to end your life.

SOCRATES: Well, Crito, I hope that it may be for the best; if the gods will it so, so be it. All the same, I don't think it will arrive today.

CRITO: What makes you think that?

SOCRATES: I will try to explain. I think I am right in saying that I have to die on the day after the boat arrives?

CRITO: That's what the authorities say, at any rate.   20

SOCRATES: Then I don't think it will arrive on this day that is just beginning, but on the day after. I am going by a dream that I had in the night, only a little while ago. It looks as though you were right not to wake me up.

CRITO: Why, what was the dream about?

SOCRATES: I thought I saw a gloriously beautiful woman dressed in white robes, who came up to me and addressed me in these words: "Socrates, to the pleasant land of Phthia on the third day thou shalt come."

CRITO: Your dream makes no sense, Socrates.

SOCRATES: To my mind, Crito, it is perfectly clear.   25

---

[1]**Delos . . . arrives** Ordinarily execution was carried out immediately after sentencing, but the day before Socrates' trial was the first day of an annual ceremony that involved sending a ship to Delos. When the ship was absent—in this case for about a month—executions could not be performed. As Crito goes on to say, Socrates could easily escape, and indeed he could have left the country before being tried. [—Ed.]

CRITO: Too clear, apparently. But look here, Socrates, it is still not too late to take my advice and escape. Your death means a double calamity for me. I shall not only lose a friend whom I can never possibly replace, but besides a great many people who don't know you and me very well will be sure to think that I let you down, because I could have saved you if I had been willing to spend the money; and what could be more contemptible than to get a name for thinking more of money than of your friends? Most people will never believe that it was you who refused to leave this place although we tried our hardest to persuade you.

SOCRATES: But my dear Crito, why should we pay so much attention to what "most people" think? The really reasonable people, who have more claim to be considered, will believe that the facts are exactly as they are.

CRITO: You can see for yourself, Socrates, that one has to think of popular opinion as well. Your present position is quite enough to show that the capacity of ordinary people for causing trouble is not confined to petty annoyances, but has hardly any limits if you once get a bad name with them.

SOCRATES: I only wish that ordinary people *had* unlimited capacity for doing harm; then they might have an unlimited power for doing good; which would be a splendid thing, if it were so. Actually they have neither. They cannot make a man wise or stupid; they simply act at random.

CRITO: Have it that way if you like; but tell me this, Socrates. I hope that 30 you aren't worrying about the possible effects on me and the rest of your friends, and thinking that if you escape we shall have trouble with informers for having helped you to get away, and have to forfeit all our property or pay an enormous fine, or even incur some further punishment? If any idea like that is troubling you, you can dismiss it altogether. We are quite entitled to run that risk in saving you, and even worse, if necessary. Take my advice, and be reasonable.

SOCRATES: All that you say is very much in my mind, Crito, and a great deal more besides.

CRITO: Very well, then, don't let it distress you. I know some people who are willing to rescue you from here and get you out of the country for quite a moderate sum. And then surely you realize how cheap these informers are to buy off; we shan't need much money to settle them; and I think you've got enough of my money for yourself already. And then even supposing that in your anxiety for my safety you feel that you oughtn't to spend my money, there are these foreign gentlemen staying in Athens who are quite willing to spend theirs. One of them, Simmias of Thebes, has actually brought the money with him for this very purpose; and Cebes and a number of others are quite ready to do the same. So as I say, you mustn't let any fears on these grounds make you slacken your efforts to escape; and you mustn't feel any misgivings about what you said at your trial, that you wouldn't know what to do with yourself if you left this country. Wherever you go, there are plenty of places where you will find a welcome; and if you choose to go to Thessaly, I have friends there who will make much of you and give you complete protection, so that no one in Thessaly can interfere with you.

Besides, Socrates, I don't even feel that it is right for you to try to do what you are doing, throwing away your life when you might save it. You are doing your best to treat yourself in exactly the same way as your enemies would, or rather did, when they wanted to ruin you. What is more, it seems to me that you are letting your sons down too. You have it in your power to finish their bringing up and education, and instead of that you are proposing to go off and desert them, and so far as you are concerned they will have to take their chance. And what sort of chance are they likely to get? The sort of thing that usually happens to orphans when they lose their parents. Either one ought not to have children at all, or one ought to see their upbringing and education through to the end. It strikes me that you are taking the line of least resistance, whereas you ought to make the choice of a good man and a brave one, considering that you profess to have made goodness your object all through life. Really, I am ashamed, both on your account and on ours your friends'; it will look as though we had played something like a coward's part all through this affair of yours. First, there was the way you came into court when it was quite unnecessary—that was the first act; than there was the conduct of the defense—that was the second; and finally, to complete the farce, we get this situation, which makes it appear that we have let you slip out of our hands through some lack of courage and enterprise on our part, because we didn't save you, and you didn't save yourself, when it would have been quite possible and practicable, if we had been any use at all.

There, Socrates; if you aren't careful, besides the suffering there will be all this disgrace for you and us to bear. Come, make up your mind. Really it's too late for that now; you ought to have it made up already. There is no alternative; the whole thing must be carried through during this coming night. If we lose any more time, it can't be done, it will be too late. I appeal to you, Socrates, on every ground; take my advice and please don't be unreasonable!

SOCRATES: My dear Crito, I appreciate your warm feelings very much— 35
that is, assuming that they have some justification; if not, the

stronger they are, the harder they will be to deal with. Very well, then; we must consider whether we ought to follow your advice or not. You know that this is not a new idea of mine; it has always been my nature never to accept advice from any of my friends unless reflection shows that it is the best course that reason offers. I cannot abandon the principles which I used to hold in the past simply because this accident has happened to me; they seem to me to be much as they were, and I respect and regard the same principles now as before. So unless we can find better principles on this occasion, you can be quite sure that I shall not agree with you; not even if the power of the people conjures up fresh hordes of bogies to terrify our childish minds, by subjecting us to chains and executions and confiscations of our property.

Well, then, how can we consider the question most reasonably? Suppose that we begin by reverting to this view which you hold about people's opinions. Was it always right to argue that some opinions should be taken seriously but not others? Or was it always wrong? Perhaps it was right before the question of my death arose, but now we can see clearly that it was a mistaken persistence in a point of view which was really irresponsible nonsense. I should like very much to inquire into this problem, Crito, with your help, and to see whether the argument will appear in any different light to me now that I am in this position, or whether it will remain the same; and whether we shall dismiss it or accept it.

Serious thinkers, I believe, have always held some such view as the one which I mentioned just now: that some of the opinions which people entertain should be respected, and others should not. Now I ask you, Crito, don't you think that this is a sound principle?—You are safe from the prospect of dying tomorrow, in all human probability; and you are not likely to have your judgment upset by this impending calamity. Consider, then; don't you think that this is a sound enough principle, that one should not regard all the opinions that people hold, but only some and not others? What do you say? Isn't that a fair statement?

CRITO: Yes, it is.

SOCRATES: In other words, one should regard the good ones and not the bad?

CRITO: Yes.

40

SOCRATES: The opinions of the wise being good, and the opinions of the foolish bad?

CRITO: Naturally.

SOCRATES: To pass on, then: What do you think of the sort of illustration that I used to employ? When a man is in training, and taking it seriously, does he pay attention to all praise and criticism and opinion indiscriminately, or only when it comes from the one qualified person, the actual doctor or trainer?

CRITO: Only when it comes from the one qualified person.

SOCRATES: Then he should be afraid of the criticism and welcome the 45 praise of the one qualified person, but not those of the general public.

CRITO: Obviously.

SOCRATES: So he ought to regulate his actions and exercises and eating and drinking by the judgment of his instructor, who has expert knowledge, rather than by the opinions of the rest of the public.

CRITO: Yes, that is so.

SOCRATES: Very well. Now if he disobeys the one man and disregards his opinion and commendations, and pays attention to the advice of the many who have no expert knowledge, surely he will suffer some bad effect?

CRITO: Certainly. 50

SOCRATES: And what is this bad effect? Where is it produced?—I mean, in what part of the disobedient person?

CRITO: His body, obviously; that is what suffers.

SOCRATES: Very good. Well now, tell me, Crito—we don't want to go through all the examples one by one—does this apply as a general rule, and above all to the sort of actions which we are trying to decide about: just and unjust, honorable and dishonorable, good and bad? Ought we to be guided and intimidated by the opinion of the many or by that of the one—assuming that there is someone with expert knowledge? Is it true that we ought to respect and fear this person more than all the rest put together; and that if we do not follow his guidance we shall spoil and mutilate that part of us which, as we used to say, is improved by right conduct and destroyed by wrong? Or is this all nonsense?

CRITO: No, I think it is true, Socrates.

SOCRATES: Then consider the next step. There is a part of us which is im- 55 proved by healthy actions and ruined by unhealthy ones. If we spoil it by taking the advice of nonexperts, will life be worth living when this part is once ruined? The part I mean is the body; do you accept this?

CRITO: Yes.

SOCRATES: Well, is life worth living with a body which is worn out and ruined by health?

CRITO: Certainly not.

SOCRATES: What about the part of us which is mutilated by wrong actions and benefited by right ones? Is life worth living with this part ruined? Or do we believe that this part of us, whatever it may be, in which right and wrong operate, is of less importance than the body?

CRITO: Certainly not. 60

SOCRATES: It is really more precious?

CRITO: Much more.

SOCRATES: In that case, my dear fellow, what we ought to consider is not so much what people in general will say about us but how we stand with the expert in right and wrong, the one authority, who represents the actual truth. So in the first place your proposition is not correct when you say that we should consider popular opinion in questions of what is right and honorable and good, or the opposite. Of course one might object "All the same, the people have the power to put us to death."

CRITO: No doubt about that! Quite true, Socrates; it is a possible objection.

SOCRATES: But so far as I can see, my dear fellow, the argument which 65 we have just been through is quite unaffected by it. At the same time I should like you to consider whether we are still satisfied on this point: that the really important thing is not to live, but to live well.

CRITO: Why, yes.

SOCRATES: And that to live well means the same thing as to live honorably or rightly?

CRITO: Yes.

SOCRATES: Then in the light of this agreement we must consider whether or not it is right for me to try to get away without an official discharge. If it turns out to be right, we must make the attempt; if not, we must let it drop. As for the considerations you raise about expense and reputation and bringing up children, I am afraid, Crito, that they represent the reflections of the ordinary public, who put people to death, and would bring them back to life if they could, with equal indifference to reason. Our real duty, I fancy, since the argument leads that way, is to consider one question only, the one which we raised just now: Shall we be acting rightly in paying money and showing gratitude to these people who are going to rescue me, and in escaping or arranging the escape ourselves, or shall we really be acting wrongly in doing all this? If it becomes clear that such conduct is wrong, I cannot help thinking that the question whether we are sure to die, or to suffer any other ill effect for that matter, if we stand our ground and take no action, ought not to weigh with us at all in comparison with the risk of doing what is wrong.

CRITO: I agree with what you say, Socrates; but I wish you would con- 70 sider what we ought to *do*.

SOCRATES: Let us look at it together, my dear fellow; and if you can challenge any of my arguments, do so and I will listen to you; but if you can't, be a good fellow and stop telling me over and over again that I ought to leave this place without official permission. I am very anxious to obtain your approval before I adopt the course which I have in mind; I don't want to act against your convictions. Now give your attention to the starting point of this inquiry—I hope that you will be satisfied with my way of stating it—and try to answer my questions to the best of your judgment.

CRITO: Well, I will try.

SOCRATES: Do we say that one must never willingly do wrong, or does it depend upon circumstance? Is it true, as we have often agreed before, that there is no sense in which wrongdoing is good or honorable? Or have we jettisoned all our former convictions in these last few days? Can you and I at our age, Crito, have spent all these years in serious discussions without realizing that we were no better than a pair of children? Surely the truth is just what we have always said. Whatever the popular view is, and whether the alternative is pleasanter than the present one or even harder to bear, the fact remains that to do wrong is in every sense bad and dishonorable for the person who does it. Is that our view, or not?

CRITO: Yes, it is.

SOCRATES: Then in no circumstances must one do wrong.   75

CRITO: No.

SOCRATES: In that case one must not even do wrong when one is wronged, which most people regard as the natural course.

CRITO: Apparently not.

SOCRATES: Tell me another thing, Crito: Ought one to do injuries or not?

CRITO: Surely not, Socrates.   80

SOCRATES: And tell me: Is it right to do an injury in retaliation, as most people believe, or not?

CRITO: No, never.

SOCRATES: Because, I suppose, there is no difference between injuring people and wronging them.

CRITO: Exactly.

SOCRATES: So one ought not to return a wrong or an injury to any per-   85 son, whatever the provocation is. Now be careful, Crito, that in making these single admissions you do not end by admitting something contrary to your real beliefs. I know that there are and always will be few people who think like this; and consequently between those who do think so and those who do not there can be no agreement on principle; they must always feel contempt when they observe one another's decisions. I want even you to consider very carefully whether you share my views and agree with me, and whether we can proceed with our discussion from the established hypothesis that it is never right to do a wrong or return a wrong or defend one's self against injury by retaliation; or whether you dissociate yourself from any share in this view as a basis for discussion. I have held it for a long time, and still hold it; but if you have formed any other opinion, say so and tell me what it is. If, on the other hand, you stand by what we have said, listen to my next point.

CRITO: Yes, I stand by it and agree with you. Go on.

SOCRATES: Well, here is my next point, or rather question. Ought one to fulfill all one's agreements, provided that they are right, or break them?

CRITO: One ought to fulfill them.

SOCRATES: Then consider the logical consequence. If we leave this place without first persuading the State to let us go, are we or are we not doing an injury, and doing it in a quarter where it is least justifiable? Are we or are we not abiding by our just agreements?

CRITO: I can't answer your question, Socrates; I am not clear in my mind.

SOCRATES: Look at it in this way. Suppose that while we were preparing to run away from here (or however one should describe it) the Laws and Constitution of Athens were to come and confront us and ask this question: "Now, Socrates, what are you proposing to do? Can you deny that by this act which you are contemplating you intend, so far as you have the power, to destroy us, the Laws, and the whole State as well? Do you imagine that a city can continue to exist and not be turned upside down, if the legal judgments which are pronounced in it have no force but are nullified and destroyed by private persons?"—how shall we answer this question, Crito, and others of the same kind? There is much that could be said, especially by a professional advocate, to protest against the invalidation of this law which enacts that judgments once pronounced shall be binding. Shall we say "Yes, I do intend to destroy the laws, because the State wronged me by passing a faulty judgment at my trial"? Is this to be our answer, or what?

CRITO: What you have just said, by all means, Socrates.

SOCRATES: Then what supposing the Laws say, "Was there provision for this in the agreement between you and us, Socrates? Or did you undertake to abide by whatever judgments the State pronounced?" If we expressed surprise at such language, they would probably say: "Never mind our language, Socrates, but answer our questions; after all, you are accustomed to the method of question and answer. Come now, what charge do you bring against us and the State, that you are trying to destroy us? Did we not give you life in the first place? Was it not through us that your father married your mother and begot you? Tell us, have you any complaint against those of us Laws that deal with marriage?" "No, none," I should say. "Well, have you any against the laws which deal with children's upbringing and education, such as you had yourself? Are you not grateful to those of us Laws which were instituted for this end, for requiring your father to give you a cultural and physical education?" "Yes," I should say. "Very good. Then since you have been born and brought up and educated, can you deny, in the first place, that you were our child and servant, both you and your ancestors? And if this is so, do you imagine that what is right for us is equally right for you, and that whatever we try to do to you, you are justified in retaliating? You did not have equality of rights with your father, or your employer (supposing that you had had one), to enable you to retaliate; you were not allowed to answer back when you were scolded or to hit back when you were beaten, or to do a great many other things of the same kind. Do you expect to have such license against your country and its laws that if we try to put you to death in the belief that it is right to do so, you on your part will try your hardest to destroy your country and us its Laws in return? And will you, the true devotee of goodness, claim that you are justified in doing so? Are you so wise as to have forgotten that compared with your mother and father and all the rest of your ancestors your country is something far more precious, more venerable, more sacred, and held in greater honor both among gods and among all reasonable men? Do you not realize that you are even more bound to respect and placate the anger of your country than your father's anger? That if you cannot persuade your country you must do whatever it orders, and patiently submit to any punishment that it imposes, whether it be flogging or imprisonment? And if it leads you out to war, to be wounded or killed, you must comply, and it is right that you should do so; you must not give way or retreat or abandon your position. Both in war and in the law courts and everywhere else you must do whatever your city and your country commands, or else persuade it in accordance with universal justice; but violence is a sin even against your parents, and it is a far greater sin against your country" — What shall we say to this, Crito? — that what the Laws say is true, or not?

CRITO: Yes, I think so.

SOCRATES: "Consider, then, Socrates," the Laws would probably continue, "whether it is also true for us to say that what you are now   95 trying to do to us is not right. Although we have brought you into the world and reared you and educated you, and given you and all your fellow citizens a share in all the good things at our disposal, nevertheless by the very fact of granting our permission we openly proclaim this principle: that any Athenian, on attaining to manhood and seeing for himself the political organization of the State and us its Laws, is permitted, if he is not satisfied with us, to take his property and go away wherever he likes. If any of you chooses to go to one of our colonies, supposing that he should not be satisfied with us and the State, or to emigrate to any other country, not one of us Laws hinders or prevents him from going away wherever he likes, without any loss of property. On the other hand, if any one of you stands his ground when he can see how we administer justice and the rest of our public organization, we hold that by so doing he has in fact undertaken to do anything that we tell him; and we maintain that anyone who disobeys is guilty of doing wrong on three separate counts: first because we are his parents, and secondly because we are his guardians; and thirdly because, after promising obedience, he is neither obeying us nor persuading us to change our decision if we are at fault in any way; and although all our orders are in the form of proposals, not of savage commands, and we give him the choice of either persuading us or doing what we say, he is actually doing neither. These are the charges, Socrates, to which we say that you will be liable if you do what you are contemplating; and you will not be the least culpable of your fellow countrymen, but one of the most guilty." If I said "Why do you say that?" they would no doubt pounce upon me with perfect justice and point out that there are very few people in Athens who have entered into this agreement with them as explicitly as I have. They would say "Socrates, we have substantial evidence that you are satisfied with us and with the State. You would not have been so exceptionally reluctant to cross the borders of your country if you had not been exceptionally attached to it. You have never left the city to attend a festival or for any other purpose, except on some military expedition; you have never traveled abroad as other people do, and you have never felt the impulse to acquaint yourself with another country or constitution; you have been content with us and with our city. You have definitely chosen us, and undertaken to observe us in all your activities as a citizen; and as the crowning proof that you are satisfied with our city, you have begotten children in it. Furthermore, even at the time of your trial you could have proposed the penalty of banishment, if you had chosen to do so; that is, you could have done then with the sanction of the State what you are now trying to do without it. But whereas at that time you made a noble show of indifference if you had to die, and in fact preferred death, as you said, to banishment, now you show no respect for your earlier professions, and no regard for us, the Laws, whom you are trying to destroy; you are behaving like the lowest type of menial, trying to run away in spite of the contracts and undertakings by which you agreed to live as a member of our State. Now first answer this question: Are we or are we not speaking the truth when we say that you have undertaken, in deed if not in word, to live your life as a citizen in obedience to us?" What are we to say to that, Crito? Are we not bound to admit it?

CRITO: We cannot help it, Socrates.

SOCRATES: "It is a fact, then," they would say, "that you are breaking covenants and undertakings made with us, although you made them under no compulsion or misunderstanding, and were not compelled to decide in a limited time; you had seventy years in which you could have left the country, if you were not satisfied with us or felt that the agreements were unfair. You did not choose Sparta or Crete—your favorite models of good government—or any other Greek or foreign state; you could not have absented yourself from the city less if you had been lame or blind or decrepit in some other way. It is quite obvious that you stand by yourself above all other Athenians in your affection for this city and for us its Laws;—who would care for a city without laws? And now, after all this, are you not going to stand by your agreement? Yes, you are, Socrates, if you will take our advice; and then you will at least escape being laughed at for leaving the city.

"We invite you to consider what good you will do to yourself or your friends if you commit this breach of faith and stain your conscience. It is fairly obvious that the risk of being banished and either losing their citizenship or having their property confiscated will extend to your friends as well. As for yourself, if you go to one of the neighboring states, such as Thebes or Megara, which are both well governed, you will enter them as an enemy to their constitution[2] and all good patriots will eye you with suspicion as a destroyer of law and order. Incidentally you will confirm the opinion of the jurors who tried you that they gave a correct verdict; a destroyer of laws might very well be supposed to have a destructive influence upon young and foolish human beings. Do you intend, then, to avoid well governed states and the higher forms of human society? And if you do, will life be worth living? Or will you approach these people and

---

[2]**as an enemy to their constitution** As a lawbreaker. [—Ed.]

have the impudence to converse with them? What arguments will you use, Socrates? The same which you used here, that goodness and integrity, institutions and laws, are the most precious possessions of mankind? Do you not think that Socrates and everything about him will appear in a disreputable light? You certainly ought to think so. But perhaps you will retire from this part of the world and go to Crito's friends in Thessaly? That is the home of indiscipline and laxity, and no doubt they would enjoy hearing the amusing story of how you managed to run away from prison by arraying yourself in some costume or putting on a shepherd's smock or some other conventional runaway's disguise, and altering your personal appearance. And will no one comment on the fact that an old man of your age, probably with only a short time left to live, should dare to cling so greedily to life, at the price of violating the most stringent laws? Perhaps not, if you avoid irritating anyone. Otherwise, Socrates, you will hear a good many humiliating comments. So you will live as the toady and slave of all the populace, literally 'roistering in Thessaly,' as though you had left this country for Thessaly to attend a banquet there; and where will your discussions about goodness and uprightness be then, we should like to know? But of course you want to live for your children's sake, so that you may be able to bring them up and educate them. Indeed! by first taking them off to Thessaly and making foreigners of them, so that they may have that additional enjoyment? Or if that is not your intention, supposing that they are brought up here with you still alive, will they be better cared for and educated without you, because of course your friends will look after them? Will they look after your children if you go away to Thessaly, and not if you go away to the next world? Surely if those who profess to be your friends are worth anything, you must believe that they would care for them.

"No, Socrates; be advised by us your guardians, and do not think more of your children or of your life or of anything else than you think of what is right; so that when you enter the next world you may have all this to plead in your defense before the authorities there. It seems clear that if you do this thing, neither you nor any of your friends will be the better for it or be more upright or have a cleaner conscience here in this world, nor will it be better for you when you reach the next. As it is, you will leave this place, when you do, as the victim of a wrong done not by us, the Laws, but by your fellow men. But if you leave in that dishonorable way, returning wrong for wrong and evil for evil, breaking your agreements and covenants with us, and injuring those whom you least ought to injure—yourself, your friends, your country, and us—then you will

have to face our anger in your lifetime, and in that place beyond
when the laws of the other world know that you have tried, so far as
you could, to destroy even us their brothers, they will not receive
you with a kindly welcome. Do not take Crito's advice, but follow
ours."

That, my dear friend Crito, I do assure you, is what I seem to 100
hear them saying, just as a mystic seems to hear the strains of
music; and the sound of their arguments rings so loudly in my head
that I cannot hear the other side. I warn you that, as my opinion
stands at present, it will be useless to urge a different view.
However, if you think that you will do any good by it, say what you
like.

CRITO: No, Socrates, I have nothing to say.

SOCRATES: Then give it up, Crito, and let us follow this course, since God
points out the way.

Topics for Critical Thinking and Writing

1. State as precisely as you can all the arguments Crito uses to try to convince Socrates that he ought to escape. Which of these arguments seems
to you to be the best? The worst? Why?

2. Socrates says to Crito, "I cannot abandon the principles which I used
to hold in the past simply because this accident [the misfortune of
being convicted by the Athenian assembly and then sentenced to death]
has happened to me" (para. 35). Does this remark strike you as self-
righteous? Stubborn? Smug? Stupid? Explain.

3. Socrates declares that "serious thinkers" have always held the view that
"some of the opinions which people entertain should be respected, and
others should not" (para. 37). There are two main alternatives to this
principle: (a) One should respect *all* the opinions that others hold, and
(b) one should respect *none* of the opinions of others. Socrates attacks
(a) but he ignores (b). What are his objections to (a)? Do you find them
convincing? Can you think of any convincing arguments against (b)?

4. As Socrates shows in his reply to Crito, he seems ready to believe (para.
63) that there are "expert[s] in right and wrong" — that is, persons with
expert opinion or even authoritative knowledge on matters of right and
wrong conduct — and that their advice should be sought and followed.
Do you agree? Consider the thesis that there are no such experts, and
write a 500-word essay defending or attacking it.

5. Socrates, as he comments to Crito, believes that "it is never right to
do a wrong or return a wrong or defend one's self against injury by

retaliation" (para. 85). He does not offer any argument for this thesis in the dialogue (although he does elsewhere). It was a very strange doctrine in his day, and even now it is not generally accepted. Write a 1,000-word essay defending or attacking this thesis.

6. Socrates seems to argue that (a) no one ought to do wrong, (b) it would injure the state for someone in Socrates' position to escape, and (c) this act would break a "just agreement" between the citizen and his state; therefore, (d) no one in Socrates' position should escape. Do you think this argument is valid? If not, what further assumptions would be needed to make it valid? Do you think the argument is sound (that is, both valid and true in all its premises)? If not, explain. If you had to attack premise (b) or (c), which do you think is the more vulnerable, and why?

7. In the imaginary speech by the Laws of Athens to Socrates, especially in paragraph 93, the Laws convey a picture of the supremacy of the state over the individual—and Socrates seems to assent to this picture. Do you? Why, or why not?

8. The Laws (para. 95) claim that if Socrates were to escape, he would be "guilty of doing wrong on three separate counts." What are they? Do you agree with all or any? Why, or why not? Read the essay by Martin Luther King Jr., "Letter from Birmingham Jail" (p. 293), and decide how King would have responded to the judgment of the Laws of Athens.

9. At the end of their peroration (para. 99), the Laws of Athens say to Socrates: Take your punishment as prescribed, and at your death "you will leave this place . . . as the victim of a wrong done not by us, the Laws, but by your fellow men." To what wrong do the Laws allude? Do you agree that it is men and not laws who perpetrated this wrong? If you were in Socrates' position, would it matter to you if you were being wronged not by laws but only by men? Explain.

10. Compose a letter from Socrates to Martin Luther King Jr. in which Socrates responds to King's "Letter from Birmingham Jail" (p. 293).

PLATO

This dialogue, from Republic, *has for its ostensible topic the nature of justice. But the reader soon learns that Socrates (who speaks for Plato) believes we cannot understand what justice is until we first understand the truth about human nature; as he explains to Glaucon, because justice can be achieved only in an ideal state, the ideal state must be constructed from a correct account of human nature. To make these issues clear, we are led into many fundamental problems of philosophy.* Republic *is thus* read not only for Plato's views on education, politics, and ethics, but also for his logical, metaphysical, and psychological theories.

At the very center of the dialogue is an examination of epistemology; that is, the nature of human knowledge. Plato's strategy is to begin by contrasting knowledge with both ignorance and belief (or opinion, doxa in Greek). The excerpt here, the "Myth [or Allegory] of the Cave," relies on the reader's having a grasp of the relations among these fundamental concepts.

The distinction among knowledge, belief, and ignorance is not peculiar to Plato, of course. We, too, need to keep clearly in mind what it is to have one or more beliefs about something, and what it is to know something. So long as we can deal with these concepts abstractly, it may not be too difficult to keep them distinct.

If pressed, we can define belief and knowledge so that they will not be confused. But as soon as we confront one of our own beliefs, and ask whether we are correct in believing it—that is, whether the belief or opinion is true, and whether we have adequate reasons or evidence for it—then it is no longer so easy at all. (How, for example, do you tell whether you know or only believe that the earth is round, or that $3 \times 5 = \frac{30}{2}$?)

In an earlier passage in Republic (not reprinted here), Plato explained these concepts by correlating them with their proper objects. The object of knowledge is Reality, and the object of ignorance is Nothing, whereas the object of belief (the most troublesome of the three) is somewhere between, the shifting and unstable world of Appearances. And so belief is sometimes true but often false. As the Myth shows, Plato believes the Good is the most important part of Reality. His account of the blinding vision of the Good—seeing the Truth and seeing it whole—vouchsafed to that rare person (the true philosopher) who succeeds in escaping the cave, has inspired later writers to see in it a foreshadowing of the mystic's vision of God. (The sun, with its blinding light, has often been used as a metaphor for divine radiance.)

The Myth of the Cave has more to teach us than a lesson in epistemology. Plato's aim is to show the nature of our lives when we fail to realize our true ignorance, and also to show the terrible price of successfully breaking free from the mental prison of mistaken belief. As the Myth shows, we become irritable and even dangerous when challenged to examine our beliefs and way of life. The Myth invites us to reevaluate our lives from beginning to end, because (if the Myth can be trusted) right now most of us dwell in darkness, unaware of our true plight. Throughout our lives we have been and probably will continue to be deceived unwittingly into thinking we really "know" the nature of reality, when in fact we don't; we foolishly "believe" we know.

A few words need to be said about the physical setting of Plato's cave. Imagine a darkened theater in which the audience is seated facing a screen. Behind the audience other persons parade back and forth with every variety of object carried on their heads. At the rear of the theater a spotlight is cleverly fixed so that it casts the shadows of these objects (but not of those carrying them) onto the screen. The shadow-show goes on endlessly, and shadows are all the audience ever sees, for they are strapped rigidly into their seats. The viewers take these shadows (mere "appearance") for "reality."

Myth of the Cave

"I want you to go on to picture the enlightenment or ignorance of our human condition somewhat as follows. Imagine an underground chamber like a cave, with a long entrance open to the daylight and as wide as the cave. In this chamber are men who have been prisoners there since they were children, their legs and necks being so fastened that they can only look straight ahead of them and cannot turn their heads. Some way off, behind and higher up, a fire is burning, and between the fire and the prisoners and above them runs a road, in front of which a curtain-wall has been built, like the screen at puppet shows between the operators and their audience, above which they show their puppets."

"I see."

"Imagine further that there are men carrying all sorts of gear along behind the curtain-wall, projecting above it and including figures of men and animals made of wood and stone and all sorts of other materials, and that some of these men, as you would expect, are talking and some not."

"An odd picture and an odd sort of prisoner."

"They are drawn from life," I replied. "For, tell me, do you think our   5 prisoners could see anything of themselves or their fellows except the shadows thrown by the fire on the wall of the cave opposite them?"

"How could they see anything else if they were prevented from moving their heads all their lives?"

"And would they see anything more of the objects carried along the road?"

"Of course not."

"Then if they were able to talk to each other, would they not assume that the shadows they saw were the real things?"

"Inevitably."   10

"And if the wall of their prison opposite them reflected sound, don't you think that they would suppose, whenever one of the passers-by on the road spoke, that the voice belonged to the shadow passing before them?"

"They would be bound to think so."

"And so in every way they would believe that the shadows of the objects we mentioned were the whole truth."

"Yes, inevitably."

"Then think what would naturally happen to them if they were re-   15
leased from their bonds and cured of their delusions. Suppose one of them were let loose, and suddenly compelled to stand up and turn his head and look and walk toward the fire; all these actions would be painful and he would be too dazzled to see properly the objects of which he used to see the shadows. What do you think he would say if he was told that what he used to see was so much empty nonsense and that he was now nearer reality and seeing more correctly, because he was turned toward objects that were more real, and if on top of that he were compelled to say what each of the passing objects was when it was pointed out to him? Don't you think he would be at a loss, and think that what he used to see was far truer than the objects now being pointed out to him?"

"Yes, far truer."

"And if he were made to look directly at the light of the fire, it would hurt his eyes and he would turn back and retreat to the things which he could see properly, which he would think really clearer than the things being shown him."

"Yes."

"And if," I went on, "he were forcibly dragged up the steep and rugged ascent and not let go till he had been dragged out into the sunlight, the process would be a painful one, to which he would much object, and when he emerged into the light his eyes would be so dazzled by the glare of it that he wouldn't be able to see a single one of the things he was now told were real."

"Certainly not at first," he agreed.   20

"Because, of course, he would need to grow accustomed to the light before he could see things in the upper world outside the cave. First he would find it easiest to look at shadows, next at the reflections of men and other objects in water, and later on at the objects themselves. After that he would find it easier to observe the heavenly bodies and the sky itself at night, and to look at the light of the moon and stars rather than at the sun and its light by day."

"Of course."

"The thing he would be able to do last would be to look directly at the sun itself, and gaze at it without using reflections in water or any other medium but as it is in itself."

"That must come last."

"Later on he would come to the conclusion that it is the sun that 25
produces the changing seasons and years and controls everything in the
visible world, and is in a sense responsible for everything that he and his
fellow-prisoners used to see."

"That is the conclusion which he would obviously reach."

"And when he thought of his first home and what passed for wisdom there, and of his fellow-prisoners, don't you think he would congratulate himself on his good fortune and be sorry for them?"

"Very much so."

"There was probably a certain amount of honor and glory to be won
among the prisoners, and prizes for keen-sightedness for those best able
to remember the order of sequence among the passing shadows and so
be best able to divine their future appearances. Will our released prisoner hanker after these prizes or envy this power or honor? Won't he be
more likely to feel, as Homer says, that he would far rather be 'a serf in
the house of some landless man,' or indeed anything else in the world,
than hold the opinions and live the life that they do?"

"Yes," he replied, "he would prefer anything to a life like theirs." 30

"Then what do you think would happen," I asked, "if he went back
to sit in his old seat in the cave? Wouldn't his eyes be blinded by the
darkness, because he had come in suddenly out of the sunlight?"

"Certainly."

"And if he had to discriminate between the shadows, in competition
with the other prisoners, while he was still blinded and before his eyes
got used to the darkness—a process that would take some time—
wouldn't he be likely to make a fool of himself? And they would say that
his visit to the upper world had ruined his sight, and that the ascent was
not worth even attempting. And if anyone tried to release them and lead
them up, they would kill him if they could lay hands on him."

"They certainly would."

"Now, my dear Glaucon," I went on, "this simile must be connected 35
throughout with what preceded it. The realm revealed by sight corre-
sponds to the prison, and the light of the fire in the prison to the power
of the sun. And you won't go wrong if you connect the ascent into the
upper world and the sight of the objects there with the upward progress
of the mind into the intelligible region. That at any rate is my interpretation, which is what you are anxious to hear; the truth of the matter is,
after all, known only to god. But in my opinion, for what it is worth, the
final thing to be perceived in the intelligible region, and perceived only
with difficulty, is the form of the good; once seen, it is inferred to be responsible for whatever is right and valuable in anything, producing in
the visible region light and the source of light, and being in the intel-

ligible region itself the controlling source of truth and intelligence. And anyone who is going to act rationally either in public or private life must have sight of it."

"I agree," he said, "so far as I am able to understand you."

"Then you will perhaps also agree with me that it won't be surprising if those who get so far are unwilling to involve themselves in human affairs, and if their minds long to remain in the realm above. That's what we should expect if our simile holds good again."

"Yes, that's to be expected."

"Nor will you think it strange that anyone who descends from contemplation of the divine to human life and its ills should blunder and make a fool of himself, if, while still blinded and unaccustomed to the surrounding darkness, he's forcibly put on trial in the law courts or elsewhere about the shadows of justice or the figures of which they are shadows, and made to dispute about the notions of them held by men who have never seen justice itself."

"There's nothing strange in that."   40

"But anyone with any sense," I said, "will remember that the eyes may be unsighted in two ways, by a transition either from light to darkness or from darkness to light, and will recognize that the same thing applies to the mind. So when he sees a mind confused and unable to see clearly he will not laugh without thinking, but will ask himself whether it has come from a clearer world and is confused by the unaccustomed darkness, or whether it is dazzled by the stronger light of the clearer world to which it has escaped from its previous ignorance. The first condition of life is a reason for congratulation, the second for sympathy, though if one wants to laugh at it one can do so with less absurdity than at the mind that has descended from the daylight of the upper world."

"You put it very reasonably."

"If this is true," I continued, "we must reject the conception of education professed by those who say that they can put into the mind knowledge that was not there before—rather as if they could put sight into blind eyes."

"It is a claim that is certainly made," he said.   45

"But our argument indicates that this is a capacity which is innate in each man's mind, and that the organ by which he learns is like an eye which cannot be turned from darkness to light unless the whole body is turned; in the same way the mind as a whole must be turned away from the world of change until its eye can bear to look straight at reality, and at the brightest of all realities which is what we call the good. Isn't that so?"

"Yes."

"Then this turning around of the mind itself might be made a subject of professional skill, which would effect the conversion as easily and effectively as possible. It would not be concerned to implant sight, but to ensure that someone who had it already was not either turned in the wrong direction or looking the wrong way."

"That may well be so."

"The rest, therefore, of what are commonly called excellences of the mind perhaps resemble those of the body, in that they are not in fact innate, but are implanted by subsequent training and practice; but knowledge, it seems, must surely have a diviner quality, something which never loses its power, but whose effects are useful and salutary or again useless and harmful according to the direction in which it is turned. Have you never noticed how shrewd is the glance of the type of men commonly called bad but clever? They have small minds, but their sight is sharp and piercing enough in matters that concern them; it's not that their sight is weak, but that they are forced to serve evil, so that the keener their sight the more effective that evil is."

"That's true." 50

"But suppose," I said, "that such natures were cut loose, when they were still children, from all the dead weights natural to this world of change and fastened on them by sensual indulgences like gluttony, which twist their minds' vision to lower things, and suppose that when so freed they were turned toward the truth, then this same part of these same individuals would have as keen a vision of truth as it has of the objects on which it is at present turned."

"Very likely."

"And is it not also likely, and indeed a necessary consequence of what we have said, that society will never be properly governed either by the uneducated, who have no knowledge of the truth, or by those who are allowed to spend all their lives in purely intellectual pursuits? The uneducated have no single aim in life to which all their actions, public and private, are to be directed; the intellectuals will take no practical action of their own accord, fancying themselves to be out of this world in some kind of earthly paradise."

"True."

"Then our job as lawgivers is to compel the best minds to attain 55 what we have called the highest form of knowledge, and to ascend to the vision of the good as we have described, and when they have achieved this and see well enough, prevent them behaving as they are now allowed to."

"What do you mean by that?"

"Remaining in the upper world, and refusing to return again to the prisoners in the cave below and share their labors and rewards, whether trivial or serious."

"But surely," he protested, "that will not be fair. We shall be compelling them to live a poorer life than they might live."

"The object of our legislation," I reminded him again, "is not the special welfare of any particular class in our society, but of the society as a whole; and it uses persuasion or compulsion to unite all citizens and make them share together the benefits which each individually can confer on the community; and its purpose in fostering this attitude is not to leave everyone to please himself, but to make each man a link in the unity of the whole."

"You are right; I had forgotten," he said.   60

"You see, then, Glaucon," I went on, "we shan't be unfair to our philosophers, but shall be quite fair in what we say when we compel them to have some care and responsibility for others. We shall tell them that philosophers born in other states can reasonably refuse to take part in the hard work of politics; for society produces them quite involuntarily and unintentionally, and it is only just that anything that grows up on its own should feel it has nothing to repay for an upbringing which it owes to no one. 'But,' we shall say, 'we have bred you both for your own sake and that of the whole community to act as leaders and king bees in a hive; you are better and more fully educated than the rest and better qualified to combine the practice of philosophy and politics. You must therefore each descend in turn and live with your fellows in the cave and get used to seeing in the dark; once you get used to it you will see a thousand times better than they do and will distinguish the various shadows, and know what they are shadows of, because you have seen the truth about things admirable and just and good. And so our state and yours will be really awake, and not merely dreaming like most societies today, with their shadow battles and their struggles for political power, which they treat as some great prize. The truth is quite different: The state whose prospective rulers come to their duties with least enthusiasm is bound to have the best and most tranquil government, and the state whose rulers are eager to rule the worst.'"

"I quite agree."

"Then will our pupils, when they hear what we say, dissent and refuse to take their share of the hard work of government, even though spending the greater part of their time together in the pure air above?"

"They cannot refuse, for we are making a just demand of just men. But of course, unlike present rulers, they will approach the business of government as an unavoidable necessity."

"Yes, of course," I agreed. "The truth is that if you want a well-   65
governed state to be possible, you must find for your future rulers some way of life they like better than government; for only then will you have

government by the truly rich, those, that is, whose riches consist not of gold, but of the true happiness of a good and rational life. If you get, in public affairs, men whose life is impoverished and destitute of personal satisfactions, but who hope to snatch some compensation for their own inadequacy from a political career, there can never be good government. They start fighting for power, and the consequent internal and domestic conflicts ruin both them and society."

"True indeed."

"Is there any life except that of true philosophy which looks down on positions of political power?"

"None whatever."

"But what we need is that the only men to get power should be men who do not love it, otherwise we shall have rivals' quarrels."

"That is certain."   70

"Who else, then, will you compel to undertake the responsibilities of Guardians of our state, if it is not to be those who know most about the principles of good government and who have other rewards and a better life than the politician's?"

"There is no one else."

Topics for Critical Thinking and Writing

1. Write an essay of 500 words in which you describe as vividly as possible, in your own language, the situation of the prisoners in the cave. You may find it helpful first to draw a rough picture of their situation as Plato describes it. Try to write your account as though you were an escaped prisoner returning to the cave.

2. Socrates claims (para. 45) that "our argument indicates that this is a capacity [i.e., for learning] which is innate in each man's mind." Explain this thesis, and state and evaluate the argument for it to which Socrates alludes.

3. The requirement that the philosophers should have to rule in the ideal state is, Glaucon suggests (para. 58), "not . . . fair." Why does he apparently think this demand is unfair, or unjust? To whom is it unjust? Evaluate Socrates' reply.

4. Socrates defends the idea (para. 61) that "the state whose prospective rulers come to their duties with least enthusiasm is bound to have the best and most tranquil government." Do you think this generalization is true? Can you think of arguments for and against it? How would you go about trying to prove or disprove it? How does Socrates argue for it?

5. Roughly midway through the essay, Socrates suggests (para. 33) that the prisoners "would kill" any of their own who escaped and returned. It is often said that in this passage Plato alludes to the historic fate of Socrates himself, who was executed under order of the Athenian government in 399 B.C. Read Plato's account of Socrates' trial in the dialogue called *Apology,* and write a 500-word essay in which you argue for or against this parallel.

THOMAS MORE

The son of a prominent London lawyer, More (1478–1535) served as a page in the household of the Archbishop of Canterbury, went to Oxford University, and then studied law in London. More's charm, brilliance, and gentle manner caused Erasmus, the great Dutch humanist who became his friend during a visit to London, to write to a friend: "Did nature ever create anything kinder, sweeter, or more harmonious than the character of Thomas More?"

More served in Parliament, became a diplomat, and after holding several important positions in the government of Henry VIII, rose to become Lord Chancellor. But when Henry married Anne Boleyn, broke from the Church of Rome, and established himself as head of the Church of England, More refused to subscribe to the Act of Succession and Supremacy. Condemned to death as a traitor, he was executed in 1535, nominally for treason but really because he would not recognize the king rather than the pope as the head of his church. A moment before the ax fell, More displayed a bit of the whimsy for which he was known: When he put his head on the block, he brushed his beard aside, commenting that his beard had done no offense to the king. In 1886 the Roman Catholic Church beatified More, and in 1935, the four-hundredth anniversary of his death, it canonized him as St. Thomas More.

More wrote Utopia *(1514–15) in Latin, the international language of the day. The book's name, however, is Greek for "no place" (*ou topos*), with a pun on "good place" (*eu topos*). Utopia owes something to Plato's* Republic *and something to then-popular accounts of voyagers such as Amerigo Vespucci. Utopia purports to record an account given by a traveler named Hytholodaeus (Greek for "learned in nonsense"), who allegedly visited Utopia. The work is playful, but it is also serious. In truth, it is hard to know exactly where it is serious and how serious it is. One inevitably wonders, for example, if More the devoted Roman*

Catholic could really have advocated euthanasia. And could More the persecutor of heretics really have approved of the religious tolerance practiced in Utopia? Is he perhaps in effect saying, "Let's see what reason, unaided by Christian revelation, can tell us about an ideal society"? But if so, is he nevertheless also saying, very strongly, that Christian countries, though blessed with the revelation of Christ's teachings, are far behind these unenlightened pagans? Utopia has been widely praised by all sorts of readers—from Roman Catholics to communists—but for all sorts of reasons. The selection presented here is about one-twelfth of the book (in a translation by Paul Turner).

From *Utopia*

[A DAY IN UTOPIA]

And now for their working conditions. Well, there's one job they all do, irrespective of sex, and that's farming. It's part of every child's education. They learn the principles of agriculture at school, and they're taken for regular outings into the fields near the town, where they not only watch farm work being done, but also do some themselves, as a form of exercise.

Besides farming which, as I say, is everybody's job, each person is taught a special trade of his own. He may be trained to process wool or flax, or he may become a stonemason, a blacksmith, or a carpenter. Those are the only trades that employ any considerable quantity of labor. They have no tailors or dressmakers, since everyone on the island wears the same sort of clothes—except that they vary slightly according to sex and marital status—and the fashion never changes. These clothes are quite pleasant to look at, they allow free movement of the limbs, they're equally suitable for hot and cold weather—and the great thing is, they're all home-made. So everybody learns one of the other trades I mentioned, and by everybody I mean the women as well as the men—though the weaker sex are given the lighter jobs, like spinning and weaving, while the men do the heavier ones.

Most children are brought up to do the same work as their parents, since they tend to have a natural feeling for it. But if a child fancies some other trade, he's adopted into a family that practices it. Of course, great care is taken, not only by the father, but also by the local authorities, to see that the foster father is a decent, respectable type. When you've learned one trade properly, you can, if you like, get permission to learn another—and when you're an expert in both, you can practice whichever you prefer, unless the other one is more essential to the public.

The chief business of the Stywards[1]—in fact, practically their only business—is to see that nobody sits around doing nothing, but that everyone gets on with his job. They don't wear people out, though, by keeping them hard at work from early morning till late at night, like cart horses. That's just slavery—and yet that's what life is like for the working classes nearly everywhere else in the world. In Utopia they have a six-hour working day—three hours in the morning, then lunch—then a two-hour break—then three more hours in the afternoon, followed by supper. They go to bed at 8 P.M., and sleep for eight hours. All the rest of the twenty-four they're free to do what they like—not to waste their time in idleness or self-indulgence, but to make good use of it in some congenial activity. Most people spend these free periods on further education, for there are public lectures first thing every morning. Attendance is quite voluntary, except for those picked out for academic training, but men and women of all classes go crowding in to hear them—I mean, different people go to different lectures, just as the spirit moves them. However, there's nothing to stop you from spending this extra time on your trade, if you want to. Lots of people do, if they haven't the capacity for intellectual work, and are much admired for such public-spirited behavior.

After supper they have an hour's recreation, either in the gardens or in the communal dining-halls, according to the time of year. Some people practice music, others just talk. They've never heard of anything so silly and demoralizing as dice, but they have two games rather like chess. The first is a sort of arithmetical contest, in which certain numbers "take" others. The second is a pitched battle between virtues and vices, which illustrates most ingeniously how vices tend to conflict with one another, but to combine against virtues. It also shows which vices are opposed to which virtues, how much strength vices can muster for a direct assault, what indirect tactics they employ, what help virtues need to overcome vices, what are the best methods of evading their attacks, and what ultimately determines the victory of one side or the other.

But here's a point that requires special attention, or you're liable to get the wrong idea. Since they only work a six-hour day, you may think there must be a shortage of essential goods. On the contrary, those six hours are enough, and more than enough to produce plenty of everything that's needed for a comfortable life. And you'll understand why it is, if you reckon up how large a proportion of the population in other

[1]**Stywards** In Utopia, each group of thirty households elects a styward; each town has two hundred stywards, who elect the mayor. [—Ed.]

countries is totally unemployed. First you have practically all the women—that gives you nearly 50 percent for a start. And in countries where the women *do* work, the men tend to lounge about instead. Then there are all the priests, and members of so-called religious orders— how much work do they do? Add all the rich, especially the landowners, popularly known as nobles and gentlemen. Include their domestic staffs—I mean those gangs of armed ruffians that I mentioned before. Finally, throw in all the beggars who are perfectly hale and hearty, but pretend to be ill as an excuse for being lazy. When you've counted them up, you'll be surprised to find how few people actually produce what the human race consumes.

And now just think how few of these few people are doing essential work—for where money is the only standard of value, there are bound to be dozens of unnecessary trades carried on, which merely supply luxury goods or entertainment. Why, even if the existing labor force were distributed among the few trades really needed to make life reasonably comfortable, there'd be so much overproduction that prices would fall too low for the workers to earn a living. Whereas, if you took all those engaged in nonessential trades, and all who are too lazy to work—each of whom consumes twice as much of the products of other people's labor as any of the producers themselves—if you put the whole lot of them on to something useful, you'd soon see how few hours' work a day would be amply sufficient to supply all the necessities and comforts of life—to which you might add all real and natural forms of pleasure.

[THE HOUSEHOLD]

But let's get back to their social organization. Each household, as I said, comes under the authority of the oldest male. Wives are subordinate to their husbands, children to their parents, and younger people generally to their elders. Every town is divided into four districts of equal size, each with its own shopping center in the middle of it. There the products of every household are collected in warehouses, and then distributed according to type among various shops. When the head of a household needs anything for himself or his family, he just goes to one of these shops and asks for it. And whatever he asks for, he's allowed to take away without any sort of payment, either in money or in kind. After all, why shouldn't he? There's more than enough of everything to go round, so there's no risk of his asking for more than he needs—for why should anyone want to start hoarding, when he knows he'll never have to go short of anything? No living creature is naturally greedy, except from fear of want—or in the case of human beings, from vanity, the notion that you're better than people if you can display more superfluous property than they can. But there's no scope for that sort of thing in Utopia.

[UTOPIAN BELIEFS]

The Utopians fail to understand why anyone should be so fascinated by the dull gleam of a tiny bit of stone, when he has all the stars in the sky to look at—or how anyone can be silly enough to think himself better than other people, because his clothes are made of finer woollen thread than theirs. After all, those fine clothes were once worn by a sheep, and they never turned it into anything better than a sheep.

Nor can they understand why a totally useless substance like gold 10 should now, all over the world, be considered far more important than human beings, who gave it such value as it has, purely for their own convenience. The result is that a man with about as much mental agility as a lump of lead or a block of wood, a man whose utter stupidity is paralleled only by his immorality, can have lots of good, intelligent people at his beck and call, just because he happens to possess a large pile of gold coins. And if by some freak of fortune or trick of the law—two equally effective methods of turning things upside down—the said coins were suddenly transferred to the most worthless member of his domestic staff, you'd soon see the present owner trotting after his money, like an extra piece of currency, and becoming his own servant's servant. But what puzzles and disgusts the Utopians even more is the idiotic way some people have of practically worshipping a rich man, not because they owe him money or are otherwise in his power, but simply because he's rich—although they know perfectly well that he's far too mean to let a single penny come their way, so long as he's alive to stop it.

They get these ideas partly from being brought up under a social system which is directly opposed to that type of nonsense, and partly from their reading and education. Admittedly, no one's allowed to become a full-time student, except for the very few in each town who appear as children to possess unusual gifts, outstanding intelligence, and a special aptitude for academic research. But every child receives a primary education, and most men and women go on educating themselves all their lives during those free periods that I told you about. . . .

In ethics they discuss the same problems as we do. Having distinguished between three types of "good," psychological, physiological, and environmental, they proceed to ask whether the term is strictly applicable to all of them, or only to the first. They also argue about such things as virtue and pleasure. But their chief subject of dispute is the nature of human happiness—on what factor or factors does it depend? Here they seem rather too much inclined to take a hedonistic view, for according to them human happiness consists largely or wholly in pleasure. Surprisingly enough, they defend this self-indulgent doctrine by arguments drawn from religion—a thing normally associated with a more serious view of life, if not with gloomy asceticism. You see, in all their discussions of happiness they invoke certain religious principles to supplement the operations of reason, which they think otherwise ill-equipped to identify true happiness.

The first principle is that every soul is immortal, and was created by a kind God, Who meant it to be happy. The second is that we shall be rewarded or punished in the next world for our good or bad behavior in this one. Although these are religious principles, the Utopians find rational grounds for accepting them. For suppose you didn't accept them? In that case, they say, any fool could tell you what you ought to do. You should go all out for your own pleasure, irrespective of right and wrong. You'd merely have to make sure that minor pleasures didn't interfere with major ones, and avoid the type of pleasure that has painful aftereffects. For what's the sense of struggling to be virtuous, denying yourself the pleasant things of life, and deliberately making yourself uncomfortable, if there's nothing you hope to gain by it? And what *can* you hope to gain by it, if you receive no compensation after death for a thoroughly unpleasant, that is, a thoroughly miserable life?

Not that they identify happiness with every type of pleasure—only with the higher ones. Nor do they identify it with virtue—unless they belong to a quite different school of thought. According to the normal view, happiness is the *summmum bonum*[2] toward which we're naturally impelled by virtue—which in their definition means following one's natural impulses, as God meant us to do. But this includes obeying the instinct to be reasonable in our likes and dislikes. And reason also teaches us, first to love and reverence Almighty God, to Whom we owe our existence and our potentiality for happiness, and secondly to get through life as comfortably and cheerfully as we can, and help all other members of our species to do so too.

The fact is, even the sternest ascetic tends to be slightly inconsistent 15 in his condemnation of pleasure. He may sentence *you* to a life of hard labor, inadequate sleep, and general discomfort, but he'll also tell you to do your best to ease the pains and privations of others. He'll regard all such attempts to improve the human situation as laudable acts of humanity—for obviously nothing could be more humane, or more natural

[2]**summum bonum** Latin for "the highest good." [—Ed.]

for a human being, than to relieve other people's sufferings, put an end to their miseries, and restore their *joie de vivre*, that is, their capacity for pleasure. So why shouldn't it be equally natural to do the same thing for oneself?

Either it's a bad thing to enjoy life, in other words, to experience pleasure—in which case you shouldn't help anyone to do it, but should try to save the whole human race from such a frightful fate—or else, if it's good for other people, and you're not only allowed, but positively obliged to make it possible for them, why shouldn't charity begin at home? After all, you've a duty to yourself as well as to your neighbor, and, if Nature says you must be kind to others, she can't turn round the next moment and say you must be cruel to yourself. The Utopians therefore regard the enjoyment of life—that is, pleasure—as the natural object of all human efforts, and natural, as they define it, is synonymous with virtuous. However, Nature also wants us to help one another to enjoy life, for the very good reason that no human being has a monopoly of her affections. She's equally anxious for the welfare of every member of the species. So of course she tells us to make quite sure that we don't pursue our own interests at the expense of other people's.

On this principle they think it right to keep one's promises in private life, and also to obey public laws for regulating the distribution of "goods"—by which I mean the raw materials of pleasure—provided such laws have been properly made by a wise ruler, or passed by common consent of a whole population, which has not been subjected to any form of violence or deception. Within these limits they say it's sensible to consult one's own interests, and a moral duty to consult those of the community as well. It's wrong to deprive someone else of a pleasure so that you can enjoy one yourself, but to deprive yourself of a pleasure so that you can add to someone else's enjoyment is an act of humanity by which you always gain more than you lose. For one thing, such benefits are usually repaid in kind. For another, the mere sense of having done somebody a kindness, and so earned his affection and goodwill, produces a spiritual satisfaction which far outweighs the loss of a physical one. And lastly—a belief that comes easily to a religious mind—God will reward us for such small sacrifices of momentary pleasure, by giving us an eternity of perfect joy. Thus they argue that, in the final analysis, pleasure is the ultimate happiness which all human beings have in view, even when they're acting most virtuously.

Pleasure they define as any state or activity, physical or mental, which is naturally enjoyable. The operative word is *naturally*. According to them, we're impelled by reason as well as an instinct to enjoy ourselves in any natural way which doesn't hurt other people, interfere with greater pleasures, or cause unpleasant aftereffects. But human beings have entered into an idiotic conspiracy to call some things enjoyable which are naturally nothing of the kind—as though facts were as easily changed as definitions. Now the Utopians believe that, so far from contributing to happiness, this type of thing makes happiness impossible—because, once you get used to it, you lose all capacity for real pleasure, and are merely obsessed by illusory forms of it. Very often these have nothing pleasant about them at all—in fact, most of them are thoroughly disagreeable. But they appeal so strongly to perverted tastes that they come to be reckoned not only among the major pleasures of life, but even among the chief reasons for living.

In the category of illusory pleasure addicts they include the kind of person I mentioned before, who thinks himself better than other people because he's better dressed than they are. Actually he's just as wrong about his clothes as he is about himself. From a practical point of view, why is it better to be dressed in fine woollen thread than in coarse? But he's got it into his head that fine thread is naturally superior, and that wearing it somehow increases his own value. So he feels entitled to far more respect than he'd ever dare to hope for, if he were less expensively dressed, and is most indignant if he fails to get it.

Talking of respect, isn't it equally idiotic to attach such importance 20 to a lot of empty gestures which do nobody any good? For what real pleasure can you get out of the sight of a bared head or a bent knee? Will it cure the rheumatism in your own knee, or make you any less weak in the head? Of course, the great believers in this type of artificial pleasure are those who pride themselves on their "nobility." Nowadays that merely means that they happen to belong to a family which has been rich for several generations, preferably in landed property. And yet they feel every bit as "noble" even if they've failed to inherit any of the said property, or if they have inherited it and then frittered it all away.

Then there's another type of person I mentioned before, who has a passion for jewels, and feels practically superhuman if he manages to get hold of a rare one, especially if it's a kind that's considered particularly precious in his country and period—for the value of such things varies according to where and when you live. But he's so terrified of being taken in by appearances that he refuses to buy any jewel until he's stripped off all the gold and inspected it in the nude. And even then he won't buy it without a solemn assurance and a written guarantee from the jeweler that the stone is genuine. But my dear sir, why shouldn't a fake give you just as much pleasure, if you can't, with your own eyes, distinguish it from a real one? It makes no difference to you whether it's genuine or not—any more than it would to a blind man!

And now, what about those people who accumulate superfluous wealth, for no better purpose than to enjoy looking at it? Is their pleasure a real one, or merely a form of delusion? The opposite type of psychopath buries his gold, so that he'll never be able to use it, and may never even see it again. In fact, he deliberately loses it in his anxiety not to lose it—for what can you call it but lost, when it's put back into the earth, where it's no good to him, or probably to anyone else? And yet he's tremendously happy when he's got it stowed away. Now, apparently, he can stop worrying. But suppose the money is stolen, and ten years later he dies without ever knowing it has gone. Then for a whole ten years he has managed to survive his loss, and during that period what difference has it made to him whether the money was there or not? It was just as little use to him either way.

Among stupid pleasures they include not only gambling—a form of idiocy that they've heard about but never practiced—but also hunting and hawking. What on earth is the fun, they ask, of throwing dice onto a table? Besides, you've done it so often that, even if there was some fun in it at first, you must surely be sick of it by now. How can you possibly enjoy listening to anything so disagreeable as the barking and howling of dogs? And why is it more amusing to watch a dog chasing a hare than to watch one dog chasing another? In each case the essential activity is running—if running is what amuses you. But if it's really the thought of being in at the death, and seeing an animal torn to pieces before your eyes, wouldn't pity be a more appropriate reaction to the sight of a weak, timid, harmless little creature like a hare being devoured by something so much stronger and fiercer?

So the Utopians consider hunting below the dignity of free men, and leave it entirely to butchers, who are, as I told you, slaves. In their view hunting is the vilest department of butchery, compared with which all the others are relatively useful and honorable. An ordinary butcher slaughters livestock far more sparingly, and only because he has to, whereas a hunter kills and mutilates poor little creatures purely for his own amusement. They say you won't find that type of blood lust even among animals, unless they're particularly savage by nature, or have become so by constantly being used for this cruel sport.

There are hundreds of things like that, which are generally regarded as pleasures, but everyone in Utopia is quite convinced that they've got nothing to do with real pleasure, because there's nothing naturally enjoyable about them. Nor is this conviction at all shaken by the argument that most people do actually enjoy them, which would seem to indicate an appreciable pleasure content. They say this is a purely subjective reaction caused by bad habits, which can make a person prefer unpleasant things to pleasant ones, just as pregnant women sometimes lose their sense of taste, and find suet or turpentine more delicious than honey. But however much one's judgment may be impaired by habit or ill health, the nature of pleasure, as of everything else, remains unchanged.

Real pleasures they divide into two categories, mental and physical. Mental pleasures include the satisfaction that one gets from understanding something, or from contemplating truth. They also include the memory of a well-spent life, and the confident expectation of good things to come. Physical pleasures are subdivided into two types. First there are those which fill the whole organism with a conscious sense of enjoyment. This may be the result of replacing physical substances which have been burnt up by the natural heat of the body, as when we eat or drink. Or else it may be caused by the discharge of some excess, as in excretion, sexual intercourse, or any relief of irritation by rubbing or scratching. However, there are also pleasures which satisfy no organic need, and relieve no previous discomfort. They merely act, in a mysterious but quite unmistakable way, directly on our senses, and monopolize their reactions. Such is the pleasure of music.

Their second type of physical pleasure arises from the calm and regular functioning of the body—that is, from a state of health undisturbed by any minor ailments. In the absence of mental discomfort, this gives one a good feeling, even without the help of external pleasures. Of course, it's less ostentatious, and forces itself less violently on one's attention than the cruder delights of eating and drinking, but even so it's often considered the greatest pleasure in life. Practically everyone in Utopia would agree that it's a very important one, because it's the basis of all the others. It's enough by itself to make you enjoy life, and unless you have it, no other pleasure is possible. However, mere freedom from pain, without positive health, they would call not pleasure but anesthesia.

Some thinkers used to maintain that a uniformly tranquil state of health couldn't properly be termed a pleasure since its presence could only be detected by contrast with its opposite—oh yes, they went very thoroughly into the whole question. But that theory was exploded long ago, and nowadays nearly everybody subscribes to the view that health is most definitely a pleasure. The argument goes like this—illness involves pain, which is the direct opposite of pleasure, and illness is the direct opposite of health, therefore health involves pleasure. They don't think it matters whether you say that illness *is* or merely *involves* pain. Either way it comes to the same thing. Similarly, whether health *is* a pleasure, or merely *produces* pleasure as inevitably as fire produces heat, it's equally logical to assume that where you have an uninterrupted state of health you cannot fail to have pleasure.

Besides, they say, when we eat something, what really happens is this. Our failing health starts fighting off the attacks of hunger, using the food as an ally. Gradually it begins to prevail, and, in this very process of winning back its normal strength, experiences the sense of enjoyment which we find so refreshing. Now, if health enjoys the actual battle, why shouldn't it also enjoy the victory? Or are we to suppose that when it has finally managed to regain its former vigor—the one thing that it has been fighting for all this time—it promptly falls into a coma, and fails to notice or take advantage of its success? As for the idea that one isn't conscious of health except through its opposite, they say that's quite untrue. Everyone's perfectly aware of feeling well, unless he's asleep or actually feeling ill. Even the most insensitive and apathetic sort of person will admit that it's delightful to be healthy—and what is delight, but a synonym for pleasure?

They're particularly fond of mental pleasures, which they consider 30 of primary importance, and attribute mostly to good behavior and a clear conscience. Their favorite physical pleasure is health. Of course, they believe in enjoying food, drink, and so forth, but purely in the interests of health, for they don't regard such things as very pleasant in themselves—only as methods of resisting the stealthy onset of disease. A sensible person, they say, prefers keeping well to taking medicine, and would rather feel cheerful than have people trying to comfort him. On the same principle it's better not to need this type of pleasure than to become addicted to it. For, if you think that sort of thing will make you happy, you'll have to admit that your idea of perfect felicity would be a life consisting entirely of hunger, thirst, itching, eating, drinking, rubbing, and scratching—which would obviously be most unpleasant as well as quite disgusting. Undoubtedly these pleasures should come right at the bottom of the list, because they're so impure. For instance, the pleasure of eating is invariably diluted with the pain of hunger, and not in equal proportions either—for the pain is both more intense and more prolonged. It starts before the pleasure, and doesn't stop until the pleasure has stopped too.

So they don't think much of pleasures like that, except insofar as they're necessary. But they enjoy them all the same, and feel most grateful to Mother Nature for encouraging her children to do things that have to be done so often, by making them so attractive. For just think how dreary life would be, if those chronic ailments, hunger and thirst, could only be cured by foul-tasting medicines, like the rarer types of disease!

They attach great value to special natural gifts such as beauty, strength, and agility. They're also keen on the pleasures of sight, hearing, and smell, which are peculiar to human beings—for no other species admires the beauty of the world, enjoys any sort of scent, except as a

,method of locating food, or can tell the difference between a harmony and a discord. They say these things give a sort of relish to life.

However, in all such matters they observe the rule that minor pleasures mustn't interfere with major ones, and that pleasure mustn't cause pain—which they think is bound to happen, if the pleasure is immoral. But they'd never dream of despising their own beauty, overtaxing their strength, converting their agility into inertia, ruining their physique by going without food, damaging their health, or spurning any other of Nature's gifts, unless they were doing it for the benefit of other people or of society, in the hope of receiving some greater pleasure from God in return. For they think it's quite absurd to torment oneself in the name of an unreal virtue, which does nobody any good, or in order to steel oneself against disasters which may never occur. They say such behavior is merely self-destructive, and shows a most ungrateful attitude toward Nature—as if one refused all her favors, because one couldn't bear the thought of being indebted to her for anything.

Well, that's their ethical theory, and short of some divine revelation, they doubt if the human mind is capable of devising a better one. We've no time to discuss whether it's right or wrong—nor is it really necessary, for all I undertook was to describe their way of life, not to defend it.

[TREATMENT OF THE DYING]

As I told you, when people are ill, they're looked after most sympa-   35
thetically, and given everything in the way of medicine or special food that could possibly assist their recovery. In the case of permanent invalids, the nurses try to make them feel better by sitting and talking to them, and do all they can to relieve their symptoms. But if, besides being incurable, the disease also causes constant excruciating pain, some priests and government officials visit the person concerned, and say something like this:

"Let's face it, you'll never be able to live a normal life. You're just a nuisance to other people and a burden to yourself—in fact you're really leading a sort of posthumous existence. So why go on feeding germs? Since your life's a misery to you, why hesitate to die? You're imprisoned in a torture chamber—why don't you break out and escape to a better world? Or say the word, and we'll arrange for your release. It's only common sense to cut your losses. It's also an act of piety to take the advice of a priest, because he speaks for God."

If the patient finds these arguments convincing, he either starves himself to death, or is given a soporific and put painlessly out of his misery. But this is strictly voluntary, and, if he prefers to stay alive, everyone will go on treating him as kindly as ever.

[THE SUMMING UP]

Well, that's the most accurate account I can give you of the Utopian Republic. To my mind, it's not only the best country in the world, but the only one that has any right to call itself a republic. Elsewhere, people are always talking about the public interest, but all they really care about is private property. In Utopia, where's there's no private property, people take their duty to the public seriously. And both attitudes are perfectly reasonable. In other "republics" practically everyone knows that, if he doesn't look out for himself, he'll starve to death, however prosperous his country may be. He's therefore compelled to give his own interests priority over those of the public; that is, of other people. But in Utopia, where everything's under public ownership, no one has any fear of going short, as long as the public storehouses are full. Everyone gets a fair share, so there are never any poor men or beggars. Nobody owns anything, but everyone is rich—for what greater wealth can there be than cheerfulness, peace of mind, and freedom from anxiety? Instead of being worried about his food supply, upset by the plaintive demands of his wife, afraid of poverty for his son, and baffled by the problem of finding a dowry for his daughter, the Utopian can feel absolutely sure that he, his wife, his children, his grandchildren, his great-grandchildren, his great-great-grandchildren, and as long a line of descendants as the proudest peer could wish to look forward to, will always have enough to eat and enough to make them happy. There's also the further point that those who are too old to work are just as well provided for as those who are still working.

Now, will anyone venture to compare these fair arrangements in Utopia with the so-called justice of other countries?—in which I'm damned if I can see the slightest trace of justice or fairness. For what sort of justice do you call this? People like aristocrats, goldsmiths, or moneylenders, who either do no work at all, or do work that's really not essential, are rewarded for their laziness or their unnecessary activities by a splendid life of luxury. But laborers, coachmen, carpenters, and farmhands, who never stop working like cart horses, at jobs so essential that, if they *did* stop working, they'd bring any country to a standstill within twelve months—what happens to them? They get so little to eat, and have such a wretched time, that they'd be almost better off if they *were* cart horses. Then at least, they wouldn't work quite such long hours, their food wouldn't be very much worse, they'd enjoy it more, and they'd have no fears for the future. As it is, they're not only ground down by unrewarding toil in the present, but also worried to death by the prospect of a poverty-stricken old age—since their daily wages aren't enough to support them for one day, let alone leave anything over to be saved up when they're old.

Can you see any fairness or gratitude in a social system which lav- 40
ishes such great rewards on so-called noblemen, goldsmiths, and people
like that, who are either totally unproductive or merely employed in
producing luxury goods or entertainment, but makes no such kind provision for farmhands, coal heavers, laborers, carters, or carpenters,
without whom society couldn't exist at all? And the climax of ingratitude
comes when they're old and ill and completely destitute. Having taken
advantage of them throughout the best years of their lives, society now
forgets all the sleepless hours they've spent in its service, and repays
them for all the vital work they've done, by letting them die in misery.
What's more, the wretched earnings of the poor are daily whittled away
by the rich, not only through private dishonesty, but through public legislation. As if it weren't unjust enough already that the man who contributes most to society should get the least in return, they make it even
worse, and then arrange for injustice to be legally described as justice.

In fact, when I consider any social system that prevails in the modern world, I can't, so help me God, see it as anything but a conspiracy of
the rich to advance their own interests under the pretext of organizing
society. They think up all sorts of tricks and dodges, first for keeping safe
their ill-gotten gains, and then for exploiting the poor by buying their
labor as cheaply as possible. Once the rich have decided that these tricks
and dodges shall be officially recognized by society—which includes the
poor as well as the rich—they acquire the force of law. Thus an unscrupulous minority is led by its insatiable greed to monopolize what
would have been enough to supply the needs of the whole population.
And yet how much happier even these people would be in Utopia! There,
with the simultaneous abolition of money and the passion for money,
how many other social problems have been solved, how many crimes
eradicated! For obviously the end of money means the end of all those
types of criminal behavior which daily punishments are powerless to
check: fraud, theft, burglary, brawls, riots, disputes, rebellion, murder,
treason, and black magic. And the moment money goes, you can also say
goodbye to fear, tension, anxiety, overwork, and sleepless nights. Why,
even poverty itself, the one problem that has always seemed to need
money for its solution, would promptly disappear if money ceased to
exist.

Let me try to make this point clearer. Just think back to one of the
years when the harvest was bad, and thousands of people died of starvation. Well, I bet if you'd inspected every rich man's barn at the end of
that lean period you'd have found enough corn to have saved all the lives
that were lost through malnutrition and disease, and prevented anyone
from suffering any ill effects whatever from the meanness of the weather
and the soil. Everyone could so easily get enough to eat, if it weren't for

that blessed nuisance, money. There you have a brilliant invention which was designed to make food more readily available. Actually it's the only thing that makes it unobtainable.

I'm sure that even the rich are well aware of all this, and realize how much better it would be to have everything one needed, than lots of things one didn't need—to be evacuated altogether from the danger area, than to dig oneself in behind a barricade of enormous wealth. And I've no doubt that either self-interest, or the authority of our Savior Christ—Who was far too wise not to know what was best for us, and far too kind to recommend anything else—would have led the whole world to adopt the Utopian system long ago, if it weren't for that beastly root of all evils, pride. For pride's criterion of prosperity is not what you've got yourself, but what other people haven't got. Pride would refuse to set foot in paradise, if she thought there'd be no underprivileged classes there to gloat over and order about—nobody whose misery could serve as a foil to her own happiness, or whose poverty she could make harder to bear, by flaunting her own riches. Pride, like a hellish serpent gliding through human hearts—or shall we say, like a sucking-fish that clings to the ship of state?—is always dragging us back, and obstructing our progress toward a better way of life.

But as this fault is too deeply ingrained in human nature to be easily eradicated, I'm glad that at least one country has managed to develop a system which I'd like to see universally adopted. The Utopian way of life provides not only the happiest basis for a civilized community, but also one which, in all human probability, will last forever. They've eliminated the root causes of ambition, political conflict, and everything like that. There's therefore no danger of internal dissension, the one thing that has destroyed so many impregnable towns. And as long as there's unity and sound administration at home, no matter how envious neighboring kings may feel, they'll never be able to shake, let alone to shatter, the power of Utopia. They've tried to do so often enough in the past, but have always been beaten back.

Topics for Critical Thinking and Writing

1. More, writing early in the sixteenth century, was living in a primarily agricultural society. Laborers were needed on farms, but might More have had any other reason for insisting (para. 1) that all people should do some farming and that farming should be "part of every child's education"? Do you think everyone should put in some time as a farmer? Why, or why not?

2. More indicates that in the England of his day many people loafed or engaged in unnecessary work (producing luxury goods, for one thing), putting an enormous burden on those who engaged in useful work. Is this condition, or any part of it, true of our society? Explain.

3. The Utopians cannot understand why the people of other nations value gems, gold, and fine clothes. If you value any of these, can you offer an explanation?

4. What arguments can you offer against the Utopians' treatment of persons who are incurably ill and in pain?

5. Take three or four paragraphs to summarize More's report of the Utopians' idea of pleasure.

6. More's Utopians cannot understand why anyone takes pleasure in gambling or in hunting. If either activity gives you pleasure, in an essay of 500 words explain why, and offer an argument on behalf of your view.

7. As More makes clear in the part we entitle "The Summing Up," in Utopia there is no private property. In a sentence or two summarize the reasons he gives for this principle, and then in a paragraph evaluate them.

NICCOLÒ MACHIAVELLI

Niccolò Machiavelli (1469–1527) was born in Florence at a time when Italy was divided into five major states: Venice, Milan, Florence, the Papal States, and Naples. Although these states often had belligerent relations with one another as well as with lesser Italian states, under the Medici family in Florence they achieved a precarious balance of power. In 1494, however, Lorenzo de' Medici, who had ruled from 1469 to 1492, died, and two years later Lorenzo's successor was exiled when the French army arrived in Florence. Italy became a field where Spain, France, and Germany competed for power. From 1498 to 1512 Machiavelli held a high post in the diplomatic service of the Florentine Republic, but when the French army reappeared and the Florentines in desperation recalled the Medici, Machiavelli lost his post, was imprisoned, tortured, and then exiled. Banished from Florence, he nevertheless lived in comfort on a small estate nearby, writing his major works and hoping to obtain an office from the Medici. In later years he was employed in a few minor diplomatic missions, but even after the collapse and expulsion of the Medici in 1527 and the restoration of the republic, he did not regain his old position of importance. He died shortly after the restoration.

Our selection comes from The Prince, *which Machiavelli wrote in 1513 during his banishment hoping that it would interest the Medici and thus restore him to favor; but the book was not published until 1532, five years after his death. In this book of twenty-six short chapters, Machiavelli begins by examining different kinds of states, but the work's enduring power resides in the discussions (in Chapters 15–18, reprinted here) of qualities necessary to a prince—that is, a head of state. Any such examination obviously is based in part on assumptions about the nature of the citizens of the realm.*

This selection was taken from a translation edited by Peter Bondanella and Mark Musa.

From *The Prince*

ON THOSE THINGS FOR WHICH MEN, AND PARTICULARLY PRINCES, ARE PRAISED OR BLAMED

Now there remains to be examined what should be the methods and procedures of a prince in dealing with his subjects and friends. And because I know that many have written about this, I am afraid that by writing about it again I shall be thought of as presumptuous, since in discussing this material I depart radically from the procedures of others. But since my intention is to write something useful for anyone who understands it, it seemed more suitable to me to search after the effectual truth of the matter rather than its imagined one. And many writers have imagined for themselves republics and principalities that have never been seen nor known to exist in reality; for there is such a gap between how one lives and how one ought to live that anyone who abandons what is done for what ought to be done learns his ruin rather than his preservation: for a man who wishes to make a vocation of being good at all times will come to ruin among so many who are not good. Hence it is necessary for a prince who wishes to maintain his position to learn how not to be good, and to use this knowledge or not to use it according to necessity.

Leaving aside, therefore, the imagined things concerning a prince, and taking into account those that are true, I say that all men, when they are spoken of, and particularly princes, since they are placed on a higher level, are judged by some of these qualities which bring them either blame or praise. And this is why one is considered generous, another miserly (to use a Tuscan word, since "avaricious" in our language is still used to mean one who wishes to acquire by means of theft; we call "miserly" one who excessively avoids using what he has); one is considered a giver, the other rapacious; one cruel, another merciful; one treacherous, another faithful; one effeminate and cowardly, another bold and courageous; one humane, another haughty; one lascivious, another chaste; one trustworthy, another cunning; one harsh, another lenient; one serious, another frivolous; one religious, another unbelieving; and the like. And I know that everyone will admit that it would be a very praiseworthy thing to find in a prince, of the qualities mentioned above, those that are held to be good; but since it is neither possible to have them nor to observe them all completely, because human nature does not permit it, a prince must be prudent enough to know how to escape the bad reputation of those vices that would lose the state for him, and must protect himself from those that will not lose it for him, if this is possible; but if he cannot, he need not concern himself unduly if he ignores these less serious vices. And, moreover, he need not worry about incurring the bad reputation of those vices without which it would be difficult to hold his state; since, carefully taking everything into account, one will discover that something which appears to be a virtue, if pursued, will end in his destruction; while some other thing which seems to be a vice, if pursued, will result in his safety and his well-being.

ON GENEROSITY AND MISERLINESS

Beginning, therefore, with the first of the above-mentioned qualities, I say that it would be good to be considered generous; nevertheless, generosity used in such a manner as to give you a reputation for it will harm you; because if it is employed virtuously and as one should employ it, it will not be recognized and you will not avoid the reproach of its opposite. And so, if a prince wants to maintain his reputation for generosity among men, it is necessary for him not to neglect any possible means of lavish display; in so doing such a prince will always use up all his resources and he will be obliged, eventually, if he wishes to maintain his reputation for generosity, to burden the people with excessive taxes and to do everything possible to raise funds. This will begin to make him hateful to his subjects, and, becoming impoverished, he will not be much esteemed by anyone; so that, as a consequence of his generosity, having offended many and rewarded few, he will feel the effects of any slight unrest and will be ruined at the first sign of danger; recognizing this and wishing to alter his policies, he immediately runs the risk of being reproached as a miser.

A prince, therefore, unable to use this virtue of generosity in a manner which will not harm himself if he is known for it, should, if he is wise, not worry about being called a miser; for with time he will come to be considered more generous once it is evident that, as a result of his parsimony, his income is sufficient, he can defend himself from anyone who makes war against him, and he can undertake enterprises without overburdening his people, so that he comes to be generous with all those from whom he takes nothing, who are countless, and miserly with all those to whom he gives nothing, who are few. In our times we have not seen great deeds accomplished except by those who were considered miserly; all others were done away with. Pope Julius II, although he made use of his reputation for generosity in order to gain the papacy, then decided not to maintain it in order to be able to wage war; the present King of France has waged many wars without imposing extra taxes on his subjects, only because his habitual parsimony has provided for the additional expenditures; the present King of Spain, if he had been considered generous, would not have engaged in nor won so many campaigns.

Therefore, in order not to have to rob his subjects, to be able to de- 5 fend himself, not to become poor and contemptible, and not to be forced to become rapacious, a prince must consider it of little importance if he incurs the name of miser, for this is one of those vices that permits him to rule. And if someone were to say: Caesar with his generosity came to rule the empire, and many others, because they were generous and known to be so, achieved very high positions; I reply: You are either already a prince or you are on the way to becoming one; in the first instance such generosity is damaging; in the second it is very necessary to be thought generous. And Caesar was one of those who wanted to gain the principality of Rome; but if, after obtaining this, he had lived and had not moderated his expenditures, he would have destroyed that empire. And if someone were to reply: There have existed many princes who have accomplished great deeds with their armies who have been reputed to be generous; I answer you: A prince either spends his own money and that of his subjects or that of others; in the first case he must be economical; in the second he must not restrain any part of his generosity. And for that prince who goes out with his soldiers and lives by looting, sacking, and ransoms, who controls the property of others, such generosity is necessary; otherwise he would not be followed by his troops. And with what does not belong to you or to your subjects you can be a more liberal giver, as were Cyrus, Caesar, and Alexander; for spending the wealth of others does not lessen your reputation but adds to it; only the spending of your own is what harms you. And there is nothing that uses itself up faster than generosity, for as you employ it you lose the means of employing it, and you become either poor or despised or, in order to escape poverty, rapacious and hated. And above all other things a prince must guard himself against being despised and hated; and generosity leads you to both one and the other. So it is wiser to live with the reputation of a miser, which produces reproach without hatred, than to be forced to incur the reputation of rapacity, which produces reproach along with hatred, because you want to be considered as generous.

ON CRUELTY AND MERCY AND WHETHER IT IS BETTER TO BE LOVED THAN TO BE FEARED OR THE CONTRARY

Proceeding to the other qualities mentioned above, I say that every prince must desire to be considered merciful and not cruel; nevertheless, he must take care not to misuse this mercy. Cesare Borgia[1] was considered cruel; nonetheless, his cruelty had brought order to Romagna, united it, restored it to peace and obedience. If we examine this carefully, we shall see that he was more merciful than the Florentine people, who, in order to avoid being considered cruel, allowed the destruction of Pistoia.[2] Therefore, a prince must not worry about the reproach of cruelty when it is a matter of keeping his subjects united and loyal; for with a very few examples of cruelty he will be more compassionate than those who, out of excessive mercy, permit disorders to continue, from which arise murders and plundering; for these usually harm the community at large, while the executions that come from the prince harm one individual in particular. And the new prince, above all other princes, cannot escape the reputation of being called cruel, since new states are full of dangers. And Virgil, through Dido, states: "My difficult condition and the newness of my rule make me act in such a manner, and to set guards over my land on all sides."[3]

Nevertheless, a prince must be cautious in believing and in acting, nor should he be afraid of his own shadow; and he should proceed in such a manner, tempered by prudence and humanity, so that too much trust may not render him imprudent nor too much distrust render him intolerable.

From this arises an argument: whether it is better to be loved than to be feared, or the contrary. I reply that one should like to be both one and the other; but since it is difficult to join them together, it is much safer to be feared than to be loved when one of the two must be lacking.

[1]**Cesare Borgia** The son of Pope Alexander VI, Cesare Borgia (1476–1507) was ruthlessly opportunistic. Encouraged by his father, in 1499 and 1500 he subdued the cities of **Romagna,** the region including Ferrara and Ravenna. [All notes are the editors' unless otherwise specified.]
[2]**Pistoia** A town near Florence; Machiavelli suggests that the Florentines failed to treat dissenting leaders with sufficient severity.
[3]In *Aeneid* I, 563–64, **Virgil** (70–19 B.C.) puts this line into the mouth of **Dido,** the queen of Carthage.

For one can generally say this about men: that they are ungrateful, fickle, simulators and deceivers, avoiders of danger, greedy for gain; and while you work for their good they are completely yours, offering you their blood, their property, their lives, and their sons, as I said earlier, when danger is far away; but when it comes nearer to you they turn away. And that prince who bases his power entirely in their words, finding himself stripped of other preparations, comes to ruin; for friendships that are acquired by a price and not by greatness and nobility of character are purchased but are not owned, and at the proper moment they cannot be spent. And men are less hesitant about harming someone who makes himself loved than one who makes himself feared because love is held together by a chain of obligation which, since men are a sorry lot, is broken on every occasion in which their own self-interest is concerned; but fear is held together by a dread of punishment which will never abandon you.

A prince must nevertheless make himself feared in such a manner that he will avoid hatred, even if he does not acquire love; since to be feared and not to be hated can very well be combined; and this will always be so when he keeps his hands off the property and the women of his citizens and his subjects. And if he must take someone's life, he should do so when there is proper justification and manifest cause; but, above all, he should avoid the property of others; for men forget more quickly the death of their father than the loss of their patrimony. Moreover, the reasons for seizing their property are never lacking; and he who begins to live by stealing always finds a reason for taking what belongs to others; on the contrary, reasons for taking a life are rarer and disappear sooner.

But when the prince is with his armies and has under his command 10 a multitude of troops, then it is absolutely necessary that he not worry about being considered cruel; for without that reputation he will never keep an army united or prepared for any combat. Among the praiseworthy deeds of Hannibal[4] is counted this: that, having a very large army, made up of all kinds of men, which he commanded in foreign lands, there never arose the slightest dissension, neither among themselves nor against their prince, both during his good and his bad fortune. This could not have arisen from anything other than his inhuman cruelty, which, along with his many other abilities, made him always respected and terrifying in the eyes of his soldiers; and without that, to attain the same effect, his other abilities would not have sufficed. And the writers of history, having considered this matter very little, on the

---

[4]**Hannibal** The Carthaginian general (247–183 B.C.) whose crossing of the Alps with elephants and full baggage train is one of the great feats of military history.

one hand admire these deeds of his and on the other condemn the main cause of them.

And that it be true that his other abilities would not have been sufficient can be seen from the example of Scipio,[5] a most extraordinary man not only in his time but in all recorded history, whose armies in Spain rebelled against him; this came about from nothing other than his excessive compassion, which gave to his soldiers more liberty than military discipline allowed. For this he was censured in the senate by Fabius Maximus, who called him the corruptor of the Roman militia. The Locrians, having been ruined by one of Scipio's officers, were not avenged by him, nor was the arrogance of that officer corrected, all because of his tolerant nature; so that someone in the senate who tried to apologize for him said that there were many men who knew how not to err better than they knew how to correct errors. Such a nature would have, in time, damaged Scipio's fame and glory if he had maintained it during the empire; but, living under the control of the senate, this harmful characteristic of his not only concealed itself but brought him fame.

I conclude, therefore, returning to the problem of being feared and loved, that since men love at their own pleasure and fear at the pleasure of the prince, a wise prince should build his foundation upon that which belongs to him, not upon that which belongs to others: He must strive only to avoid hatred, as has been said.

HOW A PRINCE SHOULD KEEP HIS WORD

How praiseworthy it is for a prince to keep his word and to live by integrity and not by deceit everyone knows; nevertheless, one sees from the experience of our times that the princes who have accomplished great deeds are those who have cared little for keeping their promises and who have known how to manipulate the minds of men by shrewdness; and in the end they have surpassed those who laid their foundations upon honesty.

You must, therefore, know that there are two means of fighting: one according to the laws, the other with force; the first way is proper to man, the second to beasts; but because the first, in many cases, is not sufficient, it becomes necessary to have recourse to the second. Therefore, a prince must know how to use wisely the natures of the beast and the man. This policy was taught to princes allegorically by the ancient writers, who described how Achilles and many other ancient

[5]**Scipio** Publius Cornelius Scipio Africanus the Elder (235–183 B.C.), the conqueror of Hannibal in the Punic Wars. The mutiny of which Machiavelli speaks took place in 206 B.C.

princes were given to Chiron[6] the Centaur to be raised and taught under his discipline. This can only mean that, having a half-beast and half-man as a teacher, a prince must know how to employ the nature of the one and the other; and the one without the other cannot endure.

Since, then, a prince must know how to make good use of the nature 15 of the beast, he should choose from among the beasts the fox and the lion; for the lion cannot defend itself from traps and the fox cannot protect itself from wolves. It is therefore necessary to be a fox in order to recognize the traps and a lion in order to frighten the wolves. Those who play only the part of the lion do not understand matters. A wise ruler, therefore, cannot and should not keep his word when such an observance of faith would be to his disadvantage and when the reasons which made him promise are removed. And if men were all good, this rule would not be good; but since men are a sorry lot and will not keep their promises to you, you likewise need not keep yours to them. A prince never lacks legitimate reasons to break his promises. Of this one could cite an endless number of modern examples to show how many pacts, how many promises have been made null and void because of the infidelity of princes; and he who has known best how to use the fox has come to a better end. But it is necessary to know how to disguise this nature well and to be a great hypocrite and a liar: and men are so simpleminded and so controlled by their present necessities that one who deceives will always find another who will allow himself to be deceived.

I do not wish to remain silent about one of these recent instances. Alexander VI[7] did nothing else, he thought about nothing else, except to deceive men, and he always found the occasion to do this. And there never was a man who had more forcefulness in his oaths, who affirmed a thing with more promises, and who honored his word less; nevertheless, his tricks always succeeded perfectly since he was well acquainted with this aspect of the world.

Therefore, it is not necessary for a prince to have all of the above-mentioned qualities, but it is very necessary for him to appear to have them. Furthermore, I shall be so bold as to assert this; that having them and practicing them at all times is harmful; and appearing to have them useful; for instance, to seem merciful, faithful, humane, forthright, religious, and to be so; but his mind should be disposed in such a way that should it become necessary not to be so, he will

---

[6]**Chiron** (Kī'ron) A centaur (half man, half horse) who was said in classical mythology to have been the teacher not only of Achilles but also of Theseus, Jason, Hercules, and other heroes.

[7]**Alexander VI** Pope from 1492 to 1503; father of Cesare Borgia.

be able and know how to change to the contrary. And it is essential to understand this: that a prince, and especially a new prince, cannot observe all those things by which men are considered good, for in order to maintain the state he is often obliged to act against his promise, against charity, against humanity, and against religion. And therefore, it is necessary that he have a mind ready to turn itself according to the way the winds of Fortune and the changeability of affairs require him; and, as I said above, as long as it is possible, he should not stray from the good, but he should know how to enter into evil when necessity commands.

A prince, therefore, must be very careful never to let anything slip from his lips which is not full of the five qualities mentioned above: He should appear, upon seeing and hearing him, to be all mercy, all faithfulness, all integrity, all kindness, all religion. And there is nothing more necessary than to seem to possess this last quality. And men in general judge more by their eyes than their hands; for everyone can see but few can feel. Everyone sees what you seem to be, few perceive what you are, and those few do not dare to contradict the opinion of the many who have the majesty of the state to defend them; and in the actions of all men, and especially of princes, where there is no impartial arbiter, one must consider the final result.[8] Let a prince therefore act to seize and to maintain the state; his methods will always be judged honorable and will be praised by all; for ordinary people are always deceived by appearances and by the outcome of a thing; and in the world there is nothing but ordinary people; and there is no room for the few, while the many have a place to lean on. A certain prince of the present day, whom I shall refrain from naming, preaches nothing but peace and faith, and to both one and the other he is entirely opposed; and both, if he had put them into practice, would have cost him many times over either his reputation or his state.

Topics for Critical Thinking and Writing

1. In the opening paragraph, Machiavelli claims that a ruler who wishes to keep in power must "learn how not to be good"—that is, must know where and when to ignore the demands of conventional morality. In the

---

[8]The Italian original, *si guarda al fine,* has often been mistranslated as "the ends justify the means," something Machiavelli never wrote. [Translator's note.]

rest of the excerpt, does he give any convincing evidence to support this claim? Can you think of any recent political event in which a political leader violated the requirements of morality, as Machiavelli advises?

2. Machiavelli says in paragraph 1 that "a man who wishes to make a vocation of being good at all times will come to ruin among so many who are not good." (By the way, the passage is ambiguous. "At all times" is, in the original, a squinting modifier. It may look backward to "being good" or forward to "will come to ruin," but Machiavelli probably means, "A man who at all times wishes to make a vocation of being good will come to ruin among so many who are not good.") Is this view realistic or cynical? (What is the difference between these two?) Assume for the moment that the view is realistic. Does it follow that society requires a ruler who must act according to the principles Machiavelli sets forth?

3. In his second paragraph Machiavelli claims that it is impossible for a ruler to exhibit *all* the conventional virtues (trustworthiness, liberality, and so on). Why does he make this claim? Do you agree with it?

4. In paragraph 4 Machiavelli cites as examples Pope Julius II, the King of France, the King of Spain, and other rulers. Is he using these examples to illustrate his generalizations or to provide evidence for them? If you think he is using them to provide evidence, how convincing do you find the evidence? (Consider: Could Machiavelli be arguing from a biased sample?)

5. In paragraphs 6 to 10 Machiavelli argues that it is sometimes necessary for a ruler to be cruel, and so he praises Cesare Borgia and Hannibal. What in human nature, according to Machiavelli, explains this need to have recourse to cruelty? (By the way, how do you think *cruelty* should be defined here?)

6. Machiavelli says that Cesare Borgia's cruelty brought peace to Romagna and that, on the other hand, the Florentines who sought to avoid being cruel in fact brought pain to Pistoia. Can you think of recent episodes supporting the view that cruelty can be beneficial to society? If so, restate Machiavelli's position, using these examples from recent history. Then go on to write two paragraphs, arguing on behalf of your two examples. Or if you believe that Machiavelli's point here is fundamentally wrong, explain why, again using current examples.

7. In *The Prince*, Machiavelli is writing about how to be a successful ruler. He explicitly says he is dealing with things as they are, not things as they should be. Do you think that in fact one can write usefully about statecraft without considering ethics? Explain. Or you may want to think about it in this way: The study of politics is often called *political science*. Machiavelli can be seen as a sort of scientist, objectively analyzing the nature of governing—without offering any moral judgments. In an essay of 500 words, argue for or against the view that the study of politics is rightly called *political science*.

8. In paragraph 18 Machiavelli declares that "one must consider the final result." Taking account of the context, do you think the meaning is that (a) any end, goal, or purpose of anyone justifies using any means to reach it or (b) the end of governing the state, nation, or country justifies using any means to achieve it? Or do you think Machiavelli means both? Something else entirely?

9. In 500 words, argue that an important contemporary political figure does or does not act according to Machiavelli's principles.

10. If you have read the selection from Thomas More's *Utopia* (p. 232), write an essay of 500 words on one of these two topics: (a) why More's book is or is not wiser than Machiavelli's or (b) why one of the books is more interesting than the other.

11. More and Machiavelli wrote their books at almost exactly the same time. Write a dialogue of two or three double-spaced typed pages in which the two men argue about the nature of the state. (During the argument, they will have to reveal their assumptions about the nature of human beings and the role of government.)

JONATHAN SWIFT

Jonathan Swift (1667–1745) was born in Ireland of English stock. An Anglican clergyman, he became Dean of St. Patrick's in Dublin in 1723, but the post he really wanted, one of high office in England, was never given to him. A prolific pamphleteer on religious and political issues, Swift today is known not as a churchman but as a satirist. His best-known works are Gulliver's Travels *(1726, a serious satire but now popularly thought of as a children's book) and "A Modest Proposal" (1729). In "A Modest Proposal," which was published anonymously, Swift addresses the great suffering that the Irish endured under the British.*

A Modest Proposal

FOR PREVENTING THE CHILDREN OF POOR PEOPLE IN IRELAND FROM BEING A BURDEN TO THEIR PARENTS OR COUNTRY, AND FOR MAKING THEM BENEFICIAL TO THE PUBLIC

It is a melancholy object to those who walk through this great town or travel in the country, when they see the streets, the roads, and cabin doors, crowded with beggars of the female sex, followed by three, four, or six children, all in rags and importuning every passenger for an alms.

These mothers, instead of being able to work for their honest livelihood, are forced to employ all their time in strolling to beg sustenance for their helpless infants: who as they grow up either turn thieves for want of work, or leave their dear native country to fight for the Pretender in Spain, or sell themselves to the Barbadoes.

I think it is agreed by all parties that this prodigious number of children in the arms, or on the backs, or at the heels of their mothers, and frequently of their fathers, is in the present deplorable state of the kingdom a very great additional grievance; and, therefore, whoever could find out a fair, cheap, and easy method of making these children sound, useful members of the commonwealth, would deserve so well of the public as to have his statue set up for a preserver of the nation.

But my intention is very far from being confined to provide only for the children of professed beggars; it is of a much greater extent, and shall take in the whole number of infants at a certain age who are born of parents in effect as little able to support them as those who demand our charity in the streets.

As to my own part, having turned my thoughts for many years upon this important subject, and maturely weighed the several schemes of our projectors,[1] I have always found them grossly mistaken in their computation. It is true, a child just dropped from its dam may be supported by her milk for a solar year, with little other nourishment; at most not above the value of 2s.,[2] which the mother may certainly get, or the value in scraps, by her lawful occupation of begging; and it is exactly at one year old that I propose to provide for them in such a manner as instead of being a charge upon their parents or the parish, or wanting food and raiment for the rest of their lives, they shall on the contrary contribute to the feeding, and partly to the clothing, of many thousands.

There is likewise another great advantage in my scheme, that it will   5
prevent those voluntary abortions, and that horrid practice of women murdering their bastard children, alas! too frequent among us! sacrificing the poor innocent babes I doubt more to avoid the expense than the shame, which would move tears and pity in the most savage and inhuman breast.

The number of souls in this kingdom being usually reckoned one million and a half, of these I calculate there may be about 200,000 couple whose wives are breeders; from which number I subtract 30,000 couple who are able to maintain their own children (although I apprehend there cannot be so many, under the present distress of the kingdom); but this being granted, there will remain 170,000 breeders. I again

[1]**projectors** Persons who devise plans. [All notes are the editors'.]
[2]**2s.** Two shillings.

subtract 50,000 for those women who miscarry, or whose children die by accident or disease within the year. There only remain 120,000 children of poor parents annually born. The question therefore is, how this number shall be reared and provided for? which, as I have already said, under the present situation of affairs, is utterly impossible by all the methods hitherto proposed. For we can neither employ them in handicraft or agriculture; we neither build houses (I mean in the country) nor cultivate land; they can very seldom pick up a livelihood by stealing, till they arrive at six years old, except where they are of towardly parts; although I confess they learn the rudiments much earlier; during which time they can, however, be properly looked upon only as probationers; as I have been informed by a principal gentleman in the county of Cavan, who protested to me that he never knew above one or two instances under the age of six, even in a part of the kingdom so renowned for the quickest proficiency in that art.

I am assured by our merchants, that a boy or a girl before twelve years old is no salable commodity; and even when they come to this age they will not yield above 3£. or 3£. 2s. 6d.[3] at most on the exchange; which cannot turn to account either to the parents or kingdom, the charge of nutriment and rags having been at least four times that value.

I shall now therefore humbly propose my own thoughts, which I hope will not be liable to the least objection.

I have been assured by a very knowing American of my acquaintance in London, that a young healthy child well nursed is at a year old a most delicious, nourishing, and wholesome food, whether stewed, roasted, baked, or broiled; and I make no doubt that it will equally serve in a fricassee or a ragout.

I do therefore humbly offer it to public consideration that of the 10 120,000 children already computed, 20,000 may be reserved for breed, whereof only one-fourth part to be males; which is more than we allow to sheep, black cattle, or swine; and my reason is, that these children are seldom the fruits of marriage, a circumstance not much regarded by our savages; therefore one male will be sufficient to serve four females. That the remaining 100,000 may, at a year old, be offered in sale to the persons of quality and fortune through the kingdom; always advising the mother to let them suck plentifully in the last month, so as to render them plump and fat for a good table. A child will make two dishes at an entertainment for friends; and when the family dines alone, the fore or hind quarter will make a reasonable dish, and seasoned with a little pepper or salt will be very good boiled on the fourth day, especially in winter.

[3]**£. . . . d.** £ is an abbreviation for "pound sterling," and *d.* for "pence."

I have reckoned upon a medium that a child just born will weigh twelve pounds, and in a solar year, if tolerably nursed, will increase to twenty-eight pounds.

I grant this food will be somewhat dear, and therefore very proper for landlords, who, as they have already devoured most of the parents, seem to have the best title to the children.

Infant's flesh will be in season throughout the year, but more plentiful in March, and a little before and after: for we are told by a grave author, an eminent French physician, that fish being a prolific diet, there are more children born in Roman Catholic countries about nine months after Lent than at any other season; therefore, reckoning a year after Lent, the markets will be more glutted than usual, because the number of popish infants is at least three to one in this kingdom: and therefore it will have one other collateral advantage, by lessening the number of papists among us.

I have already computed the charge of nursing a beggar's child (in which list I reckon all cottagers, laborers, and four-fifths of the farmers) to be about 2s. per annum, rags included; and I believe no gentleman would repine to give 10s. for the carcass of a good fat child, which, as I have said, will make four dishes of excellent nutritive meat, when he has only some particular friend or his own family to dine with him. Thus the squire will learn to be a good landlord, and grow popular among the tenants; the mother will have 8s. net profit, and be fit for work till she produces another child.

Those who are more thrifty (as I must confess the times require) 15 may flay the carcass; the skin of which artificially dressed will make admirable gloves for ladies, and summer boots for fine gentlemen.

As to our city of Dublin, shambles[4] may be appointed for this purpose in the most convenient parts of it, and butchers we may be assured will not be wanting: although I rather recommend buying the children alive, and dressing them hot from the knife as we do roasting pigs.

A very worthy person, a true lover of his country, and whose virtues I highly esteem, was lately pleased in discoursing on this matter to offer a refinement upon my scheme. He said that many gentlemen of this kingdom, having of late destroyed their deer, he conceived that the want of venison might be well supplied by the bodies of young lads and maidens, not exceeding fourteen years of age nor under twelve; so great a number of both sexes in every country being now ready to starve for want of work and service; and these to be disposed of by their parents, if alive, or otherwise by their nearest relations. But with due deference to so excellent a friend and so deserving a patriot, I cannot be altogether in

---

[4]**shambles** Slaughterhouses.

his sentiments; for as to the males, my American acquaintance assured me from frequent experience that their flesh was generally tough and lean, like that of our schoolboys by continual exercise, and their taste disagreeable; and to fatten them would not answer the charge. Then as to the females, it would, I think, with humble submission be a loss to the public, because they soon would become breeders themselves: and besides, it is not improbable that some scrupulous people might be apt to censure such a practice (although indeed very unjustly), as a little bordering upon cruelty; which, I confess, has always been with me the strongest objection against any project, how well soever intended.

But in order to justify my friend, he confessed that this expedient was put into his head by the famous Psalmanazar[5] a native of the island Formosa, who came from thence to London about twenty years ago: and in conversation told my friend, that in his country when any young person happened to be put to death, the executioner sold the carcass to persons of quality as a prime dainty; and that in his time the body of a plump girl of fifteen, who was crucified for an attempt to poison the emperor, was sold to his imperial majesty's prime minister of state, and other great mandarins of the court, in joints from the gibbet, at 400 crowns. Neither indeed can I deny, that if the same use were made of several plump young girls in this town, who without one single groat to their fortunes cannot stir abroad without a chair, and appear at the playhouse and assemblies in foreign fineries which they never will pay for, the kingdom would not be the worse.

Some persons of a depending spirit are in great concern about the vast number of poor people, who are aged, diseased, or maimed, and I have been desired to employ my thoughts what course may be taken to ease the nation of so grievous an encumbrance. But I am not in the least pain upon that matter, because it is very well known that they are every day dying and rotting by cold and famine, and filth and vermin, as fast as can be reasonably expected. And as to the young laborers, they are now in as hopeful a condition: They cannot get work, and consequently pine away for want of nourishment, to a degree that if at any time they are accidentally hired to common labor, they have not strength to perform it; and thus the country and themselves are happily delivered from the evils to come.

I have too long digressed, and therefore shall return to my subject. I think the advantages by the proposal which I have made are obvious and many, as well as of the highest importance.

[5]**Psalmanazar** George Psalmanazar (c. 1679–1763), a Frenchman who claimed to be from Formosa (now Taiwan); he wrote *An Historical and Geographical Description of Formosa* (1704). The hoax was exposed soon after publication.

For first, as I have already observed, it would greatly lessen the number of papists, with whom we are yearly overrun, being the principal breeders of the nation as well as our most dangerous enemies; and who stay at home on purpose to deliver the kingdom to the Pretender, hoping to take their advantage by the absence of so many good Protestants, who have chosen rather to leave their country than stay at home and pay tithes against their conscience to an Episcopal curate.

Secondly, The poor tenants will have something valuable of their own, which by law may be made liable to distress and help to pay their landlord's rent, their corn and cattle being already seized, and money a thing unknown.

Thirdly, Whereas the maintenance of 100,000 children from two years old and upward, cannot be computed at less than 10s. apiece per annum, the nation's stock will be thereby increased £50,000 per annum, beside the profit of a new dish introduced to the tables of all gentlemen of fortune in the kingdom who have any refinement in taste. And the money will circulate among ourselves, the goods being entirely of our own growth and manufacture.

Fourthly, The constant breeders beside the gain of 8s. sterling per annum by the sale of their children, will be rid of the charge of maintaining them after the first year.

Fifthly, This food would likewise bring great custom to taverns, 25 where the vintners will certainly be so prudent as to procure the best receipts for dressing it to perfection, and consequently have their houses frequented by all the fine gentlemen, who justly value themselves upon their knowledge in good eating; and a skilful cook who understands how to oblige his guests, will contrive to make it as expensive as they please.

Sixthly, This would be a great inducement to marriage, which all wise nations have either encouraged by rewards or enforced by laws and penalties. It would increase the care and tenderness of mothers toward their children, when they were sure of a settlement for life to the poor babes, provided in some sort by the public, to their annual profit instead of expense. We should see an honest emulation among the married women, which of them would bring the fattest child to the market. Men would become as fond of their wives during the time of their pregnancy as they are now of their mares in foal, their cows in calf, their sows when they are ready to farrow; nor offer to beat or kick them (as is too frequent a practice) for fear of a miscarriage.

Many other advantages might be enumerated. For instance, the addition of some thousand carcasses in our exportation of barreled beef, the propagation of swine's flesh, and improvement in the art of making good bacon, so much wanted among us by the great destruction of pigs, too frequent at our table; which are no way comparable in taste or magnificence to a well-grown, fat, yearling child, which roasted whole will make a considerable figure at a lord mayor's feast or any other public entertainment. But this and many others I omit, being studious of brevity.

Supposing that 1,000 families in this city would be constant customers for infants' flesh, besides others who might have it at merry-meetings, particularly at weddings and christenings, I compute that Dublin would take off annually about 20,000 carcasses; and the rest of the kingdom (where probably they will be sold somewhat cheaper) the remaining 80,000.

I can think of no one objection that will possibly be raised against this proposal, unless it should be urged that the number of people will be thereby much lessened in the kingdom. This I freely own, and it was indeed one principal design in offering it to the world. I desire the reader will observe, that I calculate my remedy for this one individual kingdom of Ireland and for no other that ever was, is, or I think ever can be upon earth. Therefore let no man talk to me of other expedients: of taxing our absentees at 5s. a pound; of using neither clothes nor household furniture except what is of our own growth and manufacture; of utterly rejecting the materials and instruments that promote foreign luxury; of curing the expensiveness of pride, vanity, idleness, and gaming in our women; of introducing a vein of parsimony, prudence, and temperance; of learning to love our country, in the want of which we differ even from Laplanders and the inhabitants of Topinamboo; of quitting our animosities and factions, nor acting any longer like the Jews, who were murdering one another at the very moment their city was taken; of being a little cautious not to sell our country and conscience for nothing; of teaching landlords to have at least one degree of mercy toward their tenants; lastly, of putting a spirit of honesty, industry, and skill into our shopkeepers; who, if a resolution could now be taken to buy only our native goods, would immediately unite to cheat and exact upon us in the price the measure, and the goodness, nor could ever yet be brought to make one fair proposal of just dealing, though often and earnestly invited to it.

Therefore I repeat, let no man talk to me of these and the like expe- 30 dients, till he has at least some glimpse of hope that there will be ever some hearty and sincere attempt to put them in practice.

But as to myself, having been wearied out for many years with offering vain, idle, visionary thoughts, and at length utterly despairing of success, I fortunately fell upon this proposal; which, as it is wholly new, so it has something solid and real, of no expense and little trouble, full in our own power, and whereby we can incur no danger in disobliging England. For this kind of commodity will not bear exportation, the flesh being of too tender a consistence to admit a long continuance in salt, although perhaps I could name a country which would be glad to eat up our whole nation without it.

After all, I am not so violently bent upon my own opinion as to reject any offer proposed by wise men, which shall be found equally innocent, cheap, easy, and effectual. But before something of that kind shall be advanced in contradiction to my scheme, and offering a better, I desire the author or authors will be pleased maturely to consider two points. First, as things now stand, how they will be able to find food and raiment for 100,000 useless mouths and backs. And secondly, there being a round million of creatures in human figure throughout this kingdom, whose subsistence put into a common stock would leave them in debt 2,000,000£. sterling, adding those who are beggars by profession to the bulk of farmers, cottagers, and laborers, with the wives and children who are beggars in effect; I desire those politicians who dislike my overture, and may perhaps be so bold as to attempt an answer, that they will first ask the parents of these mortals, whether they would not at this day think it a great happiness to have been sold for food at a year old in the manner I prescribe, and thereby have avoided such a perpetual scene of misfortunes as they have since gone through by the oppression of landlords, the impossibility of paying rent without money or trade, the want of common sustenance, with neither house nor clothes to cover them from the inclemencies of the weather, and the most inevitable prospect of entailing the like or greater miseries upon their breed for ever.

I profess, in the sincerity of my heart, that I have not the least personal interest in endeavoring to promote this necessary work, having no other motive than the public good of my country, by advancing our trade, providing for infants, relieving the poor, and giving some pleasure to the rich. I have no children by which I can propose to get a single penny; the youngest being nine years old, and my wife past childbearing.

Topics for Critical Thinking and Writing

1. In paragraph 4 the speaker of the essay mentions proposals set forth by "projectors"—that is, by advocates of other proposals or projects. On the basis of the first two paragraphs of "A Modest Proposal," how would you characterize *this* projector, the speaker of the essay? Write your characterization in one paragraph. Then, in a second paragraph, characterize the projector as you understand him, having read the entire essay. In your second paragraph, indicate what *he thinks he is* and also what the reader sees he really is.

2. The speaker or persona of "A Modest Proposal" is confident that selling children "for a good table" (para. 10) is a better idea than any of the then

current methods of disposing of unwanted children, including abortion and infanticide. Can you think of any argument that might favor abortion or infanticide for parents in dire straits, rather than the projector's scheme?

3. In paragraph 29 the speaker considers, but dismisses out of hand, several other solutions to the wretched plight of the Irish poor. Write a 500-word essay in which you explain each of these ideas and their combined merits as an alternative to the solution he favors.

4. What does the projector imply are the causes of the Irish poverty he deplores? Are there possible causes he has omitted? If so, what are they?

5. Imagine yourself as one of the poor parents to whom Swift refers, and write a 250-word essay explaining why you prefer not to sell your infant to the local butcher.

6. The modern version of the problem to which the proposal is addressed is called "population policy." How would you describe our nation's current population policy? Do we have a population policy, in fact? If not, what would you propose? If we do have one, would you propose any changes in it? Why, or why not?

7. It is sometimes suggested that just as persons need to get a license to drive a car, to hunt with a gun, or to marry, a husband and wife ought to be required to get a license to have a child. Would you favor this idea, assuming that it applied to you as a possible parent? Would Swift? Explain your answers in an essay of 500 words.

8. Consider the six arguments advanced in paragraphs 21 to 26, and write a 1,000-word essay criticizing all of them. Or if you find that one or more of the arguments is really unanswerable, explain why you find it so compelling.

9. Write your own "modest proposal," ironically suggesting a solution to a problem. Possible topics: health care or schooling for the children of illegal immigrants, overcrowded jails, children who have committed a serious crime, homeless people.

THOMAS JEFFERSON

Thomas Jefferson (1743–1826) was a congressman, the governor of Virginia, the first secretary of state, and the president of the United States, but he said he wished to be remembered for only three things: drafting the Declaration of Independence, writing the Virginia Statute for Religious Freedom, and founding the University of Virginia. All three were efforts to promote freedom.

Jefferson was born in Virginia and educated at William and Mary College in Williamsburg, Virginia. After graduating he studied law, was admitted to the bar, and in 1769 was elected to the Virginia House of Burgesses, his first political office. In 1776 he went to Philadelphia as a delegate to the second Continental Congress, where he was elected to a committee of five to write the Declaration of Independence. Jefferson drafted the document, which was then subjected to some changes by the other members of the committee and by the Congress. Although he was unhappy with the changes (especially with the deletion of a passage against slavery), his claim to have written the Declaration is just.

The Declaration of Independence

When in the course of human events, it becomes necessary for one people to dissolve the political bands which have connected them with another, and to assume among the Powers of the earth, the separate and equal station to which the Laws of Nature and of Nature's God entitle them, a decent respect to the opinions of mankind requires that they should declare the causes which impel them to the separation.

We hold these truths to be self-evident, that all men are created equal, that they are endowed by their Creator with certain unalienable Rights, that among these are Life, Liberty and the pursuit of Happiness.

That to secure these rights, Governments are instituted among Men, deriving their just powers from the consent of the governed.

That whenever any Form of Government becomes destructive of these ends, it is the Right of the People to alter or to abolish it, and to institute a new Government, laying its foundation on such principles and organizing its powers in such form, as to them shall seem most likely to effect their Safety and Happiness. Prudence, indeed, will dictate that Governments long established should not be changed for light and transient causes; and accordingly all experience hath shown that mankind are more disposed to suffer, while evils are sufferable, than to right themselves by abolishing the forms to which they are accustomed. But when a long train of abuses and usurpations pursuing invariably the same Object evinces a design to reduce them under absolute Despotism, it is their right, it is their duty, to throw off such government, and to provide new Guards for their future security.

Such has been the patient sufferance of these Colonies; and such is   5
now the necessity which constrains them to alter their former Systems of Government. The history of the present King of Great Britain is a

history of repeated injuries and usurpations, all having in direct object the establishment of an absolute Tyranny over these States. To prove this, let Facts be submitted to a candid world.

He has refused his Assent to Laws, the most wholesome and necessary for the public good.

He has forbidden his Governors to pass Laws of immediate and pressing importance, unless suspended in their operation till his Assent should be obtained; and when so suspended, he has utterly neglected to attend to them.

He has refused to pass over Laws for the accommodation of large districts of people, unless those people would relinquish the right of Representation in the Legislature, a right inestimable to them and formidable to tyrants only.

He has called together legislative bodies at places unusual, uncomfortable, and distant from the depository of their Public Records, for the sole purpose of fatiguing them into compliance with his measures.

He has dissolved Representative Houses repeatedly, for opposing   10 with manly firmness his invasions on the rights of the people.

He has refused for a long time, after such dissolutions, to cause others to be elected; whereby the Legislative Powers, incapable of Annihilation, have returned to the People at large for their exercise; the State remaining in the mean time exposed to all the dangers of invasion from without, and convulsions within.

He has endeavored to prevent the population of these States, for that purpose obstructing the Laws of Naturalization of Foreigners; refusing to pass others to encourage their migration hither, and raising the conditions of new Appropriations of Lands.

He has obstructed the Administration of Justice, by refusing his Assent to Laws for establishing Judiciary Powers.

He has made Judges dependent on his Will alone, for the tenure of their offices, and the amount and payment of their salaries.

He has erected a multitude of New Offices, and sent hither swarms   15 of Officers to harass our People, and eat out their substance.

He has kept among us, in time of peace, Standing Armies without the consent of our Legislature.

He has affected to render the Military independent of and superior to the Civil Power.

He has combined with others to subject us to jurisdictions foreign to our constitution, and unacknowledged by our laws; giving his Assent to their acts of pretended Legislation:

For quartering large bodies of armed troops among us:

For protecting them, by a mock Trial, from Punishment for any   20 Murders which they should commit on the Inhabitants of these States:

For cutting off our Trade with all parts of the world:

For imposing Taxes on us without our Consent:

For depriving us in many cases, of the benefits of Trial by Jury:

For transporting us beyond Seas to be tried for pretended offenses:

For abolishing the free System of English Laws in a Neighbouring 25 Province, establishing therein an Arbitrary government, and enlarging its boundaries so as to render it at once an example and fit instrument for introducing the same absolute rule into these Colonies:

For taking away our Charters, abolishing our most valuable Laws, and altering fundamentally the Forms of our Governments.

For suspending our own Legislatures, and declaring themselves invested with Power to legislate for us in all cases whatsoever.

He has abdicated Government here, by declaring us out of his Protection and waging War against us.

He has plundered our seas, ravaged our Coasts, burnt our towns and destroyed the Lives of our people.

He is at this time transporting large Armies of foreign Mercenaries 30 to compleat the works of death, desolation and tyranny, already begun with circumstances of Cruelty & perfidy scarcely paralleled in the most barbarous ages, and totally unworthy the Head of a civilized nation.

He has constrained our fellow Citizens taken Captive on the high Seas to bear Arms against their Country, to become the executioners of their friends and Brethren, or to fall themselves by their Hands.

He has excited domestic insurrections amongst us, and has endeavored to bring on the inhabitants of our frontiers, the merciless Indian Savages, whose known rule of warfare is an undistinguished destruction of all ages, sexes and conditions.

In every stage of these Oppressions We Have Petitioned for Redress in the most humble terms: Our repeated petitions have been answered only by repeated injury. A Prince, whose character is thus marked by every act which may define a Tyrant, is unfit to be the ruler of a free People.

Nor have We been wanting in attention to our British brethren. We have warned them from time to time of attempts by their legislature to extend an unwarrantable jurisdiction over us. We have reminded them of the circumstances of our emigration and settlement here. We have appealed to their native justice and magnanimity and we have conjured them by the ties of our common kindred to disavow these usurpations, which would inevitably interrupt our connections and correspondence. They too have been deaf to the voice of justice and of consanguinity. We must, therefore, acquiesce in the necessity, which denounces our Separation, and hold them, as we hold the rest of mankind, Enemies in War, in Peace Friends.

We, therefore, the Representatives of the United States of America, 35 in General Congress, Assembled, appealing to the Supreme Judge of the world of the rectitude of our intentions, do, in the Name, and by Authority of the good People of these Colonies, solemnly publish and declare, That these United Colonies are, and of Right ought to be, Free and Independent States; that they are Absolved from all Allegiance to the British Crown, and that all political connection between them and the State of Great Britain, is and ought to be totally dissolved; and that as Free and Independent States, they have full power to levy War, conclude Peace, contract Alliances, establish Commerce, and so all the other Acts and Things which Independent States may of right do. And for the support of this Declaration, with a firm reliance on the protection of Divine Providence, we mutually pledge to each other our lives, our Fortunes and our sacred Honor.

Topics for Critical Thinking and Writing

1. According to the first paragraph, for what audience was the Declaration written? What other audiences do you think the document was (in one way or another) addressed to?

2. The Declaration states that it is intended to "prove" that the acts of the government of George III had as their "direct object the establishment of an absolute Tyranny" in the American colonies (para. 5). Write an essay of 500 to 750 words showing whether the evidence offered in the Declaration "proves" this claim to your satisfaction. (You will, of course, want to define *absolute tyranny*.) If you think further evidence is needed to "prove" the colonists' point, indicate what this evidence might be.

3. Paying special attention to the paragraphs beginning "That whenever any Form of Government" (para. 4), "In every stage" (para. 33), and "Nor have We been wanting" (para. 34), in a sentence or two set forth the image of themselves that the colonists seek to convey.

4. In the Declaration of Independence it is argued that the colonists are entitled to certain things and that under certain conditions they may behave in a certain way. Make explicit the syllogism that Jefferson is arguing.

5. What evidence does Jefferson offer to support his major premise? His minor premise?

6. In paragraph 2 the Declaration cites "certain unalienable Rights" and mentions three: "Life, Liberty and the pursuit of Happiness." What is an unalienable right? If someone has an unalienable (or inalienable) right, does that imply that he or she also has certain duties? If so, what are

these duties? John Locke, a century earlier (1690), asserted that all men have a natural right to "life, liberty, and property." Do you think the decision to drop "property" and substitute "pursuit of Happiness" improved Locke's claim? Explain.

7. The Declaration ends thus: "We mutually pledge to each other our lives, our Fortunes and our sacred Honor." Is it surprising that honor is put in the final, climactic position? Is this a better ending than "our Fortunes, our sacred Honor, and our lives," or than "our sacred Honor, our lives, and our Fortunes?" Why?

8. King George III has asked you to reply, on his behalf, to the colonists, in 500 to 750 words. Write his reply. (Caution: A good reply will probably require you to do some reading about the period.)

9. Write a declaration of your own, setting forth in 500 to 750 words why some group is entitled to independence. You may want to argue that adolescents should not be compelled to attend school, that animals should not be confined in zoos, or that persons who use drugs should be able to buy them legally. Begin with a premise, then set forth facts illustrating the unfairness of the present condition, and conclude by stating what the new condition will mean to society.

ELIZABETH CADY STANTON

Elizabeth Cady Stanton (1815–1902), a lawyer's daughter and journalist's wife, proposed in 1848 a convention to address the "social, civil, and religious condition and rights of women." Responding to Stanton's call, women and men from all over the Northeast traveled to the Woman's Rights Convention held in the village of Seneca Falls, New York. Her Declaration, adopted by the Convention—but only after vigorous debate and some amendments by others—became the platform for the women's rights movement in this country.

Declaration of Sentiments and Resolutions

When, in the course of human events, it becomes necessary for one portion of the family of man to assume among the people of the earth a position different from that which they have hitherto occupied, but one to which the laws of nature and of nature's God entitle them, a decent respect to the opinions of mankind requires that they should declare the causes that impel them to such a course.

We hold these truths to be self-evident: that all men and women are created equal; that they are endowed by their Creator with certain inalienable rights; that among these are life, liberty and the pursuit of happiness; that to secure these rights governments are instituted, deriving their just powers from the consent of the governed. Whenever any form of government becomes destructive of these ends, it is the right of those who suffer from it to refuse allegiance to it, and to insist upon the institution of a new government, laying its foundation on such principles, and organizing its powers in such form, as to them shall seem most likely to effect their safety and happiness. Prudence, indeed, will dictate that governments long established should not be changed for light and transient causes; and accordingly all experience hath shown that mankind are more disposed to suffer, while evils are sufferable, than to right themselves by abolishing the forms to which they were accustomed. But when a long train of abuses and usurpations, pursuing invariably the same object, evinces a design to reduce them under absolute despotism, it is their duty to throw off such government, and to provide new guards for their future security. Such has been the patient sufferance of the women under this government, and such is now the necessity which constrains them to demand the equal station to which they are entitled.

The history of mankind is a history of repeated injuries and usurpations on the part of man toward woman, having in direct object the establishment of an absolute tyranny over her. To prove this, let facts be submitted to a candid world.

He has never permitted her to exercise her inalienable right to the elective franchise.

He has compelled her to submit to laws, in the formation of which   5
she had no voice.

He has withheld from her rights which are given to the most ignorant and degraded men — both natives and foreigners.

Having deprived her of this first right of a citizen, the elective franchise, thereby leaving her without representation in the halls of legislation, he has oppressed her on all sides.

He has made her, if married, in the eye of the law, civilly dead.

He has taken from her all right in property, even to the wages she earns.

He has made her, morally, an irresponsible being, as she can com-   10
mit many crimes with impunity, provided they be done in the presence of her husband. In the covenant of marriage, she is compelled to promise obedience to her husband, he becoming to all intents and purposes, her master — the law giving him power to deprive her of her liberty, and to administer chastisement.

He has so framed the laws of divorce, as to what shall be the proper causes, and in case of separation, to whom the guardianship of the children shall be given, as to be wholly regardless of the happiness of women—the law, in all cases, going upon a false supposition of the supremacy of man, and giving all power into his hands.

After depriving her of all rights as a married woman, if single, and the owner of property, he has taxed her to support a government which recognizes her only when her property can be made profitable to it.

He has monopolized nearly all the profitable employments, and from those she is permitted to follow, she receives but a scanty remuneration. He closes against her all the avenues to wealth and distinction which he considers most honorable to himself. As a teacher of theology, medicine, or law, she is not known.

He has denied her the facilities for obtaining a thorough education, all colleges being closed against her.

He allows her in Church, as well as State, but a subordinate position, claiming Apostolic authority for her exclusion from the ministry, and, with some exceptions, from any public participation in the affairs of the Church.

He has created a false public sentiment by giving to the world a different code of morals for men and women, by which moral delinquencies which exclude women from society, are not only tolerated, but deemed of little account in man.

He has usurped the prerogative of Jehovah himself, claiming it as his right to assign for her a sphere of action, when that belongs to her conscience and to her God.

He has endeavored, in every way that he could, to destroy her confidence in her own powers, to lessen her self-respect, and to make her willing to lead a dependent and abject life.

Now, in view of this entire disfranchisement of one-half the people of this country, their social and religious degradation—in view of the unjust laws above mentioned, and because women do feel themselves aggrieved, oppressed, and fraudulently deprived of their most sacred rights, we insist that they have immediate admission to all the rights and privileges which belong to them as citizens of the United States.

In entering upon the great work before us, we anticipate no small amount of misconception, misrepresentation, and ridicule; but we shall use every instrumentality within our power to effect our object. We shall employ agents, circulate tracts, petition the State and National legislatures, and endeavor to enlist the pulpit and the press in our behalf. We hope this Convention will be followed by a series of Conventions embracing every part of the country.

[The following resolutions were discussed by Lucretia Mott, Thomas and Mary Ann McClintock, Amy Post, Catharine A. F. Stebbins, and others, and were adopted:]

Whereas, The great precept of nature is conceded to be, that "man shall pursue his own true and substantial happiness." Blackstone in his Commentaries remarks, that this law of Nature being coeval with mankind, and dictated by God himself, is of course superior in obligation to any other. It is binding over all the globe, in all countries, and at all times; no human laws are of any validity if contrary to this, and such of them as are valid, derive all their force, and all their validity, and all their authority, mediately and immediately, from this original; therefore,

Resolved, That such laws as conflict, in any way, with the true and substantial happiness of woman, are contrary to the great precept of nature and of no validity, for this is "superior in obligation to any other."

Resolved, That all laws which prevent woman from occupying such a station in society as her conscience shall dictate, or which place her in a position inferior to that of man, are contrary to the great precept of nature, and therefore of no force or authority.

Resolved, That woman is man's equal — was intended to be so by the Creator, and the highest good of the race demands that she should be recognized as such.

Resolved, That the women of this country ought to be enlightened in 25 regard to the laws under which they live, that they may no longer publish their degradation by declaring themselves satisfied with their present position, nor their ignorance, by asserting that they have all the rights they want.

Resolved, That inasmuch as man, while claiming for himself intellectual superiority, does accord to woman moral superiority, it is preeminently his duty to encourage her to speak and teach, as she has an opportunity, in all religious assemblies.

Resolved, That the same amount of virtue, delicacy, and refinement of behavior that is required of woman in the social state, should also be required of man, and the same transgressions should be visited with equal severity on both man and woman.

Resolved, That the objection of indelicacy and impropriety, which is so often brought against woman when she addresses a public audience, comes with a very ill-grace from those who encourage, by their attendance, her appearance on the stage, in the concert, or in feats of the circus.

Resolved, That woman has too long rested satisfied in the circumscribed limits which corrupt customs and a perverted application of the Scriptures have marked out for her, and that it is time she should move in the enlarged sphere which her great Creator has assigned her.

Resolved, That it is the duty of the women of this country to secure   30
to themselves their sacred right to the elective franchise.

Resolved, That the equality of human rights results necessarily from
the fact of the identity of the race in capabilities and responsibilities.

Resolved, therefore, That, being invested by the Creator with the
same capabilities, and the same consciousness of responsibility for their
exercise, it is demonstrably the right and duty of woman, equally with
man, to promote every righteous cause by every righteous means; and
especially in regard to the great subjects of morals and religion, it is self-
evidently her right to participate with her brother in teaching them, both
in private and in public, by writing and by speaking, by any instrumen-
talities proper to be used, and in any assemblies proper to be held; and
this being a self-evident truth growing out of the divinely implanted
principles of human nature, any custom or authority adverse to it,
whether modern or wearing the hoary sanction of antiquity, is to be regarded as a self-evident falsehood, and at war with mankind.

[At the last session Lucretia Mott offered and spoke to the following
resolution:]

Resolved, That the speedy success of our cause depends upon the
zealous and untiring efforts of both men and women, for the overthrow
of the monopoly of the pulpit, and for the securing to woman an equal
participation with men in the various trades, professions, and commerce.

Topics for Critical Thinking and Writing

1. Stanton echoes the Declaration of Independence because she wishes to
   associate her ideas and the movement she supports with a document
   and a movement that her readers esteem. And she must have believed
   that if readers esteem the Declaration of Independence, they must grant
   the justice of her goals. Does her strategy work, or does it backfire by
   making her essay seem strained?

2. When Stanton insists that women have an "inalienable right to the elective franchise" (para. 4), what does she mean by "inalienable"?

3. Stanton complains that men have made married women, "in the eye of
   the law, civilly dead" (para. 8). What does she mean by "civilly dead"?
   How is it possible for a person to be biologically alive and yet civilly dead?

4. Stanton objects that women are "not known" as teachers of "theology,
   medicine, or law" (para. 13). Is this still true today? Do some research in
   your library, and then write three 100-word biographical sketches, one
   each on well-known woman professors of theology, medicine, and law.

5. How might you go about proving (rather than merely asserting) that, as paragraph 24 says, "woman is man's equal—was intended to be so by the Creator"?

6. The Declaration claims that women have "the same capabilities" as men (para. 32). Yet in 1848 Stanton and the others at Seneca Falls knew, or should have known, that history recorded no example of a woman philosopher comparable to Plato or Kant, a composer comparable to Beethoven or Chopin, a scientist comparable to Galileo or Newton, or a mathematician comparable to Euclid or Descartes. Do these facts contradict the Declaration's claim? If not, why not? How else but by different intellectual capabilities do you think such facts can be explained?

7. Stanton's Declaration is over 155 years old. Have all of the issues she raised been satisfactorily resolved? If not, which ones remain?

8. In our society, children have very few rights. For instance, a child cannot decide to drop out of elementary school or high school, and a child cannot decide to leave his or her parents to reside with some other family that he or she finds more compatible. Whatever your view of children's rights, compose the best Declaration of the Rights of Children that you can.

VIRGINIA WOOLF

Virginia Woolf (1882–1941) was born in London, daughter of Leslie Stephen, a distinguished Victorian scholar. She grew up in an atmosphere of learning, and after her father's death she continued to move in a world of intellectuals and writers (the Bloomsbury Group) that included economist John Maynard Keynes and novelist E. M. Forster. In 1912 she married Leonard Woolf, a writer with a special interest in politics. Together they founded the Hogarth Press, which published much important material, including Virginia's own novels and the first English translations of Sigmund Freud. In addition to writing such major novels as Mrs. Dalloway *(1925),* To the Lighthouse *(1927), and* The Waves *(1931), she wrote many essays, chiefly on literature and on feminist causes.*

The essay reprinted here was originally a talk delivered in 1931 to the Women's Service League.

Professions for Women

When your secretary invited me to come here, she told me that your Society is concerned with the employment of women and she suggested that I might tell you something about my own professional experiences.

It is true I am a woman; it is true I am employed, but what professional experiences have I had? It is difficult to say. My profession is literature; and in that profession there are fewer experiences for women than in any other, with the exception of the stage—fewer, I mean, that are peculiar to women. For the road was cut many years ago—by Fanny Burney, by Aphra Behn, by Harriet Martineau, by Jane Austen, by George Eliot—many famous women, and many more unknown and forgotten, have been before me, making the path smooth, and regulating my steps. Thus, when I came to write, there were very few material obstacles in my way. Writing was a reputable and harmless occupation. The family peace was not broken by the scratching of a pen. No demand was made upon the family purse. For ten and sixpence one can buy paper enough to write all the plays of Shakespeare—if one has a mind that way. Pianos and models, Paris, Vienna, and Berlin, masters and mistresses, are not needed by a writer. The cheapness of writing paper is, of course, the reason why women have succeeded as writers before they have succeeded in the other professions.

But to tell you my story—it is a simple one. You have only got to figure to yourselves a girl in a bedroom with a pen in her hand. She had only to move that pen from left to right—from ten o'clock to one. Then it occurred to her to do what is simple and cheap enough after all—to slip a few of those pages into an envelope, fix a penny stamp in the corner, and drop the envelope into the red box at the corner. It was thus that I became a journalist; and my effort was rewarded on the first day of the following month—a very glorious day it was for me—by a letter from an editor containing a check for one pound ten shillings and sixpence.[1] But to show you how little I deserve to be called a professional woman, how little I know of the struggles and difficulties of such lives, I have to admit that instead of spending that sum upon bread and butter, rent, shoes and stockings, or butcher's bills, I went out and bought a cat—a beautiful cat, a Persian cat, which very soon involved me in bitter disputes with my neighbors.

What could be easier than to write articles and to buy Persian cats with the profits? But wait a moment. Articles have to be about something. Mine, I seem to remember, was about a novel by a famous man. And while I was writing this review, I discovered that if I were going to review books I should need to do battle with a certain phantom. And the phantom was a woman, and when I came to know her better I called her after the heroine of a famous poem, The Angel in the House. It was she who used to come between me and my paper when I was writing

---

[1] **one pound ten shillings and sixpence** In 1930, this sum was equivalent to about $7.40. [—Ed.]

reviews. It was she who bothered me and wasted my time and so tormented me that at last I killed her. You who come of a younger and happier generation may not have heard of her—you may not know what I mean by the Angel in the House. I will describe her as shortly as I can. She was intensely sympathetic. She was immensely charming. She was utterly unselfish. She excelled in the difficult arts of family life. She sacrificed herself daily. If there was chicken, she took the leg; if there was a draught she sat in it—in short she was so constituted that she never had a mind or a wish of her own, but preferred to sympathize always with the minds and wishes of others. Above all—I need not say it—she was pure. Her purity was supposed to be her chief beauty—her blushes, her great grace. In those days—the last of Queen Victoria—every house had its Angel. And when I came to write I encountered her with the very first words. The shadow of her wings fell on my page; I heard the rustling of her skirts in the room. Directly, that is to say, I took my pen in hand to review that novel by a famous man, she slipped behind me and whispered: "My dear, you are a young woman. You are writing about a book that has been written by a man. Be sympathetic; be tender; flatter; deceive; use all the arts and wiles of our sex. Never let anybody guess that you have a mind of your own. Above all, be pure." And she made as if to guide my pen. I now record the one act for which I take some credit to myself, though the credit rightly belongs to some excellent ancestors of mine who left me a certain sum of money—shall we say five hundred pounds a year?—so that it was not necessary for me to depend solely on charm for my living. I turned upon her and caught her by the throat. I did my best to kill her. My excuse, if I were to be had up in a court of law, would be that I acted in self-defense. Had I not killed her she would have killed me. She would have plucked the heart out of my writing. For, as I found, directly I put pen to paper, you cannot review even a novel without having a mind of your own, without expressing what you think to be the truth about human relations, morality, sex. And all these questions, according to the Angel in the House, cannot be dealt with freely and openly by women; they must charm, they must conciliate, they must—to put it bluntly—tell lies if they are to succeed. Thus, whenever I felt the shadow of her wing or the radiance of her halo upon my page, I took up the inkpot and flung it at her. She died hard. Her fictitious nature was of great assistance to her. It is far harder to kill a phantom than a reality. She was always creeping back when I thought I had despatched her. Though I flatter myself that I killed her in the end, the struggle was severe; it took much time that had better have been spent upon learning Greek grammar; or in roaming the world in search of adventures. But it was a real experience; it was an experience that was bound to befall all women writers at that time. Killing the Angel in the House was part of the occupation of a woman writer.

But to continue my story. The Angel was dead; what then remained? You may say that what remained was a simple and common object—a young woman in a bedroom with an inkpot. In other words, now that she had rid herself of falsehood, that young woman had only to be herself. Ah, but what is "herself"? I mean, what is a woman? I assure you, I do not know. I do not believe that you know. I do not believe that anybody can know until she has expressed herself in all the arts and professions open to human skill. That indeed is one of the reasons why I have come here—out of respect for you, who are in process of showing us by your experiments what a woman is, who are in process of providing us, by your failures and successes, with that extremely important piece of information.

But to continue the story of my professional experiences. I made 5 one pound ten and six by my first review; and I bought a Persian cat with the proceeds. Then I grew ambitious. A Persian cat is all very well, I said; but a Persian cat is not enough. I must have a motor car. And it was thus that I became a novelist—for it is a very strange thing that people will give you a motor car if you will tell them a story. It is a still stranger thing that there is nothing so delightful in the world as telling stories. It is far pleasanter than writing reviews of famous novels. And yet, if I am to obey your secretary and tell you my professional experiences as a novelist, I must tell you about a very strange experience that befell me as a novelist. And to understand it you must try first to imagine a novelist's state of mind. I hope I am not giving away professional secrets if I say that a novelist's chief desire is to be as unconscious as possible. He has to induce in himself a state of perpetual lethargy. He wants life to proceed with the utmost quiet and regularity. He wants to see the same faces, to read the same books, to do the same things day after day, month after month, while he is writing, so that nothing may break the illusion in which he is living—so that nothing may disturb or disquiet the mysterious nosings about, feelings round, darts, dashes, and sudden discoveries of that very shy and illusive spirit, the imagination. I suspect that this state is the same both for men and women. Be that as it may, I want you to imagine me writing a novel in a state of trance. I want you to figure to yourselves a girl sitting with a pen in her hand, which for minutes, and indeed for hours, she never dips into the inkpot. The image that comes to my mind when I think of this girl is the image of a fisherman lying sunk in dreams on the verge of a deep lake with a rod held out over the water. She was letting her imagination sweep unchecked round every rock and cranny of the world that lies submerged in the depths of our unconscious being. Now came the experience, the experience that I believe to be far commoner with women writers than with men. The line raced through the girl's fingers. Her imagination had rushed away. It had sought the pools, the depths, the dark places where the largest fish slumber. And there was a smash. There was a explosion. There was foam and confusion. The imagination had dashed itself against something hard. The girl was roused from her dream. She was indeed in a state of the most acute and difficult distress. To speak without figure she had thought of something, something about the body, about the passions which it was unfitting for her as a woman to say. Men, her reason told her, would be shocked. The consciousness of what men will say of a woman who speaks the truth about her passions had roused her from her artist's state of unconsciousness. She could write no more. The trance was over. Her imagination could work no longer. This I believe to be a very common experience with women writers—they are impeded by the extreme conventionality of the other sex. For though men sensibly allow themselves great freedom in these respects, I doubt that they realize or can control the extreme severity with which they condemn such freedom in women.

These then were two very genuine experiences of my own. These were two of the adventures of my professional life. The first—killing the Angel in the House—I think I solved. She died. But the second, telling the truth about my own experiences as a body, I do not think I solved. I doubt that any woman has solved it yet. The obstacles against her are still immensely powerful—and yet they are very difficult to define. Outwardly, what is simpler than to write books? Outwardly, what obstacles are there for a woman rather than for a man? Inwardly, I think, the case is very different; she has still many ghosts to fight, many prejudices to overcome. Indeed it will be a long time still, I think, before a woman can sit down to write a book without finding a phantom to be slain, a rock to be dashed against. And if this is so in literature, the freest of all professions for women, how is it in the new professions which you are now for the first time entering?

Those are the questions that I should like, had I time, to ask you. And indeed, if I have laid stress upon these professional experiences of mine, it is because I believe that they are, though in different forms, yours also. Even when the path is nominally open—when there is nothing to prevent a woman from being a doctor, a lawyer, a civil servant—there are many phantoms and obstacles, as I believe, looming in her way. To discuss and define them is I think of great value and importance; for thus only can the labor be shared, the difficulties be solved. But besides this, it is necessary also to discuss the ends and the aims for which we are fighting, for which we are doing battle with these formidable obstacles. Those aims cannot be taken for granted; they must be perpetually questioned and examined. The whole position, as I see it—here in this hall surrounded by women practicing for the first time in history I know not how many different professions—is one of extraordinary interest and importance. You have won rooms of your own in, the house hitherto exclusively owned by men. You are able, though not without great labor and effort, to pay the rent. You are earning your five hundred pounds a year. But this freedom is only a beginning; the room is your own, but it is still bare. It has to be furnished; it has to be decorated; it has to be shared. How are you going to furnish it, how are you going to decorate it? With whom are you going to share it, and upon what terms? These, I think, are questions of the utmost importance and interest. For the first time in history you are able to ask them; for the first time you are able to decide for yourselves what the answers should be. Willingly would I stay and discuss those questions and answers—but not tonight. My time is up; and I must cease.

Topics for Critical Thinking and Writing

1. At the end of the first paragraph, Woolf purports to explain why "women have succeeded as writers before they have succeeded in the other professions." Do you think her explanation is serious? Correct? Write a 250-word essay in which you defend or attack her explanation.

2. Woolf declares herself (paras. 5 and 6) to have been unable to write comfortably about her "passions" and her "own experiences as a body," She also thinks that men have it easier in this respect. Can you think of reasons why this difference should have been true, or appeared to be true, earlier in this century? Do you think it is true today? Why, or why not?

3. In her final paragraph Woolf says that "even when the path is nominally open" for a woman to become a doctor, lawyer, or civil servant, "there are many phantoms and obstacles . . . looming in her way." In a paragraph explain what she means, and in a second paragraph indicate whether you think her point is valid today.

4. In your library find a copy of John Stuart Mill's *Subjection of Women* (written about seventy-five years before Woolf's essay), read it, and write a 500-word essay focused on one of these questions: (a) Would Mill have approved of Woolf's murdering the Angel in the House? (b) How would Mill explain Woolf's inability to answer the question, "What is a woman?"

5. In the reference section in your library find out what you can about each of the five women Woolf mentions in her first paragraph. Then

look up something about the life of Virginia Woolf herself, and write a 500-word essay in which you compare her life and career to the life and career of the one woman among these five who was most like her.

GEORGE ORWELL

George Orwell was the pen name adopted by Eric Blair (1903–1950), an Englishman born in India. Orwell was educated at Eton, in England, but in 1921 he went back to the East and served for five years as a police officer in Burma (now Myanmar). Disillusioned with colonial imperialism, he returned to Europe, doing odd jobs while writing novels and stories. In 1936 he fought in the Spanish Civil War on the side of the Republicans, an experience he reported in Homage to Catalonia *(1938). His last years were spent writing in England. His best-known work probably is the satiric allegory* 1984 *(1949), showing a totalitarian state in which the citizens are perpetually under the eye of Big Brother. The following essay is from* Shooting an Elephant and Other Essays *(1950).*

Shooting an Elephant

In Moulmein, in Lower Burma, I was hated by large numbers of people—the only time in my life that I have been important enough for this to happen to me. I was sub-divisional police officer of the town, and in an aimless, petty kind of way anti-European feeling was very bitter. No one had the guts to raise a riot, but if a European woman went through the bazaars alone somebody would probably spit betel juice over her dress. As a police officer I was an obvious target and was baited whenever it seemed safe to do so. When a nimble Burman tripped me up on the football field and the referee (another Burman) looked the other way, the crowd yelled with hideous laughter. This happened more than once. In the end the sneering yellow faces of young men that met me everywhere, the insults hooted after me when I was at a safe distance, got badly on my nerves. The young Buddhist priests were the worst of all. There were several thousands of them in the town and none of them seemed to have anything to do except stand on street corners and jeer at Europeans.

All this was perplexing and upsetting. For at that time I had already made up my mind that imperialism was an evil thing and the sooner I chucked up my job and got out of it the better. Theoretically—and secretly, of course—I was all for the Burmese and all against their oppressors, the British. As for the job I was doing, I hated it more bitterly than I can perhaps make clear. In a job like that you see the dirty work of Empire at close quarters. The wretched prisoners huddling in the stinking cages of the lock-ups, the grey, cowed faces of the long-term convicts, the scarred buttocks of the men who had been flogged with bamboos—all these oppressed me with an intolerable sense of guilt. But I could get nothing into perspective. I was young and ill-educated and I had had to think out my problems in the utter silence that is imposed on every Englishman in the East. I did not even know that the British Empire is dying, still less did I know that it is a great deal better than the younger empires that are going to supplant it. All I knew was that I was stuck between my hatred of the empire I served and my rage against the evilspirited little beasts who tried to make my job impossible. With one part of my mind I thought of the British Raj[1] as an unbreakable tyranny, as something clamped down, in *saecula saeculorum*,[2] upon the will of prostrate peoples; with another part I thought that the greatest joy in the world would be to drive a bayonet into a Buddhist priest's guts. Feelings like these are the normal by-products of imperialism; ask any Anglo-Indian official, if you can catch him off duty.

One day something happened which in a roundabout way was enlightening. It was a tiny incident in itself, but it gave me a better glimpse than I had had before of the real nature of imperialism—the real motives for which despotic governments act. Early one morning the subinspector at a police station the other end of the town rang me up on the 'phone and said that an elephant was ravaging the bazaar. Would I please come and do something about it? I did not know what I could do, but I wanted to see what was happening and I got on to a pony and started out. I took my rifle, an old .44 Winchester and much too small to kill an elephant, but I thought the noise might be useful *in terrorem*.[3] Various Burmans stopped me on the way and told me about the elephant's doings. It was not, of course, a wild elephant, but a tame one which had gone "must."[4] It had been chained up, as tame elephants always are when their attack of "must" is due, but on the previous night it had broken its chain and escaped. Its mahout, the only person who could manage it when it was in that state, had set out in pursuit, but had taken the wrong direction and was now twelve hours' journey away, and

---

[1]**British Raj** British imperial government in India and Burma. [All notes are the editors'.]
[2]**in *saecula saeculorum*** Forever (Latin). A term used in Christian liturgy.
[3]***in terrorem*** As a warning.
[4]**"must"** Into sexual heat.

in the morning the elephant had suddenly reappeared in the town. The Burmese population had no weapons and were quite helpless against it. It had already destroyed somebody's bamboo hut, killed a cow and raided some fruit-stalls and devoured the stock; also it had met the municipal rubbish van and, when the driver jumped out and took to his heels, had turned the van over and inflicted violences upon it.

The Burmese sub-inspector and some Indian constables were waiting for me in the quarter where the elephant had been seen. It was a very poor quarter, a labyrinth of squalid bamboo huts, thatched with palm-leaf, winding all over a steep hillside. I remember that it was a cloudy, stuffy morning at the beginning of the rains. We began questioning the people as to where the elephant had gone and, as usual, failed to get any definite information. That is invariably the case in the East; a story always sounds clear enough at a distance, but the nearer you get to the scene of events the vaguer it becomes. Some of the people said that the elephant had gone in one direction, some said that he had gone in another, some professed not even to have heard of any elephant. I had almost made up my mind that the whole story was a pack of lies, when we heard yells a little distance away. There was a loud, scandalized cry of "Go away, child! Go away this instant!" and an old woman with a switch in her hand came round the corner of a hut, violently shooing away a crowd of naked children. Some more women followed, clicking their tongues and exclaiming; evidently there was something that the children ought not to have seen. I rounded the hut and saw a man's dead body sprawling in the mud. He was an Indian, a black Dravidian coolie, almost naked, and he could not have been dead many minutes. The people said that the elephant had come suddenly upon him round the corner of the hut, caught him with its trunk, put its foot on his back and ground him into the earth. This was the rainy season and the ground was soft, and his face had scored a trench a foot deep and a couple of yards long. He was lying on his belly with arms crucified and head sharply twisted to one side. His face was coated with mud, the eyes wide open, the teeth bared and grinning with an expression of unendurable agony. (Never tell me, by the way, that the dead look peaceful. Most of the corpses I have seen looked devilish.) The friction of the great beast's foot had stripped the skin from his back as neatly as one skins a rabbit. As soon as I saw the dead man I sent an orderly to a friend's house nearby to borrow an elephant rifle. I had already sent back the pony, not wanting it to go mad with fright and throw me if it smelt the elephant.

The orderly came back in a few minutes with a rifle and five car-   5
tridges, and meanwhile some Burmans had arrived and told us that the elephant was in the paddy fields below, only a few hundred yards away. As I started forward practically the whole population of the quarter

flocked out of the houses and followed me. They had seen the rifle and were all shouting excitedly that I was going to shoot the elephant. They had not shown much interest in the elephant when he was merely ravaging their homes, but it was different now that he was going to be shot. It was a bit of fun to them, as it would be to an English crowd; besides they wanted the meat. It made me vaguely uneasy. I had no intention of shooting the elephant—I had merely sent for the rifle to defend myself if necessary—and it is always unnerving to have a crowd following you. I marched down the hill, looking and feeling a fool, with the rifle over my shoulder and an ever-growing army of people jostling at my heels. At the bottom, when you got away from the huts, there was a metalled road and beyond that a miry waste of paddy fields a thousand yards across, not yet ploughed but soggy from the first rains and dotted with coarse grass. The elephant was standing eight yards from the road, his left side towards us. He took not the slightest notice of the crowd's approach. He was tearing up bunches of grass, beating them against his knees to clean them and stuffing them into his mouth.

I had halted on the road. As soon as I saw the elephant I knew with perfect certainty that I ought not to shoot him. It is a serious matter to shoot a working elephant—it is comparable to destroying a huge and costly piece of machinery—and obviously one ought not to do it if it can possibly be avoided. And at that distance, peacefully eating, the elephant looked no more dangerous than a cow. I thought then and I think now that his attack of "must" was already passing off; in which case he would merely wander harmlessly about until the mahout came back and caught him. Moreover, I did not in the least want to shoot him. I decided that I would watch him for a little while to make sure that he did not turn savage again, and then go home.

But at that moment I glanced round at the crowd that had followed me. It was an immense crowd, two thousand at the least and growing every minute. It blocked the road for a long distance on either side. I looked at the sea of yellow faces above the garish clothes—faces all happy and excited over this bit of fun, all certain that the elephant was going to be shot. They were watching me as they would watch a conjurer about to perform a trick. They did not like me, but with the magical rifle in my hands I was momentarily worth watching. And suddenly I realized that I should have to shoot the elephant after all. The people expected it of me and I had got to do it; I could feel their two thousand wills pressing me forward, irresistibly. And it was at this moment, as I stood there with the rifle in my hands, that I first grasped the hollowness, the futility of the white man's dominion in the East. Here was I, the white man with his gun, standing in front of the unarmed native crowd—seemingly the leading actor of the piece; but in reality I was only an absurd puppet pushed to and fro by the will of those yellow faces behind. I perceived in this moment that when the white man turns tyrant it is his own freedom that he destroys. He becomes a sort of hollow, posing dummy, the conventionalized figure of a sahib. For it is the condition of his rule that he shall spend his life in trying to impress the "natives," and so in every crisis he has got to do what the "natives" expect of him. He wears a mask, and his face grows to fit it. I had got to shoot the elephant. I had committed myself to doing it when I sent for the rifle. A sahib has got to act like a sahib; he has got to appear resolute, to know his own mind and do definite things. To come all that way, rifle in hand, with two thousand people marching at my heels, and then to trail feebly away, having done nothing—no, that was impossible. The crowd would laugh at me. And my whole life, every white man's life in the East, was one long struggle not to be laughed at.

But I did not want to shoot the elephant. I watched him beating his bunch of grass against his knees, with that preoccupied grandmotherly air that elephants have. It seemed to me that it would be murder to shoot him. At that age I was not squeamish about killing animals, but I had never shot an elephant and never wanted to. (Somehow it always seems worse to kill a *large* animal.) Besides, there was the beast's owner to be considered. Alive, the elephant was worth at least a hundred pounds; dead, he would only be worth the value of his tusks, five pounds, possibly. But I had got to act quickly. I turned to some experienced-looking Burmans who had been there when we arrived, and asked them how the elephant had been behaving. They all said the same thing; he took no notice of you if you left him alone, but he might charge if you went too close to him.

It was perfectly clear to me what I ought to do. I ought to walk up to within, say, twenty-five yards of the elephant and test his behavior. If he charged, I could shoot; if he took no notice of me, it would be safe to leave him until the mahout came back. But also I knew that I was going to do no such thing. I was a poor shot with a rifle and the ground was soft mud into which one would sink at every step. If the elephant charged and I missed him, I should have about as much chance as a toad under a steam-roller. But even then I was not thinking particularly of my own skin, only of the watchful yellow faces behind. For at that moment, with the crowd watching me, I was not afraid in the ordinary sense, as I would have been if I had been alone. A white man mustn't be frightened in front of "natives"; and so, in general, he isn't frightened. The sole thought in my mind was that if anything went wrong those two thousand Burmans would see me pursued, caught, trampled on and reduced to a grinning corpse like that Indian up the hill. And if that happened it was quite probable that some of them would laugh. That would never do. There was only one alternative. I shoved the cartridges into the magazine and lay down on the road to get a better aim.

The crowd grew very still, and a deep, low, happy sigh, as of people who see the theatre curtain go up at last, breathed from innumerable throats. They were going to have their bit of fun after all. The rifle was a beautiful German thing with cross-hair sights. I did not then know that in shooting an elephant one would shoot to cut an imaginary bar running from ear-hole to ear-hole. I ought, therefore, as the elephant was sideways on, to have aimed straight at his ear-hole; actually I aimed several inches in front of this, thinking the brain would be further forward.

When I pulled the trigger I did not hear the bang or feel the kick—one never does when a shot goes home—but I heard the devilish roar of glee that went up from the crowd. In that instant, in too short a time, one would have thought, even for the bullet to get there, a mysterious, terrible change had come over the elephant. He neither stirred nor fell, but every line of his body had altered. He looked suddenly stricken, shrunken, immensely old, as though the frightful impact of the bullet had paralyzed him without knocking him down. At last, after what seemed a long time—it might have been five seconds, I dare say—he sagged flabbily to his knees. His mouth slobbered. An enormous senility seemed to have settled upon him. One could have imagined him thousands of years old. I fired again into the same spot. At the second shot he did not collapse but climbed with desperate slowness to his feet and stood weakly upright, with legs sagging and head dropping. I fired a third time. That was the shot that did for him. You could see the agony of it jolt his whole body and knock the last remnant of strength from his legs. But in falling he seemed for a moment to rise, for as his hind legs collapsed beneath him he seemed to tower upward like a huge rock toppling, his trunk reaching skywards like a tree. He trumpeted, for the first and only time. And then down he came, his belly towards me, with a crash that seemed to shake the ground even where I lay.

I got up. The Burmans were already racing past me across the mud. It was obvious that the elephant would never rise again, but he was not dead. He was breathing very rhythmically with long rattling gasps, his great mound of a side painfully rising and falling. His mouth was wide open—I could see far down into caverns of pale pink throat. I waited a long time for him to die, but his breathing did not weaken. Finally I fired my two remaining shots into the spot where I thought his heart must be. The thick blood welled out of him like red velvet, but still he did not die. His body did not even jerk when the shots hit him, the tortured breathing continued without a pause. He was dying, very slowly and in great agony, but in some world remote from me where not even a bullet could damage him further. I felt that I had got to put an end to that dreadful noise. It seemed dreadful to see the great beast lying there, powerless to move and yet powerless to die, and not even to be able to finish him. I sent back for my small rifle and poured shot after shot into his heart and down his throat. They seemed to make no impression. The tortured gasps continued as steadily as the ticking of a clock.

In the end I could not stand it any longer and went away. I heard later that it took him half an hour to die. Burmans were bringing dahs[5] and baskets even before I left, and I was told they had stripped his body almost to the bones by the afternoon.

Afterwards, of course, there were endless discussions about the shooting of the elephant. The owner was furious, but he was only an Indian and could do nothing. Besides, legally I had done the right thing, for a mad elephant has to be killed, like a mad dog, if its owner fails to control it. Among the Europeans opinion was divided. The older men said I was right, the younger men said it was a damn shame to shoot an elephant for killing a coolie, because an elephant was worth more than any damn Coringhee coolie. And afterwards I was very glad that the coolie had been killed; it put me legally in the right and it gave me a sufficient pretext for shooting the elephant. I often wondered whether any of the others grasped that I had done it solely to avoid looking a fool.

Topics for Critical Thinking and Writing

1. Did Orwell shoot the elephant of his own free will? Or did he shoot the elephant because he *had* to shoot it? What does he say about this? Do you find his judgment convincing or not? Write a 500-word essay explaining your answer.

2. Was Orwell justified in shooting the elephant? Did he do the right thing in killing it? In the aftermath, did he think he did the right thing? Do you? Write a 500-word essay explaining your answers.

3. Orwell says that "as soon as I saw the elephant I knew with perfect certainty that I ought not to shoot him" (para. 6). How could he claim to "know" this, when moments later he did shoot the elephant?

4. Orwell says in passing, "Somehow it always seems worse to kill a *large* animal" (para. 8). Explain why you think Orwell says this and whether you agree.

5. A biographer who did research on Orwell in Burma reported that he could find no supporting documentation, either in the local newspapers

[5]**dahs** Large knives.

or in the files of the police, that this episode ever occurred. Suppose that Orwell made it up. If so, is your response different? Explain.

6. If, pressured by circumstances, you have ever acted against what you might think is your reason or your nature, report the experience, and give your present evaluation of your behavior.

MARTIN LUTHER KING JR.

Martin Luther King Jr. (1929–1968) was born in Atlanta and edu-cated at Morehouse College, Crozer Theological Seminary, and Boston University. In 1954 he was called to serve as a Baptist minister in Montgomery, Alabama. During the next two years he achieved national fame when, using a policy of nonviolent resis-tance, he successfully led the boycott against segregated bus lines in Montgomery. He then organized the Southern Christian Leadership Conference, which furthered civil rights, first in the South and then nationwide. In 1964 he was awarded the Nobel Peace Prize. Four years later he was assassinated in Memphis, Tennessee, while supporting striking garbage workers.

The speech presented here was delivered from the steps of the Lincoln Memorial, in Washington, D.C., in 1963, the hundredth anniversary of the Emancipation Proclamation. King's immedi-ate audience consisted of more than two hundred thousand peo-ple who had come to demonstrate for civil rights.

I Have a Dream

I am happy to join with you today in what will go down in history as the greatest demonstration for freedom in the history of our nation.

Five score years ago, a great American, in whose symbolic shadow we stand today, signed the Emancipation Proclamation. This momen-tous decree came as a great beacon light of hope to millions of Negro slaves who had been seared in the flames of withering injustice. It came as a joyous daybreak to end the long night of their captivity. But one hundred years later, the Negro still is not free. One hundred years later, the life of the Negro is still sadly crippled by the manacles of segregation and the chains of discrimination. One hundred years later, the Negro lives on a lonely island of poverty in the midst of a vast ocean of material prosperity. One hundred years later, the Negro is still anguished in the corners of American society and finds himself in exile in his own land. And so we have come here today to dramatize a shameful condition.

In a sense we have come to our nation's capital to cash a check. When the architects of our republic wrote the magnificent words of the Constitution and the Declaration of Independence, they were signing a promissory note to which every American was to fall heir. This note was the promise that all men — yes, black men as well as white men — would be guaranteed the inalienable rights of life, liberty, and the pursuit of happiness.

It is obvious today that America has defaulted on this promissory note insofar as her citizens of color are concerned. Instead of honoring this sacred obligation, America has given the Negro people a bad check, a check which has come back marked "insufficient funds." But we refuse to believe that the bank of justice is bankrupt. We refuse to believe that there are insufficient funds in the great vaults of opportunity of this nation; and so we have come to cash this check, a check that will give us upon demand the riches of freedom and the security of justice.

We have also come to this hallowed spot to remind America of the   5
fierce urgency of *now*. This is no time to engage in the luxury of cooling off or to take the tranquilizing drug of gradualism. *Now* is the time to make real promises of democracy. *Now* is the time to rise from the dark and desolate valley of segregation to the sunlit path of racial justice. *Now* is the time to lift our nation from the quicksands of racial injustice to the solid rock of brotherhood. *Now* is the time to make justice a reality for all of God's children.

It would be fatal for the nation to overlook the urgency of the moment. This sweltering summer of the Negro's legitimate discontent will not pass until there is an invigorating autumn of freedom and equality. Nineteen sixty-three is not an end, but a beginning. And those who hope that the Negro needed to blow off steam and will now be content will have a rude awakening if the nation returns to business as usual. There will be neither rest nor tranquility in America until the Negro is granted his citizenship rights. The whirlwinds of revolt will continue to shake the foundations of our nation until the bright day of justice emerges.

But there is something that I must say to my people who stand on the warm threshold which leads into the palace of justice. In the process of gaining our rightful place, we must not be guilty of wrongful deeds. Let us not seek to satisfy our thirst for freedom by drinking from the cup of bitterness and hatred. We must forever conduct our struggle on the high plane of dignity and discipline. We must not allow our creative protest to degenerate into physical violence. Again and again we must rise to the majestic heights of meeting physical force with soul force. And the marvelous new militancy which has engulfed the Negro community must not lead us to a distrust of all white people; for many of our white brothers, as evidenced by their presence here today, have come to

realize that their destiny is tied up with our destiny, and they have come
to realize that their freedom is inextricably bound to our freedom.

We cannot walk alone. And as we walk we must make the pledge
that we shall always march ahead. We cannot turn back. There are those
who are asking the devotees of civil rights, "When will you be satisfied?"
We can never be satisfied as long as the Negro is the victim of the un-
speakable horrors of police brutality. We can never be satisfied as long
as our bodies, heavy with the fatigue of travel, cannot gain lodging in the
motels of the highways and the hotels of the cities. We cannot be satisfied as long as the Negro's basic mobility is from a smaller ghetto to a
larger one. We can never be satisfied as long as our children are stripped
of their selfhood and robbed of their dignity by signs stating "For Whites
Only." We cannot be satisfied as long as the Negro in Mississippi cannot
vote and a Negro in New York believes he has nothing for which to vote.
No, no, we are not satisfied, and we will not be satisfied until justice rolls
down like waters and righteousness like a mighty stream.[1]

I am not unmindful that some of you have come here out of great
trials and tribulations. Some of you have come fresh from narrow jail
cells. Some of you have come from areas where your quest for freedom
left you battered by the storms of persecution and staggered by the
winds of police brutality. You have been the veterans of creative suffering. Continue to work with the faith that unearned suffering is redemp-
tive.

Go back to Mississippi, and go back to Alabama. Go back to South   10
Carolina. Go back to Georgia. Go back to Louisiana. Go back to the
slums and ghettos of our Northern cities, knowing that somehow this
situation can and will be changed. Let us not wallow in the valley of despair.

I say to you today, my friends, even though we face the difficulties of
today and tomorrow, I still have a dream. It is a dream deeply rooted in
the American dream. I have a dream that one day this nation will rise up
and live out the true meaning of its creed: "We hold these truths to be
self-evident, that all men are created equal." I have a dream that one day,
on the red hills of Georgia, sons of former slaves and the sons of former
slave owners will be able to sit down together at the table of brotherhood. I have a dream that one day even the state of Mississippi, a state
sweltering with the heat of injustice, sweltering with the heat of oppression, will be transformed into an oasis of freedom and justice. I have a
dream that my four little children will one day live in a nation where
they will not be judged by the color of their skin, but by the content of
their character.

[1]**justice . . . stream** A quotation from the Hebrew Bible: Amos 5:24. [—Ed.]

I have a dream today. I have a dream that one day down in Alabama—with its vicious racists, with its governor's lips dripping with the words of interposition and nullification—one day right there in Alabama, little black boys and black girls will be able to join hands with little white boys and white girls as sisters and brothers.

I have a dream today. I have a dream that one day every valley shall be exalted and every hill and mountain shall be made low, the rough places will be made plain and the crooked places will be made straight, and the glory of the Lord shall be revealed, and all flesh shall see it together.[2]

This is our hope. This is the faith that I go back to the South with. And with this faith we will be able to hew out of the mountain of despair a stone of hope. With this faith we will be able to transform the jangling discords of our nation into a beautiful symphony of brotherhood. With this faith we will be able to work together, to play together, to struggle together, to go to jail together, to stand up for freedom together, knowing that we will be free one day.

And this will be the day—this will be the day when all of God's chil-   15
dren will be able to sing with new meaning:

> My country, 'tis of thee,
> Sweet land of liberty,
>   Of thee I sing;
> Land where my fathers died,
> Land of the Pilgrim's pride,
> From every mountainside
>   Let freedom ring.

And if America is to be a great nation, this must become true.

And so let freedom ring from the prodigious hilltops of New Hampshire. Let freedom ring from the mighty mountains of New York. Let freedom ring from the heightening Alleghenies of Pennsylvania. Let freedom ring from the snow-capped Rockies of Colorado. Let freedom ring from the curvaceous slopes of California.

But not only that. Let freedom ring from Stone Mountain of Georgia. Let freedom ring from Lookout Mountain of Tennessee. Let freedom ring from every hill and molehill of Mississippi. "From every mountainside let freedom ring."

And when this happens—when we allow freedom to ring, when we let it ring from every village and every hamlet, from every state and every

---

[2]**every valley . . . see it together** Another quotation from the Hebrew Bible: Isaiah 40:4–5. [—Ed.]

city—we will be able to speed up that day when all of God's children, Black men and white men, Jews and Gentiles, Protestants and Catholics, will be able to join hands and sing in the words of the old Negro spiritual: "Free at last! Free at last! Thank God Almighty. We are free at last!"

Topics for Critical Thinking and Writing

1. Analyze the rhetoric—the oratorical art—of the second paragraph. What, for instance, is gained by saying "five score years ago" instead of "a hundred years ago"? By metaphorically calling the Emancipation Proclamation "a great beacon light of hope"? By saying that "Negro slaves . . . had been seared in the flames of withering injustice"? And what of the metaphors "daybreak" and "the long night of . . . captivity"?

2. Do the first two paragraphs make an effective opening? Why?

3. In the third and fourth paragraphs King uses the metaphor of a bad check. Rewrite the third paragraph *without* using any of King's metaphors, and then in a paragraph evaluate the differences between King's version and yours.

4. King's highly metaphoric speech appeals to emotions. But it also offers *reasons*. What reasons, for instance, does King give to support his belief that African Americans should not resort to physical violence in their struggle against segregation and discrimination?

5. When King delivered the speech, his audience at the Lincoln Memorial was primarily African American. Do you think that the speech is also addressed to other Americans? Explain.

6. The speech can be divided into three parts: paragraphs 1 through 6; paragraphs 7 ("But there is") through 10; and paragraph 11 ("I say to you today, my friends") to the end. Summarize each of these three parts in a sentence or two so that the basic organization is evident.

7. King says (para. 11) that his dream is "deeply rooted in the American dream." First, what is the American dream, as King seems to understand it? Second, how does King establish his point—that is, what evidence does he use to convince us—that his dream is the American dream? (On this second issue, one might start by pointing out that in the second paragraph King refers to the Emancipation Proclamation. What other relevant documents does he refer to?)

8. King delivered his speech in 1963, more than forty years ago. In an essay of 500 words, argue that the speech still is—or is not—relevant. Or write an essay of 500 words in which you state what you take to be the "American dream," and argue that it now is or is not readily available to African Americans.

MARTIN LUTHER KING JR.

In 1963 King was arrested in Birmingham, Alabama, for partici-
pating in a march for which no parade permit had been issued by
city officials. In jail he wrote a response to a letter that eight local
clergymen had published in a newspaper. Their letter, titled "A
Call for Unity," is printed here, followed by King's response.

A CALL FOR UNITY

April 12, 1963

We the undersigned clergymen are among those who, in January, issued "An Appeal for Law and Order and Common Sense," in dealing
with racial problems in Alabama. We expressed understanding that
honest convictions in racial matters could properly be pursued in the
courts, but urged that decisions of those courts should in the meantime
be peacefully obeyed.

Since that time there had been some evidence of increased fore-
bearance and a willingness to face facts. Responsible citizens have
undertaken to work on various problems which cause racial friction and
unrest. In Birmingham, recent public events have given indication that
we all have opportunity for a new constructive and realistic approach to
racial problems.

However, we are now confronted by a series of demonstrations by
some of our Negro citizens, directed and led in part by outsiders. We
recognize the natural impatience of people who feel that their hopes are
slow in being realized. But we are convinced that these demonstrations
are unwise and untimely.

We agree rather with certain local Negro leadership which has
called for honest and open negotiation of racial issues in our area. And
we believe this kind of facing of issues can best be accomplished by citizens of our own metropolitan area, white and Negro, meeting with their
knowledge and experience of the local situation. All of us need to face
that responsibility and find proper channels for its accomplishment.

Just as we formerly pointed out that "hatred and violence have no   5
sanction in our religious and political traditions," we also point out that
such actions as incite to hatred and violence, however technically peaceful those actions may be, have not contributed to the resolution of our
local problems. We do not believe that these days of new hope are days
when extreme measures are justified in Birmingham.

We commend the community as a whole, and the local news media
and law enforcement officials in particular, on the calm manner in
which these demonstrations have been handled. We urge the public to

continue to show restraint should the demonstrations continue, and the law enforcement officials to remain calm and continue to protect our city from violence.

We further strongly urge our own Negro community to withdraw support from these demonstrations, and to unite locally in working peacefully for a better Birmingham. When rights are consistently denied, a cause should be pressed in the courts and in negotiations among local leaders, and not in the streets. We appeal to both our white and Negro citizenry to observe the principles of law and order and common sense.

> C.C.J. Carpenter, D.D., L.L.D., Bishop of Alabama; Joseph A. Durick, D.D., Auxiliary Bishop, Diocese of Mobile-Birmingham; Rabbi Milton L. Grafman, Temple Emanu-El, Birmingham, Alabama; Bishop Paul Hardin, Bishop of the Alabama-West Florida Conference of the Methodist Church; Bishop Nolan B. Harmon, Bishop of the North Alabama Conference of the Methodist Church; George M. Murray, D.D., L.L.D., Bishop Coadjutor, Episcopal Diocese of Alabama; Edward V. Ramage, Moderator, Synod of the Alabama Presbyterian Church in the United States; Earl Stallings, Pastor, First Baptist Church, Birmingham, Alabama.

Letter from Birmingham Jail

April 16, 1963

My Dear Fellow Clergymen:

While confined here in the Birmingham city jail, I came across your recent statement calling my present activities "unwise and untimely."[1] Seldom do I pause to answer criticism of my work and ideas. If I sought

---

[1]This response to a published statement by eight fellow clergymen from Alabama (Bishop C.C.J. Carpenter, Bishop Joseph A. Durick, Rabbi Milton L. Grafman, Bishop Paul Hardin, Bishop Nolan B. Harmon, the Reverend George M. Murray, the Reverend Edward V. Ramage, and the Reverend Earl Stallings) was composed under somewhat constricting circumstances. Begun on the margins of the newspaper in which the statement appeared while I was in jail, the letter was continued on scraps of writing paper supplied by a friendly Negro trusty, and concluded on a pad my attorneys were eventually permitted to leave me. Although the text remains in substance unaltered, I have indulged in the author's prerogative of polishing it for publication. [Author's note.]

to answer all the criticisms that cross my desk, my secretaries would have little time for anything other than such correspondence in the course of the day, and I would have no time for constructive work. But since I feel that you are men of genuine good will and that your criticisms are sincerely set forth, I want to try to answer your statement in what I hope will be patient and reasonable terms.

I think I should indicate why I am here in Birmingham, since you have been influenced by the view which argues against "outsiders coming in." I have the honor of serving as president of the Southern Christian Leadership Conference, an organization operating in every southern state, with headquarters in Atlanta, Georgia. We have some eighty-five affiliated organizations across the South, and one of them is the Alabama Christian Movement for Human Rights. Frequently we share staff, educational, and financial resources with our affiliates. Several months ago the affiliate here in Birmingham asked us to be on call to engage in a nonviolent direct-action program if such were deemed necessary. We readily consented, and when the hour came we lived up to our promise. So I, along with several members of my staff, am here because I was invited here. I am here because I have organizational ties here.

But more basically, I am in Birmingham because injustice is here. Just as the prophets of the eighth century B.C. left their villages and carried their "thus saith the Lord" far beyond the boundaries of their home towns, and just as the Apostle Paul left his village of Tarsus and carried the gospel of Jesus Christ to the far corners of the Greco-Roman world, so am I compelled to carry the gospel of freedom beyond my own home town. Like Paul, I must constantly respond to the Macedonian call for aid.

Moreover, I am cognizant of the interrelatedness of all communities and states. I cannot sit idly by in Atlanta and not be concerned about what happens in Birmingham. Injustice anywhere is a threat to justice everywhere. We are caught in an inescapable network of mutuality; tied in a single garment of destiny. Whatever affects one directly, affects all indirectly. Never again can we afford to live with the narrow, provincial "outside agitator" idea. Anyone who lives inside the United States can never be considered an outsider anywhere within its bounds.

You deplore the demonstrations taking place in Birmingham. But   5
your statement, I am sorry to say, fails to express a similar concern for the conditions that brought about the demonstrations. I am sure that none of you would want to rest content with the superficial kind of social analysis that deals merely with effects and does not grapple with underlying causes. It is unfortunate that demonstrations are tak-

ing place in Birmingham, but it is even more unfortunate that the city's white power structure left the Negro community with no alternative.

In any nonviolent campaign there are four basic steps: collection of the facts to determine whether injustices exist; negotiation; self-purification; and direct action. We have gone through all these steps in Birmingham. There can be no gainsaying the fact that racial injustice engulfs this community. Birmingham is probably the most thoroughly segregated city in the United States. Its ugly record of brutality is widely known. Negroes have experienced grossly unjust treatment in the courts. There have been more unsolved bombings of Negro homes and churches in Birmingham than in any other city in the nation. These are the hard, brutal facts of the case. On the basis of these conditions, Negro leaders sought to negotiate with the city fathers. But the latter consistently refused to engage in good-faith negotiation.

Then, last September, came the opportunity to talk with leaders of Birmingham's economic community. In the course of the negotiations, certain promises were made by the merchants—for example, to remove the stores' humiliating racial signs. On the basis of these promises, the Reverend Fred Shuttlesworth and the leaders of the Alabama Christian Movement for Human Rights agreed to a moratorium on all demonstrations. As the weeks and months went by, we realized that we were the victims of a broken promise. A few signs, briefly removed, returned; the others remained.

As in so many past experiences, our hopes had been blasted, and the shadow of deep disappointment settled upon us. We had no alternative except to prepare for direct action, whereby we would present our very bodies as a means of laying our case before the conscience of the local and the national community. Mindful of the difficulties involved, we decided to undertake a process of self-purification. We began a series of workshops on nonviolence, and we repeatedly asked ourselves: "Are you able to accept blows without retaliating?" "Are you able to endure the ordeal of jail?" We decided to schedule our direct-action program for the Easter season, realizing that except for Christmas, this is the main shopping period of the year. Knowing that a strong economic-withdrawal program would be the by-product of direct action, we felt that this would be the best time to bring pressure to bear on the merchants for the needed change.

Then it occurred to us that Birmingham's mayoralty election was coming up in March, and we speedily decided to postpone action until after election day. When we discovered that the Commissioner of Public Safety, Eugene "Bull" Connor, had piled up enough votes to be in the run-off, we decided again to postpone action until the day after the run-off so that the demonstrations could not be used to cloud the issues. Like many others, we waited to see Mr. Connor defeated, and to this end we endured postponement after postponement. Having aided in this community need, we felt that our direct-action program could be delayed no longer.

You may well ask: "Why direct action? Why sit-ins, marches, and so forth? Isn't negotiation a better path?" You are quite right in calling for negotiation. Indeed, this is the very purpose of direct action. Nonviolent direct action seeks to create such a crisis and foster such a tension that a community which has constantly refused to negotiate is forced to confront the issue. It seeks so to dramatize the issue that it can no longer be ignored. My citing the creation of tension as part of the work of the nonviolent-resister may sound rather shocking. But I must confess that I am not afraid of the word "tension." I have earnestly opposed violent tension, but there is a type of constructive, nonviolent tension which is necessary for growth. Just as Socrates felt that it was necessary to create a tension in the mind so that individuals could rise from the bondage of myths and half-truths to the unfettered realm of creative analysis and objective appraisal, so must we see the need for nonviolent gadflies to create the kind of tension in society that will help men rise from the dark depths of prejudice and racism to the majestic heights of understanding and brotherhood.

The purpose of our direct-action program is to create a situation so crisis-packed that it will inevitably open the door to negotiation. I therefore concur with you in your call for negotiation. Too long has our beloved Southland been bogged down in a tragic effort to live in monologue rather than dialogue.

One of the basic points in your statement is that the action that I and my associates have taken in Birmingham is untimely. Some have asked: "Why didn't you give the new city administration time to act?" The only answer that I can give to this query is that the new Birmingham administration must be prodded about as much as the outgoing one, before it will act. We are sadly mistaken if we feel that the election of Albert Boutwell as mayor will bring the millennium to Birmingham. While Mr. Boutwell is a much more gentle person than Mr. Connor, they are both segregationists, dedicated to maintenance of the status quo. I have hope that Mr. Boutwell will be reasonable enough to see the futility of massive resistance to desegregation. But he will not see this without pressure from devotees of civil rights. My friends, I must say to you that we have not made a single gain in civil rights without determined legal and nonviolent pressure. Lamentably, it is an historical fact that privileged groups seldom give up their privileges voluntarily. Individuals may see the moral light and voluntarily give up their unjust posture; but as

Reinhold Niebuhr[2] has reminded us, groups tend to be more immoral than individuals.

We know through painful experience that freedom is never voluntarily given by the oppressor; it must be demanded by the oppressed. Frankly, I have yet to engage in a direct-action campaign that was "well timed" in the view of those who have not suffered unduly from the disease of segregation. For years now I have heard the word "Wait!" It rings in the ear of every Negro with piercing familiarity. This "Wait" has almost always meant "Never." We must come to see, with one of our distinguished jurists, that "justice too long delayed is justice denied."[3]

We have waited for more than 340 years for our constitutional and God-given rights. The nations of Asia and Africa are moving with jetlike speed toward gaining political independence, but we still creep at horse-and-buggy pace toward gaining a cup of coffee at a lunch counter. Perhaps it is easy for those who have never felt the stinging darts of segregation to say, "Wait." But when you have seen vicious mobs lynch your mothers and fathers at will and drown your sisters and brothers at whim; when you have seen hate-filled policemen curse, kick, and even kill your black brothers and sisters; when you see the vast majority of your twenty million Negro brothers smothering in an airtight cage of poverty in the midst of an affluent society; when you suddenly find your tongue twisted and your speech stammering as you seek to explain to your six-year-old daughter why she can't go to the public amusement park that has just been advertised on television, and see tears welling up in her eyes when she is told that Funtown is closed to colored children, and see ominous clouds of inferiority beginning to form in her little mental sky, and see her beginning to distort her personality by developing an unconscious bitterness toward white people; when you have to concoct an answer for a five-year-old son who is asking: "Daddy, why do white people treat colored people so mean?"; when you take a cross-country drive and find it necessary to sleep night after night in the uncomfortable corners of your automobile because no motel will accept you; when you are humiliated day in and day out by nagging signs reading "white" and "colored"; when your first name becomes "nigger," your middle name becomes "boy" (however old you are) and your last name becomes "John," and your wife and mother are never given the respected title "Mrs."; when you are harried by day and haunted by night by the

[2]**Reinhold Niebuhr** Niebuhr (1892–1971) was a minister, political activist, author, and professor of applied Christianity at Union Theological Seminary. [All notes are the editors' unless otherwise specified.]
[3]**justice . . . denied** A quotation attributed to William E. Gladstone (1809–1898), British statesman and prime minister.

fact that you are a Negro, living constantly at tiptoe stance, never quite knowing what to expect next, and are plagued with inner fears and outer resentments; when you are forever fighting a degenerating sense of "no-bodiness"—then you will understand why we find it difficult to wait. There comes a time when the cup of endurance runs over, and men are no longer willing to be plunged into the abyss of despair. I hope, sirs, you can understand our legitimate and unavoidable impatience.

You express a great deal of anxiety over our willingness to break 15 laws. This is certainly a legitimate concern. Since we so diligently urge people to obey the Supreme Court's decision of 1954 outlawing segregation in the public schools, at first glance it may seem rather paradoxical for us consciously to break laws. One may well ask: "How can you advocate breaking some laws and obeying others?" The answer lies in the fact that there are two types of laws: just and unjust. I would be the first to advocate obeying just laws. One has not only a legal but a moral responsibility to obey just laws. Conversely, one has a moral responsibility to disobey unjust laws. I would agree with St. Augustine that "an unjust law is no law at all."

Now, what is the difference between the two? How does one determine whether a law is just or unjust? A just law is a man-made code that squares with the moral law or the law of God. An unjust law is a code that is out of harmony with the moral law. To put it in the terms of St. Thomas Aquinas: An unjust law is a human law that is not rooted in eternal law and natural law. Any law that uplifts human personality is just. Any law that degrades human personality is unjust. All segregation statutes are unjust because segregation distorts the soul and damages the personality. It gives the segregator a false sense of superiority and the segregated a false sense of inferiority. Segregation, to use the terminology of the Jewish philosopher Martin Buber, substitutes an "I-it" relationship for an "I-thou" relationship and ends up relegating persons to the status of things. Hence segregation is not only politically, economically, and sociologically unsound, it is morally wrong and sinful. Paul Tillich[4] has said that sin is separation. Is not segregation an existential expression of man's tragic separation, his awful estrangement, his terrible sinfulness? Thus it is that I can urge men to obey the 1954 decision of the Supreme Court, for it is morally right; and I can urge them to disobey segregation ordinances, for they are morally wrong.

[4]**Paul Tillich** Tillich (1886–1965), born in Germany, taught theology at several German universities, but in 1933 he was dismissed from his post at the University of Frankfurt because of his opposition to the Nazi regime. At the invitation of Reinhold Niebuhr, he came to the United States and taught at Union Theological Seminary.

Let us consider a more concrete example of just and unjust laws. An unjust law is a code that a numerical or power majority group compels a minority group to obey but does not make binding on itself. This is *dif-ference* made legal. By the same token, a just law is a code that a major-ity compels a minority to follow and that it is willing to follow itself. This is *sameness* made legal.

Let me give another explanation. A law is unjust if it is inflicted on a minority that, as a result of being denied the right to vote, had no part in enacting or devising the law. Who can say that the legislature of Alabama which set up that state's segregation laws was democratically elected? Throughout Alabama all sorts of devious methods are used to prevent Negroes from becoming registered voters, and there are some counties in which, even though Negroes constitute a majority of the pop-ulation, not a single Negro is registered. Can any law enacted under such circumstances be considered democratically structured?

Sometimes a law is just on its face and unjust in its application. For instance, I have been arrested on a charge of parading without a permit. Now, there is nothing wrong in having an ordinance which requires a permit for a parade. But such an ordinance becomes unjust when it is used to maintain segregation and to deny citizens the First Amendment privilege of peaceful assembly and protest.

I hope you are able to see the distinction I am trying to point out. In 20 no sense do I advocate evading or defying the law, as would the rabid segregationist. That would lead to anarchy. One who breaks an unjust law must do so openly, lovingly, and with a willingness to accept the penalty. I submit that an individual who breaks a law that conscience tells him is unjust, and who willingly accepts the penalty of imprison-ment in order to arouse the conscience of the community over its injus-tice, is in reality expressing the highest respect for law.

Of course, there is nothing new about this kind of civil disobedi-ence. It was evidenced sublimely in the refusal of Shadrach, Meshach, and Abednego to obey the laws of Nebuchadnezzar, on the ground that a higher moral law was at stake. It was practiced superbly by the early Christians, who were willing to face hungry lions and the excruciating pain of chopping blocks rather than submit to certain unjust laws of the Roman Empire. To a degree, academic freedom is a reality today be-cause Socrates practiced civil disobedience. In our own nation, the Boston Tea Party represented a massive act of civil disobedience.

We should never forget that everything Adolf Hitler did in Germany was "legal" and everything the Hungarian freedom fighters did in Hungary was "illegal." It was "illegal" to aid and comfort a Jew in Hitler's Germany. Even so, I am sure that, had I lived in Germany at the time, I would have aided and comforted my Jewish brothers. If today I lived in a Communist country where certain principles dear to the Christian faith are suppressed, I would openly advocate disobeying that country's antireligious laws.

I must make two honest confessions to you, my Christian and Jewish brothers. First, I must confess that over the past few years I have been gravely disappointed with the white moderate. I have almost reached the regrettable conclusion that the Negro's great stumbling block in his stride toward freedom is not the White Citizen's Counciler or the Ku Klux Klanner, but the white moderate, who is more devoted to "order" than to justice; who prefers a negative peace which is the absence of tension to a positive peace which is the presence of justice; who constantly says: "I agree with you in the goal you seek, but I cannot agree with your methods or direct action"; who paternalistically believes he can set the timetable for another man's freedom; who lives by a mythical concept of time and who constantly advises the Negro to wait for a "more convenient season." Shallow understanding from people of good will is more frustrating than absolute misunderstanding from people of ill will. Lukewarm acceptance is much more bewildering than outright rejection.

I had hoped that the white moderate would understand that law and order exist for the purpose of establishing justice and that when they fail in this purpose they become the dangerously structured dams that block the flow of social progress. I had hoped that the white moderate would understand that the present tension in the South is a necessary phase of the transition from an obnoxious negative peace, in which the Negro passively accepted his unjust plight, to a substantive and positive peace, in which all men will respect the dignity and worth of human personality. Actually, we who engage in nonviolent direct action are not the creators of tension. We merely bring to the surface the hidden tension that is already alive. We bring it out in the open, where it can be seen and dealt with. Like a boil that can never be cured so long as it is covered up but must be opened with all its ugliness to the natural medicines of air and light, injustice must be exposed, with all the tension its exposure creates, to the light of human conscience and the air of national opinion before it can be cured.

In your statement you assert that our actions, even though peaceful, 25 must be condemned because they precipitate violence. But is this a logical assertion? Isn't this like condemning a robbed man because his possession of money precipitated the evil act of robbery? Isn't this like condemning Socrates because his unswerving commitment to truth and his philosophical inquiries precipitated the act by the misguided populace in which they made him drink hemlock? Isn't this like condemning Jesus because his unique God-consciousness and never-ceasing devotion to

God's will precipitated the evil act of crucifixion? We must come to see that, as the federal courts have consistently affirmed, it is wrong to urge an individual to cease his efforts to gain his basic constitutional rights because the quest may precipitate violence. Society must protect the robbed and punish the robber.

I had also hoped that the white moderate would reject the myth concerning time in relation to the struggle for freedom. I have just received a letter from a white brother in Texas. He writes: "All Christians know that the colored people will receive equal rights eventually, but it is possible that you are in too great a religious hurry. It has taken Christianity almost two thousand years to accomplish what it has. The teachings of Christ take time to come to earth." Such an attitude stems from a tragic misconception of time, from the strangely irrational notion that there is something in the very flow of time that will inevitably cure all ills. Actually, time itself is neutral; it can be used either destructively or constructively. More and more I feel that the people of ill will have used time much more effectively than have the people of good will. We will have to repent in this generation not merely for the hateful words and actions of the bad people but for the appalling silence of the good people. Human progress never rolls in on wheels of inevitability; it comes through the tireless efforts of men willing to be co-workers with God, and without this hard work, time itself becomes an ally of the forces of social stagnation. We must use time creatively, in the knowledge that the time is always ripe to do right. Now is the time to make real the promise of democracy and transform our pending national elegy into a creative psalm of brotherhood. Now is the time to lift our national policy from the quicksand of racial injustice to the solid rock of human dignity.

You speak of our activity in Birmingham as extreme. At first I was rather disappointed that fellow clergymen would see my nonviolent efforts as those of an extremist. I began thinking about the fact that I stand in the middle of two opposing forces in the Negro community. One is a force of complacency, made up in part of Negroes who, as a result of long years of oppression, are so drained of self-respect and a sense of "somebodiness" that they have adjusted to segregation; and in part of a few middle-class Negroes who, because of a degree of academic and economic security and because in some ways they profit by segregation, have become insensitive to the problems of the masses. The other force is one of bitterness and hatred, and it comes perilously close to advocating violence. It is expressed in the various black nationalist groups that are springing up across the nation, the largest and best-known being Elijah Muhammad's Muslim movement. Nourished by the Negro's frustration over the continued existence of racial discrimination, this movement is made up of people who have lost faith in America, who have absolutely repudiated Christianity, and who have concluded that the white man is an incorrigible "devil."

I have tried to stand between these two forces, saying that we need emulate neither the "do-nothingism" of the complacent nor the hatred and despair of the black nationalist. For there is the more excellent way of love and nonviolent protest. I am grateful to God that, through the influence of the Negro church, the way of nonviolence became an integral part of our struggle.

If this philosophy had not emerged, by now many streets of the South should, I am convinced, be flowing with blood. And I am further convinced that if our white brothers dismiss as "rabble-rousers" and "outside agitators" those of us who employ nonviolent direct action, and if they refuse to support our nonviolent efforts, millions of Negroes will, out of frustration and despair, seek solace and security in black-nationalist ideologies—a development that would inevitably lead to a frightening racial nightmare.

Oppressed people cannot remain oppressed forever. The yearning ³⁰ for freedom eventually manifests itself, and that is what has happened to the American Negro. Something within has reminded him of his birthright of freedom, and something without has reminded him that it can be gained. Consciously or unconsciously, he has been caught up by the *Zeitgeist*,⁵ and with his black brothers of Africa and his brown and yellow brothers of Asia, South America, and the Caribbean, the United States Negro is moving with a sense of great urgency toward the promised land of racial justice. If one recognizes this vital urge that has engulfed the Negro community, one should readily understand why public demonstrations are taking place. The Negro has many pent-up resentments and latent frustrations, and he must release them. So let him march; let him make prayer pilgrimages to the city hall; let him go on freedom rides—and try to understand why he must do so. If his repressed emotions are not released in nonviolent ways, they will seek expression through violence; this is not a threat but a fact of history. So I have not said to my people: "Get rid of your discontent." Rather, I have tried to say that this normal and healthy discontent can be channeled into the creative outlet of nonviolent direct action. And now this approach is being termed extremist.

But though I was initially disappointed at being categorized as an extremist, as I continued to think about the matter I gradually gained a measure of satisfaction from the label. Was not Jesus an extremist for love: "Love your enemies, bless them that curse you, do good to them that hate you, and pray for them which despitefully use you, and perse-

⁵*Zeitgeist* Spirit of the age (German).

cute you." Was not Amos an extremist for justice: "Let justice roll down like waters and righteousness like an ever-flowing stream." Was not Paul an extremist for the Christian gospel: "I bear in my body the marks of the Lord Jesus." Was not Martin Luther an extremist: "Here I stand; I cannot do otherwise, so help me God." And John Bunyan: "I will stay in jail to the end of my days before I make a butchery of my conscience." And Abraham Lincoln: "This nation cannot survive half slave and half free." And Thomas Jefferson: "We hold these truths to be self-evident, that all men are created equal. . . ." So the question is not whether we will be extremists, but what kind of extremists we will be. Will we be extremists for hate or for love? Will we be extremists for the preservation of injustice or for the extension of justice? In that dramatic scene on Calvary's hill three men were crucified. We must never forget that all three were crucified for the same crime — the crime of extremism. Two were extremists for immorality, and thus fell below their environment. The other, Jesus Christ, was an extremist for love, truth, and goodness, and thereby rose above his environment. Perhaps the South, the nation, and the world are in dire need of creative extremists.

I had hoped that the white moderate would see this need. Perhaps I was too optimistic; perhaps I expected too much. I suppose I should have realized that few members of the oppressor race can understand the deep groans and passionate yearnings of the oppressed race, and still fewer have the vision to see that injustice must be rooted out by strong, persistent, and determined action. I am thankful, however, that some of our white brothers in the South have grasped the meaning of this social revolution and committed themselves to it. They are still all too few in quantity, but they are big in quality. Some — such as Ralph McGill, Lillian Smith, Harry Golden, James McBride Dabbs, Ann Braden, and Sarah Patton Boyle — have written about our struggle in eloquent and prophetic terms. Others have marched with us down nameless streets of the South. They have languished in filthy, roach-infested jails, suffering the abuse and brutality of policemen who view them as "dirty nigger-lovers." Unlike so many of their moderate brothers and sisters, they have recognized the urgency of the moment and sensed the need for powerful "action" antidotes to combat the disease of segregation.

Let me take note of my other major disappointment. I have been so greatly disappointed with the white church and its leadership. Of course, there are some notable exceptions. I am not unmindful of the fact that each of you has taken some significant stands on this issue. I commend you, Reverend Stallings, for your Christian stand on this past Sunday, in welcoming Negroes to your worship service on a nonsegregated basis. I commend the Catholic leaders of this state for integrating Spring Hill College several years ago.

But despite these notable exceptions, I must honestly reiterate that I have been disappointed with the church. I do not say this as one of those negative critics who can always find something wrong with the church. I say this as a minister of the gospel, who loves the church; who was nurtured in its bosom; who has been sustained by its spiritual blessings and who will remain true to it as long as the cord of life shall lengthen.

When I was suddenly catapulted into the leadership of the bus 35 protest in Montgomery, Alabama, a few years ago, I felt we would be supported by the white church. I felt that the white ministers, priests, and rabbis of the South would be among our strongest allies. Instead, some have been outright opponents, refusing to understand the freedom movement and misrepresenting its leaders; all too many others have been more cautious than courageous and have remained silent behind the anesthetizing security of stained-glass windows.

In spite of my shattered dreams, I came to Birmingham with the hope that the white religious leadership of this community would see the justice of our cause and, with deep moral concern, would serve as the channel through which our just grievances could reach the power structure. I had hoped that each of you would understand. But again I have been disappointed.

I have heard numerous southern religious leaders admonish their worshipers to comply with a desegregation decision because it is the law, but I have longed to hear white ministers declare: "Follow this decree because integration is morally right and because the Negro is your brother." In the midst of blatant injustices inflicted upon the Negro, I have watched white churchmen stand on the sideline and mouth pious irrelevancies and sanctimonious trivialities. In the midst of a mighty struggle to rid our nation of racial and economic injustice, I have heard many ministers say: "Those are social issues, with which the gospel has no real concern." And I have watched many churches commit themselves to a completely otherworldly religion which makes a strange, unbiblical distinction between body and soul, between the sacred and the secular.

I have traveled the length and breadth of Alabama, Mississippi, and all the other southern states. On sweltering summer days and crisp autumn mornings I have looked at the South's beautiful churches with their lofty spires pointing heavenward. I have beheld the impressive outlines of her massive religious-education buildings. Over and over I have found myself saying: "What kind of people worship here? Who is their God? Where were their voices when the lips of Governor Barnett dripped with words of interposition and nullification? Where were they when Governor Wallace gave a clarion call for defiance and hatred? Where were their voices of support when bruised and weary Negro men and women decided to rise from the dark dungeons of complacency to the bright hills of creative protest?"

Yes, these questions are still in my mind. In deep disappointment I have wept over the laxity of the church. But be assured that my tears have been tears of love. There can be no deep disappointment where there is not deep love. Yes, I love the church. How could I do otherwise? I am in the rather unique position of being the son, the grandson, and the great-grandson of preachers. Yes, I see the church as the body of Christ. But, Oh! How we have blemished and scarred that body through social neglect and through fear of being nonconformists.

There was a time when the church was very powerful—in the time when the early Christians rejoiced at being deemed worthy to suffer for what they believed. In those days the church was not merely a thermometer that recorded the ideas and principles of popular opinion; it was a thermostat that transformed the mores of society. Whenever the early Christians entered a town, the people in power became disturbed and immediately sought to convict the Christians for being "disturbers of the peace" and "outside agitators." But the Christians pressed on, in the conviction that they were "a colony of heaven," called to obey God rather than man. Small in number, they were big in commitment. They were too God-intoxicated to be "astronomically intimidated." By their effort and example they brought an end to such ancient evils as infanticide and gladiatorial contests.

Things are different now. So often the contemporary church is a weak, ineffectual voice with an uncertain sound. So often it is an archdefender of the status quo. Far from being disturbed by the presence of the church, the power structure of the average community is consoled by the church's silent—and often even vocal—sanction of things as they are.

But the judgment of God is upon the church as never before. If today's church does not recapture the sacrificial spirit of the early church, it will lose its authenticity, forfeit the loyalty of millions, and be dismissed as an irrelevant social club with no meaning for the twentieth century. Every day I meet young people whose disappointment with the church has turned into outright disgust.

Perhaps I have once again been too optimistic. Is organized religion too inextricably bound to the status quo to save our nation and the world? Perhaps I must turn my faith to the inner spiritual church, the church within the church, as the true *ekklesia*[6] and the hope of the world. But again I am thankful to God that some noble souls from

---

[6]*ekklesia* A gathering or assembly of citizens (Greek).

the ranks of organized religion have broken loose from the paralyzing chains of conformity and joined us as active partners in the struggle for freedom. They have left their secure congregations and walked the streets of Albany, Georgia, with us. They have gone down the highways of the South on tortuous rides for freedom. Yes, they have gone to jail with us. Some have been dismissed from their churches, have lost the support of their bishops and fellow ministers. But they have acted in the faith that right defeated is stronger than evil triumphant. Their witness has been the spiritual salt that has preserved the true meaning of the gospel in these troubled times. They have carved a tunnel of hope through the dark mountain of disappointment.

I hope the church as a whole will meet the challenge of this decisive hour. But even if the church does not come to the aid of justice, I have no despair about the future. I have no fear about the outcome of our struggle in Birmingham, even if our motives are at present misunderstood. We will reach the goal of freedom in Birmingham and all over the nation, because the goal of America is freedom. Abused and scorned though we may be, our destiny is tied up with America's destiny. Before the pilgrims landed at Plymouth, we were here. Before the pen of Jefferson etched the majestic words of the Declaration of Independence across the pages of history, we were here. For more than two centuries our forebears labored in this country without wages; they made cotton king; they built the homes of their masters while suffering gross injustice and shameful humiliation—and yet out of a bottomless vitality they continue to thrive and develop. If the inexpressible cruelties of slavery could not stop us, the opposition we now face will surely fail. We will win our freedom because the sacred heritage of our nation and the eternal will of God are embodied in our echoing demands.

Before closing I feel impelled to mention one other point in your 45 statement that has troubled me profoundly. You warmly commended the Birmingham police force for keeping "order" and "preventing violence." I doubt that you would have so warmly commended the police force if you had seen its dogs sinking their teeth into unarmed, nonviolent Negroes. I doubt that you would so quickly commend the policemen if you were to observe their ugly and inhumane treatment of Negroes here in the city jail; if you were to watch them push and curse old Negro women and young Negro girls; if you were to see them slap and kick old Negro men and young boys; if you were to observe them, as they did on two occasions, refuse to give us food because we wanted to sing our grace together. I cannot join you in your praise of the Birmingham police department.

It is true that the police have exercised a degree of discipline in handling the demonstrators. In this sense they have conducted themselves rather "nonviolently" in public. But for what purpose? To preserve the evil system of segregation. Over the past few years I have consistently preached that nonviolence demands that the means we use must be as pure as the ends we seek. I have tried to make clear that it is wrong to use immoral means to attain moral ends. But now I must affirm that it is just as wrong, or perhaps even more so, to use moral means to preserve immoral ends. Perhaps Mr. Connor and his policemen have been rather nonviolent in public, as was Chief Pritchett in Albany, Georgia, but they used the moral means of nonviolence to maintain the immoral end of racial injustice. As T. S. Eliot has said: "The last temptation is the greatest treason: To do the right deed for the wrong reason."

I wish you had commended the Negro sit-inners and demonstrators of Birmingham for their sublime courage, their willingness to suffer, and their amazing discipline in the midst of great provocation. One day the South will recognize its real heroes. They will be the James Merediths, with the noble sense of purpose that enables them to face jeering and hostile mobs, and with the agonizing loneliness that characterizes the life of the pioneer. They will be old, oppressed, battered Negro women, symbolized in a seventy-two-year-old woman in Montgomery, Alabama, who rose up with a sense of dignity and with her people decided not to ride segregated buses, and who responded with ungrammatical profundity to one who inquired about her weariness: "My feets is tired, but my soul is at rest." They will be the young high school and college students, the young ministers of the gospel and a host of their elders, courageously and nonviolently sitting in at lunch counters and willingly going to jail for conscience's sake. One day the South will know that when these disinherited children of God sat down at lunch counters, they were in reality standing up for what is best in the American dream and for the most sacred values in our Judaeo-Christian heritage, thereby bringing our nation back to those great wells of democracy which were dug deep by the founding fathers in their formulation of the Constitution and the Declaration of Independence.

Never before have I written so long a letter. I'm afraid it is much too long to take your precious time. I can assure you that it would have been much shorter if I had been writing from a comfortable desk, but what else can one do when he is alone in a narrow jail cell, other than write long letters, think long thoughts, and pray long prayers?

If I have said anything in this letter that overstates the truth and indicates an unreasonable impatience, I beg you to forgive me. If I have said anything that understates the truth and indicates my having a patience that allows me to settle for anything less than brotherhood, I beg God to forgive me.

I hope this letter finds you strong in the faith. I also hope that circumstances will soon make it possible for me to meet each of you, not as an integrationist or a civil-rights leader but as a fellow clergyman and a Christian brother. Let us all hope that the dark clouds of racial prejudice will soon pass away and the deep fog of misunderstanding will be lifted from our fear-drenched communities, and in some not too distant tomorrow the radiant stars of love and brotherhood will shine over our great nation with all their scintillating beauty.

Yours for the cause of Peace and Brotherhood,

Martin Luther King Jr.

Topics for Critical Thinking and Writing

1. In his first five paragraphs of the "Letter," how does King assure his audience that he is not a meddlesome intruder but a man of good will?

2. In paragraph 3 King refers to Hebrew prophets and to the Apostle Paul and later (para. 10) to Socrates. What is the point of these references?

3. In paragraph 11 what does King mean when he says that "our beloved Southland" has long tried to "live in monologue rather than dialogue"?

4. King begins paragraph 23 with "I must make two honest confessions to you, my Christian and Jewish brothers." What would have been gained or lost if he had used this paragraph as his opening?

5. King's last three paragraphs do not advance his argument. What do they do?

6. Why does King advocate breaking unjust laws "openly, lovingly" (para. 20)? What does he mean by these words? What other motives or attitudes do these words rule out?

7. Construct two definitions of *civil disobedience*, and explain whether and to what extent it is easier (or harder) to justify civil disobedience, depending on how you have defined the expression.

8. If you feel that you wish to respond to King's letter on some point, write a letter nominally addressed to King. You may, if you wish, adopt the persona of one of the eight clergymen whom King initially addressed.

9. King writes (para. 46) that "nonviolence demands that the means we use must be as pure as the ends we seek." How do you think King would evaluate the following acts: (a) occupying a college administration building to protest the administration's unsatisfactory response to a racial incident on campus or its failure to hire minority persons as staff and faculty; (b) occupying an abortion clinic to protest abortion? Set down your answer in an essay of 500 words.

10. Compose a letter from Martin Luther King Jr. in which King responds to Plato's "Crito" (p. 208).

JUDY BRADY

Born in San Francisco in 1937, Judy Brady married in 1960 and two years later earned a bachelor's degree in painting at the University of Iowa. Active in the women's movement and in other political causes, she has worked as an author, an editor, and a secretary. The essay reprinted here, written before she and her husband separated, appeared originally in the first issue of Ms. Magazine *in 1971.*

I Want a Wife

I belong to that classification of people known as wives. I am a Wife. And, not altogether incidentally, I am a mother.

Not too long ago a male friend of mine appeared on the scene fresh from a recent divorce. He had one child, who is, of course, with his ex-wife. He is looking for another wife. As I thought about him while I was ironing one evening, it suddenly occurred to me that I, too, would like to have a wife. Why do I want a wife?

I would like to go back to school so that I can become economically independent, support myself, and, if need be, support those dependent upon me. I want a wife who will work and send me to school. And while I am going to school I want a wife to take care of my children. I want a wife to keep track of the children's doctor and dentist appointments. And to keep track of mine, too. I want a wife to make sure my children eat properly and are kept clean. I want a wife who will wash the children's clothes and keep them mended. I want a wife who is a good nurturant attendant to my children, who arranges for their schooling, makes sure that they have an adequate social life with their peers, takes them to the park, the zoo, etc. I want a wife who takes care of the children when they are sick, a wife who arranges to be around when the children need special care, because, of course, I cannot miss classes at school. My wife must arrange to lose time at work and not lose the job. It may mean a small cut in my wife's income from time to time, but I guess I can tolerate that. Needless to say, my wife will arrange and pay for the care of the children while my wife is working.

I want a wife who will take care of *my* physical needs. I want a wife who will keep my house clean. A wife who will pick up after my children, a wife who will pick up after me. I want a wife who will keep my clothes clean, ironed, mended, replaced when need be, and who will see to it that my personal things are kept in their proper place so that I can find what I need the minute I need it. I want a wife who cooks the meals, a wife who is a *good* cook. I want a wife who will plan the menus, do the necessary grocery shopping, prepare the meals, serve them pleasantly, and then do the cleaning up while I do my studying. I want a wife who will care for me when I am sick and sympathize with my pain and loss of time from school. I want a wife to go along when our family takes a vacation so that someone can continue to care for me and my children when I need a rest and change of scene.

I want a wife who will not bother me with rambling complaints   5
about a wife's duties. But I want a wife who will listen to me when I feel the need to explain a rather difficult point I have come across in my course of studies. And I want a wife who will type my papers for me when I have written them.

I want a wife who will take care of the details of my social life. When my wife and I are invited out by my friends, I want a wife who will take care of the babysitting arrangements. When I meet people at school that I like and want to entertain, I want a wife who will have the house clean, will prepare a special meal, serve it to me and my friends, and not interrupt when I talk about things that interest me and my friends. I want a wife who will have arranged that the children are fed and ready for bed before my guests arrive so that the children do not bother us. I want a wife who takes care of the needs of my guests so that they feel comfortable, who makes sure that they have an ashtray, that they are passed the hors d'oeuvres, that they are offered a second helping of the food, that their wine glasses are replenished when necessary, that their coffee is served to them as they like it. And I want a wife who knows that sometimes I need a night out by myself.

I want a wife who is sensitive to my sexual needs, a wife who makes love passionately and eagerly when I feel like it, a wife who makes sure that I am satisfied. And, of course, I want a wife who will not demand sexual attention when I am not in the mood for it. I want a wife who assumes the complete responsibility for birth control, because I do not want more children. I want a wife who will remain sexually faithful to me so that I do not have to clutter up my intellectual life with jealousies. And I want a wife who understands that *my* sexual needs may entail more than strict adherence to monogamy. I must, after all, be able to relate to people as fully as possible.

If, by chance, I find another person more suitable as a wife than the wife I already have, I want the liberty to replace my present wife with another one. Naturally, I will expect a fresh, new life; my wife will take the children and be solely responsible for them so that I am left free.

When I am through with school and have a job, I want my wife to quit working and remain at home so that my wife can more fully and completely take care of a wife's duties.

My God, who *wouldn't* want a wife?   10

Topics for Critical Thinking and Writing

1. If one were to summarize Brady's first paragraph, one might say it adds up to "I am a wife and a mother." But analyze it closely. Exactly what does the second sentence add to the first? And what does "not altogether incidentally" add to the third sentence?

2. Brady uses the word *wife* in sentences where one ordinarily would use *she* or *her*. Why? And why does she begin paragraphs 4, 5, 6, and 7 with the same words, "I want a wife"?

3. In her second paragraph Brady says that the child of her divorced male friend "is, of course, with his ex-wife." In the context of the entire essay, what does this sentence mean?

4. Complete the following sentence by offering a definition: "According to Judy Brady, a wife is. . . ."

5. Try to state the essential argument of Brady's essay in a simple syllogism. (*Hint:* Start by identifying the thesis or conclusion you think she is trying to establish, and then try to formulate two premises, based on what she has written, that would establish the conclusion.)

6. Drawing on your experience as observer of the world around you (and perhaps as husband, wife, or former spouse), do you think Brady's picture of a wife's role is grossly exaggerated? Or is it (allowing for some serious playfulness) fairly accurate, even though it was written in 1971? If grossly exaggerated, is the essay therefore meaningless? If fairly accurate, what attitudes and practices does it encourage you to support? Explain.

7. Whether or not you agree with Brady's vision of marriage in our society, write an essay (500 words) titled "I Want a Husband," imitating her style and approach. Write the best possible essay, and then decide which of the two essays—yours or hers—makes a fairer comment on current society. Or if you believe Brady is utterly misleading, write an essay titled "I Want a Wife," seeing the matter in a different light.

8. If you feel that you have been pressed into an unappreciated, unreasonable role—built-in babysitter, listening post, or girl (or boy or man or woman) Friday—write an essay of 500 words that will help the reader to see both your plight and the injustice of the system. (*Hint:* A little humor will help to keep your essay from seeming to be a prolonged whine.)

PETER SINGER

Peter Singer is the Ira W. DeCamp Professor of Bioethics at Princeton University. A native of Australia, he is a graduate of the University of Melbourne and Oxford University and the author or editor of more than two dozen books, including Animal Liberation *(1975),* Practical Ethics *(1979),* Rethinking Life and Death *(1995), and* One World: The Ethics of Globalization *(2002). He has written on a variety of ethical issues, but he is especially known for caring about the welfare of animals.*

This essay originally appeared in the New York Review of Books *(April 5, 1973), as a review of* Animals, Men and Morals, *edited by Stanley and Roslind Godlovitch and John Harris.*

Animal Liberation

I

We are familiar with Black Liberation, Gay Liberation, and a variety of other movements. With Women's Liberation some thought we had come to the end of the road. Discrimination on the basis of sex, it has been said, is the last form of discrimination that is universally accepted and practiced without pretense, even in those liberal circles which have long prided themselves on their freedom from racial discrimination. But one should always be wary of talking of "the last remaining form of discrimination." If we have learned anything from the liberation movements, we should have learned how difficult it is to be aware of the ways in which we discriminate until they are forcefully pointed out to us. A liberation movement demands an expansion of our moral horizons, so that practices that were previously regarded as natural and inevitable are now seen as intolerable.

Animals, Men and Morals is a manifesto for an Animal Liberation movement. The contributors to the book may not all see the issue this way. They are a varied group. Philosophers, ranging from professors to graduate students, make up the largest contingent. There are five of them, including the three editors, and there is also an extract from the unjustly neglected German philosopher with an English name, Leonard Nelson, who died in 1927. There are essays by two novelist/critics, Brigid Brophy and Maureen Duffy, and another by Muriel the Lady Dowding, widow of Dowding of Battle of Britain fame and the founder of "Beauty without Cruelty," a movement that campaigns against the use of animals for furs and cosmetics. The other pieces are by a psychologist, a botanist, a sociologist, and Ruth Harrison, who is probably best described as a professional campaigner for animal welfare.

Whether or not these people, as individuals, would all agree that they are launching a liberation movement for animals, the book as a whole amounts to no less. It is a demand for a complete change in our attitudes to nonhumans. It is a demand that we cease to regard the exploitation of other species as natural and inevitable, and that, instead, we see it as a continuing moral outrage. Patrick Corbett, Professor of Philosophy at Sussex University, captures the spirit of the book in his closing words:

> We require now to extend the great principles of liberty, equality, and fraternity over the lives of animals. Let animal slavery join human slavery in the graveyard of the past.

The reader is likely to be skeptical. "Animal Liberation" sounds more like a parody of liberation movements than a serious objective. The reader may think: We support the claims of blacks and women for equality because blacks and women really are equal to whites and males—equal in intelligence and in abilities, capacity for leadership, rationality, and so on. Humans and nonhumans obviously are not equal in these respects. Since justice demands only that we treat equals equally, unequal treatment of humans and nonhumans cannot be an injustice.

This is a tempting reply, but a dangerous one. It commits the non-   5
racist and nonsexist to a dogmatic belief that blacks and women really are just as intelligent, able, etc., as whites and males—and no more. Quite possibly this happens to be the case. Certainly attempts to prove that racial or sexual differences in these respects have a genetic origin have not been conclusive. But do we really want to stake our demand for equality on the assumption that there are no genetic differences of this kind between the different races or sexes? Surely the appropriate response to those who claim to have found evidence for such genetic differences is not to stick to the belief that there are no differences, whatever the evidence to the contrary; rather one should be clear that the claim to equality does not depend on IQ. Moral equality is distinct from factual equality. Otherwise it would be nonsense to talk to the equality of human beings, since humans, as individuals, obviously differ in intelligence and almost any ability one cares to name. If possessing greater intelligence does not entitle one human to exploit another, why should it entitle humans to exploit nonhumans?

Jeremy Bentham expressed the essential basis of equality in his famous formula: "Each to count for one and none for more than one." In other words, the interests of every being that has interests are to be taken into account and treated equally with the like interests of any other being. Other moral philosophers, before and after Bentham, have made the same point in different ways. Our concern for others must not depend on whether they possess certain characteristics, though just what that concern involves may, of course, vary according to such characteristics.

Bentham, incidentally, was well aware that the logic of the demand for racial equality did not stop at the equality of humans. He wrote:

> The day *may* come when the rest of the animal creation may acquire those rights which never could have been withholden from them but by the hand of tyranny. The French have already discovered that the blackness of the skin is no reason why a human being should be abandoned without redress to the caprice of a tormentor. It may one day come to be recognized that the number of the legs, the villosity of the skin, or the termination of the *os sacrum*, are reasons equally insufficient for abandoning a sensitive being to the same fate. What else is it that should trace the insuperable line? Is it the faculty of reason, or perhaps the faculty of discourse? But a full-grown horse or dog is beyond comparison a more rational, as well as a more conversable animal, than an infant of a day, or a week, or even a month, old. But suppose they were otherwise, what would it avail? The question is not, Can they *reason?* nor Can they *talk?* but, Can they *suffer?*[1]

Surely Bentham was right. If a being suffers, there can be no moral justification for refusing to take that suffering into consideration, and, indeed, to count it equally with the like suffering (if rough comparisons can be made) of any other being.

So the only question is: Do animals other than man suffer? Most people agree unhesitatingly that animals like cats and dogs can and do suffer, and this seems also to be assumed by those laws that prohibit wanton cruelty to such animals. Personally, I have no doubt at all about this and find it hard to take seriously the doubts that a few people apparently do have. The editors and contributors of *Animals, Men and Morals* seem to feel the same way, for although the question is raised more than once, doubts are quickly dismissed each time. Nevertheless, because this is such a fundamental point, it is worth asking what grounds we have for attributing suffering to other animals.

It is best to begin by asking what grounds any individual human has for supposing that other humans feel pain. Since pain is a state of consciousness, a "mental event," it can never be directly observed. No observations, whether behavioral signs such as writing or screaming or physiological or neurological recordings, are observations of pain itself. Pain is something one feels, and one can only infer that others are feeling it from various external indications. The fact that only philosophers

---

[1] *The Principles of Morals and Legislation*, ch. XVII, sec. 1, footnote to paragraph 4. [All notes are the author's unless otherwise specified.]

are ever skeptical about whether other humans feel pain shows that we regard such inference as justifiable in the case of humans.

Is there any reason why the same inference should be unjustifiable 10 for other animals? Nearly all the external signs which lead us to infer pain in other humans can be seen in other species, especially "higher" animals such as mammals and birds. Behavioral signs—writhing, yelping, or other forms of calling, attempts to avoid the source of pain, and many others—are present. We know, too, that these animals are biologically similar in the relevant respects, having nervous systems like ours which can be observed to function as ours do.

So the grounds for inferring that these animals can feel pain are nearly as good as the grounds for inferring other humans do. Only nearly, for there is one behavioral sign that humans have but nonhumans, with the exception of one or two specially raised chimpanzees, do not have. This, of course, is a developed language. As the quotation from Bentham indicates, this has long been regarded as an important distinction between man and other animals. Other animals may communicate with each other, but not in the way we do. Following Chomsky,[2] many people now mark this distinction by saying that only humans communicate in a form that is governed by rules of syntax. (For the purposes of this argument, linguists allow those chimpanzees who have learned a syntactic sign language to rank as honorary humans.) Nevertheless, as Bentham pointed out, this distinction is not relevant to the question of how animals ought to be treated, unless it can be linked to the issue of whether animals suffer.

This link may be attempted in two ways. First, there is a hazy line of philosophical thought, stemming perhaps from some doctrines associated with Wittgenstein, which maintains that we cannot meaningfully attribute states of consciousness to beings without language. I have not seen this argument made explicit in print, though I have come across it in conversation. This position seems to me very implausible, and I doubt that it would be held at all if it were not thought to be a consequence of a broader view of the significance of language. It may be that the use of a public, rule-governed language is a precondition of conceptual thought. It may even be, although personally I doubt it, that we cannot meaningfully speak of a creature having an intention unless that creature can use a language. But states like pain, surely, are more primitive than either of these, and seem to have nothing to do with language.

Indeed, as Jane Goodall points out in her study of chimpanzees, when it comes to the expression of feelings and emotions, humans tend

[2]**Chomsky** Noam Chomsky (b. 1928), a professor of linguistics and the author of (among other books) *Language and Mind* (1972). [—Ed.]

to fall back on nonlinguistic modes of communication which are often found among apes, such as a cheering pat on the back, an exuberant embrace, a clasp of hands, and so on.[3] Michael Peters makes a similar point in his contribution to *Animals, Men and Morals* when he notes that the basic signals we use to convey pain, fear, sexual arousal, and so on are not specific to our species. So there seems to be no reason at all to believe that a creature without language cannot suffer.

The second, and more easily appreciated way of linking language and the existence of pain is to say that the best evidence that we can have that another creature is in pain is when he tells us that he is. This is a distinct line of argument, for it is not being denied that a non-language-user conceivably could suffer, but only that we could know that he is suffering. Still, this line of argument seems to me to fail, and for reasons similar to those just given. "I am in pain" is not the best possible evidence that the speaker is in pain (he might be lying) and it is certainly not the only possible evidence. Behavioral signs and knowledge of the animal's biological similarity to ourselves together provide adequate evidence that animals do suffer. After all, we would not accept linguistic evidence if it contradicted the rest of the evidence. If a man was severely burned, and behaved as if he were in pain, writhing, groaning, being very careful not to let his burned skin touch anything, and so on, but later said he had not been in pain at all, we would be more likely to conclude that he was lying or suffering from amnesia than that he had not been in pain.

Even if there were stronger grounds for refusing to attribute pain to those who do not have a language, the consequences of this refusal might lead us to examine these grounds unusually critically. Human infants, as well as some adults, are unable to use language. Are we to deny that a year-old infant can suffer? If not, how can language be crucial? Of course, most parents can understand the responses of even very young infants better than they understand the responses of other animals, and sometimes infant responses can be understood in the light of later development.   15

This, however, is just a fact about the relative knowledge we have of our own species and other species, and most of this knowledge is simply derived from closer contact. Those who have studied the behavior of other animals soon learn to understand their responses at least as well as we understand those of an infant. (I am not referring to Jane Goodall's and other well-known studies of apes. Consider, for example, the degree of understanding achieved by Tinbergen from watching her-

[3]Jane van Lawick-Goodall, *In the Shadow of Man* (Houghton Mifflin, 1971), p. 225.

ring gulls.[4]) Just as we can understand infant human behavior in the light of adult human behavior, so we can understand the behavior of other species in the light of our own behavior (and sometimes we can understand our own behavior better in the light of the behavior of other species).

The grounds we have for believing that other mammals and birds suffer are, then, closely analogous to the grounds we have for believing that other humans suffer. It remains to consider how far down the evolutionary scale this analogy holds. Obviously it becomes poorer when we get further away from man. To be more precise would require a detailed examination of all that we know about other forms of life. With fish, reptiles, and other vertebrates the analogy still seems strong, with molluscs like oysters it is much weaker. Insects are more difficult, and it may be that in our present state of knowledge we must be agnostic about whether they are capable of suffering.

If there is no moral justification for ignoring suffering when it occurs, and it does occur in other species, what are we to say of our attitudes toward these other species? Richard Ryder, one of the contributors to *Animals, Men and Morals*, uses the term "speciesism" to describe the belief that we are entitled to treat members of other species in a way in which it would be wrong to treat members of our own species. The term is not euphonious, but it neatly makes the analogy with racism. The nonracist would do well to bear the analogy in mind when he is inclined to defend human behavior toward nonhumans. "Shouldn't we worry about improving the lot of our own species before we concern ourselves with other species?" he may ask. If we substitute "race" for "species" we shall see that the question is better not asked. "Is a vegetarian diet nutritionally adequate?" resembles the slaveowner's claim that he and the whole economy of the South would be ruined without slave labor. There is even a parallel with skeptical doubts about whether animals suffer, for some defenders of slavery professed to doubt whether blacks really suffer in the way whites do.

I do not want to give the impression, however, that the case for Animal Liberation is based on the analogy with racism and no more. On the contrary, *Animals, Men and Morals* describes the various ways in which humans exploit nonhumans, and several contributors consider the defenses that have been offered, including the defense of meat-eating mentioned in the last paragraph. Sometimes the rebuttals are scornfully dismissive, rather than carefully designed to convince the detached critic. This may be a fault, but it is a fault that is inevitable, given the

---

[4]N. Tinbergen, *The Herring Gull's World* (Basic Books, 1961).

kind of book this is. The issue is not one on which one can remain detached. As the editors state in their Introduction:

> Once the full force of moral assessment has been made explicit there can be no rational excuse left for killing animals, be they killed for food, science, or sheer personal indulgence. We have not assembled this book to provide the reader with yet another manual on how to make brutalities less brutal. Compromise, in the traditional sense of the term, is simple unthinking weakness when one considers the actual reasons for our crude relationships with the other animals.

The point is that on this issue there are few critics who are genuinely 20 detached. People who eat pieces of slaughtered nonhumans every day find it hard to believe that they are doing wrong; and they also find it hard to imagine what else they could eat. So for those who do not place nonhumans beyond the pale of morality, there comes a stage when further argument seems pointless, a stage at which one can only accuse one's opponent of hypocrisy and reach for the sort of sociological account of our practices and the way we defend them that is attempted by David Wood in his contribution to his book. On the other hand, to those unconvinced by the arguments, and unable to accept that they are merely rationalizing their dietary preferences and their fear of being thought peculiar, such sociological explanations can only seem insultingly arrogant.

II

The logic of speciesism is most apparent in the practice of experimenting on nonhumans in order to benefit humans. This is because the issue is rarely obscured by allegations that nonhumans are so different from humans that we cannot know anything about whether they suffer. The defender of vivisection cannot use this argument because he needs to stress the similarities between man and other animals in order to justify the usefulness to the former of experiments on the latter. The researcher who makes rats choose between starvation and electric shocks to see if they develop ulcers (they do) does so because he knows that the rat has a nervous system very similar to man's, and presumably feels an electric shock in a similar way.

Richard Ryder's restrained account of experiments on animals made me angrier with my fellow men than anything else in this book. Ryder, a clinical psychologist by profession, himself experimented on animals before he came to hold the view he puts forward in his essay. Experimenting on animals is now a large industry, both academic and commercial. In 1969, more than 5 million experiments were performed in Britain, the vast majority without anesthetic (though how many of these involved pain is not known). There are no accurate U.S. figures, since there is no federal law on the subject, and in many cases no state law either. Estimates vary from 20 million to 200 million. Ryder suggests that 80 million may be the best guess. We tend to think that this is all for vital medical research, but of course it is not. Huge numbers of animals are used in university departments from Forestry to Psychology, and even more are used for commercial purposes, to test whether cosmetics can cause skin damage, or shampoos eye damage, or to test food additives or laxatives or sleeping pills or anything else.

A standard test for foodstuffs is the "LD50." The object of this test is to find the dosage level at which 50 percent of the test animals will die. This means that nearly all of them will become very sick before finally succumbing or surviving. When the substance is a harmless one, it may be necessary to force huge doses down the animals, until in some cases sheer volume or concentration causes death.

Ryder gives a selection of experiments, taken from recent scientific journals. I will quote two, not for the sake of indulging in gory details, but in order to give an idea of what normal researchers think they may legitimately do to other species. The point is not that the individual researchers are cruel men, but that they are behaving in a way that is allowed by our speciesist attitudes. As Ryder points out, even if only 1 percent of the experiments involve severe pain, that is 50,000 experiments in Britain each year, or nearly 150 every day (and about fifteen times as many in the United States, if Ryder's guess is right). Here then are two experiments:

O. S. Ray and R. J. Barrett of Pittsburgh gave electric shocks to the feet of 1,042 mice. They then caused convulsions by giving more intense shocks through cup-shaped electrodes applied to the animals' eyes or through pressure spring clips attached to their ears. Unfortunately some of the mice who "successfully completed Day One training were found sick or dead prior to testing on Day Two." [*Journal of Comparative and Physiological Psychology*, 1969, vol. 67, pp. 110–116]

At the National Institute for Medical Research, Mill Hill, London, W. Feldberg and S. L. Sherwood injected chemicals into the brains of cats—"with a number of widely different substances, recurrent patterns of reaction were obtained. Retching, vomiting, defecation, increased salivation and greatly accelerated respiration leading to panting were common features." . . .

The injection into the brain of a large dose of Tubocuraine caused the cat to jump "from the table to the floor and then straight into its cage, where it started calling more and more noisily whilst moving about restlessly and jerkily . . . finally the cat fell with legs and neck flexed, jerking in rapid clonic movements, the condition being that of a major [epileptic] convulsion . . . within a few seconds the cat got up, ran for a few yards at high speed, and fell in another fit. The whole process was repeated several times within the next ten minutes, during which the cat lost faeces and foamed at the mouth."

This animal finally died thirty-five minutes after the brain injection. [*Journal of Physiology*, 1954, vol. 123, pp. 148–167]

There is nothing secret about these experiments. One has only to open any recent volume of a learned journal, such as the *Journal of Comparative and Physiological Psychology*, to find full descriptions of experiments of this sort, together with the results obtained — results that are frequently trivial and obvious. The experiments are often supported by public funds.

It is a significant indication of the level of acceptability of these practices that, although these experiments are taking place at this moment on university campuses throughout the country, there has, so far as I know, not been the slightest protest from the student movement. Students have been rightly concerned that their universities should not discriminate on grounds of race or sex, and that they should not serve the purposes of the military or big business. Speciesism continues undisturbed, and many students participate in it. There may be a few qualms at first, but since everyone regards it as normal, and it may even be a required part of a course, the student soon becomes hardened and, dismissing his earlier feelings as "mere sentiment," comes to regard animals as statistics rather than sentient beings with interests that warrant consideration.

Argument about vivisection has often missed the point because it has been put in absolutist terms: Would the abolitionist be prepared to let thousands die if they could be saved by experimenting on a single animal? The way to reply to this purely hypothetical question is to pose another: Would the experimenter be prepared to experiment on a human orphan under six months old, if it were the only way to save many lives? (I say "orphan" to avoid the complication of parental feelings, although in doing so I am being overfair to the experimenter, since the nonhuman subjects of experiments are not orphans.) A negative answer to this question indicates that the experimenter's readiness to use nonhumans is simple discrimination, for adult apes, cats, mice, and other mammals are more conscious of what is happening to them, more self-directing, and, so far as we can tell, just as sensitive to pain as a human infant. There is no characteristic that human infants possess that adult mammals do not have to the same or a higher degree.

(It might be possible to hold that what makes it wrong to experiment on a human infant is that the infant will in time develop into more than the nonhuman, but one would then, to be consistent, have to oppose abortion, and perhaps contraception, too, for the fetus and the egg and sperm have the same potential as the infant. Moreover, one would still have no reason for experimenting on a nonhuman rather than a human with brain damage severe enough to make it impossible for him to rise above infant level.)

The experimenter, then, shows a bias for his own species whenever he carries out an experiment on a nonhuman for a purpose that he would not think justified him in using a human being at an equal or lower level of sentience, awareness, ability to be self-directing, etc. No one familiar with the kind of results yielded by these experiments can have the slightest doubt that if this bias were eliminated the number of experiments performed would be zero or very close to it.

III

If it is vivisection that shows the logic of speciesism most clearly, it is the use of other species for food that is at the heart of our attitudes toward them. Most of *Animals, Men and Morals* is an attack on meat eating—an attack which is based solely on concern for nonhumans, without reference to arguments derived from consideration of ecology, macrobiotics, health, or religion.

The idea that nonhumans are utilities, means to our ends, pervades our thought. Even conservationists who are concerned about the slaughter of wildfowl but not about the vastly greater slaughter of chickens for our tables are thinking in this way—they are worried about what we would lose if there were less wildlife. Stanley Godlovitch, pursuing the Marxist idea that our thinking is formed by the activities we undertake in satisfying our needs, suggests that man's first classification of his environment was into Edibles and Inedibles. Most animals came into the first category, and there they have remained.

Man may always have killed other species for food, but he has never exploited them so ruthlessly as he does today. Farming has succumbed to business methods, the objective being to get the highest possible ratio of output (meat, eggs, milk) to input (fodder, labor costs, etc.). Ruth Harrison's essay "On Factory Farming" gives an account of some aspects of modern methods, and of the unsuccessful British campaigns for effective controls, a campaign which was sparked off by her *Animal Machines* (London: Stuart, 1964).

Her article is in no way a substitute for her earlier book. This is a pity since, as she says, "Farm produce is still associated with mental pictures of animals browsing in the fields . . . of hens having a last forage before going to roost. . . ." Yet neither in her article nor elsewhere in *Animals, Men and Morals* is this false image replaced by a clear idea of the nature and extent of factory farming. We learn of this only indirectly, when we hear of the code of reform proposed by an advisory committee set up by the British government.

Among the proposals, which the government refused to implement on the grounds that they were too idealistic, were: *"Any animal should at least have room to turn around freely."*

Factory farm animals need liberation in the most literal sense. Veal   35 calves are kept in stalls 5 feet by 2 feet. They are usually slaughtered when about four months old, and have been too big to turn in their stalls for at least a month. Intensive beef herds, kept in stalls only proportionately larger for much longer periods, account for a growing percentage of beef production. Sows are often similarly confined when pregnant, which, because of artificial methods of increasing fertility, can be most of the time. Animals confined in this way do not waste food by exercising, nor do they develop unpalatable muscle.

"A dry bedded area should be provided for all stock." Intensively kept animals usually have to stand and sleep in slatted floors without straw, because this makes cleaning easier.

"Palatable roughage must be readily available to all calves after one week of age." In order to produce the pale veal housewives are said to prefer, calves are fed on an all-liquid diet until slaughter, even though they are long past the age at which they would normally eat grass. They develop a craving for roughage, evidenced by attempts to gnaw wood from their stalls. (For the same reason, their diet is deficient in iron.)

"Battery cages for poultry should be large enough for a bird to be able to stretch one wing at a time." Under current British practice, a cage for four or five laying hens has a floor area of 20 inches by 18 inches, scarcely larger than a double page of the *New York Review of Books*. In this space, on a sloping wire floor (sloping so the eggs roll down, wire so the dung drips through) the birds live for a year or eighteen months while artificial lighting and temperature conditions combine with drugs in their food to squeeze the maximum number of eggs out of them. Table birds are also sometimes kept in cages. More often they are reared in sheds, no less crowded. Under these conditions all the birds' natural activities are frustrated, and they develop "vices" such as pecking each other to death. To prevent this, beaks are often cut off, and the sheds kept dark.

How many of those who support factory farming by buying its produce know anything about the way it is produced? How many have heard something about it, but are reluctant to check up for fear that it will make them uncomfortable? To nonspeciesists, the typical consumer's mixture of ignorance, reluctance to find out the truth, and vague belief that nothing really bad could be allowed seems analogous to the attitudes of "decent Germans" to the death camps.

There are, of course, some defenders of factory farming. Their arguments are considered, though again rather sketchily, by John Harris. Among the most common: "Since they have never known anything else, they don't suffer." This argument will not be put by anyone who knows anything about animal behavior, since he will know that not all behavior has to be learned. Chickens attempt to stretch wings, walk around, scratch, and even dustbathe or build a nest, even though they have never lived under conditions that allowed these activities. Calves can suffer from maternal deprivation no matter at what age they were taken from their mothers. "We need these intensive methods to provide protein for a growing population." As ecologists and famine relief organizations know, we can produce far more protein per acre if we grow the right vegetable crop, soy beans for instance, than if we use the land to grow crops to be converted into protein by animals who use nearly 90 percent of the protein themselves, even when unable to exercise.

There will be many readers of this book who will agree that factory farming involves an unjustifiable degree of exploitation of sentient creatures, and yet will want to say that there is nothing wrong with rearing animals for food, provided it is done "humanely." These people are saying, in effect, that although we should not cause animals to suffer, there is nothing wrong with killing them.

There are two possible replies to this view. One is to attempt to show that this combination of attitudes is absurd. Roslind Godlovitch takes this course in her essay, which is an examination of some common attitudes to animals. She argues that from the combination of "animal suffering is to be avoided" and "there is nothing wrong with killing animals" it follows that all animal life ought to be exterminated (since all sentient creatures will suffer to some degree at some point in their lives). Euthanasia is a contentious issue only because we place some value on living. If we did not, the least amount of suffering would justify it. Accordingly, if we deny that we have a duty to exterminate all animal life, we must concede that we are placing some value on animal life.

This argument seems to me valid, although one could still reply that the value of animal life is to be derived from the pleasures that life can have for them, so that, provided their lives have a balance of pleasure over pain, we are justified in rearing them. But this would imply that we ought to produce animals and let them live as pleasantly as possible, without suffering.

At this point, one can make the second of the two possible replies to the view that rearing and killing animals for food is all right so long as it is done humanely. This second reply is that so long as we think that a nonhuman may be killed simply so that a human can satisfy his taste for meat, we are still thinking of nonhumans as means rather than as ends in themselves. The factory farm is nothing more than the application of technology to this concept. Even traditional methods involve castration, the separation of mothers and their young, the breaking up of herds, branding or earpunching, and of course transportation to the abattoirs and the final moments of terror when the animal smells blood and senses danger. If we were to try rearing animals so that they lived and died without suffering, we should find that to do so on anything like the scale of today's meat industry would be a sheer impossibility. Meat would become the prerogative of the rich.

I have been able to discuss only some of the contributions to this 45 book, saying nothing about, for instance, the essays on killing for furs and for sport. Nor have I considered all the detailed questions that need to be asked once we start thinking about other species in the radically different way presented by this book. What, for instance, are we to do about genuine conflicts of interest like rats biting slum children? I am not sure of the answer, but the essential point is just that we *do* see this as a conflict of interests, that we recognize that rats have interests too. Then we may begin to think about other ways of resolving the conflict — perhaps by leaving out rat baits that sterilize the rats instead of killing them.

I have not discussed such problems because they are side issues compared with the exploitation of other species for food and for experimental purposes. On these central matters, I hope that I have said enough to show that this book, despite its flaws, is a challenge to every human to recognize his attitudes to nonhumans as a form of prejudice no less objectionable than racism or sexism. It is a challenge that demands not just a change of attitudes, but a change in our way of life, for it requires us to become vegetarians.

Can a purely moral demand of this kind succeed? The odds are certainly against it. The book holds out no inducements. It does not tell us that we will become healthier, or enjoy life more, if we cease exploiting animals. Animal Liberation will require greater altruism on the part of mankind than any other liberation movement, since animals are incapable of demanding it for themselves, or of protesting against their exploitation by votes, demonstrations, or bombs. Is man capable of such genuine altruism? Who knows? If this book does have a significant effect, however, it will be a vindication of all those who have believed that man has within himself the potential for more than cruelty and selfishness.

Topics for Critical Thinking and Writing

1. In his fourth paragraph Singer formulates an argument on behalf of the skeptical reader. Examine that argument closely, restate it in your own words, and evaluate it. Which of its premises is most vulnerable to criticism? Why?

2. Singer quotes with approval (para. 7) Bentham's comment, "The question is not, Can they *reason?* nor Can they *talk?* but, Can they *suffer?*" Do you find this argument persuasive? Can you think of any effective challenge to it?

3. Singer allows that although developed linguistic capacity is not necessary for a creature to have pain, perhaps such a capacity is necessary for "having an intention" (para. 12). Do you think this concession is correct? Have you ever seen animal behavior that you would be willing to describe or explain as evidence that the animal has an intention to do something, despite knowing that the animal cannot talk?

4. Singer thinks that the readiness to experiment on animals argues against believing that animals don't suffer pain (see para. 21). Do you agree with this reasoning?

5. Singer confesses (para. 22) to being made especially angry "with my fellow men" after reading the accounts of animal experimentation. What is it that aroused his anger? Do such feelings, and the acknowledgment that one has them, have any place in a sober discussion about the merits of animal experimentation? Why, or why not?

6. What is "factory farming" (paras. 32–40)? Why is Singer opposed to it?

7. To the claim that there is nothing wrong with "rearing animals for food," provided it is done "humanely" (para. 41), Singer offers two replies (paras. 42–44). In an essay of 250 words summarize them briefly, and then indicate whether either persuades you and why or why not.

8. Suppose someone were to say to Singer: "You claim that capacity to suffer is the relevant factor in deciding whether a creature deserves to be treated as my moral equal. But you're wrong. The relevant factor is whether the creature is *alive*. Being alive is what matters, not being capable of feeling pain." In one or two paragraphs declare what you think would be Singer's reply.

9. Do you think it is worse to kill an animal for its fur than to kill, cook, and eat an animal? Is it worse to kill an animal for sport than to kill it for medical experimentation? What is Singer's view? Explain your view, making use of Singer's if you wish, in an essay of 500 words.

10. Are there any arguments, in your opinion, that show the immorality of eating human flesh (cannibalism) but that do not show a similar

objection to eating animal flesh? Write a 500-word essay in which you discuss the issue.

GARRETT HARDIN

Garrett Hardin (1915–2003) was Emeritus Professor of Human Ecology at the University of California, Santa Barbara. Born in Dallas, Texas, he received his Ph.D. in biology from Stanford in 1941 and is the author of several books, including The Limits of Altruism *(1977),* Managing the Commons *(1977),* Filters Against Folly *(1988), and* The Ostrich Factor *(1998). The essay reprinted here originally appeared in* Psychology Today *(September 1974).*

Lifeboat Ethics: The Case against Helping the Poor

Environmentalists use the metaphor of the earth as a "spaceship" in trying to persuade countries, industries, and people to stop wasting and polluting our natural resources. Since we all share life on this planet, they argue, no single person or institution has the right to destroy, waste, or use more than a fair share of its resources.

But does everyone on earth have an equal right to an equal share of its resources? The spaceship metaphor can be dangerous when used by misguided idealists to justify suicidal policies for sharing our resources through uncontrolled immigration and foreign aid. In their enthusiastic but unrealistic generosity, they confuse the ethics of a spaceship with those of a lifeboat.

A true spaceship would have to be under the control of a captain, since no ship could possibly survive if its course were determined by committee. Spaceship Earth certainly has no captain; the United Nations is merely a toothless tiger, with little power to enforce any policy upon its bickering members.

If we divide the world crudely into rich nations and poor nations, two thirds of them are desperately poor, and only one third comparatively rich, with the United States the wealthiest of all. Metaphorically each nation can be seen as a lifeboat full of comparatively rich people. In the ocean outside each lifeboat swim the poor of the world, who would like to get in, or at least to share some of the wealth. What should the lifeboat passengers do?

First, we must recognize the limited capacity of any lifeboat. For example, a nation's land has a limited capacity to support a population and as the current energy crisis has shown us, in some ways we have already exceeded the carrying capacity of our land.

ADRIFT IN A MORAL SEA

So here we sit, say fifty people in our lifeboat. To be generous, let us assume it has room for ten more, making a total capacity of sixty. Suppose the fifty of us in the lifeboat see 100 others swimming in the water outside, begging for admission to our boat or for handouts. We have several options: We may be tempted to try to live by the Christian ideal of being "our brother's keeper," or by the Marxist ideal of "to each according to his needs." Since the needs of all in the water are the same, and since they can all be seen as "our brothers," we could take them all into our boat, making a total of 150 in a boat designed for sixty. The boat swamps, everyone drowns. Complete justice, complete catastrophe.

Since the boat has an unused excess capacity of ten more passengers, we could admit just ten more to it. But which ten do we let in? How do we choose? Do we pick the best ten, the neediest ten, "first come, first served"? And what do we say to the ninety we exclude? If we do let an extra ten into our lifeboat, we will have lost our "safety factor," an engineering principle of critical importance. For example, if we don't leave room for excess capacity as a safety factor in our country's agriculture, a new plant disease or a bad change in the weather could have disastrous consequences.

Suppose we decide to preserve our small safety factor and admit no more to the lifeboat. Our survival is then possible, although we shall have to be constantly on guard against boarding parties.

While this last solution clearly offers the only means of our survival, it is morally abhorrent to many people. Some say they feel guilty about their good luck. My reply is simple: "Get out and yield your place to others." This may solve the problem of the guilt-ridden person's conscience, but it does not change the ethics of the lifeboat. The needy person to whom the guilt-ridden person yields his place will not himself feel guilty about his good luck. If he did, he would not climb aboard. The net result of conscience-stricken people giving up their unjustly held seats is the elimination of that sort of conscience from the lifeboat.

This is the basic metaphor within which we must work out our solutions. Let us now enrich the image, step by step, with substantive additions from the real world, a world that must solve real and pressing problems of overpopulation and hunger.

The harsh ethics of the lifeboat become even harsher when we consider the reproductive differences between the rich nations and the poor nations. The people inside the lifeboats are doubling in numbers every eighty-seven years; those swimming around outside are doubling, on the average, every thirty-five years, more than twice as fast as the rich. And since the world's resources are dwindling, the difference in prosperity between the rich and the poor can only increase.

As of 1973, the United States had a population of 210 million people, who were increasing by 0.8 percent per year. Outside our lifeboat, let us imagine another 210 million people (say the combined populations of Colombia, Ecuador, Venezuela, Morocco, Pakistan, Thailand, and the Philippines), who are increasing at a rate of 3.3 percent year. Put differently, the doubling time for this aggregate population is twenty-one years, compared to eighty-seven years for the United States.

MULTIPLYING THE RICH AND THE POOR

Now suppose the United States agreed to pool its resources with those seven countries, with everyone receiving an equal share. Initially the ratio of Americans to non-Americans in this model would be one-to-one. But consider what the ratio would be after eighty-seven years, by which time the Americans would have doubled to a population of 420 million. By then, doubling every twenty-one years, the other group would have swollen to 354 billion. Each American would have to share the available resource with more than eight people.

But, one could argue, this discussion assumes that current population trends will continue, and they may not. Quite so. Most likely the rate of population increase will decline much faster in the United States than it will in the other countries, and there does not seem to be much we can do about it. In sharing with "each according to his needs," we must recognize that needs are determined by population size, which is determined by the rate of reproduction, which at present is regarded as a sovereign right of every nation, poor or not. This being so, the philanthropic load created by the sharing ethic of the spaceship can only increase.

THE TRAGEDY OF THE COMMONS

The fundamental error of spaceship ethics, and the sharing it requires, is that it leads to what I call "the tragedy of the commons." Under a system of private property, the men who own property recognize their responsibility to care for it, for if they don't they will eventually suffer. A farmer, for instance, will allow no more cattle in a pasture than its carrying capacity justifies. If he overloads it, erosion sets in, weeds take over, and he loses the use of the pasture.

If a pasture becomes a commons open to all, the right of each to use it may not be matched by a corresponding responsibility to protect it. Asking everyone to use it with discretion will hardly do, for the considerate herdsman who refrains from overloading the commons suffers more than a selfish one who says his needs are greater. If everyone would restrain himself, all would be well; but it takes only one less than everyone to ruin a system of voluntary restraint. In a crowded world of less than perfect human beings, mutual ruin is inevitable if there are no controls. This is the tragedy of the commons.

One of the major tasks of education today should be the creation of such an acute awareness of the dangers of the commons that people will recognize its many varieties. For example, the air and water have become polluted because they are treated as commons. Further growth in the population or per-capita conversion of natural resources into pollutants will only make the problem worse. The same holds true for the fish of the oceans. Fishing fleets have nearly disappeared in many parts of the world, technological improvements in the art of fishing are hastening the day of complete ruin. Only the replacement of the system of the commons with a responsible system of control will save the land, air, water, and oceanic fisheries.

THE WORLD FOOD BANK

In recent years there has been a push to create a new commons called a World Food Bank, an international depository of food reserves to which nations would contribute according to their abilities and from which they would draw according to their needs. This humanitarian proposal has received support from many liberal international groups, and from such prominent citizens as Margaret Mead, U.N. Secretary General Kurt Waldheim, and Senators Edward Kennedy and George McGovern.

A world food bank appeals powerfully to our humanitarian impulses. But before we rush ahead with such a plan, let us recognize where the greatest political push comes from, lest we be disillusioned later. Our experience with the "Food for Peace program," or Public Law 480, gives us the answer. This program moved billions of dollars' worth of U.S. surplus grain to food-short, population-long countries during the past two decades. But when PL 480 first became law, a headline in the business magazine *Forbes* revealed the real power behind it: "Feeding the World's Hungry Millions: How It Will Mean Billions for U.S. Business."

And indeed it did. In the years 1960 to 1970, U.S. taxpayers spent a   20
total of $7.9 billion on the Food for Peace program. Between 1948 and
1970, they also paid an additional $50 billion for other economic-aid
programs, some of which went for food and food-producing machinery
and technology. Though all U.S. taxpayers were forced to contribute to
the cost of PL 480, certain special interest groups gained handsomely
under the program. Farmers did not have to contribute the grain; the
government, or rather the taxpayers, bought it from them at full market
prices. The increased demand raised prices of farm products generally.
The manufacturers of farm machinery, fertilizers, and pesticides benefited by the farmers' extra efforts to grow more food. Grain elevators
profited from storing the surplus until it could be shipped. Railroads
made money hauling it to ports, and shipping lines profited from carrying it overseas. The implementation of PL 480 required the creation of a
vast government bureaucracy, which then acquired its own vested interest in continuing the program regardless of its merits.

EXTRACTING DOLLARS

Those who proposed and defended the Food for Peace program in
public rarely mentioned its importance to any of these special interests.
The public emphasis was always on its humanitarian effects. The combination of silent selfish interests and highly vocal humanitarian apolo-
gists made a powerful and successful lobby for extracting money from
taxpayers. We can expect the same lobby to push now for the creation of
a World Food Bank.

However great the potential benefit to selfish interests, it should not
be a decisive argument against a truly humanitarian program. We must
ask if such a program would actually do more good than harm, not only
momentarily but also in the long run. Those who propose the food bank
usually refer to a current "emergency" or "crisis" in terms of world food
supply. But what is an emergency? Although they may be infrequent and
sudden, everyone knows that emergencies will occur from time to time.
A well-run family, company, organization, or country prepares for the
likelihood of accidents and emergencies. It expects them, it budgets for
them, it saves for them.

LEARNING THE HARD WAY

What happens if some organizations or countries budget for accidents and others do not? If each country is solely responsible for its own
well-being, poorly managed ones will suffer. But they can learn from ex-

perience. They may mend their ways, and learn to budget for infrequent but certain emergencies. For example, the weather varies from year to year, and periodic crop failures are certain. A wise and competent government saves out of the production of the good years in anticipation of bad years to come. Joseph taught this policy to Pharaoh in Egypt more than 2,000 years ago. Yet the great majority of the governments in the world today do not follow such a policy. They lack either the wisdom or the competence, or both. Should those nations that do manage to put something aside be forced to come to the rescue each time an emergency occurs among the poor nations?

"But it isn't their fault!" some kindhearted liberals argue. "How can we blame the poor people who are caught in an emergency? Why must they suffer for the sins of their governments?" The concept of blame is simply not relevant here. The real question is, what are the operational consequences of establishing a world food bank? If it is open to every country every time a need develops, slovenly rulers will not be motivated to take Joseph's advice. Someone will always come to their aid. Some countries will deposit food in the world food bank, and others will withdraw it. There will be almost no overlap. As a result of such solutions to food shortage emergencies, the poor countries will not learn to mend their ways, and will suffer progressively greater emergencies as their populations grow.

POPULATION CONTROL THE CRUDE WAY

On the average, poor countries undergo a 2.5 percent increase in population each year; rich countries, about 0.8 percent. Only rich countries have anything in the way of food reserves set aside, and even they do not have as much as they should. Poor countries have none. If poor countries received no food from the outside, the rate of their population growth would be periodically checked by crop failures and famines. But if they can always draw on a world food bank in time of need, their populations can continue to grow unchecked, and so will their "need" for aid. In the short run, a world food bank may diminish that need, but in the long run it actually increases the need without limit.

Without some system of worldwide food sharing, the proportion of people in the rich and poor nations might eventually stabilize. The overpopulated poor countries would decrease in numbers, while the rich countries that had room for more people would increase. But with a well-meaning system of sharing, such as a world food bank, the growth differential between the rich and the poor countries will not only persist, it will increase. Because of the higher rate of population growth in the poor countries of the world, 88 percent of today's children are born poor, and only 12 percent rich. Year by year the ratio becomes worse, as the fast-reproducing poor outnumber the slow-reproducing rich.

A world food bank is thus a commons in disguise. People will have more motivation to draw from it than to add to any common store. The less provident and less able will multiply at the expense of the abler and more provident, bringing eventual ruin upon all who share in the commons. Besides, any system of "sharing" that amounts to foreign aid from the rich nations to the poor nations will carry the taint of charity, which will contribute little to the world peace so devoutly desired by those who support the idea of a world food bank.

As past U.S. foreign-aid programs have amply and depressingly demonstrated, international charity frequently inspires mistrust and antagonism rather than gratitude on the part of the recipient nation.

CHINESE FISH AND MIRACLE RICE

The modern approach to foreign aid stresses the export of technology and advice, rather than money and food. As an ancient Chinese proverb goes: "Give a man a fish and he will eat for a day; teach him how to fish and he will eat for the rest of his days." Acting on this advice, the Rockefeller and Ford foundations have financed a number of programs for improving agriculture in the hungry nations. Known as the "Green Revolution," these programs have led to the development of "miracle rice" and "miracle wheat," new strains that offer bigger harvests and greater resistance to crop damage. Norman Borlaug, the Nobel Prize–winning agronomist who, supported by the Rockefeller Foundation, developed "miracle wheat," is one of the most prominent advocates of a world food bank.

Whether or not the Green Revolution can increase food production as much as its champions claim is a debatable but possibly irrelevant point. Those who support this well-intended humanitarian effort should first consider some of the fundamentals of human ecology. Ironically, one man who did was the late Alan Gregg, a vice president of the Rockefeller Foundation. Two decades ago he expressed strong doubts about the wisdom of such attempts to increase food production. He likened the growth and spread of humanity over the surface of the earth to the spread of cancer in the human body, remarking that "cancerous growths demand food; but, as far as I know, they have never been cured by getting it." 30

OVERLOADING THE ENVIRONMENT

Every human born constitutes a draft on all aspects of the environment: food, air, water, forests, beaches, wildlife, scenery, and solitude. Food can, perhaps, be significantly increased to meet a growing demand. But what about clean beaches, unspoiled forests, and solitude? If we satisfy a growing population's need for food, we necessarily decrease its per-capita supply of the other resources needed by men.

India, for example, now has a population of 600 million, which increases by 15 million each year. This population already puts a huge load on a relatively impoverished environment. The country's forests are now only a small fraction of what they were three centuries ago, and floods and erosion continually destroy the insufficient farmland that remains. Every one of the 15 million new lives added to India's population puts an additional burden on the environment, and increases the economic and social costs of crowding. However humanitarian our intent, every Indian life saved through medical or nutritional assistance from abroad diminishes the quality of life for those who remain, and for subsequent generations. If rich countries make it possible, through foreign aid, for 600 million Indians to swell to 1.2 billion in a mere twenty-eight years, as their current growth rate threatens, will future generations of Indians thank us for hastening the destruction of their environment? Will our good intentions be sufficient excuse for the consequences of our actions?

My final example of a commons in action is one for which the public has the least desire for rational discussion—immigration. Anyone who publicly questions the wisdom of current U.S. immigration policy is promptly charged with bigotry, prejudice, ethnocentrism, chauvinism, isolationism, or selfishness. Rather than encounter such accusations, one would rather talk about other matters, leaving immigration policy to wallow in the crosscurrents of special interests that take no account of the good of the whole, or the interest of posterity.

Perhaps we still feel guilty about things we said in the past. Two generations ago the popular press frequently referred to Dagos, Wops, Polacks, Chinks, and Krauts, in articles about how America was being "overrun" by foreigners of supposedly inferior genetic stock. But because the implied inferiority of foreigners was used then as justification for keeping them out, people now assume that restrictive policies could only be based on such misguided notions. There are no other grounds.

A NATION OF IMMIGRANTS

Just consider the numbers involved. Our government acknowledges 35 a net inflow of 400,000 immigrants a year. While we have no hard data on the extent of illegal entries, educated guesses put the figure at about 600,000 a year. Since the natural increase (excess of births over deaths) of the resident population now runs about 1.7 million per year, the yearly gain from immigration amounts to at least 19 percent of the total annual increase, and may be as much as 37 percent if we include the estimate for illegal immigrants. Considering the growing use of birth-control devices, the potential effect of educational campaigns by such organizations as Planned Parenthood Federation of America and Zero Population Growth, and the influence of inflation and the housing shortage, the fertility rate of American women may decline so much that immigration could account for all the yearly increase in population. Should we not at least ask if that is what we want?

For the sake of those who worry about whether the "quality" of the average immigrant compares favorably with the quality of the average resident, let us assume that immigrants and native-born citizens are of exactly equal quality, however one defines that term. We will focus here only on quantity; and since our conclusions will depend on nothing else, all charges of bigotry and chauvinism become irrelevant.

IMMIGRATION VS. FOOD SUPPLY

World food banks *move food to the people*, hastening the exhaustion of the environment of the poor countries. Unrestricted immigration, on the other hand, *moves people to the food*, thus speeding up the destruction of the environment of the rich countries. We can easily understand why poor people should want to make this latter transfer, but why should rich hosts encourage it?

As in the case of foreign-aid programs, immigration receives support from selfish interests and humanitarian impulses. The primary selfish interest in unimpeded immigration is the desire of employers for cheap labor, particularly in industries and trades that offer degrading work. In the past, one wave of foreigners after another was brought into the United States to work at wretched jobs for wretched wages. In recent years, the Cubans, Puerto Ricans, and Mexicans have had this dubious honor. The interests of the employers of cheap labor mesh well with the guilty silence of the country's liberal intelligentsia. White Anglo-Saxon Protestants are particularly reluctant to call for a closing of the doors to immigration for fear of being called bigots.

But not all countries have such reluctant leadership. Most educated Hawaiians, for example, are keenly aware of the limits of their environment, particularly in terms of population growth. There is only so much room on the islands, and the islanders know it. To Hawaiians, immigrants from the other forty-nine states present as great a threat as those from other nations. At a recent meeting of Hawaiian government officials in Honolulu, I had the ironic delight of hearing a speaker, who like most of his audience was of Japanese ancestry, ask how the country might practically and constitutionally close its doors to further immigration. One member of the audience countered: "How can we shut the doors now? We have many friends and relatives in Japan that we'd like to bring here some day so that they can enjoy Hawaii too." The Japanese-American speaker smiled sympathetically and answered: "Yes, but we have children now, and someday we'll have grandchildren too. We can bring more people here from Japan only by giving away some of the land that we hope to pass on to our grandchildren some day. What right do we have to do that?"

At this point, I can hear U.S. liberals asking: "How can you justify   40 slamming the door once you're inside? You say that immigrants should be kept out. But aren't we all immigrants, or the descendants of immigrants? If we insist on staying, must we not admit all others?" Our craving for intellectual order leads us to seek and prefer symmetrical rules and morals: a single rule for me and everybody else; the same rule yesterday, today, and tomorrow. Justice, we feel, should not change with time and place.

We Americans of non-Indian ancestry can look upon ourselves as the descendants of thieves who are guilty morally, if not legally, of stealing this land from its Indian owners. Should we then give back the land to the now living American descendants of those Indians? However morally or logically sound this proposal may be, I, for one, am unwilling to live by it and I know no one else who is. Besides, the logical consequence would be absurd. Suppose that, intoxicated with a sense of pure justice, we should decide to turn our land over to the Indians. Since all our wealth has also been derived from the land, wouldn't we be morally obliged to give that back to the Indians too?

PURE JUSTICE VS. REALITY

Clearly, the concept of pure justice produces an infinite regression to absurdity. Centuries ago, wise men invented statutes of limitations to justify the rejection of such pure justice, in the interest of preventing continual disorder. The law zealously defends property rights, but only relatively recent property rights. Drawing a line after an arbitrary time has elapsed may be unjust, but the alternatives are worse.

We are all descendants of thieves, and the world's resources are inequitably distributed. But we must begin the journey to tomorrow from the point where we are today. We cannot remake the past. We cannot safely divide the wealth equitably among all peoples so long as people reproduce at different rates. To do so would guarantee that our grandchildren, and everyone else's grandchildren, would have only a ruined world to inhabit.

To be generous with one's own possessions is quite different from being generous with those of posterity. We should call this point to the attention of those who, from a commendable love of justice and equality, would institute a system of the commons, either in the form of a world food bank, or of unrestricted immigration. We must convince them if we wish to save at least some parts of the world from environmental ruin.

Without a true world government to control reproduction and the 45 use of available resources, the sharing ethic of the spaceship is impossible. For the foreseeable future, our survival demands that we govern our actions by the ethics of a lifeboat, harsh though they may be. Posterity will be satisfied with nothing less.

Topics for Critical Thinking and Writing

1. Hardin says that "in some ways we have already exceeded the carrying capacity of our land" (para. 5). Does he tell us later what some of those ways are? Can you think of others?

2. The central analogy on which Hardin's argument rests is that human life on planet Earth is like living in an overcrowded lifeboat. Evaluate this analogy.

3. What does Hardin mean by "ethics" in the title of his essay? What, if any, ethical principle does Hardin believe should guide our conduct in lifeboat Earth?

4. What is "the tragedy" and what is "the commons" in what Hardin calls "the tragedy of the commons" (paras. 15–17)?

5. What does Hardin mean by "a truly humanitarian program" (para. 22) to alleviate future problems of hunger and starvation? Why does he think a World Food Bank would aggravate, rather than alleviate, the problem?

6. How do you react to the analogy that compares the growth of the human race over the earth to "the spread of cancer in the human body" (para. 30)?

7. Hardin's view of the relationship between population growth and available resources can be described (though he doesn't) as a zero-sum game. Do you agree with such a description? Why, or why not?

8. Hardin refers to an organization named Zero Population Growth (para. 35). In your public or college library find out about this organization, and then write a 250-word essay describing its origin and aims.

9. Hardin offers a reductio ad absurdum argument against large-scale restitution by the current nonnative American population to the surviv-

ing native Americans (para. 41). Evaluate this argument in an essay of 250 words.

10. Hardin refers frequently (for example, para. 42) and unsympathetically to what he calls "pure justice." To what principle, exactly, is he referring by this phrase? Would you agree that this principle is, indeed, well described as "pure justice"? Why, or why not?

11. Suppose someone, after reading Hardin's essay, described it as nothing more than selfishness on a national scale. Would Hardin agree? Would he consider this a serious criticism of his analysis and proposals?

JAMES RACHELS

James Rachels (1941–2003) was a professor of philosophy at the University of Alabama at Birmingham and the author of several books, including The End of Life: Euthanasia and Morality *(1986) and* Can Ethics Provide Answers? And Other Essays in Moral Philosophy *(1997). The article reprinted here appeared in the* New England Journal of Medicine *in 1975.*

Active and Passive Euthanasia

The distinction between active and passive euthanasia is thought to be crucial for medical ethics. The idea is that it is permissible, at least in some cases, to withhold treatment and allow a patient to die, but it is never permissible to take any direct action designed to kill the patient. This doctrine seems to be accepted by most doctors, and it is endorsed in a statement adopted by the House of Delegates of the American Medical Association on December 4, 1973:

> The intentional termination of the life of one human being by another—mercy killing—is contrary to that for which the medical profession stands and is contrary to the policy of the American Medical Association. The cessation of the employment of extraordinary means to prolong the life of the body when there is irrefutable evidence that biological death is imminent is the decision of the patient and/or his immediate family. The advice and judgment of the physician should be freely available to the patient and/or his immediate family.

However, a strong case can be made against this doctrine. In what follows I will set out some of the relevant arguments, and urge doctors to reconsider their views on this matter.

To begin with a familiar type of situation, a patient who is dying of incurable cancer of the throat is in terrible pain, which can no longer be satisfactorily alleviated. He is certain to die within a few days, even if present treatment is continued, but he does not want to go on living for those days since the pain is unbearable. So he asks the doctor for an end to it, and his family joins in the request.

Suppose the doctor agrees to withhold treatment, as the conventional doctrine says he may. The justification for his doing so is that the patient is in terrible agony, and since he is going to die anyway, it would be wrong to prolong his suffering needlessly. But now notice this. If one simply withholds treatment, it may take the patient longer to die, and so he may suffer more than he would if more direct action were taken and a lethal injection given. This fact provides strong reason for thinking that, once the initial decision not to prolong his agony has been made, active euthanasia is actually preferable to passive euthanasia, rather than the reverse. To say otherwise is to endorse the option that leads to more suffering rather than less, and is contrary to the humanitarian impulse that prompts the decision not to prolong his life in the first place.

Part of my point is that the process of being "allowed to die" can be relatively slow and painful, whereas being given a lethal injection is relatively quick and painless. Let me give a different sort of example. In the United States about one in six hundred babies is born with Down's syndrome. Most of these babies are otherwise healthy—that is, with only the usual pediatric care, they will proceed to an otherwise normal infancy. Some, however, are born with congenital defects such as intestinal obstructions that require operations if they are to live. Sometimes, the parents and the doctor will decide not to operate, and let the infant die. Anthony Shaw describes what happens then:

> When surgery is denied [the doctor] must try to keep the infant from suffering while natural forces sap the baby's life away. As a surgeon whose natural inclination is to use the scalpel to fight off death, standing by and watching a salvageable baby die is the most emotionally exhausting experience I know. It is easy at a conference, in a theoretical discussion to decide that such infants should be allowed to die. It is altogether different to stand by in the nursery and watch as dehydration and infection wither a tiny being over hours and days. This is a terrible ordeal for me and the hospital staff—much more so than for the parents who never set foot in the nursery.[1]

[1]Anthony Shaw, "Doctor, Do We Have a Choice?" *New York Times Magazine*, January 30, 1972, p. 54. [Author's note.]

I can understand why some people are opposed to all euthanasia, and insist that such infants must be allowed to live. I think I can also understand why other people favor destroying these babies quickly and painlessly. But why should anyone favor letting "dehydration and infection wither a tiny being over hours and days"? The doctrine that says that a baby may be allowed to dehydrate and wither, but may not be given an injection that would end its life without suffering, seems so patently cruel as to require no further refutation. The strong language is not intended to offend, but only to put the point in the clearest possible way.

My second argument is that the conventional doctrine leads to decisions concerning life and death made on irrelevant grounds. 5

Consider again the case of the infants with Down's syndrome who need operations for congenital defects unrelated to the syndrome to live. Sometimes, there is no operation, and the baby dies, but when there is no such defect, the baby lives on. Now, an operation such as that to remove an intestinal obstruction is not prohibitively difficult. The reason why such operations are not performed in these cases is, clearly, that the child has Down's syndrome and the parents and the doctor judge that because of that fact it is better for the child to die.

But notice that this situation is absurd, no matter what view one takes of the lives and potentials of such babies. If the life of such an infant is worth preserving, what does it matter if it needs a simple operation? Or, if one thinks it better that such a baby should not live on, what difference does it make that it happens to have an unobstructed intestinal tract? In either case, the matter of life and death is being decided on irrelevant grounds. It is the Down's syndrome, and not the intestines, that is the issue. The matter should be decided, if at all, on that basis, and not be allowed to depend on the essentially irrelevant question of whether the intestinal tract is blocked.

What makes this situation possible, of course, is the idea that when there is an intestinal blockage, one can "let the baby die," but when there is no such defect there is nothing that can be done, for one must not "kill" it. The fact that this idea leads to such results as deciding life or death on irrelevant grounds is another good reason why the doctrine would be rejected.

One reason why so many people think that there is an important moral difference between active and passive euthanasia is that they think killing someone is morally worse than letting someone die. But is it? Is killing, in itself, worse than letting die? To investigate this issue, two cases may be considered that are exactly alike except that one involves killing whereas the other involves letting someone die. Then, it can be asked whether this difference makes any difference to the moral assessments. It is important that the cases be exactly alike, except for this one difference, since otherwise one cannot be confident that it is this difference and not some other that accounts for any variation in the assessments of the two cases. So, let us consider this pair of cases:

In the first, Smith stands to gain a large inheritance if anything 10 should happen to his six-year-old cousin. One evening while the child is taking his bath, Smith sneaks into the bathroom and drowns the child, and then arranges things so that it will look like an accident.

In the second, Jones also stands to gain if anything should happen to his six-year-old cousin. Like Smith, Jones sneaks in planning to drown the child in his bath. However, just as he enters the bathroom Jones sees the child slip and hit his head, and fall face down in the water. Jones is delighted; he stands by, ready to push the child's head back under if it is necessary, but it is not necessary. With only a little thrashing about, the child drowns all by himself, "accidentally," as Jones watches and does nothing.

Now Smith killed the child, whereas Jones "merely" let the child die. That is the only difference between them. Did either man behave better, from a moral point of view? If the difference between killing and letting die were in itself a morally important matter, one should say that Jones's behavior was less reprehensible than Smith's. But does one really want to say that? I think not. In the first place, both men acted from the same motive, personal gain, and both had exactly the same end in view when they acted. It may be inferred from Smith's conduct that he is a bad man, although the judgment may be withdrawn or modified if certain further facts are learned about him—for example, that he is mentally deranged. But would not the very same thing be inferred about Jones from his conduct? And would not the same further considerations also be relevant to any modification of this judgment? Moreover, suppose Jones pleaded, in his own defense, "After all, I didn't do anything except just stand there and watch the child drown. I didn't kill him; I only let him die." Again, if letting die were in itself less bad than killing, this defense should have at least some weight. But it does not. Such a "defense" can only be regarded as a grotesque perversion of moral reasoning. Morally speaking, it is no defense at all.

Now, it may be pointed out, quite properly, that the cases of euthanasia with which doctors are concerned are not like this at all. They do not involve personal gain or the destruction of normal healthy children. Doctors are concerned only with cases in which the patient's life is of no further use to him, or in which the patient's life has become or will soon become a terrible burden. However, the point is the same in these cases: The bare difference between killing and letting die does not, in itself, make a moral difference. If a doctor lets a patient die, for humane reasons, he is in the same moral position as if he had given the patient a lethal injection for humane reasons. If his decision was wrong—if, for example, the patient's illness was in fact curable—the decision would be equally regrettable no matter which method was used to carry it out. And if the doctor's decision was the right one, the method used is not in itself important.

The AMA policy statement isolates the crucial issue very well; the crucial issue is "the intentional termination of the life of one human being by another." But after identifying this issue, and forbidding "mercy killing," the statement goes on to deny that the cessation of treatment is the intentional termination of life. This is where the mistake comes in, for what is the cessation of treatment, in these circumstances, if it is not "the intentional termination of the life of one human being by another?" Of course it is exactly that, and if it were not, there would be no point to it.

Many people will find this judgment hard to accept. One reason, I 15 think, is that it is very easy to conflate the question of whether killing is, in itself, worse than letting die, with the very different question of whether most actual cases of killing are more reprehensible than most actual cases of letting die. Most actual cases of killing are clearly terrible (think, for example, of all the murders reported in the newspapers), and one hears of such cases every day. On the other hand, one hardly ever hears of a case of letting die, except for the actions of doctors who are motivated by humanitarian reasons. So one learns to think of killing in a much worse light than of letting die. But this does not mean that there is something about killing that makes it in itself worse than letting die, for it is not the bare difference between killing and letting die that makes the difference in these cases. Rather, the other factors—the murderer's motive of personal gain, for example, contrasted with the doctor's humanitarian motivation—account for different reactions to the different cases.

I have argued that killing is not in itself any worse than letting die; if my contention is right, it follows that active euthanasia is not any worse than passive euthanasia. What arguments can be given on the other side? The most common, I believe, is the following:

> The important difference between active and passive euthanasia is that, in passive euthanasia, the doctor does not do anything to bring about the patient's death. The doctor does nothing, and the patient dies of whatever ills already afflict him. In active euthanasia, however, the doctor does something to bring about the patient's death: He kills him. The doctor who gives the patient with cancer a lethal injection has himself caused his patient's death; whereas if he merely ceases treatment, the cancer is the cause of the death.

A number of points need to be made here. This first is that it is not exactly correct to say that in passive euthanasia the doctor does nothing, for he does do one thing that is very important: He lets the patient die. "Letting someone die" is certainly different, in some respects, from other types of action — mainly in that it is a kind of action that one may perform by way of not performing certain other actions. For example, one may let a patient die by way of not giving medication, just as one may insult someone by way of not shaking his hand. But for any purpose of moral assessment, it is a type of action nonetheless. The decision to let a patient die is subject to moral appraisal in the same way that a decision to kill him would be subject to moral appraisal: It may be assessed as wise or unwise, compassionate or sadistic, right or wrong. If a doctor deliberately let a patient die who was suffering from a routinely curable illness, the doctor would certainly be to blame for what he had done, just as he would be to blame if he had needlessly killed the patient. Charges against him would then be appropriate. If so, it would be no defense at all for him to insist that he didn't "do anything." He would have done something very serious indeed, for he let his patient die.

Fixing the cause of death may be very important from a legal point of view, for it may determine whether criminal charges are brought against the doctor. But I do not think that this notion can be used to show a moral difference between active and passive euthanasia. The reason why it is considered bad to be the cause of someone's death is that death is regarded as a great evil — and so it is. However, if it has been decided that euthanasia — even passive euthanasia — is desirable in a given case, it has also been decided that in this instance death is not greater an evil than the patient's continued existence. And if this is true, the usual reason for not wanting to be the cause of someone's death simply does not apply.

Finally, doctors may think that all of this is only of academic interest — the sort of thing that philosophers may worry about but that has no practical bearing on their own work. After all, doctors must be concerned about the legal consequences of what they do, and active euthanasia is clearly forbidden by the law. But even so, doctors should also be concerned with the fact that the law is forcing upon them a moral doctrine that may be indefensible, and has a considerable effect on their practices. Of course, most doctors are not now in the position of being coerced in this matter, for they do not regard themselves as merely going along with what the law requires. Rather, in statements such as the AMA policy statement that I have quoted, they are endorsing this doctrine as a central point of medical ethics. In that statement, active euthanasia is condemned not merely as illegal but as "contrary to that for which the medical profession stands," whereas passive euthanasia is approved. However, the preceding considerations suggest that there is really no moral difference between the two, considered in themselves (there may be important moral differences in some cases in their *consequences*, but, as I pointed out, these differences may make active euthanasia, and not passive euthanasia, the morally preferable option). So, whereas doctors may have to discriminate between active and passive euthanasia to satisfy the law, they should not do any more than that. In particular, they should not give the distinction any added authority and weight by writing it into official statements of medical ethics.

Topics for Critical Thinking and Writing

1. Explain "the distinction between active and passive euthanasia" (para. 1). Why do you think the American Medical Association attaches importance to the distinction?

2. Rachels argues that in certain cases, "active euthanasia is actually preferable to passive euthanasia" (para. 3). What is his argument? Do you think it ought to persuade a person who already favors "passive" euthanasia to perform "active" euthanasia in cases of the sort Rachels describes? Why, or why not?

3. What is Rachels's "second argument" (para. 5), and what is it supposed to prove? Do you think it succeeds? Explain.

4. Rachels asks whether "killing someone is morally worse than letting someone die" (para. 9). He argues that it is not. What is his argument? Does it persuade you? Why, or why not?

5. Rachels opens his essay by discussing a genuine case of a newborn with Down's syndrome (para. 4), but eventually he is forced to construct purely hypothetical cases (paras. 10–11). Do you think that the persuasive power of his argument suffers when he shifts to hypothetical cases? Or does it improve? Or doesn't it matter whether he is discussing actual or only hypothetical cases? Explain.

6. The principal thesis of Rachels's essay is that "the bare difference between killing and letting die does not, in itself, make a moral difference" (para. 13). Summarize his argument for this thesis.

Acknowledgments continued from copyright page.

David Bruck. "The Death Penalty." From *The New Republic*, May 20, 1985. Copyright © 1985 by The New Republic, Inc. Reprinted by permission of *The New Republic*.

David Burt. "Yes, Install Filters." Copyright © 2001 The CQ Researcher, published by CQ Press, a division of Congressional Quarterly, Inc.

Elliott Currie. "Toward a Policy on Drugs." Excerpt from "Rethinking Criminal Justice" in *Reckoning, Drugs, The Cities, and the American Future* by Elliott Currie. Copyright © 1993 by Elliott Currie. Reprinted by permission of Hill and Wang, a division of Farrar, Straus and Giroux, LLC.

Judith Wagner DeCew. "The Feminist Critique of Privacy." From *In Pursuit of Privacy: Law, Ethics, and the Rise of Technology*. Copyright © 1997 by Cornell University. Used by permission of the publisher, Cornell University Press.

Alan M. Dershowitz. "Yes, It Should Be 'On the Books.'" Originally titled, "Why Fear National ID Cards?" Originally published in the *Boston Globe*, February 16, 2002. Reprinted by permission of the author.

Terry Eastland. "Ending Affirmative Action: The Case for Colorblind Justice." (paper). Copyright © 1996 By Perseus Books Group. Reproduced with permission of Perseus Books Group in the format Textbook Via Copyright Clearance Center.

Amitai Etzioni. "Less Privacy Is Good for Us (and You)." From *Privacy Journal*, April 1999, pp. 3–5. Copyright © 1999 Amitai Etizioni. Reprinted by permission of the author.

Milton Friedman. "There's No Justice in the War on Drugs." From *The New York Times*, January 11, 1998. Copyright © 1998 The New York Times. Reprinted by permission.

William Galston. "The Perils of Preemptive War." Reprinted with permission from *The American Prospect*, Volume 13, Number 17: September 23, 2002. The American Prospect, 5 Broad Street, Boston, MA 02109. All rights reserved.

Ellen Goodman. "The Reasonable Woman Standard." © 1980, 1991 The Washington Post Writers Group. Reprinted with permission.

Robert W. Hahn and Paul Tetlock. "No, Don't Prohibit Their Use." Copyright © 2001 The CQ Researcher, published by CQ Press, a division of Congressional Quarterly, Inc.

Garrett Hardin. "Lifeboat Ethics." From *Psychology Today* magazine, September 1974. Copyright © 1974 Sussex Publishers, Inc. Reprinted by permission of the publisher.

Philip B. Heymann. "Torture Should Not Be Authorized." From the *Boston Globe*, February 16, 2002. Reprinted by permission of the author.

Vincent Iacopino. "It Should Not Be Permissible to Torture Suspected Terrorists to Gather Information." Copyright © 2003 The CQ Researcher. Published by CQ Press, a division of Congressional Quarterly Inc.

Martin Luther King Jr. "I Have a Dream" and "Letter from Birmingham Jail." Copyright © 1968 Martin Luther King Jr. Copyright renewed 1996

Coretta Scott King. Reprinted by arrangement with the Estate of Martin Luther King Jr., c/o Writers House as agent for the proprietor, New York, NY.

Edward I. Koch. "Death and Justice: How Capital Punishment Affirms Life." Originally published in *The New Republic*, April 15, 1985. Copyright © 1985 by The New Republic, Inc. Reprinted with permission.

Alex Kozinski/Sean Gallagher. "For an Honest Death Penalty." From *The New York Times*, March 8, 1995. Copyright © 1995 The New York Times. Reprinted by permission.

Nancy Kranich. "No, Do Not Install Filters." Copyright © 2001 The CQ Researcher, published by CQ Press, a division of Congressional Quarterly, Inc.

Michael Levin. "The Case for Torture." From *Newsweek*, June 7, 1982. Reprinted by permission of the author.

George A. Lopez. "Iraq and Just-War Thinking." From *Commonweal*, September 27, 2002. Copyright © 2002 Commonweal Foundation. Reprinted with permission.

Niccolò Machiavelli. Excerpt from "The Prince." From *The Portable Machiavelli* edited by Peter Bondanella & Mark Musa. Translated by Mark Musa & Peter Bondanella. Copyright © 1979 by Viking Penguin, Inc. Used by permission of Viking Penguin, a division of Penguin Group (USA) Inc.

Burke Marshall and Nicholas deB. Katzenbach. "Not Color Blind: Just Blind." From *The New York Times*, February 22, 1998. Copyright © 1998 Burke Marshall and Nicholas deB. Katzenbach.

Sarah J. McCarthy. "Cultural Facism." From *Forbes*, December 9, 1991. © 2003 Forbes, Inc. Reprinted by permission of *Forbes Magazine*.

Thomas More. "A Day in Utopia." From *Utopia* by Thomas More, translated by Paul Turner (Penguin Classics, 1961). Copyright © Paul Turner, 1961. Reprinted by permission of Penguin Book Ltd.

George Orwell. "Shooting an Elephant." From *Shooting an Elephant and Other Essays* by George Orwell. Copyright 1950 by Sonia Brownell Orwell and renewed 1978 by Sonia Pitt-Rivers. Reprinted by permission of Harcourt, Inc. Copyright © George Orwell 1936 by permission of Bill Hamilton as the Literary Executor of the Estate of the Late Sonia Brownell Orwell and Seeker & Warburg Ltd.

Ellen Frankel Paul. "Bared Buttocks and Federal Cases." From *Society*, May/June 1991. Copyright © 1991. Reprinted with the permission of Transaction Publishers.

Plato, "Myth of the Cave." From *Plato: The Republic* translated by Desmond Lee (Penguin Classics, 1955, second edition 1974) pp. 317–325, copyright © H. D. P. Lee, 1955, 1974. Reproduced by permission of Penguin Books Ltd.

Helen Prejean. "Executions Are Too Costly—Morally." Excerpt from *Dead Man Walking* by Helen Prejean. Copyright © 1993 by Helen Prejean. Used by permission of Random House, Inc.

James Rachels. "Active and Passive Euthanasia." From the *New England Journal of Medicine*, January 1, 1975. Copyright © 1975 Massachusetts Medical Society. All rights reserved.

Index of Authors
and Titles